LATINO FIRSTS

Trailblazers and Milestones in United States History

Nicolás Kanellos

DETROIT

ABOUT THE AUTHOR

Nicolás Kanellos is founding publisher of the noted Latino literary journal *The Americas Review* (formerly *Revista Chicano-Riqueña*) and of the nation's oldest and most esteemed Latino publishing house, Arte Público Press. He has been professor of literature at the University of Houston since 1980. In 1994 Dr. Kanellos was appointed by President Clinton to the council for the National Endowment for the Humanities (NEH).

Kanellos's four-volume reference book, *Handbook of Hispanic Cultures in the United States,* has received two awards: the American Library Association Denali Press Award for best reference work and the Outstanding Reference Work of 1994 by *Choice*. His work *The Hispanic American Almanac* won a Reference and Adult Services Division (RASD) Award for Outstanding Reference Source of the Year from the American Library Association in 1993. His book *Hispanic Immigrant Literature: El Sueño del Retorno* (2011) was named an Outstanding Academic Title by *Choice* and won the PEN Southwest Award for Non-Fiction. He is also the author of Visible Ink Press' *Latino Almanac: From Early Explorers to Corporate Leaders.*

Dr. Kanellos is also the founder of a major national research project Recovering the Hispanic Literary Heritage of the United States, a program to identify, preserve, study, and make accessible tens of thousands of documents from the colonial period to 1980. In 2008 he was elected to the Spanish American Royal Academy of Literature, Arts and Sciences. In 2014 he was awarded the Anderson Imbert Lifetime Achievement Award by the North American Academy of the Spanish Language. In 2016 he was awarded the Cross of the Order of Isabella the Catholic Queen, the highest decoration given to a civilian by the Spanish government. In 2024, President Jose Biden awarded Dr. Kanellos the National Humanities Medal.

LATINO FIRSTS

Trailblazers and Milestones in United States History

Nicolás Kanellos

Copyright © 2025 by Visible Ink Press®

This publication is a creative work fully protected by all applicable copyright laws, as well as by misappropriation, trade secret, unfair competition, and other applicable laws.

No part of this book may be reproduced in any form without permission in writing from the publisher, except by a reviewer who wishes to quote brief passages in connection with a review written for inclusion in a magazine, newspaper, or website.

All rights to this publication will be vigorously defended.

Visible Ink Press®
43311 Joy Rd., #414
Canton, MI 48187-2075

Visible Ink Press is a registered trademark of Visible Ink Press LLC.

Most Visible Ink Press books are available at special quantity discounts when purchased in bulk by corporations, organizations, or groups. Customized printings, special imprints, messages, and excerpts can be produced to meet your needs. For more information, contact Special Markets Director, Visible Ink Press, www.visibleink.com, or 734-667-3211.

Managing Editor: Kevin S. Hile
Cover Design: John Gouin
Page Design and Typesetting: Kevin S. Hile
Proofreaders: Christa Gainor and Shoshanna Hurwitz
Indexer: Shoshanna Hurwitz

Cover images: Shutterstock.

ISBNs
Paperback: 978-1-57859-848-9
Library Hardback: 978-1-57859-870-0
eBook: 978-1-57859-871-7

Cataloging-in-Publication Data is on file at the Library of Congress.

Printed in the United States of America.

10 9 8 7 6 5 4 3 2 1

DEDICATION

This volume of firsts is dedicated to the next two generations, who will create their own firsts: Elyse, John Michael, Laura, Luzia, Miguel José, Teo, and Sonja. And as always, I thank my wife, Cristelia, the love of my life.

Also from Visible Ink Press

African American Almanac: 400 Years of Black Excellence
by Lean'tin Bracks, PhD
ISBN: 978-1-57859-780-2

The American Women's Almanac: 500 Years of Making History
by Deborah G Felder
ISBN: 978-1-57859-636-2

Black Firsts: 500 Years of Trailblazing Achievements and Ground-Breaking Events
by Jessie Carney Smith, Ph.D.
ISBN: 978-1-57859-688-1

Black Heroes
by Jessie Carney Smith, Ph.D.
ISBN: 978-1-57859-136-7

Freedom Facts and Firsts: 400 Years of the African American Civil Rights Experience
by Jessie Carney Smith, Ph.D. and Linda T Wynn
ISBN: 978-1-57859-192-3

The Handy African American History Answer Book
by Jessie Carney Smith, Ph.D.
ISBN: 978-1-57859-452-8

The Handy Islam Answer Book
by John Renard, PhD
ISBN: 978-1-57859-510-5

Indigenous Firsts: A History of Native American Achievement and Events
by Yvonne Wakim Dennis, Arlene Hirschfelder and Paulette F Molin
ISBN: 978-1-57859-712-3

Latino Almanac: From Early Explorers to Corporate Leaders
by Nicolás Kanellos, Ph.D.
ISBN: 978-1-57859-611-9

Native American Almanac: More Than 50,000 Years of the Cultures and Histories of Indigenous Peoples
by Yvonne Wakim Dennis, Arlene Hirschfelder, and Shannon Rothenberger Flynn
ISBN: 978-1-57859-507-5

Native American Landmarks and Festivals: A Traveler's Guide to Indigenous United States and Canada
by Yvonne Wakim Dennis and Arlene Hirschfelder
ISBN: 978-1-57859-641-6

Originals! Black Women Breaking Barriers
by Jessie Carney Smith, Ph.D.
ISBN: 978-1-57859-759-8

Trailblazing Women! Amazing Americans Who Made History
by Deborah G Felder
ISBN: 978-1-57859-729-1

Please visit us at www.visibleinkpress.com.

Contents

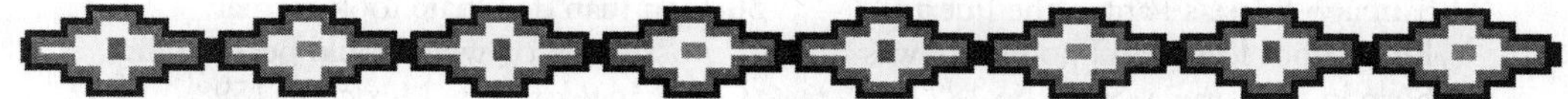

CALENDAR OF FIRSTS

JANUARY

2 Manuel Ortiz of El Centro, California, became the first Latino to win the bantamweight boxing championship in 1942

4 Lauro F. Cavazos, the first Latin Secretary of Education, was born in Kingsville, Texas, in 1927

5 Oscar Muñoz, who served as CEO for United Airlines, was born in Southern California, in 1959

6 One of the greatest women's golf champions of all time, Nancy López, was born to Mexican American parents in Torrence, California, in 1957

8 José Ferrer, the first Hispanic actor to win an Academy Award, was born in Santurce, Puerto Rico. in 1912

9 Robert "Bobby" García, the first Puerto Rican born in the continental United States to serve as a congressman, was born in Bronx, New York, in 1977

14 Texas general Antonio Canales and followers proclaimed in 1840 the independence of the Republic of the Rio Grande, to comprise a part of Texas and the Mexican state of Tamaulipas

16 Lin-Manuel Miranda, the author and director of the greatest Broadway money-making show *Hamilton*, was born in New York City in 1980

17 Hector García Pérez, the Mexican American civil rights leader and founder of the American G.I. Forum, was born in Llera, Tamaulipas, Mexico, in 1914

☼ The first Chicano political party, La Raza Unida Party (United Hispanic People's Party) was founded in 1970 in Crystal City, Texas

21 Rolando Hinojosa, the most prolific and bilingual of the Latino novelists of the United States, was born in Mercedes, Texas, in 1929

23 Broadway legend, dancer-actress Chita Rivera was born in Washington, D.C., in 1933

28 Poet, writer, and lawyer Jose Martí was born in Havana, Cuba, in 1853. Martí became the leading figure in the Cuban revolutionary movement for independence from Spain and the most important precursor of the modernist literary movement

31 Publisher and scholar Nicolás Kanellos, the founder of Arte Público Press and Recovering the U.S. Hispanic Literary Heritage was born in New York City in 1945

FEBRUARY

4 The Gulf Stream was discovered in 1517 by pilot Antonio de Alaminos during Juan Ponce de León's voyage to Florida

6 Ramón Novarro, the first Latino romantic leading man, rivaled only by Rudolph Valentino, was born in Durango, Mexico, in 1899

10 Edward R. Roybal, who held his seat in Congress longer than any other Latino, was born in Albuquerque, New Mexico, in 1916

18 Luis Muñoz Marín, the first popularly elected native governor of Puerto Rico, was born in San Juan in 1898

☼ Armando Ramos became the first Mexican American boxer to win the world lightweight championship in 1969

20 On this date in 1915 a general uprising among Mexican Americans known as The Plan of San Diego was begun in order to retake lans that once belonged to Mexico. The rebellion was organized under the Supreme Revolutionary Congress of San Diego

22 Santiago Iglesias Pantín, the Puerto Rican labor leader and politician, was born in La Coruña, Spain, in 1872

24 Poet and novelist Judith Ortiz Cofer was born in 1952 in San Germán, Puerto Rico

MARCH

15 Federico Peña, the first Latino to become the secretary of transportation and the first to serve as mayor of Denver, Colorado, was born in Laredo, Texas, in 1947

☼ Eva Longoria, movie and TV actress, director, and producer, was born in Corpus Christi, Texas, in 1975

21 Arte Público Press became the first Latino publishing house to win the Ivan Sandrof National Book Critics Circle Lifetime Achievement Award in 2018

27 Denver's Crusade for Justice sponsored the first national Chicano Youth Liberation Conference in 1969

31 César Chávez, the first labor activist to organize a successful union of farm workers, was born in 1927 near Yuma, Arizona, into a family of migrant farmworkers

APRIL

1 Juan Ponce de León landed on the shores of Florida in 1515, exploring most of the coastal regions up to Apalachi Bay

7 Gabriela Mistral, the first Latin American writer to win the Nobel Prize, was born in Vicuña, Chile, in 1889

14 Mexican American parents won a 1947 lawsuit alleging segregation in four Orange County elementary school districts (*Mendez et al. v. Westminster School District et al.*) in California

21 Anthony Quinn, two-time Academy Award-winning actor, was born in Chihuahua, Mexico, in 1915

☼ Puerto Rico's Carlos Ortiz became the first Puerto Rican boxer to win the lightweight boxing championship in 1962

30 Don Juan de Oñate took formal possession of what would become the Province of New Mexico in 1598

MAY

3 Workers struck the Farah Manufacturing Company in El Paso, Texas, and initiated a national boycott that lasted from 1972 to 1974

5 The Gregory Nava film *My Family* (1995) had the highest average revenue ($5,375) for all movies released on the weekend beginning on this date

6 Astros batting-champ José Altuve was born in 1990 in Maracay, Venezuela

8 Hernando de Soto discovered and crossed the Mississippi River in 1541

9 One of the greatest tennis professionals ever, Richard Alonso "Pancho" González, was born in Los Angeles, California, in 1928

10 Ellen Ochoa, the first Latina astronaut, was born in Los Angeles, California, in 1958

14 Tania J. León, Cuban singer and director of classical music, was born in Havana, Cuba, in 1943

16 Juan Nepomuceno Cortina, who was a rancher, a revolutionary who started the "Cortina War," and a Mexican governor, was born in Camargo on the Mexican side of the Rio Grande from Brownsville, Texas, in 1824

24 The first permanent Spanish settlement in Texas, San Francisco de los Tejas, was founded in 1690

JUNE

1 One of the earliest and most important copper mine strikes in the Southwest occurred in 1903, when mostly Mexican and Mexican American workers walked out at Clifton-Morenci

11 Henry G. Cisneros, the first Latino secretary of Housing and Urban Development and former mayor of San Antonio, Texas, was born in San Antonio, Texas, in 1947

13 Luis Walter Alvarez, the first Latino to win the Nobel Prize for physics, was born in San Francisco, California, in 1911

19 Julián Nava, the first Mexican American to serve as ambassador to Mexico, was born in Los Angeles, California, in 1927

26 Luis Valdez, the father of Chicano theater, was born in Delano, California, in 1940

JULY

3 In 1769, Fray Junípero Serra established the first mission, Mission San Diego de Alcalá, in what would become San Diego

9 Lawyer Anthony Romero, the first Latino director of the American Civil Liberties Union, was born in 1965 in New York City

10 The first Latino ballplayer was selected for the 1951 All-Star game: Venezuelan short stop Alfonso (Chico) Carrasquel

15 Juan de Oñate founded the first town in 1598, in what would become the U.S. Southwest, and became the first governor of what would become the Spanish colonial province of New Mexico

☼ In 1931, Cuba's Eligio "Kid Chocolate" Sardiñas became the first Latino boxer to win a world title

☼ In 1963 Dominican pitcher Juan Marichal became the first Latino to throw a no-hitter in U.S. professional baseball

17 Francisco Manuel Oller y Cestero, the distinguished painter and introducer of Impressionism and art education in Puerto Rico, was born in San Juan in 1833

18 Lupe Vélez (María Guadalupe Vélez de Villalobos), one of the most famous Latin American screen actresses of all time, was born in San Luis Potosí, Mexico, in 1908

19 Vikki Carr, the internationally famous singer of popular music, was born in El Paso, Texas, in 1940

20 Neuroscientist Albert Mark Galaburda was born in Santiago, Chile, in 1948

26 Patricio F. Flores, the first Mexican American to be named a bishop of the Catholic church, was born in Ganado, Texas, in 1929

27 Alex "A-Rod" Rodríguez, the highest paid baseball player, was born in Washington Heights, New York, in 1975

29 After prolonged strikes and national boycotts, the United Farmworkers Organizing Committee (UFWOC), under the leadership of César Chávez and Dolores Huerta, signed contracts in 1970 with most of the Central Valley table grape growers of California

AUGUST

1 Sarah Elizabeth Robles, the first Latina Olympic weightlifter, was born in San Diego, California, in 1988

3 Dolores del Río, the first Latin American leading lady in Hollywood films, was born in Durango, Mexico, in 1904

18 One of the greatest baseball players of all time, Roberto Clemente, was born in Carolina, Puerto Rico, in 1934

23 Antonia Novello, the first Latina Surgeon General of the United States, was born in Fajardo, Puerto Rico, in 1944

20 Beatriz Escalona, known by her stage name of La Chata Noloesca and the greatest Latina vaudeville star in the United States, was born in San Antonio, Texas, in 1903

☼ In 1970 Los Angeles, more than 20,000 Chicanos and supporters participated in a Chicano Moratorium to the Vietnam War

24 Oscar Hijuelos, the first Latino writer to win the Pulitzer Prize for fiction, was born in New York City in 1951

25 In 1954, explorer Francisco Vásquez de Coronado encountered the Grand Canyon

29 ASPIRA obtained a consent decree in 1974 mandating bilingual education programs in the New York City schools

31 In 1936 Sixto Escobar became the first Puerto Rican boxer to win a world championship

SEPTEMBER

8 Saint Augustine, Florida, the oldest permanent European settlement in what is today the mainland United States, was founded in 1565 by Pedro Menéndez de Avilés

☼ In 1965 César Chávez and Dolores Huerta led the National Farm Workers Association into a strike started by Filipino grape pickers in Delano, California; this was the beginning of the most successful farm worker union in history

12 Pedro Alvizu Campos, the greatest activist for Puerto Rican independence from the United States, was born in Ponce in 1893

14 Puerto Rican patriot and poet Lola Rodríguez de Tió was born in San Germán in 1843

17 José Moraga founded San Francisco, California, in 1776

28 In 1542 Juan Rodríguez de Cabrillo explored what he described as an excellent port—present-day San Diego, California

OCTOBER

1 Pulitzer Prize-winning memoirist Cristina Rivera Garza was born in Matamoros, Mexico, in 1964

6 Rebecca Lobo, the greatest Latina basketball player, was born in Hartford, Connecticut, in 1973

12 In 1492 Columbus landed on an island he called San Salvador—either present-day Watling Island or Samana Cay in the eastern Bahamas

17 Rita Hayworth (Magarita Carmen Cansino), the first Latina actress to be seen as an American sex goddess, was born in Brooklyn, New York, in 1918

23 One of golf's all-time greats, Juan "Chi Chi" Rodríguez, was born in Río Piedras, Puerto Rico, in 1935

25 José Angel Gutiérrez, Chicano civil Rights leader and founder of La Raza Unida Party, was born in Crystal City, Texas, in 1944

30 Academy Award-winning cinematographer and director, Nestor Almendros, was born in Barcelona, Spain, in 1930

NOVEMBER

1 Journalist Carlos Lozada wins the Pulitzer Prize for Criticism in 2019

☼ Nicholasa Mohr, the first Latina to have developed a long career as a creative writer for the major publishing houses, was born in Bronx, New York, in 1938

10 Zoologist Evelyn Margaret Rivera was born in Hollister, California, in 1929

15 Alberto Vinicio Baez, the noted physicist, was born in Puebla, Mexico, in 1912

25 Actor Ricardo Montalbán, founder of the first organization to work for increasing the number of Latinos in Hollywood and improving their screen image, was born in Mexico City, in 1920

29 Hall of Fame pitcher Mariano Rivera was born in Puerto Caimito, Panama, in 1969

DECEMBER

1 The famous Mexican American golfer, Lee Buck Treviño, was born in Garland, Texas, in 1929

11 Famed actor Gilbert Roland was born in Ciudad Juárez, Mexico, in 1905

16 Neurobiologist Rodolfo Llinas was born in Bogotá, Colombia, in 1934

19 Academy Award-winning actress, dancer, and singer Rita Moreno (Rosita Dolores Alverio) was born on in Humacao, Puerto Rico, in 1931

☼ Miguel Piñero, the most famous dramatist to come out of the Nuyorican school, was born in Gurabo, Puerto Rico, in 1946

22 Mexican American novelist Tomás Rivera, one of the principal founders of Chicano literature as a concept and the first Latino chancellor in the University of California system, was born in Crystal City, Texas, in 1935

23 One of the greatest colonial artists, José Campeche, was born in San Juan, Puerto Rico, in 1751

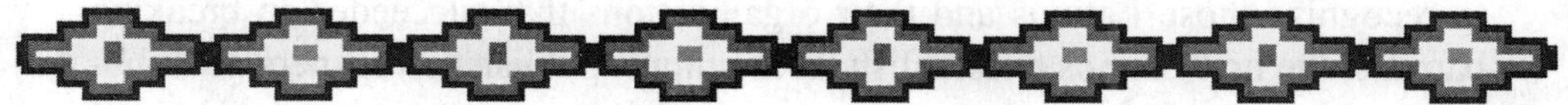

Introduction

Latino Firsts: Trailblazers and Milestones in United States History is an effort to organize the contributions and achievements of Latinos as pioneers of American culture. In an easily readable and digestible form, these pages document and detail the accomplishments of Latinos chronologically according to the various fields of their endeavors, from the arts to the sciences. Whereas what has reigned in popular culture and even the teaching of history for more than a century is a stereotypical vision of Latinos as less than desirable neighbors and citizens, the record clearly shows that Hispanic peoples are responsible for laying the foundation for much of American industry and civilization. Although Latinos make up the largest minority group in the United States and are forecast to become one-third of the population by 2050, little is generally known of their contributions to U.S. culture and civilization, and far too little is known about their current participation in every field and at every level of the American enterprise.

The writing of *Latino Firsts* is governed by two concepts: (1) The development of U.S. civilization owes much to pioneering Hispanic peoples; and (2) Latinos are also pioneers for breaking barriers to success in American society. Therefore, most of the entries for the early years in this book represent the coming of the Spanish and their Afro- and Indo-Hispanic progeny to areas that would become the United States. These Hispanic peoples introduced European concepts of agriculture, architecture, city planning, education, law, literature, religion, science, writing, and almost every other social organization and intellectual endeavor that was imported to the New World or was developed here as the product of the wedding of European, African, and Amerindian cultures. Once the thirteen colonies that became the United States began to expand southward and westward, Hispanic civilization in North America and the Caribbean was the object of conquest, subjugation, and, to some extent, assimilation. Despite Hispanic peoples having been conquered and incorporated as citizens of the United States, and despite their having been imported for a century and a half to toil in factories, fields, and mines, they too often remained outsiders, seen as foreigners and even enemies.

Their accomplishments as a people in North America have often been maligned, ignored, or forgotten, even while the United States benefitted from their pioneering work and genius. Thus, the second organizing principle of this book is to recognize those Latinos and their organizations that succeeded in breaking barriers; the first Latinos to establish labor unions, publish newspapers, run publishing houses, gain entrance to major sports and even be named to the Halls of Fame; the first Latinos to discover scientific processes and to fly into outer space; and most important, the first Latinos to make important gains in civil rights and government and to fight for the dignity of people everywhere.

Most entries are brief mentions of important historical achievements; however, events of greatest resonance are highlighted in the text and are often accompanied by an illustration or photograph. To enable easier scanning and identification of the various achievements of Latinos, a detailed index is included in the back of this book. Also, each entry is accompanied by a reference to sources of information or books and articles for further reading. A complete bibliography is also included for those readers who desire to continue learning about the history of Hispanic peoples in the United States.

In conducting the research for *Latino Firsts*, it became obvious that many of the great accomplishments by Latinos in the United States could not be included simply because they were not the first in history but had built on already existing traditions. Therefore, some very important names of extraordinary people are absent from this text. Also, there are many deeds that have gone unrecorded, many accomplishments for which we do not have a precise date or the name of the individual or individuals involved. For instance, which Hispanic pioneer established the first mine in the Southwest? Who was the first to grow wheat, or cotton, or rice? At this time in history, many of the documentary sources are lost—perhaps forever. Hundreds of newspapers and books were written and published in Latino communities of the United States but were never collected or preserved by libraries and institutions of learning in this society. How much more information could they have added to our storehouse of historical data? How much will we never know about the life and culture of Hispanic peoples in this land?

As a pioneering effort unto itself, *Latino Firsts* relies on a wide variety of sources, some of which may have erred in precision. If any errors are detected, I beg the reader's indulgence and forgiveness and invite the reader to forward corrections to Visible Ink Press in order that the following editions of the work may be corrected. But in all, both Visible Ink Press and I believe that we have broadened the scope of American history and helped to provide more detail and accuracy as to its actual development by acknowledging and documenting the Latino contribution that has been absent for so long!

—Nicolás Kanellos; Houston, Texas

GOVERNMENT

1539 ♦ Hernando de Soto (c. 1500–1542) led some 600 soldiers, priests, and followers into Florida and built a winter camp on the site of today's city of Tallahassee, making it the oldest known European building site in what has become the United States. Excavations at Tallahassee's Lafayette Street have uncovered some of the remains of that camp.

Sources: Henderson and Mormino, *Spanish Pathways in Florida*, p. 87.

1560 ♦ The Spanish founded Santa Elena in what is today the state of South Carolina; it was the first European settlement in what became the continental United States. Both Santa Elena and Saint Augustine predate Jamestown, which was founded in 1607 by the British, and the arrival of the *Mayflower* in 1620. Santa Elena did not last as a settlement.

Sources: Kanellos, *Chronology of Hispanic American History*, p. 45.

1565 ♦ The first permanent town settlement and government (not counting Native American settlements, of course) in what became the continental United States was San Agustín (Saint Augustine), Florida, founded by Pedro Menéndez de Avilés (1519–1574) on the eastern Florida coast. It served to protect Spanish shipping around the islands of the Caribbean. (The English did not establish the town of Jamestown in Virginia until 1607.) During the 17th century, Saint Augustine and other areas of Florida received a considerable amount of migration from Spain and the Spanish Caribbean. The population of Saint Augustine grew to 2,000 by the turn of the 18th century. The city was afforded more security by the building of the San Marcos Fort, begun in 1672 and finished in

Pedro Menéndez de Avilés

1756. In 1763, the region of the Florida peninsula called Eastern Florida—as opposed to Western Florida, which ranged from the Georgia coast to the Mississippi River—came under British control as a result of the Treaty of Paris. This included Saint Augustine. In 1783, under the Treaty of Versailles, Eastern Florida was returned to Spain. It remained a possession of Spain until 1821, when it was surrendered to the United States.

Sources: Cruz, *Let There Be Towns*, p. 19; Kanellos, *Chronology of Hispanic American History*, p. 45.

1565 ♦ With the founding of Saint Augustine, the Spanish system of local government was instituted in what became part of the continental United States; it would be extended to all new towns and municipalities founded over the next two centuries. The system included an elected town council (*cabildo*) and an elected mayor (*alcalde*); thus, the first democratic municipal elections in what would become the continental United States were introduced by the Spanish *mestizo* colonizers. (However, the Spanish Crown had the power to confirm or nullify the elections.) Among the rights of citizens (*fueros*) was that of holding open town meetings (*cabildo abierto*) for the discussion of issues affecting the community and for decision making regarding the issues; these represented the first town meetings in what would become the United States.

The roots of the *cabildo abierto* lay in the rights of medieval Spanish towns. Typically, the town councils on the Spanish frontier consisted of four annually elected councilmen (*regidores*). The council selected two magistrates (*alcaldes ordinarios*) to preside over the *cabildo* and to try local cases, one citizen to serve as a constable (*alguacil*), one as a city clerk (*escribano*), and another as a royal standard bearer (*alferez real*). In addition to executing local governance, the *cabildos* came to serve as advisory boards for the governors of the provinces, and they served as spokesmen for the community to the authorities of the church, the higher government, and the royalty.

In the larger municipalities, such as San Antonio, the *alcalde* held court daily except for Sundays; in frontier municipalities, the judges convened the court whenever it was needed. The first lawyers in what became the United States date to this period, and in the later colonial period, the first public defenders were appointed by the *cabildos* at the city's expense to serve citizens who could not afford legal fees. The *cabildo* also appointed a *fiel executor*, a person in charge of weights and measures, thus regulating the marketplace, and a person in charge of surveying lands. All of these positions and institutions were the first of their kind in areas that became the United States. In the Southwest, another type of governing organization was the local ditch (*acequia*) association, which is extant today in some parts of New Mexico. These associations maintained and governed the use of the irrigation systems, which were essential to the agriculture and economy of each of the villages. Representatives were elected to a commission, and a supervisor administered the flow and usage of the water on an equitable basis.

Sources: Cruz, *Let There Be Towns*, pp. 74–76, 133–134, 148–151; Gómez-Quiñones, *Roots of Chicano Politics, 1600–1940*, pp. 24–25, 40.

Don Juan de Oñate

1598 ♦ On April 30, 1598, Don Juan de Oñate (c. 1550–1630) took formal possession of what would become the province of New Mexico in a pass on the Rio Grande, dividing New Spain (Mexico) from what would eventually become the southwestern United States. The pass would serve as a weigh station for colonizers traveling north into the new province; it eventually became the town of El Paso, today a large city in Texas that still serves as a vital commercial link between Mexico and the United States.

Sources: Cruz, *Let There Be Towns*, pp. 36–37.

1598 ♦ On July 15, 1598, Don Juan de Oñate (c. 1550–1630) founded the first town in what would become the southwestern United States and became the first governor of what would soon be the Spanish colonial province of New Mexico. He chose a site known as Caypa on the east bank of the Rio Grande by a friendly Indian pueblo and christened the town San Juan de los Caballeros. Three years later, he founded another town across the river from San Juan, baptized it San Gabriel, and set up his governor's residency there.

Sources: Cruz, *Let There Be Towns*, pp. 19–22.

1610 ♦ Don Juan de Oñate (c. 1550–1630) founded the capital of the province of New Mexico in Santa Fe. This became the first capital on what would later be U.S. soil. The founding of Santa Fe was carried out according to the Spanish Ordinances of 1573, calling for the establishment of a mayor (*alcalde*) and council (*cabildo*) elected by the citizens, a municipal court, a constable, and a clerk.

Sources: Cruz, *Let There Be Towns*, pp. 19–29.

1691 ♦ Domingo Terán de los Ríos was named the first governor of the province of Texas. As a response to French exploration and incursions, Spain decided to rapidly settle Texas. Terán de los Ríos was empowered to establish eight missions among the Indian nations in east Texas.

Sources: Blake, Robert Bruce, "Terán de los Ríos, Domingo," *Handbook of Texas*: https://www.tshaonline.org/handbook/entries/teran-de-los-rios-domingo.

1718 ♦ Martín de Alarcón, a knight of the Order of Santiago and governor of Coahuila, founded the San Antonio de Béxar Presidio (or fort), which would become the city of San Antonio. The San Antonio de Valero Mission was founded that same year. It became the most important and most prosperous settlement in Texas. During the 1730s and 1740s, missions spread from eastern Texas westward. The eastern Texas missions had been partially abandoned and moved to San Antonio, with San Antonio de Valero, San Juan Capistrano, San Francisco de la Espada, and Purísima Concepcion being established along the San Antonio River. The area developed into an important center for trade.

Sources: Jasinski, Laurie E., "San Antonio, Tx.," *Handbook of Texas*: https://www.tshaonline.org/handbook/entries/san-antonio-tx.

José de Gálvez

1761 ♦ The province of Alta California was founded through the leadership of José de Gálvez (1720–1787) who, besides convincing the Crown to colonize the area, also outfitted two ships, which occupied what would become the port of San Diego in April. After establishing missions and settlements in San Diego, Gáspar de Pórtola (1716–1786), who became the first governor of California, and Father Junípero Serra (1713–1784) set out for Monterey Bay in July. After discovering San Francisco Bay, they reached Monterey Bay in March 1770.

Sources: Hackel, Steven W., Ju*nipero Serra: California's Founding Father*, New York: Hill and Wang, 2013.

1773 ♦ The first European settlements in Alaska were established by the Spanish. Spanish expeditions began to explore the Canadian coast up into Alaska over the next few years, making contact with Russians. Their explorations eventually led to the establishment of a base at Nutka on the coast of Vancouver Island. This was the only European outpost in the expanse from San Francisco to Alaska.

Sources: Kanellos, *Chronology of Hispanic American History*, p. 58.

1776 ♦ On September 17, 1776, José Moraga (1745–1785), a lieutenant in Juan Bautista de Anza's (1736–1788) colonizing mission to Alta California consisting of 20 families (240 people), 700 horses, and 350 cattle, founded

San Francisco. In 1777, the governor of Alta California, Felipe de Neve (1724–1784), established his capital in Monterey and also founded the village of San Jose with some of the settlers brought by Moraga. In 1781, de Neve went south with other settlers and established Nuestra Señora la Reina de los Angeles de Porciúncula (Los Angeles).

Sources: Kanellos, *Chronology of Hispanic American History*, pp. 58–59.

1822 ♦ Joseph Hernández (1793–1857), from the Territory of Florida, was elected the first Latino representative to the U.S. Congress. He was the son of Spanish immigrants who had settled in Florida in 1768. Two years later, Hernández, a Whig Party member, was elected president of the legislative council of Florida. Hernández ran unsuccessfully for the U.S. Senate in 1845.

Joseph Hernández

Sources: Hispanics in U.S. History, p. 70.

Pío de Jesús Pico

1832 ♦ Pío de Jesús Pico (1801–1894) became the first governor of African heritage in what became the United States. Born on May 5, 1801, at Mission San Gabriel, Pico also had the distinction of being the last governor of California under Mexican rule. As a young man, he became a successful businessman in Los Angeles. In 1828, he was elected to the territorial legislature and assumed grand stature as a southern Californio political leader. From January to February 1832, he was governor briefly but then became the civilian administrator of the San Luis Rey Mission. In 1845, he once again became governor, this time at the seat in Los Angeles instead of at Monterey. He was attacked on various occasions for land grants that he made and for his sale of mission lands. When the Americans invaded, Pico at first offered some resistance but soon fled to Baja California. After signing a peace treaty, Pico returned to California and assumed the peaceful life of a rancher. He, like many other Californios, lost all of his lands to mortgage companies when he had to raise funds to defend the titles to the properties from squatters and other usurpers. Under American rule, Pico continued his interest in politics, serving on the Los Angeles City Council and as the Los Angeles County tax assessor. He also owned a large hotel, the Pico House, which still stands in downtown Los Angeles. Pico died penniless on September 11, 1894.

Sources: Salomon, Carlos Manuel, *Pio Pico: The Last Governor of Mexican California,* University of Oklahoma Press, 2010.

1836 ♦ Politician and statesman Lorenzo de Zavala (1788–1836), one of the main leaders of the revolt against the central government in Mexico, became the first vice president of the Republic of Texas.

Sources: Meier and Rivera, *Dictionary of Mexican American History*, p. 374.

1850 ♦ Manuel Requena (1802–1876) was elected to the first Los Angeles City Council. Under Mexican rule, he had served as mayor (*alcalde*). In 1856, he became president of the council. His terms on the council were 1850–1854, 1856, and 1864–1868.

Sources: Schmal, John P., "The Four Latino Mayors of Los Angeles," *Hispanic Vista*, 23 May 2005.

José Manuel Gallegos

1853 ♦ The second Latino to serve in the U.S. House of Representatives was the first elected representative of New Mexico Territory, José Manuel Gallegos (1815–1875). An ordained priest who had studied under Antonio José Martínez, Gallegos ministered to the San Juan Pueblo and was later transferred to Albuquerque. Gallegos became a delegate to the New Mexican assembly in 1843, when the province still belonged to Mexico. In 1851, under U.S. rule, he was elected to the territorial senate and two years later became a representative to U.S. Congress, despite his inability to speak English. While in his second term in Congress, Gallegos was unseated (in 1856) by the House as a result of appeals from Miguel A. Otero Jr., who had opposed Gallegos in the close election. Gallegos returned to New Mexico and continued his political career, serving as the speaker of the New Mexico House from 1860 to 1862. In 1870, he again won a seat in U.S. Congress and served until 1873.

Sources: Gómez-Quiñones, *Roots of Chicano Politics, 1600–1940*, p. 240; Meier and Rivera, *Dictionary of Mexican American History*, pp. 141–142.

1856 ♦ When the Los Angeles mayor resigned, Manuel Requena, serving as president of the city council, became mayor until an election was held 11 days later. For a brief time, then, he was the only Mexican American to serve as mayor of Los Angeles under U.S. rule until recent times.

Sources: Schmal, John P., "The Four Latino Mayors of Los Angeles," *Hispanic Vista*, 23 May 2005.

1875 ♦ Romualdo Pacheco (1831–1899) became the first Latino governor of California under U.S. rule. After being elected to the lieutenant governorship in 1871, Pacheco succeeded to the position of governor when Governor Newton Booth was elected to the Senate in 1875. After serving for nine months, Pacheco failed to gain the Republican nomination for governor in the next election. Pacheco was the son of a Mexican army officer from Guadalajara; he was raised in Hawaii, where he received his English-language education. After the Mexican War, he supervised his family's ranch in San Luis Obispo and entered politics. He was first elected to the California Assembly in 1853; he won a seat in the state senate in 1858 and then won the lieutenant governorship in 1871. After serving as governor, he served two terms in the U.S. House of Representatives between 1878 and 1882.

Romualdo Pacheco

Sources: Gómez-Quiñones, *Roots of Chicano Politics, 1600–1940*, p. 256; Meier and Rivera, *Dictionary of Mexican American History*, p. 268.

1875 ♦ Casimiro Barela (1847–1920) was the only Latino elected as a delegate to the state constitutional convention of Colorado. Barela secured a provision in the state constitution protecting the civil rights of the Spanish-speaking citizens as well as a rule providing for the publication of laws in Spanish, English, and German. The state constitution was written and published in both languages. In 1876, he was elected a state senator; he served until 1916. A native of New Mexico whose family had moved to Colorado in 1867, Barela held various other elected posts before becoming a state senator. While serving in politics, he kept up his interests in banking and other businesses and became one of the wealthiest men in the state.

Casimiro Barela

Sources: Gómez-Quiñones, *Roots of Chicano Politics, 1600–1940*, pp. 265–266.

1875 ♦ Four years after Tucson was incorporated as a city (in 1871), its first Hispanic mayor was elected. Estevan Ochoa (1831–1888), a wealthy freighter, was the only Mexican mayor of Tucson elected following the Gadsden Purchase in 1854. From a wealthy Chihuahua family, Ochoa became a loyal American, so loyal in fact that he fiercely opposed the Confederacy. He grew up learning the freighting business and developing bilingual-bicultural skills that allowed him to prosper in business both in the United States and Mexico as well as to win the confidence of both the Anglo and Mexican electorates in Tucson. During the 1860s and 1870s, he served in the territorial legislature and on the city council.

Sources: Gómez-Quiñones, *Roots of Chicano Politics, 1600–1940*, p. 268.

1890: First Latino Third Party in America

Félix Martínez Jr. (1857–1916) founded the first Latino third party in U.S. history in 1890. The New Mexico businessman and newspaper publisher, after breaking with the Democratic Party, ran in 1890 and 1892 as a candidate of El Partido del Pueblo Unido (The United People's Party) and won a seat on the territorial council in the second election. In addition, the party swept all offices in San Miguel County in 1890. The principal issues of the party were land tenure and the common people's mistreatment by the dominant political leaders, both Anglo and Mexican. In 1899, Martínez moved to El Paso, Texas, where he furthered his business and publishing interests and was later appointed by President William Howard Taft as U.S. commissioner general to South America. *Sources:* Gómez-Quiñones, *Roots of Chicano Politics, 1600–1940*, p. 281; Meier and Rivera, *Dictionary of Mexican American History*, pp. 213-214, 270.

1877 ♦ Romualdo Pacheco (1831–1899) became the first Latino regular member of the U.S. House of Representatives and served until 1882. Pancheco was elected as a Republican, but his Democratic opponent contested the election and was seated in his place on February 7, 1878. Pacheco again ran for the position in 1878 and was elected again; this time, he served out his term and another full term until 1833. In 1890, he was named minister plenipotentiary to Central America by President Benjamin Harrison.

Sources: "Romualdo Pacheco," *Dictionary of the United States Congress*, p. 1418.

1897 ♦ President William McKinley's appointment made Miguel A. Otero Jr. (1859–1944) the youngest and only Latino governor of New Mexico Territory. He served until January 1907. Otero was a politician and businessman born in Albuquerque, New Mexico, into the distinguished family of his father and namesake, Miguel A. Otero Sr., an outstanding business and political figure. Educated in St. Louis and Annapolis and at Notre Dame University, the younger Otero developed his business acumen in the offices of his father's company, Otero, Sellar & Company, which served him well when he took a major role in the firm after his father's death. With significant business interests in mining, ranching, real estate, and banking, Otero entered politics as a Republican. During the course of his early career, he held various elected and appointed positions and was even a candidate for the Republican vice presidential nomination in 1894. In 1897, Otero was appointed by President William McKinley to the governorship of New Mex-

Miguel A. Otero Jr.

ico Territory. Because he opposed President Theodore Roosevelt's National Forest Project, Otero was not reappointed to a second term as governor. At this point, Otero switched to the Democratic Party. Under President Woodrow Wilson, Otero was appointed U.S. marshal of the Panama Canal Zone in 1917. Otero remained active in politics into the 1920s. He also found time during his busy career to author various memoirs of historical value: *My Life on the Frontier, 1864–1882* (1935), *My Life on the Frontier, 1882–1897* (1939), and *My Nine Years as Governor of the Territory of New Mexico, 1897–1906* (1940). Four years after the publication of his last book, Otero died in Albuquerque at the age of 84.

Sources: Meier and Rivera, *Dictionary of Mexican American History*, pp. 267–268.

1913 ♦ Ladislao Lázaro (1872–1927) became Louisiana's first Latino congressman. A medical doctor, Lázaro had served in the Louisiana state senate from 1908 to 1912. Lázaro served eight successive terms in U.S. Congress until his death in 1927.

Sources: "Ladislas Lázaro." *Biographical Dictionary of the United States Congress*, p. 882.

Ezequiel Cabeza de Vaca

1916 ♦ Ezequiel Cabeza de Vaca (1864–1917) became the first Mexican American governor of the state of New Mexico. He died shortly after assuming the office. When New Mexico became a state in 1912, he served as its first lieutenant governor. He had also been a delegate to the state constitutional convention and worked toward establishing bilingual education for all New Mexicans.

Sources: "Ezequiel Cabeza de Baca," *New Mexico History:* https://newmexicohistory.org/2012/06/30/ezequiel-cabeza-de-baca/.

1922 ♦ Soledad C. Chacón (1890–1936) became the first Latina to win a state office; the Mexican American was elected New Mexico's secretary of state. In 1924, Chacón served as acting governor for two weeks.

Sources: Gómez-Quiñones, *Roots of Chicano Politics, 1600–1940*, p. 358.

Octaviano Larrazolo

1928 ♦ Octaviano Larrazolo (1859–1930) was the first Latino to become a U.S. senator. The native of Allende, Chihuahua, Mexico, was elected to complete the term of A. A. Jones, a New Mexico senator who died in office. Larrazolo graduated from Saint Michael's College in Arizona and had worked as a teacher and principal of an elementary school in Texas when he was appointed in 1885 as clerk of the U.S. District and Circuit Courts in El Paso. In Texas, he was also elected district attorney twice and served on the school board. He was an early, strong advocate for Mexican American civil rights. Larrazolo's political career rose and, after his move to New Mexico in 1895, continued until he became governor of the state and a U.S. senator in November 1928. He was elected to the U.S. Senate again in 1929 but did not complete the term because of poor health.

Sources: Cordova and Judah, *Octaviano Larrazolo*, pp. 16–21, 22–28; Gómez-Quiñones, *Roots of Chicano Politics, 1600–1940*, pp. 330–331; Rosales, *Chicano! History of the Mexican American Civil Rights Movement*, p. 109.

Dennis Chávez

1935 ♦ Dennis Chávez (1888–1962) became the first Latino elected to the U.S. Senate to serve a full term. Born to a poor family in a village to the west of Albuquerque, New Mexico, Chávez attended school in Albuquerque but was forced to drop out of school to work. Chávez continued his education on his own and eventually enrolled in law school; he graduated with a law degree from Georgetown University in 1920. He returned to New Mexico, established a private practice, and ran for office. In 1930, he won a seat in the U.S. House of Representatives; that was followed by his election to the Senate in 1935, where the Democrat was a staunch supporter of education and civil rights. In all, Chávez was elected to the Senate five times.

Sources: Coy, Cassie, *Dennis Chávez, The First Hispanic Senator*, Houston: Arte Público Press, 2017.

1946 ♦ Jesús T. Piñero (1897–1952) became the first native Puerto Rican to be appointed governor of Puerto Rico. He was appointed by President Harry S. Truman. Since 1940, he had been serving as the resident commissioner of Puerto Rico, an advisory position without a vote to the U.S. House of Representatives.

Jesús T. Piñero

Sources: "Jesús T. Piñero, 1897–1952," *Biographical Dictionary of the United States Congress*: https://bioguide.congress.gov/search/bio/P000361.

1946 ♦ Felisa Rincón de Gautier became the first woman to serve as mayor of San Juan, the capital of Puerto Rico. Because Puerto Rico, although not a state, is part of the United States, she was the first female mayor of a major

American city. As mayor, Rincón de Gautier was a populist who opened the doors of city government to the people. She was so beloved that she served until 1969 and was named one of the 100 outstanding women of the world.

Sources: Hispanics in U.S. History, p. 46.

Luis Muñoz Marín

1949 ♦ The first native governor of Puerto Rico under American rule was Luis Muñoz Marín (1898–1980). Muñoz Marín received his early education on the island and then attended Georgetown University, where he studied journalism and also earned a degree in law. Besides developing his career as a politician, Muñoz Marín worked as a journalist, serving as publisher of the *Revista de Indias* (Review of the Indies) and editor of various newspapers, including *El Imparcial* (The Imparcial), *El Batey* (The Beaten Ground), and *La Democracia* (Democracy). Muñoz Marín also served as secretary to the resident commissioner for Puerto Rico in Washington, D.C. (1916–1918). He was a labor organizer, served in the secretariat of the Pan American Union, was first elected to the Puerto Rican senate in 1932, and founded the Popular Democratic Party in 1940. In 1941, he was elected president of the senate. He served as the first governor of Puerto Rico from 1949 to 1965 and was one of the principal architects of the Commonwealth of Puerto Rico, a political and governmental organization that established Puerto Rico as a free associated state of the United States—a contradiction in terms that really was a liberal definition of a colony. He was also a chief architect of Operation Bootstrap, a program that offered tax incentives for American industries to locate in Puerto Rico and thus contribute to the economic development of the island. Muñoz Marín spearheaded many reforms and programs that improved the economy, the transportation infrastructure, and the educational and health delivery systems in Puerto Rico. One constant criticism, however, has been that much of the success of his programs and the improvement of the Puerto Rican economy came at the high cost of shifting its working-class population to the urban centers of the United States, most notably New York City and its surrounding areas. Muñoz Marín died of a heart attack on April 30, 1980.

Sources: Muñoz Marín, *Memorias: Autobiografía pública.*

1949 ♦ Edward R. Roybal (1916–2005) became the first Mexican American to be elected to the Los Angeles City Council since 1881. A representative from East Los Angeles, his election was very much a part of the effort by returning Mexican American veterans of World War II to get representation. Born into a middle-class Mexican American family in Albuquerque,

Edward R. Roybal

New Mexico, Roybal began his education in the Los Angeles public schools after his parents moved there. After attending the University of California and Southwestern University, Roybal became a healthcare educator in the 1930s. He served in World War II and returned to Los Angeles to continue his profession when a group of Mexican American citizens approached him about running for city council. He was successful on his second attempt.

Sources: Rosales, *Chicano! History of the Mexican American Civil Rights Movement*, p. 106.

1951 ♦ President Harry S. Truman appointed the first Latino to the U.S. Court of Appeals for the 2nd Circuit: Judge Harold R. Medina Sr. (1888–1990). Born in Brooklyn, New York, of Mexican American and Dutch American parents, Medina graduated from Princeton University with honors in 1909 and received his law degree from Columbia University Law School in 1912. In 1918, Medina formed his own law firm and specialized in appeals. The most famous case argued by Medina was the Cramer treason case during World War II. Medina won the case on appeal to the U.S. Supreme Court. After World War II, Medina was appointed to the U.S. District Court for the District of New York.

Harold R. Medina Sr.

Sources: "Harold Medina, U.S. Judge, Dies at 102," *New York Times*, 16 March 1990.

1956 ♦ San Antonio native Henry B. González (1916–2000) became the first Mexican American to be elected to the Texas state senate in 110 years. Similar to his previous advocacy on the San Antonio City Council, González was a champion of civil rights for minorities. González was born in San Antonio into a family of refugees from the Mexican Revolution who stressed education and intellectual pursuits. After graduating from the University of Texas, González went on to get his law degree from Saint Mary's University in San Antonio in 1943. His first elected office was that of city councilman in 1953.

Sources: Meier and Rivera, *Dictionary of Mexican American History*, p. 148; Rosales, *Chicano! History of the Mexican American Civil Rights Movement*, p. 107.

1957 ♦ One of the most significant electoral gains for Mexican Americans was the election of Raymond L. Telles Jr. (1915–2013) as mayor of El Paso, Texas. Telles had served as El Paso county clerk since 1948. Telles's election signified that Mexican Americans could vote as a bloc if the candidate was one of their own. Although more than half of El Paso's population was Mexican American, low voter registration meant that Telles had to carry a sizable percentage of the white vote, which he did by running a campaign that minimized racial and ethnic differences.

Raymond L. Telles Jr.

Sources: Rosales, *Chicano! History of the Mexican American Civil Rights Movement*, p. 107.

1961 ♦ President John F. Kennedy appointed the first Latino judge to the U.S. District Court for the Southern District of Texas. Judge Reynaldo G. Garza (1915–2004), the son of Mexican immigrants, was born in Brownsville, Texas, and attended the University of Texas, where he received his law degree in 1901. In 1974, he became the chief judge of the U.S. District Court for the Southern District of Texas. From 1979 to 1982, he served on the U.S. Court of Appeals for the 5th Circuit.

Sources: "Reynaldo Guerra Garza," Federal Judicial Center: https://www.fjc.gov/history/judges/garza-reynaldo-guerra.

1961 ♦ Henry B. González (1916–2000) was elected to U.S. Congress, becoming the first Texan of Mexican American descent to serve in the U.S. House of Representatives. He became one of the longest tenured representatives in U.S. history. He was a staunch protector of civil rights, adequate housing, and adult education, among many other causes.

Henry B. González

Sources: Kanellos, *Latino Almanac*, p. 146.

1954: First Latinos to Argue before the U.S. Supreme Court

In 1954, the first Latinos—three Mexican American lawyers—argued a case before the U.S. Supreme Court: Gustavo C. García (1915-1964), Carlos Cadena (1917-2001), and John J. Herrera (1910-1986). Working pro bono but with trial expenses and transportation covered by fundraising from the League of United Latin American Citizens and the American G.I. Forum, this inexperienced legal team was able to go to the nation's capital and argue *Hernandez v. Texas* (1954) and prevail to have juries in the state of Texas desegregated. The decision was far-reaching for all ethnic and minority groups and became a precedent for many other cases, including *Brown v. Board of Education* (1954), which desegregated public education throughout the United States. *Sources:* Olivas, Michael A., ed., *"Colored men" and "hombres aquí": Hernández v. Texas and the Emergence of Mexican-American Lawyering*, Houston: Arte Público Press, 2006.

1961 ♦ Leon Baqueiro Poullada (1913–1987), a career Foreign Service officer, was the first Latino to be appointed a U.S. ambassador. He was ambassador to Togo from 1961 to 1964 during the Kennedy administration. The son of a Mexican immigrant doctor, Poullada also held the distinction of having served as legal counsel during the Nuremberg trials at the end of World War II. He followed his life as a diplomat by obtaining a Ph.D. in political science and teaching at Northern Arizona University.

Sources: "Leon B. Poullada, Ex-Envoy and Afghan Expert, Is Dead," *New York Times,* 23 July 1987.

1961 ♦ Teodoro Moscoso (1910–1992) became the first Puerto Rican to be appointed an ambassador of the United States. President John F. Kennedy named the former pharmacist to the post of ambassador to Venezuela on March 29, 1961. Moscoso only served for a few months. Based on his success in Venezuela, President Kennedy named him to the position of coordinator for the Alliance for Progress, a 10-year, multibillion-dollar cooperative enterprise for the social and economic development of Latin America. Moscoso was born to Puerto Rican parents in Barcelona, Spain, but grew up in Ponce, Puerto Rico, where he followed in his father's footsteps to run the family pharmacy. He found his way into politics in Puerto Rico, where he distinguished himself in the economic development program known as Operation Bootstrap.

Teodoro Moscoso

Sources: Moritz, Charles. *Current Biography Yearbook, 1963*, pp. 283–285.

1961 ♦ Raymond L. Telles Jr. (1915–2013) was one of three Latino ambassadors named in 1961 by President John F. Kennedy. He was appointed ambassador to Costa Rica. Telles had also been the first Mexican American mayor in modern times of a major U.S. city: El Paso (1959–1961). In 1971, he became chairman of the Equal Employment Opportunity Commission under President Richard Nixon. His daughter, Cynthia Telles, would follow in her father's footprints, becoming ambassador to Costa Rica.

Sources: García, Mario T., *The Making of a Mexican American Mayor: Raymond L. Telles of El Paso*, Texas Western Press, 1998.

1962 ♦ Edward R. Roybal (1916–2005) became the first Mexican American from California's 25th Congressional District to be elected to U.S. Congress, where he served for more than three decades. During his tenure in Congress, Roybal worked for social and economic reform. In 1967, he introduced legislation that became the first bilingual education act. In 1982, as chairman of the Congressional Hispanic Caucus, he led the opposition to sanctions against employers for hiring undocumented workers, which ultimately was enacted as the Immigration Reform and Control Act of 1986.

Sources: Rosales, *Chicano! History of the Mexican American Civil Rights Movement*, p. 106.

1970 ♦ Herman Badillo (1929–2014) became the first Puerto Rican ever elected as a voting member of Congress. Orphaned in Puerto Rico, he was sent to New York to live with relatives in 1940. He acquired all of his education in city schools, earning his bachelor's degree at City College of New York and his law degree at Brooklyn Law School. Badillo entered politics in 1961, losing in a run for state assembly. He later made a strong showing in a race for mayor and finally became a congressman in 1970, eventually serving four terms. Badillo resigned from Congress in 1977 to serve as an appointed deputy mayor of New York City under Mayor Ed Koch until September 1979; he was one of seven deputy mayors.

Herman Badillo

Sources: McFadden, Robert D., "Herman Badillo, Congressman and Fixture of New York Politics, Dies at 85," *New York Times*, 4 December 2014.

1970 ♦ José Angel Gutiérrez (1944–) and others founded the first successful third party in Texas, La Raza Unida (The United Race), which was also the first Mexican American political party in Texas. He and two other Chicanos were elected to the Crystal City City Council. In 1974, Gutiérrez was elected judge of Zavala County, a position from which he resigned in 1981. La Raza Unida won some initial victories, especially in Texas towns and counties densely populated with Mexican Americans, but by the 1980s, much of its pioneering reforms were absorbed by the Democratic Party, which finally became more open to Mexican Americans in Texas and other southwestern states.

Sources: Meier and Rivera, *Dictionary of Mexican American History*, pp. 157–158, 294–296; Pendas and Ring, *Toward Chicano Power.*

1971 ♦ Phillip V. Sánchez (1929–2017), the son of Mexican immigrants, became the first Latino to direct the Office of Economic Opportunity. He was appointed by President Richard M. Nixon. President Nixon later appointed him ambassador to Honduras (1973–1976).

Sources: Meier and Rivera, *Dictionary of Mexican American History*, p. 318.

1972 ♦ Romana Acosta Bañuelos (1925–2018) became the first Latina treasurer of the United States. Born in Miami, Arizona, Acosta Bañuelos was forcefully deported with her parents during the Depression. In 1944, she resettled in Los Angeles and soon thereafter founded a tortilla factory. By 1969, she was named Outstanding Businesswoman of the Year in Los Angeles. She was sworn in as treasurer on December 17, 1971.

Romana Acosta Bañuelos

Sources: Meier and Rivera, *Dictionary of Mexican American History*, p. 33.

Maurice Ferré

1973 ♦ Puerto Rican Maurice Ferré (1935–2019) became the first Hispanic mayor of Miami. His election as mayor was a sign of the emergence of a Latino voting bloc in Miami. Ferré was reelected five times but ultimately lost in 1985 to a Cuban-born candidate. During his tenure, he presided over the city's growth as an important center of international trade and banking. The wealthy businessman's electoral career started in the mid-1960s with his election to the Miami City Council; he later served in the state legislature.

Sources: Henderson and Mormino, *Spanish Pathways in Florida*, pp. 305, 308, 310–315.

1974 ♦ Jerry Apodaca (1934–) became the first Latino governor of New Mexico in 50 years. After his term as governor, President Jimmy Carter appointed him chairman of the President's Council on Physical Fitness and Sports. Born and raised in Las Cruces, Apodaca entered politics in 1966 as a Democratic state senator.

Sources: Kanellos, *Latino Almanac*, pp. 149–150, 234.

1975 ♦ Raúl Héctor Castro (1916–2015) became the first Latino governor of Arizona. Born on June 12, 1916, in Cananea, Mexico, he moved as a child with his poverty-stricken parents to Pertleville, Arizona, where he became the family's wage earner after his father died. Despite working as a migrant laborer, miner, and rancher, he was able to earn a degree from Arizona State College in 1939 and went to Washington, D.C., to work for the State Department. He returned to Arizona in

Raúl Héctor Castro

1971: First Feminist Mexican American Conference

The first national feminist conference of Mexican Americans was held in Houston in 1971. The Conferencia de Mujeres por la Raza, also known as the National Chicana Conference, was held at the Magnolia Park YWCA in Houston from May 28 to 30, 1971, with some 600 women in attendance from 23 states. Four major workshops were organized on education and employment, sex and birth control, marriage and childcare, and religion. Among the issues discussed were gender discrimination, abortion, birth control, inadequate educational opportunities, racism, welfare support, and employment discrimination. *Sources:* Palomo Acosta, Teresa, "Conferencia de Mujeres por la Raza," *Handbook of Texas:* https://www.tshaonline.org/handbook/entries/conferencia-de-mujeres-por-la-raza.

1946 and earned a law degree from the University of Arizona in 1949. He entered politics and served in various elected positions. In 1964, he was appointed ambassador to El Salvador and, in 1968, ambassador to Bolivia. He ran unsuccessfully for governor in 1970 but was victorious in 1974. In 1977, he resigned from his office to serve as ambassador to Argentina.

Sources: Meier and Rivera, *Dictionary of Mexican American History*, pp. 72–73; Rivera-Ashford, Roni Capi, *Raulito, the First Hispanic Governor of Arizona*, Houston: Arte Público Press, 2021.

1976 ♦ Largely through the efforts of New York congressman Herman Badillo (1929–2014), the Congressional Hispanic Caucus was organized. This signified that for the first time, there were enough Hispanic congressional representatives to have a caucus: a total of five. The caucus is dedicated to voicing and advancing, through the legislative process, issues affecting Hispanic Americans in the United States and its territories.

Sources: Enciso et al., *The History of the Congressional Hispanic Caucus*, p. 7.

1977 ♦ Mari-Luci Jaramillo (1928–2019) became the first Latina to be named an ambassador. The native of Las Vegas, New Mexico, and education professor at the University of New Mexico was appointed by President Jimmy Carter as ambassador to Honduras. Born into a poor family in Las Vegas,

Mari-Luci Jaramillo

New Mexico, on June 19, 1928, Jaramillo became an outstanding student but went on to receive a college education only after her three children were old enough to allow her to continue studying. She also held jobs while studying and raising a family. In 1955, Jaramillo obtained her degree in education from New Mexico Highlands University and became a teacher. She later worked her way up into university teaching, and through her involvement in international education, she came to the attention of President Jimmy Carter, who named her to an ambassadorship. In 1990, the Mexican American Women's National Association honored her with the Primera Award as the first Hispanic woman to be appointed an ambassador.

Sources: Meier and Rivera, *Dictionary of Mexican American History*, p. 176; Telgen and Kamp, *Latinas! Women of Achievement*, pp. 210–215.

1977 ♦ Leonel Castillo (1939–2013) became the first Latino to direct the U.S. Immigration and Naturalization Service. Born in Victoria, Texas, Castillo received his B.A. from Saint Mary's University in San Antonio and his M.S.W. from the University of Pittsburgh in 1967. After graduating from Saint Mary's in 1961, Castillo served in the Peace Corps in the Philippines from 1961 to 1965. After the Peace Corps, Castillo returned to Houston and, in 1970, won a surprise victory in the race for city comptroller against a 25-year incumbent. In 1974, he was named treasurer of the Texas Democratic Party.

Sources: Meier and Rivera, *Dictionary of Mexican American History*, p. 72.

1977 ♦ Lawyer Graciela Olivárez was the first Latina to serve as director of the Community Services Administration under President Jimmy Carter. She was the highest-ranking Latina in the Carter administration.

Sources: Telgen and Kamp, *Latinas! Women of Achievement*, p. 288.

Robert "Bobby" García

1978 ♦ Robert "Bobby" García (1933–1917) became the first Puerto Rican born in the continental United States to be elected to the U.S. House of Representatives. He served from 1978 to 1990. García was born to Puerto Rican/Spanish working-class parents in the Bronx, in the same south Bronx district he represented, first as a state assemblyman (1966–1967), then as a state senator (1968–1978), and then as a congressman. García was a major implementer of the 1965 Voting Rights Act and other equal rights legislation; he was one of the founders of the Congressional Hispanic Caucus.

Sources: García, Robert, *Man of the People: The Autobiography of Robert García*, Houston: Arte Público Press, 2023.

José A. Cabranés

1979 ♦ President Jimmy Carter appointed the first native Puerto Rican, José A. Cabranés (1940–), to the federal court within the continental United States. Born in Mayagüez, Puerto Rico, Cabranés moved as a child with his family to New York City. He attended public schools and graduated from Columbia College in 1961 and from Yale University Law School in 1965. He received his LL.M. degree from the University of Cambridge in England in 1967. Cabranés practiced law and also taught at Rutgers University Law School in New Jersey. He served on the President's Commission on Mental Health from 1977 to 1978 and in a variety of other governmental advisory positions. In 1979, President Carter appointed Cabranés to the U.S. District Court for the District of Connecticut. In 1988, U.S. Supreme Court Chief Justice William H. Rehnquist named Judge Cabranés as one of five federal judges for the 15-member Federal Court Study Committee, created by an act of Congress "to examine problems facing the federal courts and develop a long-range plan for the future of the federal judiciary." In 2000, he received the Federal Bar Council's Learned Hand Medal for Excellence in Federal Jurisprudence and, in 2023, the Edward J. Devitt Distinguished Service to Justice Award.

Sources: Kanellos, *Latino Almanac,* p. 166.

1979 ♦ President Jimmy Carter appointed the first Latino judge to the U.S. Court of Appeals for the 5th Circuit, Judge Reynaldo G. Garza (1915–2004), who was also the first Mexican American appointed to the federal bench, in 1961. He served on the appeals court until 1981.

Sources: Kanellos, *Latino Almanac,* p. 170.

1979 ♦ President Jimmy Carter appointed the first Latino secretary of the U.S. Navy, Edward Hidalgo (1912–1995), a native of Mexico City.

Sources: Kanellos, *Latino Almanac,* p. 154.

Julian Nava

1980 ♦ President Jimmy Carter named Julian Nava (1927–1922) U.S. ambassador to Mexico. Nava thus became the first Mexican American to serve in that position. Born in Mexico but raised in East Los Angeles, Nava had previously created a successful career as an educator, author, and politician. After receiving his doctorate in history from Harvard University in 1955, Nava taught at the University of Puerto Rico and later at California State College at Northridge. He served on the Los Angeles school board for various terms and wrote books on Mexican American history.

Sources: Nava, Julian, *Julian Nava: My Mexican-American Journey*, Houston: Arte Público Press, 2002.

1980 ♦ President Jimmy Carter appointed Hipólito Frank García (1925–2002) to the U.S. District Court for the Western District of Texas, making him the first Latino to serve in that position. He served from 1964 to 1980 as a Texas county court judge. He graduated from Saint Mary's University Law School in 1951.

Sources: Kanellos, *Latino Almanac*, p. 169.

1980 ♦ Carmen Consuelo Cerezo (1940–) became the first Latina to serve on a federal bench when President Jimmy Carter appointed her to the U.S. District Court for the District of Puerto Rico. She served until her retirement in 2012; she was chief judge from 1994 to 1999.

Sources: Kanellos, *Latino Almanac*, p. 167.

1981 ♦ Henry G. Cisneros (1947–) became the first modern-day Latino mayor of San Antonio, Texas, the nation's ninth largest city. Born in a Mexican barrio of San Antonio, the son of a civil servant, Cisneros was educated in the city's parochial schools and attended Texas A&M University, where he received a B.A. and then a master's degree in urban planning in 1970. In 1971, Cisneros moved to Washington, D.C., where he worked for the National League of Cities and began full-time graduate studies in public administration at George Washington University. At the age of 22, Cisneros became the youngest White House fellow in U.S. history. When his fellowship ended, he earned a second master's degree, in public administration, at Harvard University. He went on to complete his work at George Washington University and received a Ph.D. in public administration. He then returned to San Antonio to teach government at the University of Texas. In 1975, Cisneros ran for the city council on the Good Government League ticket and won. He gained a reputation as a bright young politician, and in 1977, he was reelected by a landslide. In 1981, Cisneros was elected mayor of San Antonio with 62 percent of the vote. In 1983, he was reelected

Henry G. Cisneros

1981: The Cuban American National Foundation

In 1981 wealthy Cuban businessmen formed the first organization to influence U.S. policy through lobbying and financial contributions to campaigns: the Cuban American National Foundation (CANF). It established its center in Washington, D.C., under the chairmanship of Jorge Mas Canosa (1939–1997). The CANF began influencing U.S. policy toward Cuba principally through its political action committee, Free Cuba, which donated to the campaign funds of congressmen and senators who maintained a hard line toward Castro's Cuba. The CANF also became a principal lobbyist for the establishment by the U.S. government of Radio Martí, a radio station founded to broadcast news and features to Cuba and serve as a supplement to the censored or ideologically biased transmissions that characterized the Cuban broadcast media. *Sources:* García, *Havana USA*, pp. 147–148.

with 94 percent of the vote, again in 1985 with 72 percent, and again in 1987 with twice as many votes as his closest opponent. Although Cisneros won numerous national awards for his leadership and vision as mayor, he did not thereafter seek reelection as mayor.

Sources: "Henry Cisneros," Bipartisan Policy Center: https://bipartisanpolicy.org/person/henry-cisneros/.

1982 ♦ Cruz Reynoso (1931–2021) became the first Latino appointed to the Supreme Court of California. The Mexican American, born in Brea, California, was the son of farm workers. He received his law degree from University of California Law School in 1958 and immediately entered private practice. He worked in the government in the 1960s both in California and Washington, D.C. After serving as the director of the California Rural Legal Assistance program, in 1972, he accepted a teaching position at University of New Mexico Law School. In 1976, he was appointed to the California Courts of Appeal in Sacramento, and in 1982, Governor Jerry Brown appointed him to the California Supreme Court, where he served until 1986. In 1990, he was appointed to the law faculty at the University of California. In 2000, President Clinton awarded Reynoso the Presidential Medal of Freedom.

Sources: Kanellos, *Latino Almanac*, p. 179.

1982 ♦ Dorothy Comstock Riley (1924–2004) became the first Latina supreme court judge of any state. Born to Latino parents in Detroit, Michigan, Riley attended Wayne State University, where she received both her B.A. and her law degree. After a career in private practice, including running her own firm, Riley sat on the Michigan Courts of Appeal from 1976 to 1982, when she was elevated to the Michigan Supreme Court as an associate justice.

Sources: Kanellos, *Latino Almanac*, p. 179.

Gloria Molina

1982 ♦ Gloria Molina (1948–2023) of Los Angeles became the first Latina ever to be elected to the California state legislature. She continued her political career in 1987 by being elected to the Los Angeles City Council, on which she served until she was elected to the Los Angeles County Board of Supervisors in 1991. The daughter of Mexican immigrants, Molina grew up in the Los Angeles area. Although she became the principal provider for her family when her father became ill, she was able to finish her college education at California State College in Los Angeles.

Sources: Kanellos, *Latino Almanac*, p. 156.

1983 ♦ Federico Peña (1947–) became the first Latino mayor of Denver, Colorado, one of the nation's major cities. At the age of 36, Peña was elected Denver's 37th mayor and was reelected to a second term in 1987. At the time he entered office, he was among the youngest chief executives in Denver history. Mayor Peña's efforts to strengthen Denver's economy placed the city in the national spotlight. The U.S. Conference of Mayors selected Denver over 100 other cities as the winner of its prestigious City Livability Award.

Sources: Kanellos, *Chronology of Hispanic American History*, p. 226.

1985 ♦ Miami elected its first Cuban-born mayor, Xavier Suárez (1949–). By then, Latinos controlled three of the five seats on the city commission and held many of the city's most important administrative and patronage positions. Born in Las Villas, Cuba, the son of a university professor, Suárez moved as an exile to Washington, D.C., with his family in 1961. After studying law and public policy at Harvard University, Suárez moved to Miami to become involved in politics. After unsuccessfully challenging Maurice Ferré for the office of mayor in 1983, he was finally successful by creating coalitions of blacks, Anglos, and Latinos.

Xavier Suárez

Sources: Henderson and Mormino, *Spanish Pathways in Florida*, pp. 314–322.

1985 ♦ Mexican American Frances García (1938–) became the first Latina mayor in the Midwest when she took office in Hutchinson, Kansas. Hutchinson had a population of 41,000, of which only two percent were Latinos.

Sources: Tardiff and Mabunda, *Dictionary of Hispanic Biography*, pp. 368–369.

1987 ♦ Tampa native Bob Martínez (1934–) became the first Catholic and first Latino to be elected governor of Florida. He served until January 1991.

Sources: Tardiff and Mabunda, *Dictionary of Hispanic Biography*, p. 527.

1987 ♦ Gloria Molina (1948–2023) became the first Mexican American woman ever elected to the Los Angeles City Council.

Sources: Tardiff and Mabunda, *Dictionary of Hispanic Biography*, p. 559.

1988 ♦ President Ronald Reagan appointed Dr. Lauro F. Cavazos (1927–2022), the former president of Texas Tech University, to the cabinet post of secretary of education. He became the first Hispanic to hold the post and the first Hispanic ever to become a member of the presidential cabinet.

Sources: Kanellos, *Latino Almanac*, p. 152.

1989 ♦ For the first time in history, a Cuban American was elected to U.S. Congress. Miami's Ileana Ros-Lehtinen (1952–) was also the first Latina to become a congresswoman. Ros-Lehtinen received bachelor's and master's degrees from Florida International University in Miami and went on to teach in her own private school. In 1982, she was elected to the Florida legislature as a Republican. She was elected to the Florida state senate in 1986.

Ileana Ros-Lehtinen

Sources: Telgen and Kamp, *Latinas! Women of Achievement*, pp. 327–331.

Manuel Luján Jr.

1989 ♦ President George H. W. Bush appointed the first Latino secretary of the interior, Manuel Luján Jr. (1928–2019). The Santa Fe, New Mexico, native had served as a Republican congressman from 1969 to 1989 and, at the time of his appointment, was the ranking minority member of the House Interior Committee.

Sources: Kanellos, *Latino Almanac*, pp. 154–155.

1989 ♦ The first Latino to be appointed chief of police of a major metropolitan police department was Philip Arreola (1940–), when he assumed the leadership of the Milwaukee Police Department. Born on February 4, 1940, in Acambaro, Guanajuato, Mexico, Arreola had previously served as chief of the Port Huron Police Department in Michigan. Arreola's education includes a bachelor of science (cum laude) degree and a law degree from Wayne State University, conferred in 1974 and 1985, respectively. He is also a graduate of the FBI National Academy (1977) and was a fellow of Harvard University School of Law (1970–1971). He served as chief until 1996, when he took the job as chief of police for Tacoma, Washington.

Sources: "Milwaukee Police Chief Philip Arreola," Milwaukee Public Library: https://www.mpl.org/blog/now/milwaukee-police-chief-philip-arreola

1989 ♦ Raymond E. Orozco (1933–) became the first fire commissioner of a major metropolitan fire department when he assumed the leadership of the Chicago Fire Department. Born in Chicago, Illinois, on December 7, 1933, Orozco rose through the ranks to become chief. He served as chief until his retirement in 1996; he had served as a fireman for 38 years. In 2008, he became the executive director of the Office of Emergency Management and Communications for the City of Chicago and, in 2013, the mayor's chief of staff.

Sources: "Orozco Retiring as Chicago Fire Chief at Month's End," *Chicago Tribune:* https://www.chicagotribune.com/1996/11/03/orozco-retiring-as-chicago-fire-chief-at-months-end/.

1990 ♦ Ecuadoran American lawyer Lourdes Baird (1935–) became U.S. attorney for the U.S. District Court for the Central District of California, the largest federal district in the nation. In that position, she would oversee the work of 150 attorneys. Born on May 12, 1935, in Quito, Ecuador, Baird was educated in a Catholic school for girls in Los Angeles. She married a businessman and raised children, becoming a lawyer later in life, in 1977. By 1986, she had become a judge in the East Los Angeles Municipal Court. She became a Los Angeles Superior Court judge in 1988 until her appointment as U.S. attorney.

Sources: Tardiff and Mabunda, *Dictionary of Hispanic Biography*, pp. 85–86; Telgen and Kamp, *Latinas! Women of Achievement*, pp. 45–50.

1990 ♦ President George H. W. Bush appointed the first woman and the first Latino surgeon general of the United States, Antonia C. Novello (1944–). Born in Fajardo, Puerto Rico, Novello received her B.A. (1965) and M.D.

Antonia C. Novello

(1970) degrees from the University of Puerto Rico. She received a master's degree in public health from Johns Hopkins University in 1982. Novello joined the U.S. Public Health Service in 1978 and served in various capacities at the National Institutes of Health, including serving as deputy director of the National Institute of Child Health and Human Development. In 2020, *USA Today* named Novello among "100 Women of the Century," citing among other achievements: "As Surgeon General, Dr. Novello was among the first to recognize the need to focus on women with AIDS and on neonatal transmission of HIV."

Sources: "Antonia Novello," National Women's Hall of Fame: https://www.womenofthehall.org/inductee/antonia-novello/.

1991 ♦ Gloria Molina (1984–2023) became the first woman ever elected to the Los Angeles County Board of Supervisors. She was the first Latino since 1875 to serve in that position.

Sources: Tardiff and Mabunda, *Dictionary of Hispanic Biography*, p. 560.

1991 ♦ Ed Pastor (1943–2018) became Arizona's first Latino congressman when he was appointed and then elected to fill the House seat vacated by Morris K. Udall. The former chemistry teacher and lawyer began his political career when elected to the Maricopa County Board of Supervisors in 1977.

Sources: "Ed Pastor, Arizona's First Hispanic Congressman, Dies at 75," *Washington Post*, 28 November 2018.

1992 ♦ Henry G. Cisneros (1947–) was named by President Bill Clinton to the cabinet position of secretary of housing and urban development and became the first Latino to hold that post.

Sources: Kanellos, *Chronology of Hispanic American History*, p. 279.

1992 ♦ Federico Peña was named by President Bill Clinton to the cabinet position of secretary of transportation and became the first Latino to hold that post.

Sources: Kanellos, *Chronology of Hispanic American History*, p. 279.

1992 ♦ Brooklyn's Nydia Margarita Velázquez (1953–) became the first Puerto Rican woman and the second Latina to be elected to U.S. Congress.

Nydia Margarita Velázquez

Born and raised in Puerto Rico, Velázquez received her B.A. from the University of Puerto Rico and her M.A. in political science from New York University. From 1984 to 1986, Velázquez served on the New York City Council. In 1986, she became the director of the Migration Division of the Commonwealth of Puerto Rico.

Sources: "Loyalty and Labor: Nydia Margarita Velázquez," *New York Times*, 16 September 1992, p. B6; "Congresswoman Nydia Velázquez: Biography": https://velazquez.house.gov/about/full-biography.

1992 ♦ Lucille Roybal-Allard (1941–) became the first Mexican American woman to be elected to the U.S. House of Representatives, representing California's 33rd Congressional District (then 34th and lastly 40th), which was previously represented by her father, Edward Roybal. She served until 2023.

Sources: Telgen and Kamp, *Latinas! Women of Achievement*, pp. 333–337.

1992 ♦ Aeronautical engineer Ana Sol Gutiérrez (1942–) became the first Latina elected to a board of education in the state of Maryland and the first Salvadoran American ever elected to a public office in the United States. She served four terms.

Sources: Tardiff and Mabunda, *Dictionary of Hispanic Biography*, p. 410.

Sylvia García

1994 ♦ Judge Sylvia García (1950–) became the first Latina judge to direct a major municipal court system. She served as director and presiding judge of the Houston Municipal Courts. Born on September 6, 1950, in San Diego, Texas, García received her law degree from Thurgood Marshall School of Law at Texas Southern University. García served as Houston city controller (1998) and went on to be elected to the Harris County Commissioners Court (2002), the Texas Senate (2013), and the U.S. House of Representatives (2019). In 2020, García served as one of seven mangers of the impeachment of President Donald Trump.

Sources: "Congresswoman Sylvia García": https://sylviaGarcía.house.gov/about; *Texas Hispanic*, 5/26 (1995), p. 53.

1996 ♦ John M. Bernal (1994–2000) became the first Latino (and the first Mexican American) to head the International Boundary and Water Commission in its 106-year history. This U.S. federal agency was created to handle boundary and water disputes between the United States and Mexico. The Tucson engineer was appointed to the post by President Bill Clinton.

Sources: Hispanic, March 1996, p. 9.

Alex Castellanos

1996 ♦ The first Latino to direct a presidential election advertising campaign was Cuban American Alex Castellanos (1954–), who was selected by Republican presidential nominee Bob Dole to lead his advertising campaign against incumbent president Bill Clinton. Born in Havana, Castellanos fled Cuba with his parents at the age of 6. They settled in North Carolina, where Castellanos attended the University of North Carolina. He dropped out during his senior year to work on the Ronald Reagan campaign and has been involved in Republican Party politics ever since. He was widely credited with inventing a lucrative direct-mail operation for Senator Jesse Helms in the late 1970s and continued putting successful campaigns together for the conservative senator. After working on the Dole campaign, he served as a media consultant for the Bush and Romney campaigns.

Sources: Duffy, Michael, "Campaign '96: Alex Castellanos Has a Crisp, Clear Way of Going for the Jugular," *Time*, 16 September 1996, p. 44.

1996 ♦ Adriano Espaillat (1954–) became the first Dominican American elected to a state legislature (New York).

Sources: Lombardi, Frank, "Freshman State Sen. Espaillat Going to Bat for More Than 1M Tenants from Rent Regulation Changes," *Daily News New York*, 14 April 2011.

1997 ♦ Former Denver mayor Federico Peña (1947–) became the first Latino to serve as the secretary of energy. The new energy czar had previously served as secretary of transportation during President Bill Clinton's first term.

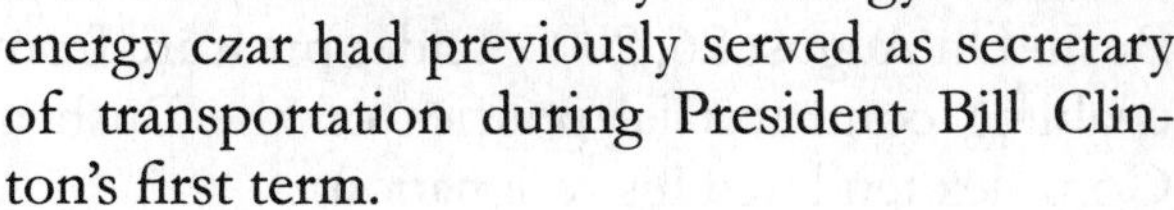

Federico Peña

Sources: Kanellos, *Chronology of Hispanic American History*, p. 226.

Loretta Sánchez

1997 ♦ Loretta Sánchez (1960–) became the first Mexican American U.S. congresswoman. She was elected in a very close race in one of the nation's most conservative districts: Orange County, California. In 2016, she decided not to run again for the House of Representatives.

Sources: Hispanic, December 1996, pp. 8–9.

Bill Richardson

1997 ♦ Bill Richardson (1947–2023) was the first Latino to serve as U.S. ambassador to the United Nations. Born on November 15, 1947, in Pasadena, California, Richardson spent his boyhood in Mexico City. He graduated from Tufts University in 1970 and received a master's degree from the Fletcher School of Law and Diplomacy in 1971. Richardson served as governor of New Mexico from 2003 to 2011. He had also served as secretary of energy in the Clinton administration and was a U.S. congressman representing New Mexico. Richardson was the first Latino to serve as secretary of energy (1998–2001).

Sources: Richardson, Bill, with Michael Ruby, *Between Worlds: The Making of an American Life—An Autobiography*, G. P. Putnam's Sons, 2005.

2003 ♦ When President George W. Bush appointed Cecilia M. Altonaga (1962–) a judge of the U.S. District Court for the Southern District of Florida, she became the first Cuban American woman to be appointed as a federal judge in the United States. She became chief judge of the court in 2021.

Sources: García, Lisette, "County Judge Attains New Benchmark," *Miami Herald*, 29 August 1999.

Alberto R. González

2005 ♦ Alberto R. González (1955–) became the first Latino attorney general of the United States when he was appointed by President George W. Bush. The son of a Mexican migrant worker and a homemaker, he first served under Governor Bush of Texas and later as White House counsel to President Bush. On August 26, 2007, under pressure from Congress for enabling controversial policies of the Bush administration, González tendered his resignation.

Sources: McElroy, Lisa Tucker, *Alberto Gonzales, Attorney General*, Minneapolis: Millbrook Press, 2006.

2009 ♦ Sonia Sotomayor (1954–) became the first and only Latino to be appointed to the U.S. Supreme Court. The Puerto Rican native of New York's South Bronx also became the first nonwhite woman and the first

Sonia Sotomayor

Latina to serve on the court. Sotomayor graduated from Princeton University (1976) and Yale University Law School (1979), where she was the editor of the law journal. Sotomayor worked as a district attorney in New York City before becoming a judge in 1991, when President George H. W. Bush nominated her to the U.S. District Court for the Southern District of New York. When she was confirmed by the U.S. Senate, she became the youngest judge in the Southern District and the first Latina federal judge in New York State, as well as the first Puerto Rican to serve as a federal judge. Among her numerous awards and special recognition, in 2006, Sotomayor was named to *Esquire* magazine's list of "The 75 Most Influential People of the 21st Century." In 2008, she was elected to the National Women's Hall of Fame.

Sources: Sotomayor, Sonia, *Turning Pages: My Life Story*, New York: Philomel Books, 2018.

Hilda L. Solís

2009 ♦ Hilda L. Solís (1957–) became the first Latino to serve as the U.S. secretary of labor in President Barack Obama's cabinet; she served until 2013. She was also the first woman of Central American descent to be appointed to a presidential cabinet. Prior to her appointment, she served as a U.S congresswoman from 2001 to 2009. Solís was also the first woman to receive the John F. Kennedy Profile in Courage Award in 2000 for her pioneering work on environmental justice issues. In 2014, Solís won a seat on the Los Angeles County Board of Supervisors; she became its chair in 2015. She has been reelected to the board since then.

Sources: Kimitch, Rebecca, "Solis, a Woman of Many Firsts, Had a Steady Rise through California's Political Ranks," *San Gabriel Tribune*, 7 January 2009.

Mari Carmen Aponte

2010 ♦ Jaime Herrera-Beutler (1978–) was the first Latino to be elected to Congress from the state of Washington. She was only 31 years of age at the time and soon became the 15th ranked most bipartisan representative.

Sources: Kanellos, *Latino Almanac*, pp. 137–138.

2010 ♦ Mari Carmen Aponte (1946–) became the first Puerto Rican to serve as U.S. ambassador. President Barack Obama appointed Aponte ambassador to El Salvador. She served from August 2010 until December 2011 and again from June 14, 2012, until December 2015. She served as U.S. ambassador to Panama from 2022 to 2025, having been nominated by President Joe Biden.

Sources: Mead, Kevin, "Obama Names Aponte to Top US Post at Organization of American States," *Caribbean Business,* 3 August 2012: http://www.caribbeanbusinesspr.com/news/obama-names-aponte-to-top-us-post-at-organization-of-4merican-states-99225.html.

Julissa Reynoso Pantaleón

2012 ♦ Julissa Reynoso Pantaleón (1975–) was the first Dominican-born American U.S. ambassador. Attorney Reynoso Pantaleón was appointed U.S. ambassador to Uruguay in 2012. She later served as chief of staff to First Lady Jill Biden and then in December 2021 was appointed U.S. ambassador to Spain and Andorra.

Sources: "Ambassador Julissa Reynoso," U.S. Embassy & Consulate in Spain and Andorra: https://es.usembassy.gov/ambassador-julissa-reynoso/.

2013 ♦ Tony Cárdenas (1963–) became the first Latino elected to Congress to represent the San Fernando Valley district of California. With a background in engineering and business, Cárdenas had served three terms in the California Assembly before being elected to Congress.

Sources: Kanellos, *Latino Almanac*, p. 132.

Alex Mooney

2014 ♦ Alex Mooney (1971–) was the first Latino elected to represent West Virginia in the U.S. House of Representative, where he served from 2015 to 2025. Alex's mother, Lala (Suárez) Mooney, was born and raised in Fidel Castro's Cuba, where she was thrown into jail for seven weeks for opposing Castro's communist regime. When she was 20 years old, Lala escaped Cuba and fled to the United States to restart her life. Alex's father, Vincent, was sent to Vietnam when Lala was expecting their first child. Mooney's uncle is former Miami mayor Xavier Suárez. From 1999 to 2011, Mooney served in the Maryland Senate but was defeated in the 2010 election. He nevertheless became chair of the Maryland Republican Party. In 2013, Mooney moved to West Virginia and declared his intention to run for Congress.

Sources: Sonmez, Felicia, Amy B. Wang, and Marianna Sotomayor, "House

Ethics Committee Investigating Reps. Cawthorn, Jackson, Mooney," *Washington Post*, 23 May 2022.

Norma J. Torres

2014 ♦ Norma J. Torres (1965–) became the first immigrant from Guatemala to be elected to U.S. Congress. Torres immigrated to the United States with family members when she was five years old. Torres became a U.S. citizen in 1992. She worked as a labor union activist and served as the shop steward for Local 3090 of the municipal employees' union. Prior to being elected congresswoman, she had served as mayor of Pomona, California; she had also served as a state senator and assemblywoman. Notably, her amendment to require the secretary of state to send Congress a list of corrupt officials in Honduras, Guatemala, and El Salvador became part of the Defense Authorization Act signed into law in 2019.

Sources: Huetteman, Emmarie, "Dangers Propelled Norma Torres to Move to U.S., Then to Politics," *New York Times*, 15 February 2015.

Linda T. Sánchez

2015 ♦ During the 115th Congress (2015–2017), Linda T. Sánchez (1969–) served as vice chair of the House Democratic Caucus. She is the first Latina elected to a leadership position in U.S. Congress. In 2009, Sánchez introduced the Gender Equity in Health Premiums Act to bar health insurance companies from charging women more for healthcare premiums than men. The Gender Equity in Health Premiums Act became part of the Affordable Care Act, which President Obama signed into law in 2010. She was reelected, most recently, in 2024.

Sources: Sánchez, Linda, and Loretta Sánchez, *Dream in Color: How the Sánchez Sisters Are Making History in Congress*, New York: Grand Central Publishing, 2008.

2016 ♦ Catherine Cortez Masto became the first woman from Nevada and the first Latina ever elected to the U.S. Senate. Previously, she had served two terms as Nevada's attorney general. She was reelected in 2022.

Sources: Philipps, Dave. "Catherine Cortez Masto Wins Nevada to Become First Latina Senator," *New York Times*, 9 November 2016.

Adriano Espaillat

2017 ♦ Adriano Espaillat (1954–) became the first Dominican American to be elected to the House of Representatives. He was also the first undocumented immigrant to serve in U.S. Congress—he received his green card residency in 1965. Espaillat is an avid promoter of the American Dream and Promise Act that would legalize residency for children brought to the United States by undocumented parents.

Sources: Eligon, John, "Running for the House on Pride in His Roots, and Pure Energy," *New York Times*, 18 June 2012.

Debbie Murcasel-Powell

2019 ♦ Debbie Murcasel-Powell (1971–) became the first Ecuadorian American and the first South American immigrant member of Congress, representing portions of South Florida. Born on January 18, 1971, in Guayaquil, Ecuador, Mucarsel-Powell immigrated to the United States from Ecuador as a young girl with her mother and sisters. She learned the struggles immigrants face at an early age when her mother worked double shifts while attending night school to learn English. At the age of 15, Mucarsel-Powell started helping her mother by working at a doughnut shop before school. She worked her way through high school and college and earned her bachelor's degree in political science from Pitzer College. She then gained her master's degree in international political economy from Claremont Graduate University. She returned to Miami and, from 2003 to 2007, served as the director of development at Florida International University. From 2007 to 2011, she was the associate vice president for advancement at FIU's Herbert Wertheim College of Medicine and the associate dean at the College of Medicine, where she worked to grow programs that improve healthcare access for Floridians. She was defeated for reelection in 2020. She ran for the U.S. Senate in 2024 and became the first Latina nominee for Senate in Florida, but she was defeated by Republican Rick Scott.

Sources: Clark, Lesley, "Citing Health Care, Debbie Mucarsel-Powell Wants to Be Part of Florida's Blue Wave," *McClatchyDC*: https://www.mcclatchydc.com/latest-news/article219016890.html.

2019 ♦ When Alexandria Ocasio-Cortez (1989–), the daughter of Puerto Rican parents, was elected to the U.S. House of Representatives, she became the youngest woman to ever serve in Congress. After high school, Ocasio-Cortez attended and graduated cum laude from Boston University (2011) with degrees in economics and international relations. During her university studies, she also had the opportunity to work in the office of the late Senator Ted Kennedy. During the 2016 presidential election, she worked as a volunteer organizer for

Alexandria Ocasio-Cortez

Bernie Sanders in the South Bronx, expanding her skills in electoral organizing and activism that served as experience to launch her people-funded, grassroots campaign for Congress. Ocasio-Cortez is a member of the Democratic Socialists of America and is committed to serving working-class people over corporate interests and advocating for social, racial, economic, and environmental justice.

Sources: Givhan, Robin, "Alexandria Ocasio-Cortez Shared Her Personal Story and Revealed Our Collective Trauma," *Washington Post*, 2 February 2021.

2020 ♦ A new milestone was set: there were 128 Latinos serving in U.S. Congress.

Sources: Kanellos, *Latino Almanac*, p. 127.

2021 ♦ Attorney General of California Xavier Becerra (1958–) became the first Latino to serve as secretary of health and human services, a presidential cabinet position, when President Joe Biden nominated him and the Senate confirmed him for the position. He had previously served in Congress from 1992 to 2001.

Sources: Kanellos, *Latino Almanac*, p. 151.

Alejandro Mayorkas

2021 ♦ Alejandro Mayorkas (1959–) became the first Latino to head the U.S. Department of Homeland Security when President Joe Biden nominated him and the Senate confirmed him for that position. A Cuban born to Jewish parents, Mayorkas and his family came to the United States in 1960 as refugees from the Cuban Revolution. After receiving his degree from Loyola Law School in 1985, he spent the majority of his career in government service. In 1998, he became the youngest U.S. attorney in history. In 2009, he was appointed director of the U.S. Citizenship and Immigration Service by President Barack Obama, thus becoming the highest-ranking Cuban American in government at that time. It was under his directorship that the Deferred Action for Childhood Arrivals (DACA) was developed to shield minors from deportation. From 2013 to 2016, he served as deputy secretary of the U.S. Department of Homeland Security.

Sources: Kanellos, *Latino Almanac*, pp. 157–158.

2022 ♦ Jason Stuart Miyares (1976–), the son of Cuban refugees, was the first Latino elected to serve as the attorney general of Virginia. Actually, he was the first Latino elected statewide to any office. In 2015, he had been elected and served in the Virgina House of Delegates.

Sources: "In U.S. Politics, Even the Storied Phrase 'the American Dream' Divides," *New York Times*, 21 August 2022.

2022 ♦ Republican Lori Michelle Chavez-DeRemer (1968–) and Democrat Andrea Salinas (1969–), Mexican Americans, became the first Latinas elected to represent Oregon in U.S. Congress.

Sources: "The Latinos Who Made History in the Midterm Elections," *Axios*: www.axios/2022/11/09/midterms-latinos-firsts.

Yadira D. Caraveo

2022 ♦ Democrat Yadira D. Caraveo (1980–) became the first Latina elected to represent Colorado in the U.S. House of Representatives. Born to Mexican undocumented parents who benefited from amnesty, Caraveo was able to become a medical doctor but entered politics first, working for Barack Obama's 2008 election campaign. In 2018, she was elected to the Colorado House and served until her election to Congress.

Sources: "The Latinos Who Made History in the Midterm Elections," *Axios*: www.axios/2022/11/09/midterms-latinos-firsts.

2022 ♦ Republican Anna Paulina Luna (1989–) became the first Mexican American (via a maternal grandparent) elected to Congress from Florida. Born in Santa Ana, California, she received her higher education in Florida.

Sources: "The Latinos Who Made History in the Midterm Elections," *Axios*: www.axios/2022/11/09/midterms-latinos-firsts

2022 ♦ Democrat Alejandro "Alex" Padilla (1973–) became the first Mexican American in modern times elected to the U.S. Senate. Both of his parents were immigrants from Mexico, and he was born in Los Angeles. From 2015 to 2021, he had previously served as the California secretary of state. In 2021, Governor Gavin Newsome had appointed Padilla to serve out Senator Kamala Harris's term when she became vice president. He subsequently won the special election to fill the Senate seat.

Alex Padilla

Sources: "The Latinos Who Made History in the Midterm Elections," *Axios*: www.axios/2022/11/09/midterms-latinos-firsts.

2022 ♦ The daughter of immigrants from Guatemala, Democrat Delia Ramírez became the first Latina elected to represent Illinois in the U.S. Congress. Prior to that, she had served in the Illinois House from 2018 to 2023, where she was the first Guatemalan elected to that body.

Sources: "The Latinos Who Made History in the Midterm Elections," *Axios*: www.axios/2022/11/09/midterms-latinos-firsts.

Robert García

2022 ♦ Democrat Robert García (1977–) became the first openly gay man and the first Peruvian elected to Congress to represent California. García was born in Lima, Peru, and immigrated with his mother when he was five years old. With a doctorate in education, he had taught at the college level and also served on the Long Beach City Council, then as mayor of Long Beach from 2014 to 2022.

Sources: "The Latinos Who Made History in the Midterm Elections," *Axios*: www.axios/2022/11/09/midterms-latinos-firsts

2022 ♦ Adriana Kugler (1970–) became the first Latina to serve on the board of governors of the Federal Reserve. Of Latino and Jewish ancestry, she was born in the United States but raised in Colombia. Previously, the renowned economist taught economics at Georgetown University and served as the U.S. executive director at World Bank. From 2011 to 2013, she served as chief economist at the U.S. Department of Labor.

Sources: "Biden Taps 2, Including 1st Hispanic, For Roles in Fed Board," *Houston Chronicle*, 13 May 2023.

2022 ♦ Mayra Flores (1986–) became the first Mexican-born U.S. congresswoman when she won a special election in June 2022 for Texas' 34th Congressional District. The Republican, who had immigrated to the United States at six years old and became a citizen at 14, subsequently lost the seat in the regular election in 2023.

Mayra Flores

Sources: "Rematch Is Set for Valley Seat," *Houston Chronicle*, 16 July 2023.

2022 ♦ Mexican American Robert Luis Santos (1957–) became the first Latino director of the U.S. Census Bureau. President Joe Biden nominated Santos at a particularly sensitive time, when there was much debate and controversy over how to count Latinos and immigrants. The San Antonio native had previously served as the president of the American Statistical Association (2013–2014) and the American Association of Public Opinion Research.

Robert Luis Santos

Sources: "President Biden Announces His Intent to Nominate Robert Santos for Director of the U.S. Census Bureau," The White House: https://www.whitehouse.gov/briefing-room/statements-releases/2021/04/13/president-biden-announces-his-intent-to-nominate-robert-santos-for-director-of-the-u-s-census-bureau/.

Irma Carrillo Ramírez

2023 ♦ Judge Irma Carrillo Ramírez (1964–) became the first Latina appointed to the 5th Circuit Court of Appeals; the daughter of Mexican immigrants, she was nominated by President Joe Biden and confirmed by the U.S. Senate. She had been serving as a magistrate judge for the U.S. District Court for the Northern District of Texas (2002–2023). She had also served as a U.S. assistant attorney from 1995 to 2002.

Sources: "Texan Becomes First Latina on Appeals Court," *Houston Chronicle*, 5 December 2023.

LAW AND CIVIL RIGHTS

LAW

1610 ♦ With the founding of Santa Fe, New Mexico, many Spanish laws governing all facets of life were introduced to what would become the culture of the Southwest. Foremost among those laws were those concerning water and its management; many of these Spanish laws would pass into the legal codes of the United States. In the Spanish and Mexican judicial systems, the rights of the community weighed more heavily than those of the individual concerning the precious resource of water in the arid Southwest. The water in Spanish and Mexican towns and cities was held in trust for the benefit of the entire community. The *cabildo*, a democratically elected town council, held the authority over local water usage. Usually, each pueblo was invested with special rights in respect to water. Title to the water in streams flowing through the pueblo's common lands was reserved to the pueblo and its inhabitants for both domestic and public use, as in parks and for nonagricultural purposes. The Treaty of Guadalupe Hidalgo passed these rights to posterity after the Mexican War (1846–1848). The City of Los Angeles, which inherited the pueblo rights, was able to obtain a favorable ruling from the U.S. Supreme Court over a water dispute with landowners of the San Fernando Valley. The court ruled that the city had prior claim to all waters originating within the watershed of the Los Angeles River; thus, the court asserted that pueblo rights took precedence over the common-law rights of the landowners.

Sources: Meyer, *Water in the Hispanic Southwest*, pp. 156–157; Rosaldo et al., *Chicano*, p. 13.

1681 ♦ The Spanish government issued the first compilation of laws that governed settlement of their colonies in the New World, including those in areas that became the United States. The *Recopilación de las leyes de las Indias* (Compilation of the Laws of the Indies) organized and reduced to a total of 6,400 the laws applicable to its American colonies. By 1635, there had been issued some 400,000 edicts. The *Recopilación* was reissued with changes in 1774 and revised again in 1791. In these codes and laws, the granting of land and the details of founding of towns were prescribed, including the physical layouts of the towns and the powers of the municipal authorities.

Sources: Gómez-Quiñones, *Roots of Chicano Politics, 1600–1940*, p. 18; Kanellos, *Chronology of Hispanic American History*, p. 52.

1767 ♦ Spanish laws governing water usage became the foundation for current Texas law regarding water usage and rights. Spain began making grants of Texas land to colonizers; it is estimated that some 26 million of Texas's 170 million acres were granted by Spain and Mexico, and various titles of water rights were attached to these land grants. The water rights that go with these grants are covered by Texas law but determined by the terms of the original grants. After the founding of the Republic of Texas in 1836 and then the later admission of Texas as a state to the union, the Spanish and Mexican laws regarding water usage were incorporated into the state constitution. This Spanish heritage was the basis of the Irrigation Act of 1852, which is the basis for Texas statutory irrigation law.

Sources: Dobkins, *The Spanish Element in Texas Water Law*, pp. 124–125.

1840 ♦ The Texas legislature adopted the Hispano-Mexican system of a single court rather than continuing the dual court system (courts of law and courts of equity) of Anglo-American law. Under the Hispanic system, all issues could be considered simultaneously rather than divided between two jurisdictions. Thus, the Republic of Texas became the first English-speaking country to adopt a permanent and full unitary system of justice. This system passed into Texas law after it became a state.

Sources: Chipman, *Spanish Texas, 1519–1821*, pp. 250–251.

1840 ♦ The Texas legislature adopted from the Hispanic legal system the requirement that a person be sued in the locale in which he resides for his convenience. This principle passed into Texas state law.

Sources: Chipman, *Spanish Texas, 1519–1821*, p. 251.

1839: The First Homestead Law

Texas adopted the first Homestead law in the United States on January 26, 1839. The principle of protecting certain pieces of personal property from creditors has its roots in Castilian practices that date to the 13th century and passed into Texas law from the Hispano-Mexican legal codes. This made it possible for a debtor to protect the principal residence of the family from seizure by creditors; it also protected other basic items, such as clothing and implements of trade needed for the debtor to make a living. Today, Texas continues to have one of the strongest property-exemption laws of any state. Texas also accepted the Mexican and Spanish land-use system via this law, which called for large tracts of land with access to water that could be used for ranching cattle and sheep. *Sources:* Chipman, *Spanish Texas, 1519–1821*, pp. 253–254; McKnight, *The Spanish Elements in Modern Texas Law*, p. 9.

1840 ♦ The legislature of the Republic of Texas adopted and subsequently passed on to the state legal code the Spanish legal concept of community property. Husband and wife were to share equally in the profits and fruits of their marriage. Under Anglo-American law, however, property was owned exclusively by the husband, and on the death of her spouse, the wife was protected only by a life interest in one-third of the lands of her deceased spouse. The Republic of Texas recognized this inequity and specifically excluded the Anglo-American law of matrimonial property. The previously Hispanic provinces of Texas and Louisiana were the first to protect wives through common-law statutes. Today, community property law is prevalent in states that have a Hispanic heritage: Texas, Louisiana, New Mexico, Arizona, Nevada, and California. It has also been pointed out that even the right to file a joint income tax return derives from this Spanish principle.

Sources: Chipman, *Spanish Texas, 1519–1821*, p. 253; McKnight, *The Spanish Elements in Modern Texas Law*, p. 8.

1840 ♦ The legal code of Texas incorporated the Spanish concept of "independent executor" in relation to probate matters (i.e., wills). This did away with the Anglo-American legal practice that allowed executors to obtain court orders to perform acts not specifically called for in the testament. Placing confidence in an executor was more expedient and saved legal expenses both for the legal system and the individuals involved. This Spanish judicial procedure later spread from Texas to Arizona, Washington, Idaho, and some 10 other states as provisions of the Uniform Probate Code.

Sources: Chipman, *Spanish Texas, 1519–1821*, p. 251.

1841 ♦ Numerous principles of Spanish family law were incorporated into the legal code of Texas, covering the rights of partners in marriage as well as the adoption of children. Included among these principles was the protection of the rights of parties in a common-law relationship. Furthermore, children of such marriages, even if the marriages were declared invalid later, were considered legitimate, and a fair division of the profits of the marriages resulted. This legitimation of children is still part of Texas family law today.

Sources: Chipman, *Spanish Texas, 1519–1821*, p. 252.

1849 ♦ At the California Constitutional Convention, Anglos resisted giving the vote to Indians, blacks, and *mestizos*. Largely through the leadership of Pablo de la Guerra and other Mexican delegates, however, the convention came to an agreement that any man who had been considered a Mexican citizen, regardless of race, would be so considered under the Constitution of California. This was the first time that a state constitution defined citizenship based on the inclusiveness of all races, as was practiced in Mexico. However, those blacks and Indians who had not been Mexicans would be excluded.

Sources: Gómez-Quiñones, *Roots of Chicano Politics, 1600–1940*, pp. 226–227.

Colton Hall in Monterey was the site of the first California Constitutional Convention in 1849.

1849 ♦ The Constitution of California required that all laws be printed in English and Spanish. However, disenfranchisement of the Spanish-speaking population progressed over the years in California as the legislature mandated English-only ballots, enacted English literacy requirements, and, in 1890, amended the constitution to declare English the official language of the state.

Sources: Gómez-Quiñones, *Roots of Chicano Politics, 1600–1940*, p. 228.

1849 ♦ The California legislature adopted Anglo-American law, except for the community property system as prescribed by Hispanic legal tradition. The American regimes in both Texas and Louisiana also adopted the Hispanic community property system.

Sources: McKnight, Joseph, "Law without Lawyers on the Hispano Mexican Frontier," *The West Texas Historical Association Yearbook*, 64 (1990), pp. 51–65.

1850 ♦ Texas reinstated in its legal code the Spanish principle of adoption of children, after it had been dropped 10 years earlier, under the new legal code of the Republic of Texas. The concept of adoption was not recognized in English law, and Anglo-American law continued this glaring gap. Because of numerous petitions for specific rulings on adoptions during the years of the republic and early statehood of Texas, the legislature decided to reinstate the Hispanic concept of adoption, including the right of adopted children to inherit their adopted parents' estates. In Texas, as in the Hispanic world, the rights of an adopted child became the same as those of biological children, and they could still claim inheritance from their natural parents. After Mississippi, Texas was the second Anglo-American state to permanently recognize and codify adoption.

Sources: Chipman, *Spanish Texas, 1519–1821*, pp. 252–253; McKnight, *The Spanish Elements in Modern Texas Law*, p. 7.

1916 ♦ The first state constitution was written specifically protecting the rights of citizens to speak and vote in Spanish. Article 7 of the Constitution of New Mexico provides that the "right of any citizen to vote, hold office, or sit upon juries, shall never be restricted, abridged or impaired on account of religion, race, language or color, or inability to speak, read or write the English or Spanish languages." The constitution, under Article 2, specifically incorporated the rights of the people of New Mexico under the Treaty of Guadalupe Hidalgo, which was a product of the war with Mexico. In addition, the state was officially bilingual, as provided for by its constitution: "All laws passed by the Legislature shall be published in both the English and

1968: The Bilingual Education Act

The first federal law mandating bilingual education, the Bilingual Education Act, which became Title VII of the Elementary and Secondary Education Act, was sponsored by Senators Joseph M. Montoya of New Mexico and Ralph Yarborough of Texas. The law authorized grants to local school districts to develop and implement instruction of all subjects in both languages until the limited-English-speaking child was able to continue his or her education in English. It also called for teaching the history and culture associated with the native language. *Sources:* Vigil, *Los Patrones*, pp. 157-163.

Spanish languages." The legislature was also mandated to provide funds for the training of teachers to be proficient in both English and Spanish (Article 12). Article 12 also prohibited segregation of the children of Spanish descent.

Sources: Gómez-Quiñones, *Roots of Chicano Politics, 1600–1940*, pp. 325–328.

1974 ♦ Senator Joseph M. Montoya (1915–1978) was one of the authors of a new Bilingual Education Act, which expanded bilingual education by financing the preparation of bilingual teachers and the development of curricula.

Sources: Vigil, *Los Patrones*, pp. 157–163.

CIVIL RIGHTS

1687 ♦ The first of what would become a consistent stream of runaway slaves from the British Carolinas took refuge in Spanish Florida. From that point on, Spanish Florida, and Saint Augustine in particular, would become a well-known haven for escaped slaves from the British colonies on the North American mainland. Eight men, three women, and a three-year-old child had escaped from British Georgia by boat and were accepted in Saint Augustine, where they were given work and instruction in the Catholic religion. One year later, the slaves were claimed, but the Spanish governor in Saint Augustine refused to return them since they had gainful employment, were now Catholics, and had married locally.

Sources: Henderson and Mormino, *Spanish Pathways in Florida*, p. 192.

1693 ♦ Sanctuary for runaway slaves as a state policy in the Americas became official. King Charles III of Spain issued an edict stating that runaway slaves would be given their liberty "so that by their example and my liberality others will do the same." This stimulated the flow of runaway slaves from the British southern colonies into Florida. The British opposed this policy and in 1728 attacked Saint Augustine in retaliation. Black soldiers fought so bravely in defending the town that the governor freed all slaves who were soldiers and abolished the slave market.

Sources: Henderson and Mormino, *Spanish Pathways in Florida*, p. 192.

1728 ♦ Saint Augustine was the first town in what became the United States to abolish its slave market. This was in partial recognition of black Spanish militia who had defended the town so bravely against British invaders from Georgia.

Sources: Henderson and Mormino, *Spanish Pathways in Florida*, p. 192.

1738 ♦ The first free black community in what became the mainland United States was established at Fort Mose in Spanish Florida. Made up of free black families and escaped slaves from the British Carolinas and Georgia, Fort Mose was established north of Saint Augustine as a first line of defense against invading British soldiers and escaped-slave hunters. Many of the colonists of Florida were free black craftsmen and black soldiers in the Spanish army. Under Spanish law and practice, slaves had certain rights, and Spanish culture and the Catholic Church were more inclined to release slaves than were British culture and Protestant religions. A black militia was present in Florida by the 17th century, with both free and enslaved blacks serving as soldiers and officers. By the late 17th century, slaves in southern British colonies became fully aware of the advantages of escaping to Florida and living under Spanish rule. The first of these fugitives had arrived in Saint Augustine in 1687. In 1738, the governor of Florida decreed that all fugitives from South Carolina would be guaranteed their freedom in Florida, and he authorized the establishment of the village of Gracia Real de Santa Teresa de Mose as their home. Initially, 38 men and their families moved in, but the village soon grew much larger, and a small fort was built. A 1759 census showed that 67 people lived in 22 houses in the community.

Sources: Henderson and Mormino, *Spanish Pathways in Florida*, pp. 188–203.

1855 ♦ Mariano G. Vallejo (1807–1890), who became one of the first Californios to be elected to the state legislature and then to the state senate, was also one of the first Californios to have his extensive land grants validated in 1855. But his happiness was short-lived because squatters and speculators appealed the court decision all the way up to the U.S. Supreme Court, which invalidated his title to the large Soscol land grant. In addition to the land, much of the family wealth was lost in defending his rights to the grant in court. Vallejo thus became one of the first of a long line of Latinos and Mexicans in the southwestern states and territories to lose their lands in similar processes. When he died, he only owned 280 acres.

Mariano G. Vallejo

Sources: Meier and Rivera, *Dictionary of Mexican American History*, pp. 361–362.

Ramón Emeterio Betances

1856 ♦ Ramón Emeterio Betances (1827–1898), the indefatigable mover for Puerto Rican independence from Spain, was the principal founder of the Secret Abolitionist Societies, an alliance of organizations pushing for the abolition of slavery. Betances penned the influential proclamation *Los Diez Mandamientos de los Hombres Libres* (The Ten Commandments of Free Men), demanding the abolition of slavery and the right to freedom of speech, worship, and elections. Of mixed African and European heritage, for his writings and activism Betances was exiled a number of times. In 1867, during one of those exiles in the Dominican Republic, he founded and led the Revolutionary Committee of Puerto Rico and the next year planned *El Grito de Lares* (The Lares Shout for Independence), which was the most important armed revolt against Spanish colonial rule on the island. Due in great part to Betances's organizational and intellectual leadership, the Spanish government abolished slavery in 1873.

Sources: Kanellos, *Latino Almanac*, p. 61.

1863 ♦ Chipita Rodriguez (1799–1863) became the only woman legally hanged in Texas history. Found guilty of having murdered a horse trader, John Savage, Rodriguez was hanged despite the jury's recommendation for mercy because the evidence against her was weak and because of her tender age. The first woman hanged in California was Josefa Segovia, who during the gold rush killed an Anglo man who had made advances to her; she was hanged despite being pregnant.

Sources: Gómez-Quiñones, *Roots of Chicano Politics, 1600–1940*, p. 246; Meier and Rivera, *Dictionary of Mexican American History*, pp. 305–306.

1868 ♦ The 14th Amendment to the U.S. Constitution was adopted, declaring all people of Hispanic origin born in the United States as U.S. citizens.

Sources: Kanellos, *Chronology of Hispanic American History*, p. 108.

Lola Rodríguez de Tió

1877 ♦ Puerto Rican patriot and poet Lola Rodríguez de Tió (1843–1924) became the first Latina to be sent into political exile for her leadership in the Puerto Rican independence movement from Spain. Born on September 14, 1843, in San Germán, Rodríguez de Tió received an education at religious schools and from private tutors. In 1865, she married Bonocio Tió, a journalist who shared Rodríguez de Tió's desire for Puerto Rican independence, and they held literary and political meetings regularly at their home in Mayagüez. In 1868, she wrote the lyrics to what would become the Puerto Rican national anthem, "La Borinqueña."

In 1877, the government exiled Rodríguez de Tió; she and her family took refuge in Venezuela for three years and then returned to Puerto Rico. In 1889, she was exiled once again, this time to Cuba, where she continued her revolutionary activities until 1895, when she was again exiled. This time, she took up residence in New York and again continued to conspire with the leading revolutionaries for Puerto Rican and Cuban independence. In 1899, after the Spanish-American War, she returned to a hero's reception in Cuba. She remained in Cuba and began to work on fashioning a new society, one in which women would have greater liberty and opportunity.

In 1910, she was elected a member of the Cuban Academy of Arts and Letters. Lola Rodríguez de Tió was a romantic poet, as her three books of poems readily attest: *Mis cantares* (My Songs), 1876; *Claros y nieblas* (Clarities and Cloudiness), 1885; and *Mi libro de Cuba* (My Book of Cuba), 1893. Rodríguez de Tió was a beloved patriotic and literary figure, as well as an early feminist, in both Puerto Rico and Cuba. She died on November 10, 1924, in Cuba.

Sources: Kanellos, *Chronology of Hispanic American History*, p. 93.

1883 ♦ An early fight, possibly the first in the Southwest, against segregation in Texas took place when a veteran, Juan Cárdenas, organized a successful protest against prohibiting the use of a dance floor to Mexicans in San Pedro Park, San Antonio.

Sources: Gómez-Quiñones, *Roots of Chicano Politics, 1600–1940*, p. 270.

1889 ♦ The first underground guerrilla movement to protect the rights of native New Mexicans was founded. It was called *Las Gorras Blancas* (The White Caps). Bands of Mexican Americans wearing white caps or masks would sally out at night to pull down fences, destroy crops, burn buildings, tear up tracks on the Atchison, Topeka, and Santa Fe Railway, and even shoot people to stem the tide of Anglo-American encroachment on common land and abuse of the natural resources. Beginning in Las Vegas, New Mexico, but growing throughout San Miguel County and to other parts of the territory, the movement, made up of poor Hispanos, was principally aimed at protecting land use and ownership by the Mexican Americans and fighting the disruption of their traditional lifestyle.

The nearly two years of activity of *Las Gorras Blancas* represented the most widespread, well-organized, and effective resistance to Anglo-American control during territorial days, and the movement did succeed in temporarily halting the Anglo advance. In addition, the agitation created by *Las Gorras Blancas* led to the formation of the first Hispanic third party in U.S. history: *El Partido del Pueblo Unido* (The United People's Party).

One man who served as a catalyst for the movement was Juan José Herrera, a union organizer for the Knights of Labor, who was able to use the labor association as a base for organizing the disaffected native New Mexicans. He established 20 local assemblies in San Miguel County, rallying the members' opposition to land speculation and large landowners. It is believed that *Las Gorras Blancas* was the clandestine militant arm of the Knights of Labor assemblies in New Mexico. Local bands of *Las Gorras Blancas* continued to ride at least until 1926.

Sources: Rosaldo et al., *Chicano*, pp. 128–133.

1894 ♦ The Alianza Hispano Americana, one of the first Hispanic civil rights organizations, was founded in Tucson, Arizona, and quickly spread throughout the Southwest. The Alianza originally was a mutualist society, or alliance of mutualist societies, that was organized along masonic lines through the leadership of Carlos Velasco, editor of the Tucson newspaper *El Fronterizo* (The Frontier), as well as some 48 other prominent Mexican citizens of Tucson. At first, the organization was directed by middle- and upper-class businessmen and intellectuals, who realized that Mexicans were losing political and economic power as Anglos flooded into Arizona with the coming of the railroads. They were also responding to extensive discrimination and nativist attacks perpetrated by such organizations as the American Protective Association. Over the years, the Alianza included more working-class Mexicans and became involved more in the protection of civil rights and in furthering the rights of workers. In the 1890s and 1900s, numerous Alianza members were successfully elected to office. By 1930, it had spread throughout the

Southwest and had grown to include more than 17,000 members. In the post–World War II period, the organization became very active in protecting the civil rights of Mexican Americans. Today, it still counts over 300 chapters in its membership.

Sources: Gómez-Quiñones, *Roots of Chicano Politics, 1600–1940*, pp. 284–285; Sheridan, *Los Tucsonenses*, pp. 108–110, 112–116.

1911 ♦ The first large convention of Mexicans for action against social injustice, *El Primer Congreso Mexicanista* (The First Mexicanist Congress), was held in Laredo, Texas, on September 14–20, 1911, led by Nicasio Idar (1855–1914), editor and publisher of *La crónica* newspaper. Several women were prominent in shaping the policies of *El Primer Congreso Mexicanista*, including Hortencia Moncayo and Soledad Flores de la Peña (1889–1972). The program created both an agenda for labor organization and for protection of civil rights of Mexicans and Mexican Americans in the United States through such strategies as organizing and joining trade unions, soliciting the support of the Mexican consular system, having schools that taught in Spanish and taught Mexican culture, improving the plight of Mexican women in the United States, and developing other strategies to protect Mexican lives and economic interests. The congress concluded by establishing an ongoing organization, *La Liga Mexicanista* (The Mexicanist League).

Sources: Gómez-Quiñones, *Roots of Chicano Politics, 1600–1940*, pp. 314–323.

1911 ♦ Mexican American journalist Jovita Idar (1885–1946) helped organize and became president of the first Latina organization for women's civil rights: the League of Mexican Women. It was born as an offshoot of women getting together during *El Primer Congreso Mexicanista* (The First Mexicanist Congress) held in Laredo, organized in part by her family. Jovita Idar's leadership came to the fore because of her pioneering journalism, in which she denounced the social, educational, and economic conditions of Mexicans in Texas. As president of the organization, she led the way to providing free education for Mexican and Mexican American children and furthering Latina women's causes.

Jovita Idar

Sources: "Texas Originals/Jovita Idar," HumanitiesTexas: https://www.humanitiestexas.org/programs/tx-originals/list/jovita-idar.

1911 ♦ María Guadalupe Evangelina de López (1881–1977) became president of the College Equal Suffrage League in 1911 and led efforts to en-

The Plan of San Diego

In 1915 the first widespread plot to overthrow U.S. rule of the territories taken from Mexico—including Arizona, California, Colorado, New Mexico, and Texas—and create a separate republic was uncovered. The Plan de San Diego, supposedly organized in San Diego, Texas, was a reaction against civil rights abuses and expropriation of lands from Mexicans in Texas and called for an armed revolt. The plan also included clauses addressed to the African American, Indian, and Asian populations, in which provision for their liberation was made. There were, in fact, a series of raids, destruction of bridges, and encounters with the Texas Rangers that were effected by bands of armed riders in the lower Rio Grande Valley. But in all, the plan and its promoters remained cloaked in secrecy, and not much is known to this date about the perpetrators. *Sources:* Gómez-Quiñones, *Roots of Chicano Politics, 1600–1940*, pp. 347–349; Rosaldo et al., *Chicano*, p. 124.

María Guadalupe Evangelina de López

franchise California's women, especially by speaking, publishing, and translating suffrage materials into Spanish in order to reach Latinas. She is remembered for her eloquent and fiery speech given at a 1911 Votes for Women Club rally in Los Angeles Plaza, which she gave entirely in Spanish, reportedly the first in the state to do so. She traveled throughout southern California speaking and distributing suffrage materials in Spanish. In an opinion article she wrote, published in the *Los Angeles Herald* on August 20, 1911, she argued that California could not call itself a democracy while disenfranchising half its citizens. On October 10, 1911, the suffrage proposition passed, and California became the sixth state in the nation to approve suffrage for women, nine years before the passage of the 19th Amendment to the Constitution passed. De López was chosen by the suffragists in Los Angeles to serve as a representative from California to the 1913 Woman Suffrage Parade in Washington, D.C.

Sources: "María Guadalupe Evangelina de López," National Women's History Museum: https://www.womenshistory.org/education-resources/biographies/maria-guadalupe-evangelina-de-lopez.

1917 ♦ Puerto Ricans, who had existed under the military rule of the United States since the end of the war with Spain, became citizens of the United States with the passage of the Jones Act by U.S. Congress. While the island of Puerto Rico remained a colony of the United States and had very limited self-determination, individual Puerto Ricans were entitled to the full civil rights enjoyed by any other U.S. citizen—except that islanders then, as now, were not entitled to elected representation in Congress.

Sources: Kanellos, *Latino Almanac*, pp. 72–75.

1917 ♦ Ana Roqué de Duprey (1853–1933) led Puerto Rican women on the island in founding the *Liga Femínea Puertorriqueña* (Women's Feminist League), the first organization in Puerto Rico promoting women's rights. The immediate cause for its establishment was the Jones Act, passed by U.S. Congress in 1917, which allowed Puerto Rican men to vote as U.S. citizens but, of course, not women. Roqué de Duprey, who was a distinguished scientist, educator, and author, persisted in leading the women's suffrage movement through her teaching, organizing, and publishing; in 1898, she had founded the first women's magazine on the island: *La Mujer* (Women). In 1920, when women gained the vote in the United States, Puerto Rican women did not enjoy the same right. In 1921, the *Liga Femínea* exerted all its efforts toward women's suffrage and civil and political rights and became the Suffragist Social League, which in 1924 became the Association of Women Suffragists. By 1935, the movement had succeeded, and women gained the vote and the right to run for office.

Sources: "Ana Roqué de Duprey," National Women's History Museum: https://www.womenshistory.org/education-resources/biographies/ana-roque-de-duprey.

Adelina Otero-Warren

1917 ♦ Adelina Otero-Warren (1881–1965) became chair of the New Mexico chapter of the Congressional Union, soon to be the National Women's Party. She was also serving as chair of the New Mexico Republican State Committee's women's division and chair of the legislative committee of the New Mexico Federation of Women's Clubs. Otero-Warren was a leader of the women's suffrage movement in New Mexico and insisted that all efforts, publications, and organizing be implemented in Spanish as well as English in order to reach Latinas. Due to Otero-Warren and the organizations she led in lobbying the state legislature for women's suffrage, the New Mexico state legislature ratified the 19th Amendment on February 21, 1920.

Sources: "Adelina 'Nina' Otero-Warren," National Women's History Museum: https://www.womenshistory.org/education-resources/biographies/adelina-nina-otero-warren.

1920 ♦ One of the first Mexican American civil rights organizations founded in Texas was the Order of the Sons of America, which existed in the early 1920s and had been organized by José de la Luz Saenz (1888–1953), a teacher and World War I veteran. The organization, made up mostly of U.S.-born members, concentrated on encouraging naturalization and participation in U.S. institutions for all Mexicans.

Sources: Rosales, *Chicano! History of the Mexican American Civil Rights Movement*, pp. 90–91.

1921 ♦ One of the first organizations comprising both Hispanics and Anglos to combat discrimination was San Antonio's Pan American Round Table, which was made up of businessmen who promoted a positive image for Latinos and fought anti–Latin American attitudes.

Sources: Rosales, *Chicano! History of the Mexican American Civil Rights Movement*, p. 91.

1922 ♦ Adelina Otero-Warren became the first Latina to run for Congress when she won the Republican Party's nomination by defeating her male opponent. Unfortunately, she lost the general election by fewer than 10,000 votes, in part due to the revelation that she was divorced rather than widowed. Otero-Warren was well known throughout the state because of her suffragist activities and because of her election as the first Mexican American superintendent of Santa Fe schools in 1918; she served until 1929. As superintendent, she opposed assimilationist pressures and emphasized bicultural education.

Sources: "Adelina 'Nina' Otero-Warren," National Women's History Museum: https://www.womenshistory.org/education-resources/biographies/adelina-nina-otero-warren.

1924 ♦ The first battle against segregation of Mexicans in the Midwest was fought in the Argentine, Kansas, schools. Mexican parents and the Mexican consul protested when white parents petitioned the local school board to separate the Mexican children from theirs. The result was only a partial victory: Mexican children were allowed to attend high school with whites, but segregation was maintained in the elementary schools.

Sources: Rosales, *Chicano! History of the Mexican American Civil Rights Movement*, p. 71.

1926 ♦ Mexican women in Los Angeles founded the first civil rights organization operated by Latinas on the West Coast, *La Sociedad de Madres Mexicanas* (The Society of Mexican Mothers). The SMM's purpose was to help

1929: The League of United Latin American Citizens

In 1929 the largest and longest-lasting Latino civil rights organization, the League of United Latin American Citizens (LULAC), was founded in Texas. LULAC was founded as a mainly middle-class organization that only accepted citizens for membership. Among its most important goals was to fight segregation; another main concern was discrimination in the judicial system. A constant issue for LULAC was equal treatment under the law for Mexicans and Mexican Americans. *Sources:* Rosales, *Chicano! History of the Mexican American Civil Rights Movement*, pp. 93–97.

finance the legal defense of compatriots facing civil or criminal charges. The SMM often held fundraising events in local theaters, and its members were known for bringing toiletries and sundries to the Mexican prisoners in city and county jails; they also provided contacts and communication with the families of the incarcerated, most of whom still resided in Mexico.

Sources: Balderrama and Rodríguez, *Decade of Betrayal*, pp. 42–43.

1929 ♦ Mexican parents won the first battle to stop a local school board from segregating their children with blacks in the De Olivera Elementary School in San Bernardino, California. They did not accept the rationale given by County Superintendent of Public Instructions Ida Collins: that the purpose for the separation was to help the children learn English.

Sources: Rosales, *Chicano! History of the Mexican American Civil Rights Movement*, p. 71.

1929 ♦ Mexican Americans María L. de Hernández (1896–1986) and Pedro Hernández Barrera (1892–1980) founded one of the earliest Latino civil rights organizations, Orden de Caballeros de America (Order of the Knights of America). This was the first Latino civil rights organization that had a specifically feminist viewpoint.

Sources: Tardiff and Mabunda, *Dictionary of Hispanic Biography*, p. 422.

1930 ♦ Mexican American parents, with support from the League of United Latin American Citizens (LULAC), won their first discrimination suit, attacking segregation in the Texas schools in the case of *Salvatierra v. Del Rio Independent School District*, brought by Jesús Salvatierra against the Del Rio, Texas, school district. The courts found that Mexican American children

1932: The Mexican American Movement

The first significant civil rights organization of high school and college youth, the Mexican American Movement (MAM), was formed in 1932. With the support of Protestant church affiliates and the Young Men's Christian Association (YMCA), young Los Angeles Mexican Americans banded together to lead the way to obtaining a secure and respected place in society through Americanization. They especially believed that discrimination would disappear through education. Some of MAM's most dynamic leadership came from its female members, such as Dora Ibáñez (dates unknown), who encouraged Mexican American women to strive for education and professional careers. *Sources:* Gómez-Quiñones, *Roots of Chicano Politics, 1600–1940*, pp. 391–397; Rosales, *Chicano! History of the Mexican American Civil Rights Movement*, pp. 100–102.

had been segregated without regard to individual ability; they said that the only legitimate use of segregation should be for special education. The case put an end to the practice of labeling certain schools Mexican, but in most instances, segregation did not end, just the labeling of the schools.

Sources: "Del Rio ISD v. Salvatierra," Texas State Historical Association: https://www.tshaonline.org/handbook/entries/del-rio-isd-v-salvatierra.

1930 ♦ Parents successfully desegregated the schools in Lemon Grove, California, via a court suit; this was the first desegregation victory in California for Mexican Americans. It was heard at about the same time as the Salvatierra case.

Sources: Gómez-Quiñones, *Roots of Chicano Politics, 1600–1940*, p. 374.

1939 ♦ *El Congreso Nacional del Pueblo de Habla Hispana* (The National Congress of Spanish-Speaking Peoples) was founded; it was the first national effort to bring together Latino workers from diverse ethnic backgrounds: Cubans and Spaniards from Florida, Puerto Ricans from New York, Mexicans and Mexican Americans from the Southwest, and other groups. The prime mover in bringing the diverse Latino labor and community organizations together and in founding the congress was Luisa Moreno (1906–1992), who developed the organization under the auspices of the Congress of Industrial Organizations (CIO). The result of the first national convention of the Congress, held in Los Angeles in 1939, was that Spanish-speaking people in the United States began to realize that they constituted a national minority whose civil and labor rights were being violated consistently across the country. Another important result of the convention was highlighting the role of Latinas, who had been leaders in organizing the congress and the convention.

Sources: García, *Memories of Chicano History*, pp. 109–113.

1944 ♦ Senator Dennis Chávez introduced the first Fair Employment Practices Bill, which prohibited discrimination because of race, creed, or national origin. Although the bill was voted down by the conservative majority, it was an important predecessor of the 1964 Civil Rights Act. Chávez consistently promoted and supported civil rights legislation in Congress.

Sources: Coy, Cassie, *Dennis Chávez: The First Hispanic US Senator / El primer senador hispano de los Estados Unidos*, Piñata Books, 2017.

1945 ♦ Latino parents in California won their first suit against segregation of Mexican and Latino children on constitutional grounds in *Mendez et al. v. Westminster School District et al.* against four Orange County school districts. The parents argued that the districts were depriving the students of due process and equal protection under the law. Although the school districts appealed the decision to the higher courts, the lower court decision was upheld in 1947 in the Court of Appeals for the 9th Circuit in San Francisco. Some 5,000 Mexican American children were affected. The case set an important precedent for National Association for the Advancement of Colored People (NAACP) lawyers arguing the historic case *Brown v. Board of Education* in 1954.

Sources: Meier and Rivera, *Dictionary of Mexican American History*, p. 218; Rosales, *Chicano! History of the Mexican American Civil Rights Movement*, pp. 104–105.

1947 ♦ The Community Services Organization (CSO) was founded; it was the first predominantly Latino civil rights group to adopt the tactics that would characterize American civil rights movements in the post–World War II period and would form the backbone of the Chicano Movement. Mainly made up of Mexican Americans, many of its leaders were trained in the dramatic, confrontational tactics developed by Saul Alinsky and his Industrial Areas Foundation: mass demonstrations, picketing, confronting those in "the system" for its malfunction. Alinsky, in fact, hired César Chávez (1927–1993) and Fred Ross (1910–1992) to organize the CSO. Other important Mexican American leaders who would make history in the struggles of future decades became involved, notably Dolores Huerta (1930–) and Tony Ríos (1915–1999). The CSO also obtained the support of the Catholic Church. The CSO's first major victory came in 1949, when it organized and led the movement to elect Edward Roybal (1916–2005) to the Los Angeles

City Council. Beyond the political realm, the CSO concentrated on neighborhood services and community health issues. To effect these ends, they organized door to door in working-class and lower-middle-class neighborhoods, with many women in leadership positions. César Chávez was later successful in taking many of the tactics and philosophy of the CSO and the Industrial Areas Foundation into the struggle to unionize farm workers.

Sources: García, *Memories of Chicano History*, pp. 163–168.

1948 ♦ Mexican American doctor and World War II veteran Hector P. García (1914–1996) founded the American G.I. Forum, organizing veterans to fight for educational and medical benefits and, later, against poll taxes and school segregation. It also raised funds to combat discrimination in many spheres, including jury selection. The organization became one of two long-standing and effective Latino civil rights organizations, the other being the League of United Latin American Citizens, founded in 1929. García was appointed to the U.S. Commission on Civil Rights in 1968. In 1984, President Ronald Reagan presented García the Presidential Medal of Freedom.

Hector P. García

Sources: García, Ignacio M. *Héctor P. García: In Relentless Pursuit of Justice*. Houston: Arte Público Press, 2002.

1951 ♦ Mexican American educator George I. Sánchez (1906–1972) organized the American Council of Spanish Speaking People (ACSSP), a national Mexican American civil rights organization based in Austin, Texas. The ACSSP, funded by the Robert C. Marshall Trust Fund of New York, provided grants-in-aid, legal assistance, and research to Mexican American civil rights groups across the nation. Among the cases it funded was *Hernández v. Texas* (1954), integrating juries that provided a precedent for *Brown v. Board of Education*. Other cases included the Anthony Ríos police brutality case in Los Angeles (1954), the Robert Galván alleged communist alien deportation case in California (1954), and the Winslow, Arizona, swimming pool desegregation case (1954). In Texas, ACSSP helped desegregate Austin and Houston public housing and Zavala and Nixon schools (1951).

Sources: "The American Council of Spanish Speaking People," Texas State Historical Association: https://www.tshaonline.org/handbook/entries/american-council-of-spanish-speaking-people.

1954 ♦ *Hernandez v. Texas* was the first Mexican American discrimination case to reach the U.S. Supreme Court. The suit against Texas claimed that Pete

Hernández, a convicted murderer, had been denied equal protection under the law because he had faced a jury that did not include Mexican Americans. The court found that Jackson County, Texas, had not chosen a Mexican American juror in 25 years, despite having a Mexican American population of 14 percent. This was also the first case before the U.S. Supreme Court that was argued by Mexican American attorneys: Gustavo C. García (1915–1964), Carlos Cadena (1917–2001), and John J. Herrera (1910–1986). The decision also was the first to recognize Latinos as a separate class of people suffering profound discrimination. Previously, Hispanics were officially recognized as "white" and, therefore, not a separate minority class. The 1954 decision paved the way for Latinos to use legal means to attack all types of discrimination throughout the United States.

Sources: Olivas, Michael A., ed. *"Colored men" and "hombres aquí":* Hernández v. Texas *and the Emergence of Mexican-American Lawyering.* Houston: Arte Público Press, 2006.

1957 ♦ The National Puerto Rican Forum was founded in New York City and created and operated successful economic development projects, especially employment training and education programs.

Sources: Kanellos, *Chronology of Hispanic American History*, p. 240.

Vicente Treviño Ximenes

1960 ♦ Vicente Treviño Ximenes (1919–2014), a research economist and politician from Texas, received the United Nations Human Rights Award. Treviño Ximenes was one of the founders and most productive promoters of the American G.I. Forum, having organized some 23 chapters in New Mexico, Arizona, California, and Kansas. He was elected the chair of the G.I. Forum in 1952. He went on to serve in various po-

1959: The Mexican American Political Association

The first Mexican American civil rights organization to acknowledge racism as the major enemy confronting Latinos—the Mexican American Political Association (MAPA)—was founded in 1959 in southern California and spread rapidly throughout the Southwest. Among its main organizers were Edward Roybal (1916-2005), who later became the first Latino in modern times elected to the Los Angeles City Council, and labor organizer Bert Corona (1918-2001). *Sources:* Rosales, *Chicano! History of the Mexican American Civil Rights Movement*, p. 111.

sitions in the Kennedy, Johnson, and Carter presidential administrations. In 1967, President Johnson created the Cabinet Committee for Mexican American Affairs, chaired by Treviño Ximenes, to promote Mexican American issues throughout the federal government.

Sources: "Ximenes Traviño, Vicente (1919–2014)," Texas State Historical Association. https://www.tshaonline.org/handbook/entries/ximenes-vicente-trevino.

1960 ♦ For the first time in history, Mexican Americans had become a sizable portion of the voting population, and they organized extensive support for the Kennedy–Johnson ticket in the national elections. Mexican American political and labor organizers throughout the Southwest established Viva Kennedy Clubs to help deliver the presidential victory to Kennedy. Before this, Mexican Americans had been taken for granted as a modest part of the Democratic Party. The success of the Kennedy–Johnson ticket was seen by Mexican Americans as an ethnic victory. As a result of representing the voting margin putting John F. Kennedy and Lyndon B. Johnson into office, Mexican Americans and Latinos made many civil rights gains and won a greater representation in government during the Kennedy and Johnson administrations than ever before.

Sources: Rosales, *Chicano! History of the Mexican American Civil Rights Movement*, p. 111.

1963 ♦ In Crystal City, Texas, where Mexican Americans made up 85 percent of the population, the community ousted five Anglo-American city council members and elected five Mexican Americans. The slate of Mexican Americans had defeated the old Anglo establishment that had been in power since the town's founding in 1907. Crystal City became the only community in the Southwest where Anglos had been ousted from decades of rule. This was the first time that Latino political action had had such a success in the United States. With the assistance of the Teamsters Union at the local Del Monte cannery and the Political Association of Spanish-Speaking Organizations, the new city government made important positive reforms, but Anglo resistance and factionalism made the job difficult. A second revolt took place in 1969 and led to greater, more successful reforms. As a result of this revolt and a protest against discrimination in the Crystal City schools, a political party was formed, La Raza Unida, which expanded quickly throughout Texas under the leadership of José Angel Gutiérrez (1944–). Crystal City became the first city in the United States to have a Chicano third party controlling the local government. La Raza Unida went on to gain control of the government of Zavala County and made inroads into other areas. By

1981, however, the party was in decline, especially as the Democratic Party began to make reforms and become more inclusive of Mexican Americans and their issues. La Raza Unida and Crystal City are important historically for bringing about political change and forcing the two-party system in the United States to take Latinos into account.

Sources: Rosaldo et al., *Chicano*, pp. 303–326; Rosales, *Chicano! History of the Mexican American Civil Rights Movement*, pp. 228–247.

1964 ♦ The Supreme Court reversed the conviction for murder of Daniel Escobedo, ruling that the police had violated his constitutional rights by refusing his request to see a lawyer before he confessed. The landmark decision established a suspect's right to legal counsel during questioning and laid the foundation for the *Miranda* decision two years later that required police to inform suspects of their rights.

Sources: "*Escobedo v. Illinois*, 378 U.S. 478 (1964)," Justia U.S. Supreme Court: https://supreme.justia.com/cases/federal/us/378/478/.

1966 ♦ Rodolfo "Corky" Gonzales (1928–2005) founded the Crusade for Justice in Denver, Colorado. It was one of the most militant Chicano civil rights organizations.

Sources: Rosales, *Chicano! History of the Mexican American Civil Rights Movement*, pp. 175–182.

1967 ♦ Reies López Tijerina (1926–2015) and his *Alianza Federal de Mercedes* (Federal Land Grant Alliance) members raided and took over the Rio Arriba County Courthouse in Tierra Amarilla, New Mexico, to dramatize the plight of New Mexican small farmers attempting to recover their families' Spanish-Mexican land grants. The event became a landmark in the development of the Chicano civil rights movement and López Tijerina a symbol of the civil disobedience that would force authorities to react to demands. Eventually, the *Alianza* waned as López Tijerina and some of his followers were arrested and sentenced to prison terms for their illegal acts, which were among the most militant of the Chicano Movement.

Sources: Rosaldo et al., *Chicano*, pp. 267–277; Rosales, *Chicano! History of the Mexican American Civil Rights Movement*, pp. 153–170.

1968 ♦ The first national legal fund to pursue protection of the civil rights of Mexican Americans, the Mexican American Legal Defense and Education Fund (MALDEF), was cofounded by lawyers Pete Tijerina (1923–2003)

1967: The Mexican American Youth Organization

In 1967, young, well-educated Mexican Americans in San Antonio, Texas, founded the Mexican American Youth Organization (MAYO), whose chapters would spread throughout Texas and become the basis for the creation of the first Hispanic third party in the 20th century: La Raza Unida. Under the leadership of José Angel Gutiérrez (1944–) and other graduate students, MAYO chapters sprung up on college campuses throughout the state. Its program included ousting Anglo-Americans from economic and political control. One of the first battles won was the takeover of the school board in Crystal City in the 1970 elections under the banner of the La Raza Unida Party. *Sources:* Rosaldo et al., *Chicano*, pp. 314–326; Rosales, *Chicano! History of the Mexican American Civil Rights Movement*, pp. 228–247.

and Mario Guerra Obledo (1932–2010). With initial funding from the Ford Foundation, MALDEF has grown to file and win some of the most important suits in education and political representation in the history of Mexican American civil rights. Pete Tijerina served as its first director.

Sources: Rosales, *Chicano! History of the Mexican American Civil Rights Movement*, p. 265.

1968 ♦ The Young Lords Organization, the first militant politicized street gang made up of Puerto Rican youth, was founded in Chicago, Illinois. Similar to the Black Panthers, the party soon spread to other cities in the Northeast. Led by José "Cha Cha" Jiménez (1948–2025), the Young Lords street gang evolved into a community-based organization to advocate for minority access to health care, education, housing, and employment. It was in New York City that college students adopted the model and added "party" to the organization's title.

Sources: "The Young Lord's Organization/Party," Library of Congress Research Guides: https://guides.loc.gov/latinx-civil-rights/young-lords-organization.

1969 ♦ The first National Chicano Youth Liberation Conference was held in Denver, Colorado. The historic meeting, sponsored by Denver's Crusade for Justice under the leadership of Rodolfo "Corky" Gonzales (1928–2005), brought Mexican American activist youth together from throughout the Southwest to plan a coordinated civil rights strategy. The conference drafted and issued a spiritual plan for Chicano nationalism, *El Plan Espiritual de Aztlán* (The Spiritual Plan of Aztlán), using the name of the mythical place of origin, Aztlán, of the Aztec tribes, which corresponded roughly to the five Southwestern states where the majority of Chicanos live. The plan emphasized cultural pride and the need for self-determination. The conference also called for the creation of a Chicano political party; it called for making La Raza Unida, which had been organized in Texas, into a national third party.

Sources: García, *Memories of Chicano History*, p. 264; Rosales, *Chicano! History of the Mexican American Civil Rights Movement*, pp. 210, 228, 230.

1969 ♦ Nosotros, a Hollywood-based organization of Hispanic actors and other film media people, was created to advocate for a more positive portrayal of Latinos in film and television and to integrate the movie and television industries. Its first president and guiding force was actor Ricardo Montalbán (1920–2009).

Sources: Kanellos, *Latino Almanac*, p. 440.

1970 ♦ The first national march to protest the disproportionately high casualty rate among Mexican Americans serving in Vietnam while the community's civil rights were being denied at home took place in Los Angeles, California. The National Chicano Moratorium on the Vietnam War drew between 20,000 and 30,000 marchers from throughout the Southwest, making it the largest public demonstration in U.S. Latino history. The principal organizer of the event was a young graduate of the University of California at Los Angeles (UCLA) who had served as student body president, Rosalío Muñoz (1938–2012). Unfortunately, police, the California National Guard, and other law enforcement agencies severely repressed the march by rioting and dispersing the crowd. Numerous protesters were injured, and the leading Chicano journalist, Rubén Salazar (1928–1970), was killed when he was struck by a tear gas canister shot into a bar. The moratorium became a watershed in the Chicano civil rights movement, and Salazar was erected as a martyr.

Sources: García, *Memories of Chicano History*, pp. 275–279; Rosales, *Chicano! History of the Mexican American Civil Rights Movement*, pp. 197–208.

1971 ♦ Latinos win the first suit against schools being financed through property taxes. In *Serrano v. Priest*, John Serrano sued the California state treasurer, alleging that his son was receiving an inferior education in East Los Angeles because schools were financed by local property taxes. The

California courts found in August—and in April 1974 and December 1977 (California Supreme Court)—that financing schools through local property taxes did not provide equal education opportunities and, therefore, the financing system had to be changed. After that, the state legislature mandated that income taxes be used for financing education.

Sources: Reinhold, Robert, "John Serrano Jr., et al., and School Tax Equality," *New York Times*, 10 January 1972.

1972 ♦ Mexican American voters replaced an all Anglo-American city council for the first time in California history in the small, predominantly Mexican American town of Parlier, where discrimination against them had run high.

Sources: Meier and Rivera, *Dictionary of Mexican American History*, p. 270.

Vilma Martínez

1972 ♦ Lawyers Vilma Martínez (1943–) and Graciela Olivárez (1928–1987) became the first women to join the board of the Mexican American Legal Defense and Education Fund (MALDEF). In 1973, Martínez became the first woman to serve as its president and general counsel. During her presidency, one of Martínez's major accomplishments was her campaign toward expanding the U.S. Voting Rights Act, which, since its passage in 1965, had only applied to blacks and Puerto Ricans. Thanks to her coalition building and concerted pressure levied by organizations that she mobilized, Congress extended the act to Mexican Americans in 1975. Martínez was also successful in spearheading efforts to guarantee bilingual education for non-English-speaking children in public schools, which was secured in 1974.

Sources: Telgen and Kamp, *Latinas! Women of Achievement*, pp. 241–246.

1972 ♦ The National Conference of Puerto Rican Women was founded in Washington, D.C. It seeks justice and gives voice "to the preservation of civil, health, educational and other rights through the dissemination of information, networking, collaboration and advocacy with other national and local groups, and through education, celebration, community and civil involvement."

Sources: "Our History and Mission," National Conference on Puerto Rican Women: https://www.nacoprw.org/about/our-history-and-mission.

1972 ♦ National Image, Inc., was founded in Washington, D.C., by federal employees to end employment discrimination against Mexican Americans.

Equal Educational Opportunity Act of 1974

U.S. Congress passed the Equal Educational Opportunity Act of 1974 to create equality in public schools by making bilingual education available to Hispanic youths. According to the framers of the act, equal education means more than equal facilities and equal access to teachers. Students who have trouble with the English language must be given programs to help them overcome their difficulties with English. *Sources:* Kanellos, *Chronology of Hispanic American History*, p. 260.

The organization now works to combat discrimination against all Latinos. Its mission is "promoting Hispanic employment in the Federal, State and local government through training, leadership development, education and the advancement of Civil Rights for all."

Sources: National Image, Inc: https://national-image.org/.

1973 ♦ The right of the Puerto Rican people to decide their own future as a nation was approved by the United Nations. In 1973, the United Nations officially recognized Puerto Rico as a colony of the United States. This finding by the United Nations was of great support to the independence movement on the island and in the United States.

Sources: Kanellos, *Chronology of Hispanic American History*, p. 259.

1974 ♦ The first large Latino voter registration organization was founded, the Southwest Voter Registration Education Project, which has registered millions of Latinos to vote. Centered in San Antonio, Texas, the project has offices throughout the Southwest and has made significant strides in empowering Latinos to vote by conducting hundreds of voter registration drives in 14 states. In addition, the organization has been instrumental in the formation of voting districts with majority-Latino populations. Its founder and first director, Willie Velásquez (1944–1988), was its initial driving force; he laid the groundwork for the organization's outstanding success.

Sources: "New Mission, New Leaders for Hispanics," *Houston Chronicle*, 7 January 1996, pp. A23–24; Rosales, *Chicano! History of the Mexican American Civil Rights Movement*, pp. 264, 266.

1975 ♦ Thanks to the lobbying efforts of the Mexican American Legal Defense and Education Fund (MALDEF), under the directorship of Vilma

1975: The Congressional Hispanic Caucus

The Congressional Hispanic Caucus was founded in 1975 by Latino congressmen and senators to "to develop programs ... to increase opportunities for Hispanics to participate in and contribute to the American political system" and to "reverse the national pattern of neglect, exclusion and indifference suffered for decades by Spanish-speaking citizens of the United States." The caucus also strives to strengthen the roles of Latinos at all levels of government. It publishes the monthly *Legislative Review*, runs an institute, and has a yearly national conference. *Sources:* "History of the CHC," Congressional Hispanic Caucus: https://chc.house.gov/history-of-the-chc.

Martínez, U.S. Congress voted to expand the U.S. Voting Rights Act to include Mexican Americans. The original act, passed in 1965, had only applied to blacks and Puerto Ricans. The act also made bilingual ballots a requirement in certain locations of the United States.

Sources: Tardiff and Mabunda, *Dictionary of Hispanic Biography*, p. 529.

1976 ♦ Attorney Vilma Martínez was the first Latina to win the Jefferson Award from the American Institute for Public Service in recognition of her pioneering work in civil rights as director of the Mexican American Legal Defense and Education Fund (MALDEF).

Sources: Tardiff and Mabunda, *Dictionary of Hispanic Biography*, p. 530; Telgen and Kamp, *Latinas! Women of Achievement*, pp. 241–246.

1982 ♦ Through the work of the Mexican American Legal Defense and Education Fund (MALDEF), the *Plyler v. Doe* case was won, giving the children of undocumented workers in Texas the right to free public education. Before this decision, Texas required tuition of $1,000 for each undocumented child.

Sources: Tardiff and Mabunda, *Dictionary of Hispanic Biography*, p. 529.

1983 ♦ After the passage of the Voting Rights Act Amendments of 1982, one of the first cases to challenge vote dilution of minorities was *Velasquez v. City of Abilene* in 1983. Prominent Judge Reynaldo G. Garza delivered the opinion of the U.S. Court of Appeals for the 5th Circuit, stating that the intention of Congress was clear in cases of vote dilution. He ruled that the City of Abilene's use of at-large voting, bloc voting, and other voting mechanisms resulted in vote dilution and had a discriminatory effect on Hispanic American voters in the city.

Sources: Kanellos, *Latino Almanac*, pp. 129, 170.

Hector Pérez García received the Presidential Medal of Freedom from President Ronald Reagan in 1984.

1984 ♦ Hector Pérez García (1914–1996) became the first Latino to be awarded the Presidential Medal of Freedom for his years of work on behalf of civil rights for Latinos. Born in Llera, Tamaulipas, Mexico, García was educated in the United States after his parents immigrated to Texas. He received his B.A. in 1936 and his M.D. in 1940, both from the University of Texas. During World War II, he served with distinction in the Army Medical Corps, earning the Bronze Star and six battle stars. At the end of the war, he opened a medical practice in Corpus Christi and, outraged at the refusal of local authorities to bury a Mexican American veteran in the city cemetery at Three Rivers, Texas, he organized the American G.I. Forum, which is still one of the largest and most influential Latino civil rights organizations. In 1967, President Lyndon B. Johnson named García alternate delegate to the United Nations with the rank of ambassador, and he also appointed him the first Mexican American member of the U.S. Commission on Civil Rights. In 1965, the president of Panama awarded García the Order of Vasco Núñez de Balboa in recognition of his services to humanity. In 1984, he was awarded the Presidential Medal of Freedom.

Sources: "García, Hector Pérez (1914–1996)," Texas State Historical Association: https://www.tshaonline.org/handbook/entries/García-hector-perez.

1984 ♦ Ernesto Cortés Jr. became the first community organizer to receive the MacArthur Fellowship, commonly known as the "genius" grant, for his more than 20 years dedicated to organizing grassroots communities to empower them to make changes in the structure of authority in their schools and communities. After receiving training at the Industrial Areas Foundation in 1973, Cortés went on to help working-class people found Communities Organized for Public Service in his native San Antonio. He later created grassroots organizations and movements in Los Angeles, Houston, El Paso, Dallas, Tucson, Phoenix, Albuquerque, New Orleans, and other cities in the Southwest and built them into a network. Today, he is the Southwest director for the Industrial Areas Foundation. Thanks to his efforts, the government has been more responsive to providing services for poor people, and educational access and achievement have improved for low-income neighborhoods because of the concerted community organizing and pressure exerted by the organizations he pioneered.

Sources: Meier, Matt S., and Gutiérrez, Margo, *Encyclopedia of the Mexican American Civil Rights Movement.* Greenwood Press, 2000, pp. 64–65.

1991 ♦ As a result of the Voting Rights Act, its 1982 amendments, and the cases of *Velasquez v. City of Abilene* and *Jones v. City of Lubbock*, for the first time in history, the City of Abilene, Texas, elected two Hispanics to its city council in 1991 and the City of Lubbock elected one. The act and these court cases resulted in many Hispanics being elected to local positions throughout the United States.

Sources: "Voting Rights Act (1965)," National Archives: https://www.archives.gov/milestone-documents/voting-rights-act.

1994 ♦ The Mexican American Legal Defense and Education Fund (MALDEF) and a coalition of other civil rights organizations were successful in curtailing the effects of a voter referendum in California, Proposition 187, which banned undocumented immigrants and their children from receiving public education and social services.

Sources: Kanellos, *Chronology of Hispanic American History*, p. 282.

1995 ♦ The Presidential Medal of Freedom was awarded posthumously to Willie Velásquez (1944–1988), the founder and director of the Southwest Voter Registration Education Project. The medal, which is the nation's highest civilian honor, was presented by President Bill Clinton to Velásquez's widow in recognition of the deceased activist's lifetime commitment and contributions to democracy. Willie Velásquez is recognized as the single most influential organizer of Latinos on the road to political power and representation. In an effort to continue the legacy of Velásquez, the Southwest Voter Registration and Education Project committed itself to the ambitious goal of registering one million new Latino voters for the general elections in November 1974.

Sources: Southwest Voter Research Notes, (fall 1995/winter 1996), p. 1.

1995 ♦ Anita Pérez Ferguson became the first Latina to serve as president of the National Women's Political Caucus.

Sources: Hispanic Link Weekly Report, 14 August 1995, p. 1.

1996 ♦ Antonia Pantoja (1922–2002), educator and founder of Aspira, Inc., which counsels and provides support services for students on their way to higher education, became the first Latina to receive the Presidential Medal of Freedom, which was presented by President Bill Clinton. Born and raised in Puerto Rico but active as a community organizer in the United States—principally in New York City and Washington, D.C.— Pantoja received the award for promoting community development. In 1991, she also received the John W. Gardner Leadership Award from the independent sector.

Sources: Pantoja, Antonia. *Memoir of a Visionary*. Houston: Arte Público Press, 2002.

Anthony D. Romero

2001 ♦ Anthony D. Romero (1965–) became the executive director of the American Civil Liberties Union (ACLU), the largest and most prominent civil rights organization in the United States; he was the first Latino to lead the organization. Under his leadership, the ACLU has experienced the fastest and largest growth in its history, with a generously increased budget that allows it to address issues of racial justice, religious freedom, privacy rights, reproductive freedom, and LGBTQ+ rights. Born on July 9, 1965, in the Bronx, New York, to Puerto Rican parents, Romero was the first in his family to receive a high school education. He went on to graduate with a B.A. degree from Princeton University's Woodrow Wilson School of Public and International Affairs in 1987 and a J.D. from Stanford University Law School in 1990. Romero began his career by working on civil rights issues at the Rockefeller Foundation and then at the Ford Foundation. In 1996, he became the director of the Ford Foundation's Civil Rights and Social Justice Program. He later directed the Human Rights and International Cooperation Program, making it the largest in the foundation.

Sources: "Anthony D. Romero Is New ACLU Executive Director; First Latino to Head Premier Civil Liberties Group," ACLU: https://www.aclu.org/press-releases/anthony-d-romero-new-aclu-executive-director-first-latino-head-premier-civil.

2024 ♦ The National Park Service National Underground Network to Freedom added Mission San José in San Antonio to commemorate the role played by Mexican Texans in assisting runaway slaves from the southern United States to make their way to freedom in Mexico. In particular, the Park Service cites the role played by Mission San José in defending Mexico's antislavery laws in 1833. The citation states, "Five freedom seekers from Louisiana completed a treacherous 400-mile journey to safety in San Antonio, which was part of Mexico at the time. The Mexican Army protected the five men by opening fire on the slave catchers pursuing them."

Sources: "National Park Service Announces 19 Additions to the Underground Railroad Network to Freedom in 10 States," National Park Service: https://www.nps.gov/subjects/undergroundrailroad/national-park-service-announces-19-additions-to-the-underground-railroad-network-to-freedom-in-10-states.htm.

LABOR

1883 ♦ The first Latino labor organizing activity recorded in U.S. history was Juan Gómez's organizing of cowboys in the panhandle of Texas. He led several hundred cowboys on strike against ranch owners.

Sources: McWilliams, *North from Mexico*, p. 190.

Santiago Yglesias Pantín

1899 ♦ Santiago Yglesias Pantín (1872–1939) became the first labor organizer under U.S. rule. Yglesias Pantín was born in La Coruña, Spain, where he received an elementary education and became a carpenter. He relocated to Cuba, where he became active in organizing labor through the Círculo de Trabajadores de la Habana (Havana Workers' Circle) from 1889 to 1896. In 1899, he moved to Puerto Rico, where he was instrumental in organizing the Partido Obrero Social (Workers' Socialist Party) and later became an organizer for the American Federation of Labor for Puerto Rico and Cuba. In 1917, Yglesias Pantín founded the Federación Libre de Trabajadores de Puerto Rico (Free Federation of Puerto Rican Workers) and the Socialist Party. From 1917 to 1933, Yglesias Pantín served as a legislator in the Puerto Rican senate. From 1925 to 1933, he served as secretary of the Federación Panamericana de Trabajo (Panamerican Federation of Labor). In 1932 and 1936, he was elected resident commissioner to represent Puerto Rico in Washington, D.C. During his years as a labor organizer, Yglesias Pantín also founded and directed three newspapers: *El Porvenir Social* (The Future of Society, 1898); *La Unión Obrera* (Worker Unity, 1903); and *Justicia* (Justice). He died on December 16, 1939, in Washington, D.C.

Sources: Kanellos, *Chronology of Hispanic American History*, p. 140.

1899 ♦ The first large strike in the cigar industry occurred in Ybor City (Tampa), Florida, where Spanish and Cuban entrepreneurs had relocated their industry in 1886, in part to avoid labor unrest and organizing. The cigar industry relied on extensive manual, but skilled, labor by tobacco rollers. The cigar workers were among the most radicalized and educated, through a system whereby they supported professional *lectores*, or readers, who read to them throughout the day from world literature and newspapers while they hand-rolled cigars at their tables. The cigar rollers developed the strongest unions of any Latino workers and became the most influenced by socialist ideology. They struck again in 1901, 1910, 1920, and 1931.

Sources: Henderson and Mormino, *Spanish Pathways in Florida*, pp. 40–45.

1900 ♦ At the turn of the 20th century, American railway companies began recruiting Mexican workers in El Paso, Texas, for six-month contracts to work on the construction of lines in the North. The most active recruiters and employers of Mexican labor were the Southern Pacific Railroad and the Atchison, Topeka, and Santa Fe Railway, which heavily recruited workers to lay track in California. It is estimated that some 16,000 Mexicans were working on the railroads in the Southwest and West by 1908. The importation of Mexican labor by the railroads reached its peak between 1910 and 1912. During World War I, thousands of Mexican workers were brought to the Midwest to construct railways there. During World War II, the Bracero Program authorized further recruitment of Mexican workers for the railroads; during the war, more than 80,000 Mexican nationals were employed on some 30 American railroads. More than half of these worked on the Southern Pacific and Santa Fe lines. By April 1964, all of the Bracero Program workers were repatriated.

Between 1942 and 1964, the federal government's Bracero Program imported laborers from Mexico.

Sources: Kanellos, *Chronology of Hispanic American History*, p. 144.

1901 ♦ The American Federation of Labor (AFL) broke its pattern of exclusion of nonwhites by allowing affiliation of the Federación Libre de Trabajadores de Puerto Rico (Free Federation of Puerto Rican Workers).

Sources: Kanellos, *Chronology of Hispanic American History*, p. 146.

1903 ♦ One of the earliest and most important copper mine strikes in the Southwest occurred during the first two weeks in June 1903 in Arizona, when mostly Mexican and Mexican American workers walked out. Although the territorial legislature had reduced the work day from 10 to eight hours and prohibited the mines from cutting wages, mining officials in Clifton, Morenci, and Metcalf reduced their workers' wages. A few thousand miners walked out in protest; 80 to 90 percent of them were Mexicans, whom the unions had resolved not to organize, for they had been characterized as taking work away from Americans. Despite the absence of unions, the Mexicans were well organized, with the help of mutual aid societies, and withstood hundreds of national guardsmen, Arizona Rangers, and federal troops. But the Clifton-Morenci strike failed because Anglo workers did not join the Mexicans in the walkout and also because a flood wreaked havoc in Clifton on June 9.

Sources: Rosales, *Chicano! History of the Mexican American Civil Rights Movement*, pp. 115–117.

1903 ♦ More than 1,200 Mexican and Japanese farm workers organized the first farm worker union, the Japanese-Mexican Labor Association (JMLA), during February, in Oxnard, California. It was also the first to win a strike against the strong agricultural industry in California. The rapid development of the sugar beet industry in Ventura County, with its dependence on cheap seasonal labor amid the highly racist European American society that had moved into the area, resulted in unfair and racist labor practices by the contractors and the association of farmers and refiners.

The banding together of the Japanese and Mexican farm workers marked the first time in history that two ethnic groups united when faced with Anglo-American discrimination and labor exploitation. Their founding of the union was not an easy task, given the enormous linguistic and cultural barriers that the organizers had to overcome. The JMLA press release about the history-making strike spoke eloquently to the relationship of the workers to the industry owners and managers: "Many of us have families, were born in the country, and are lawfully seeking to protect the only property that we have—our labor. It is just as necessary for the welfare of the valley that we get a decent living wage, as it is that the machines in the great sugar factory be properly oiled—if the machine stops, the wealth of the valley stops, and likewise if the laborers are not given a decent wage, they too, must stop work and the whole people of the country will suffer with them."

By the first week in March, the JMLA had recruited more than 1,200 workers, over 90 percent of the entire sugar beet work force. Despite strikebreaking efforts, violence, and repression by the industry owners supported by the judicial system, the JMLA won an overwhelming victory and ended the strike on March 30. Because of the success of the JMLA, labor unions began to rethink their policy of not organizing nonwhite labor or farm labor. One of the important benefits for Mexican workers was that they learned some doctrines and techniques from the Wobblies (members of the labor organization and Industrial Workers of the World) that were involved and were able to apply them in their own Mexican unions.

Sources: Almaguer, *Racial Fault Lines*, pp. 183–203; Jamieson, *Labor Unionism in American Agriculture*, pp. 76–77; Kushner, *Long Road to Delano*, pp. 20–21; McWilliams, *North from Mexico*, p. 190; Rosales, *Chicano! History of the Mexican American Civil Rights Movement*, p. 117.

Luisa Capetillo

1907 ♦ Luisa Capetillo (1880–1922) became the first Puerto Rican woman to be a leader in the labor movement, with her participation in a strike of tobacco factories in Arecibo, Puerto Rico. She joined the Federación Libre de Trabajadores de Puerto Rico (Free Federation of Puerto Rican Workers) and, in 1910, founded the newspaper *La mujer* (The Woman). For the next two decades, she was active as an organizer in New York, Florida, and again in Puerto Rico. She is also known as one of Puerto Rico's first feminists.

Sources: Tardiff and Mabunda, *Dictionary of Hispanic Biography*, p. 166.

1910 ♦ The first strikes in the railroad industry led by Mexicans were a series of strikes that led to the bombing of the *Los Angeles Times* building. The wave of strikes was initiated when Mexicans working on the city's street railroad system walked out.

Sources: McWilliams, *North from Mexico*, p. 190.

1915 ♦ Labor organizer and feminist Luisa Capetillo (1880–1922) became known as the first woman in Puerto Rico to wear slacks in public as an exterior sign of her rebellion. In addition to becoming one of the first female labor organizers in Puerto Rico, she was probably the first feminist, in the modern sense of the term. Capetillo was born in Arecibo in 1880 or 1882. She received her early education in a private school, where she won prizes in grammar, history, and geography. Shortly after graduating, she worked as a journalist and labor organizer. In 1912, she lived in New York City, and in 1913, moved to Ybor City, Florida, to organize cigar workers. From 1914 to 1915, she lived in Cuba, presumably continuing her organizing among cigar workers. Thereafter, she returned to Puerto Rico and became involved in the labor and feminist movements as a socialist. She was particularly outstand-

1927: Federation of Mexican Worker Unions

In 1927 The first large-scale effort to organize and consolidate Mexican workers took place at a meeting of federated Mexican societies in Los Angeles. The result was the Confederación de Uniones Obreras Mexicanas (Federation of Mexican Worker Unions—CUOM), which was joined by more than 20 unions representing both agricultural and industrial workers throughout southern California. By May 1929, the federation had some 3,000 members organized in 20 locals throughout the region, but because many of its members were migrants without a stable residential base, the union had difficulties in surviving. The first strike called by the union, in the Imperial Valley, was broken by arrests and the deportation of Mexican workers. Two years later, the union struck again by surprise, and the growers were forced to settle. *Sources:* Jamieson, *Labor Unionism in American Agriculture*, pp. 76–77; Kushner, *Long Road to Delano*, pp. 55–56; McWilliams, *North from Mexico*, p. 191; Rosales, *Chicano! History of the Mexican American Civil Rights Movement*, pp. 119–120.

ing in militating for women's suffrage. She advocated free love, had children out of wedlock, and worked for a society without social classes. She was the founder and editor of the magazine *La Mujer* (Woman) and wrote various books: *Ensayos libertarios* (Libertarian Essays), 1909; *La humanidad en el futuro* (Humanity in the Future), 1910; *Mi opinión sobre las libertades, derechos y deberes de la mujer* (My Opinion on the Liberties, Rights and Duties of Women), 1911; and *Influencia de las ideas modernas* (The Influence of Modern Ideas, 1916). She died of tuberculosis in Rio Piedras, Puerto Rico, in 1922.

Sources: Kanellos, *Chronology of Hispanic American History*, p. 117.

1922 ♦ The first strikes of grape pickers unsuccessfully attempting to organize a union took place in Fresno, California. A three-day celebration in honor of Mexican independence turned into a union-organizing activity, but the effort ultimately failed. A small union was organized by Mexicans in the cantaloupe fields of Brawley as another early attempt at creating a farm worker union.

Sources: Jamieson, *Labor Unionism in American Agriculture*, p. 76; McWilliams, *North from Mexico*, pp. 190–191.

1928 ♦ The first union to organize farm workers in Imperial Valley, California, was one formed under the leadership of the Mexican vice consul in Calexico: the Union of the United Workers of the Imperial Valley. The Imperial Valley Cantaloupe Workers' strike was the first attempt at work stoppage by Mexican farm workers in modern California. The vice consul, Carlos Ariza, had been called upon so often to intervene in labor disputes that he thought establishing a union might be a solution. The strike was broken easily, primarily through threats and violence. Most growers agreed to pay the 15 cents per crate wage requested by the workers; however, the growers did not recognize the union as a bargaining agent.

Sources: Rosaldo et al., *Chicano*, pp. 181–182, 185–192; Rosales, *Chicano! History of the Mexican American Civil Rights Movement*, p. 120.

1931 ♦ The first labor strike in the United States over a cultural issue took place in Ybor City (Tampa), Florida, when the owners of the cigar factories abolished the *lectores* (readers), who read aloud all day from a wide variety of books and periodicals to help cigar rollers pass the time in their boring manual task. The owners accused the *lectores* of radicalizing the workers and replaced them with radios; the workers walked out, but the owners were victorious. The demand for cigars had fallen greatly due to the massive change by Americans to smoking cigarettes. The cigar industry was beginning to decline.

Sources: Henderson and Mormino, *Spanish Pathways in Florida*, p. 42.

1933 ♦ The El Monte Berry Strike in 1933, possibly the largest agricultural strike thus far, was led by Mexican unions in California. In June, members of the Mexican Farm Labor Union, an affiliate of the Confederación de Uniones Obreras Mexicanas (CUOM), officially sanctioned the strike and called for a minimum wage of 25 cents per hour. The strike spread from Los Angeles County to Orange County, and the union grew rapidly. In June, the strike ended with the concession of a small increase in wages and recognition of the Confederación. That same year, the confederation became the largest and most active agricultural union in California. In 1935, the Confederación was responsible for six of the 18 strikes in California agriculture and was also effective in winning negotiations without striking. In 1936, it was a leader in establishing the Federation of Agricultural Workers Union of America. By the end of the 1930s, however, the confederation's power had waned in the face of increased resistance from the growers, legislators, jurisdictional disputes between the American Federation of Labor and the Congress of Industrial Organizations, and a surplus of workers.

Sources: Kushner, *Long Road to Delano*, pp. 68–76; McWilliams, *North from Mexico*, p. 191.

1933 ♦ In October 1933, Mexican farm workers struck the cotton industry in the counties of Central Valley, California. The San Joaquin cotton strike was the largest and best organized of labor actions initiated by the radical Cannery and Agricultural Workers Industrial Union (CAWIU) in the 1930s. Some 12,000 to 18,000 pickers walked out, demanding a raise from 60 cents to one dollar a pound for picked cotton. Growers and vigilante groups attempted to repress the strike violently and, in fact, killed two strikers and wounded various others. California governor James Rolf called in the National Guard and established a fact-finding board, which eventually created the basis for a compromise: 75 cents per pound and a condemnation of the growers for a violation of the strikers' civil rights.

Sources: Jamieson, *Labor Unionism in American Agriculture*, pp. 100–105; Kushner, *Long Road to Delano*, pp. 57–70.

1933 ♦ Mexican working women as a group became very active for the first time as women in organizing workers in the garment industry. Rose Pessota (1896–1965) recruited heavily among Mexican women for the International Ladies' Garment Workers Union (ILGWU), which in 1933 launched a massive strike that brought garment production to a halt in Los Angeles. The strike prevailed despite harassment by city officials, spurred on by the sweatshop owners. The union prevailed, and a contract was signed with a number of shops for an increase in wages.

Sources: Rosales, *Chicano! History of the Mexican American Civil Rights Movement*, p. 119.

1933 ♦ Mexican and Mexican American workers in Texas organized one of the broadest unions in the history of Latino labor in the United States, La Asociación de Jornaleros (The Journeymen's Association), which represented everything from hatmakers to farm workers. But the union's very diversity was the cause of its failure, and it died after Texas Rangers arrested leaders of a strike in the onion fields of Laredo in 1934.

Sources: Rosales, *Chicano! History of the Mexican American Civil Rights Movement*, p. 121.

Rose Pessota speaks at an ILGWU meeting in 1965.

1935 ♦ The *Liga Obrera de Habla Espanola* (Spanish-Speaking Labor League) was

1935: The Cannery and Agricultural Workers Industrial Union

By 1935, the most effective agricultural labor unions were those organized among Mexican farm workers. Most of the membership of the Cannery and Agricultural Workers Industrial Union (CAWIU) had been Mexican since 1933. What was learned through the CAWIU was applied to the other Mexican unions that existed. The *Confederacion de Uniones de Campesinos y Obreros Mexicanos del Estado de California* (Federation of Mexican Farmworker and Industrial Worker Unions of California) became the most active farm worker organization in the state. The federation, which had developed out of the general strike in the strawberry, celery, and other crops in June 1933, by now claimed 10,000 members. It coordinated its strategies with the CSAWIU and carried out at least one strike under a united front with its partner. *Sources:* Rosales, *Chicano! History of the Mexican American Civil Rights Movement*, p. 122.

organized in Gallup, New Mexico, among coal miners in an effort to save miners arrested or charged with a variety of offenses stemming from their long-lasting strike against the Gallup-American Company (a subsidiary of Kennecott Copper Company). Jesús Pallares, a miner originally from Chihuahua, was the main organizer. With some 8,000 members, the league succeeded in forcing the authorities to abandon criminal syndicalism proceedings and won relief rights for the strikers. The personal price for this victory was the one paid by Pallares—and often meted out to Mexican-origin organizers—when he was arrested and deported.

Sources: McWilliams, *North from Mexico*, p. 195; Rosales, *Chicano! History of the Mexican American Civil Rights Movement*, p. 122.

1936 ♦ Mexican workers struck the celery fields in southern California, which led to police violently attacking and suppressing 2,000 strikers with a force of 1,500 armed men. Injured strikers were refused aid at local hospitals, and taxpayer dollars were employed by local authorities to hire field agents to visit growers and urge them not to settle. The growers themselves spent thousands of dollars to hire armed guards from a local strikebreaking detective agency.

Sources: McWilliams, *North from Mexico*, p. 192.

1936 ♦ Some 2,500 Mexican farm workers tied up a $20 million citrus crop in Orange County, California, for several weeks with a strike. More than 400 special armed guards were recruited. Some 200 arrested strikers were formally arraigned in an outdoor bullpen that served as a courtroom. Orange County remained in a state of virtual siege for several weeks as local newspapers celebrated the vigilantism used against the farm workers on strike.

Sources: McWilliams, *North from Mexico*, pp. 192–193.

1937 ♦ Bert Corona (1918–2001) became one of the founders of the International Longshoremen's and Warehousemen's Union (ILWU), serving as the secretary of Local 26. From there, Corona became the leading Latino voice in mainstream labor unions and in creating a place for Latinos in the American labor movement.

Sources: García, *Memories of Chicano History*, p. 89.

1937 ♦ Mexican workers had increasingly been recruited for the steel and automobile industries in the Midwest. Mexicans and Mexican Americans were among the most militant members of the Steel Workers Organizing Committee in the Chicago area. Their involvement meant that Mexicans were finding that racially mixed organizing was becoming a better solution to improving their lot as workers. Mexicans participated significantly in the Little Steel Strike of 1937, one of the most famous events in the labor history of the United States. In this strike, workers from throughout the Midwest walked off the job, including thousands of Mexicans, who also suffered heavy losses and injuries in the famed Republic Steel Massacre.

Sources: Rosales, *Chicano! History of the Mexican American Civil Rights Movement*, p. 122.

1938 ♦ Luisa Moreno (1907–1992), a Guatemalan immigrant who came to the United States as a child and was educated at the College of the Holy Names in Oakland, California, became the first Hispanic vice president of a major labor union, the United Cannery, Agricultural, Packing, and Allied Workers of America (UCAPAWA). Moreno had broad experience in organizing tobacco workers in Florida, factory workers in New York City, cane workers in Louisiana, cotton pickers in Texas, and sugar beet workers in Colorado. While she was organizing cannery workers in California, she developed the idea to create a national congress of Hispanic workers and communities, which she was able to accomplish under the auspices of the Congress of Industrial Organizations (CIO) and with many other union organizers, especially women. She was a leader in bringing the UCAPAWA into giant canneries in California, such as Calpak, Del Monte, Campbell, and Libby. During the McCarthy era, Moreno was severely persecuted for her politics and her labor activities. She was ordered to face a deportation hearing, and rather than let the authorities create negative publicity for the unions, she went into exile in Guatemala voluntarily. In Guatemala, she supported the democratic government of Jacobo Arbenz before he was overthrown. After the triumph of the communist revolution in Cuba, she went there to work in the educational system. Moreno died in Guatemala in 1992.

Sources: García, *Memories of Chicano History*, pp. 116–120; Kushner, *Long Road to Delano*, pp. 89–94.

1938 ♦ The first large Mexican and Mexican American agricultural workers' strike in Texas occurred in the pecan-shelling plants of San Antonio. Since the late 19th century, the Texas pecan industry had been centered in San Antonio and had traditionally used predominantly Mexican American labor. Paying only two or three cents a pound for shelling pecans, the industry rejected the National Recovery Administration's higher-wage code. By 1937, various unions had made incursions into the pecan industry, and in January 1938, the announcement of a 15 percent wage cut led to spontaneous strikes throughout the industry. Fully half of all the pecan workers in some 130 plants walked out. More than 1,000 picketers were arrested, and tear gas was used against picketing strikers six times within the first two weeks of the strike. A Mexican American pecan sheller, Emma Tenayuca (1916–1999), emerged as a leader. Known as "La Pasionaria" because of her fervor, Tenayuca joined the Communist Party because she believed that it was the only entity willing to help the shellers. The strike and the management's reaction to it became increasingly strife-ridden. More than 1,000 out of 6,000 strikers were arrested, and much violence was employed against the strikers. In March, the strike was settled through arbitration; the union was recognized, but there was a 7.5 percent decrease in wages. This decision was rendered moot in October when the Fair Labor Standards Act enforced a 25 cents per hour minimum wage. This was a stimulus for the industry to mechanize and eventually reduce its labor force drastically. When the dispute began in 1938, the Southern Pecan Shelling Company had employed some 10,000 workers; by 1941, the company had only 600 employees.

Emma Tenayuca with her husband, Homer Brooks.

Sources: Rosaldo et al., *Chicano*, pp. 192–202; Rosales, *Chicano! History of the Mexican American Civil Rights Movement*, pp. 121–122.

1939 ♦ *El Congreso Nacional del Pueblo de Habla Hispana* (The National Congress of Spanish-Speaking Peoples) was founded. It was the first national effort to bring together Latino workers from diverse ethnic backgrounds: Cubans and Spaniards from Florida, Puerto Ricans from New York, and Mexicans and Mexican Americans from the Southwest.

The prime mover in bringing the diverse Latino labor and community organizations together and in founding the congress was Luisa Moreno (1907–1992), who developed the organization under the auspices of the Congress of Industrial Organizations (CIO). Moreno developed her idea for a national Latino civil rights and labor organization while working for the United Cannery, Agricultural, Packing, and Allied Workers of America (UCAPAWA). The first convention of the congress was held in Los Angeles in April 1939, with a wide variety of labor people, educators, religious leaders, and community organizers attending. Anglo representatives from CIO unions also attended as well as representatives from the movie industry and from African American organizations.

The result of the convention and the organization of the congress itself was that Spanish-speaking people in the United States began to realize that they constituted a national minority whose civil and labor rights were being violated consistently across the country. Another important result of the convention was a highlighting of the role of Hispanic women, who had been leaders in organizing the congress and the convention. In addition to Luisa Moreno, Josefina Fierro (1914–1998) took a notable leadership role in including regional leaders, such as Linda Silva and Marta Cásares. Fierro became the key administrator of the congress as executive secretary.

World War II led to the demise of the congress, when the organization restricted its civil rights protests in order to support the war effort; it also lost numerous members to enlistment in the armed services. Although the organization attempted its revival after the war, McCarthyism and political persecution led to leaders such as Moreno and Fierro going into voluntary exile rather than being grilled by the House Un-American Activities Committee or being deported.

Sources: García, *Memories of Chicano History*, pp. 109–116; Rosales, *Chicano! History of the Mexican American Civil Rights Movement*, pp. 123–124.

1939 ♦ The celebrated organizer of the San Antonio pecan shellers strike Emma Tenayuca (1916–1999), along with Homer Brooks (his real surname was Bartchy), published the first document analyzing the condition of Mexican workers in the United States from a worker's point of view, "The Mexican Question in the Southwest." Although Tenayuca and Brooks were both communists, they described the distinctive commonality of Mexican people in the Southwest because of class and cultural oppression. The document promoted the enlistment of Mexican workers in labor unions and the Communist Party.

Sources: Gómez-Quiñones, *Roots of Chicano Politics, 1600–1940*, p. 393.

1940 ♦ The Committee on Spanish-Speaking Workers, founded and headed by Luisa Moreno (1907–1992), was the first, or one of the first, to function within a mainstream labor union. It operated during the 1940s within the California Congress of Industrial Organizations (CIO) to combat discrimination against Latinos.

Sources: García, *Memories of Chicano History*, p. 105.

1950 ♦ The Salt of the Earth Strike was the first major strike conducted by women and children. From October 1950 until January 1952, the predominantly Mexican Mine-Mill Workers Union struck the mines in southern New Mexico. A local judge issued an injunction prohibiting the mine workers from picketing the mines, but the women's auxiliary of the union continued to picket and organize, quite often with their children at their sides and in their arms and suffering abuse, violence, and arrest. The strike ended when the union was able to obtain minor concessions. In addition to the importance of the leadership role taken by women, the strike was historically important because it focused on the pattern of discrimination against Mexican workers that prevailed throughout the Southwest.

Sources: García, *Memories of Chicano History*, pp. 174–175.

1951 ♦ In California, the first union of Mexican immigrant workers was founded, *La Hermandad Mexicana Nacional* (The Mexican National Brotherhood). The lead organizers, Felipe and Alberto Usquiano, organized a quasi-union made up of a large membership of undocumented workers who were, for the most part, members of the Carpenters' Union or the Laborers' Union. The *Hermandad* was organized in response to the Immigration and Naturalization Service's program to cancel work visas of Mexican nationals.

Sources: García, *Memories of Chicano History*, pp. 290–291.

1956 ♦ California union organizer Ernesto Galarza (1905–1984) published the first exposé of abuses in the Bracero Program and the inhuman conditions under which growers employed Mexican farm workers. *Strangers in Our Fields*, published by the Joint U.S.-Mexico Trade Union Committee, was so successful that it went through two editions for a total of 10,000 copies, and it was condensed in three national magazines, receiving widespread publicity. Galarza's book even spurred the American Federation of Labor and Congress of Industrial Organizations (AFL-CIO) to begin supporting the unionization of farm workers by granting $25,000 to Galarza's National Agricultural Workers Union. The book was one of the most damaging documents to the visitor worker program so favored by California agribusiness and helped to force both the United States and Mexico to allow the program to expire in 1964. The termination of the Bracero Program, in turn, led to the successful unionizing of farm workers that would begin in 1962.

Sources: Rosaldo et al., *Chicano*, pp. 286–287; Rosales, *Chicano! History of the Mexican American Civil Rights Movement*, pp. 131–133.

César Chávez

1962 ♦ César Chávez (1927–1993) began organizing the first successful farm workers' union in U.S. history. Born near Yuma, Arizona, to a family of migrant farm workers, Chávez attended nearly 30 schools, eventually achieving a seventh-grade education. During World War II, he served in the U.S. Navy, after which he returned to migrant farm labor. He eventually settled down in 1948 in the barrio of Sal Si Puedes (Get Out If You Can) in San Jose, California. It was in San Jose that he began working for the Community Services Organization (CSO) as a community organizer. By 1958, he had become the general director of the CSO in California and Arizona. In 1962, wishing to organize farm workers, he resigned the CSO directorship and moved to Delano, California, where he became the head of the United Farm Workers Organizing Committee, which today has become the United Farm Workers, AFL-CIO. The fledgling union embarked on a number of history-making strikes and national boycotts of agricultural products that have become the most successful in the history of farm labor in the United States. Chávez was known as a selfless and spiritual leader of farm workers everywhere, bringing their plight to national attention through media appearances and interviews, hunger strikes, and well-organized boycotts. In 1993, Chávez died of a heart attack near the place of his birth. In 1994, President Bill Clinton bestowed the Presidential Medal of Freedom upon him posthumously; he became the first Latino to win the award for labor-organizing activities.

Sources: Griswold and García, *César Chávez*, pp. 22–40; Kushner, *Long Road to Delano*, pp. 106–114; Rosaldo et al., *Chicano*, pp. 170–173.

1965 ♦ The largest and most important farm worker union was founded in Delano, California, under the leadership of César Chávez (1927–1993) and Dolores Huerta (1930–), who led the organization into a strike started by Filipino grape pickers in Delano. Their United Farm Workers (UFW) group successfully converted the strike into one of the most significant movements for social justice for farm workers, especially the Mexican and Mexican American farm workers, who formed the majority of pickers. From this humble beginning, the UFW was able to develop into the largest union of agricultural workers through more than a decade of struggles, national boycotts, court cases, and legislative action in California. From table grapes, the labor actions spread to lettuce and other crops and eventually successfully won concessions and contracts on wages, working conditions, safe use of pesticides, and the right to unionize and strike. Due principally to these labor organizing efforts, the California legislature passed the California Agricultural Labor Relations Act in 1975, which provided secret ballot union elections for farm workers. Also because of this union, there have been many improvements in wage, health, and housing conditions for farm workers in California and Arizona.

Sources: Griswold and García, *César Chávez*, pp. 41–58.

Dolores Huerta

1965 ♦ Dolores Huerta (1930–) became the first female leader of a farm worker union. She cofounded the United Farm Workers with César Chávez (1927–1993) and became its contract negotiator. Huerta had worked with the Community Services Organization (CSO), a Mexican American self-help organization, as an organizer and had unsuccessfully tried to bring it into farm labor organizing. In 1965, with the United Farm Workers Organizing Committee, Huerta became the unmovable contract negotiator for the new union and its strikes. Born on April 10, 1930, in Dawson, New Mexico, Huerta came from a middle-class background, learning organizational skills from her mother and stepfather, who owned and administered two restaurants in California. Her divorced and estranged father, however, lived as an impoverished farm worker; Huerta's accompanying him in his migrations and in labor camps sensitized her to the conditions faced by agricultural workers. She became further politicized working as a teacher of very poor children and then became swept up in the growing Chicano Movement, so much so that she joined the CSO, becoming its lobbyist in Sacramento. Over the years, Huerta has been one of the most successful contract negotiators, lobbyists, and fundraisers for the union. In 2012, President Obama awarded Huerta the Presidential Medal of Freedom.

Sources: Telgen and Kamp, *Latinas! Women of Achievement*, pp. 193–199.

1969 ♦ Screen actor Ricardo Montalbán (1920–2009) founded the first organization, Nosotros, to promote equal opportunity for Latino actors and technicians in the motion picture and television industries. The organization also had as a mission the improvement of the image of Latinos on the screen.

Sources: Meier and Rivera, *Dictionary of Mexican American History*, p. 237.

Sylvia Rivera

1971 ♦ Sylvia Rivera (1951–2002) cofounded the Street Transvestite Action Revolutionaries (STAR), which became a space to organize and discuss issues facing the transgender community in New York City; STAR also became a refuge to house transgender people who were in crisis or homeless. In 1997, she also started Transy House, modeled after STAR House in Park Slope, Brooklyn. An activist in the gay rights movement who participated directly in the 1969 Stonewall Inn uprising that is considered the beginning of the gay pride movement, Rivera struggled against the discrimination of transgender people in society and in the gay movement itself and especially discrimination against transgender people of color. Assigned male at birth to a Puerto Rican mother and a Venezuelan father, she was orphaned by the age of four and raised by her grandmother in a hostile school and Latino cultural environment. After her activity at Stonewall, she led protests against the police raid and was very active in the gay movement but continually marginalized because of her transition. She nevertheless persisted, and finally, when the gay rights movement was now expanding to embrace the LGBTQ+ community, she was given a place of honor in the 25th Anniversary Stonewall Inn march of 1994.

Sources: "Sylvia Rivera," National Women's History Museum: https://www.womenshistory.org/education-resources/biographies/sylvia-rivera.

1974 ♦ Through implementing a strike in 1972 and a national boycott, the heavily Mexican and Mexican American Amalgamated Clothing Workers of America succeeded in unionizing the workers of the Farah Manufacturing Company in El Paso, Texas.

Sources: Kanellos, *Chronology of Hispanic American History*, p. 258.

1975 ♦ Continued strikes and boycotts by the Mexican American–led United Farm Workers Association (UFWA) resulted for the first time in California history in a pro-union legislative act: the California Agricultural Labor Relations Act. After prolonged strikes and national boycotts, the UFWA, under the leadership of César Chávez (1927–1993), signed contracts with most of the Central Valley table grape growers of California and immediately chose the Salinas Valley lettuce growers for the organization's next labor action. In response, some 70 growers signed "sweetheart" contracts with the International Brotherhood of Teamsters. Despite the Teamsters contracts, some 7,000 farm workers struck in August. In September, the UFWA launched a national boycott of lettuce. Strikes and lettuce and grape boycotts continued—as did the jurisdictional battle with the Teamsters—through 1975, when newly elected governor Jerry Brown pioneered the passage of the California Agricultural Labor Relations Act. Under this legislation, union elections could be held by workers; the result was that the UFWA won 65 percent of the elections and regained many lost contracts. In 1977, the UFWA–Teamsters dispute was resolved, but the lettuce boycott did not end until February 1978. Definitive victory at unionizing the lettuce fields, for the first time, came in September 1979, when the UFWA successfully signed contracts with major lettuce farmers in the state.

Sources: Griswold and García, *César Chávez*, pp. 22–40; Kushner, *Long Road to Delano*, pp. 106–114; Rosaldo et al., *Chicano*, pp. 170–173.

1983 ♦ Mexican American lawyer Patricia Díaz Dennis (1946–) became the first Latina and only the second female to serve on the National Labor Relations Board. She was appointed by President Ronald Reagan after she had developed a background of representing television management in labor issues.

Sources: Tardiff and Mabunda, *Dictionary of Hispanic Biography*, p. 285.

1989 ♦ Dennis Rivera (1950–) was the first Latino president of the 1199 National Health and Human Services Employees Union, which has a membership of some 117,000 workers, primarily residing in New York and New Jersey. By 2009, the union had more than 300,000 members working in hospitals, home care agencies, clinics, etc., in the Northeast. As president, Rivera became one of the nation's most respected and powerful labor leaders. Rivera has been a leader in signing up new members during a time when unions in the United States have waned. He has also been successful in making the union's political action department a powerhouse, especially in registering voters. Rivera is also cochair of the union's National Benefit Fund, which provides health care to 450,000 working people in New York; it is the largest self-insured union health-care plan in the United States. Rivera is the only Latino who serves on the board of the Children's Defense Fund, and he has served as the chairperson of the Rainbow Coalition since 1993. Born in Arecibo, Puerto Rico, in 1950, Rivera was active in Puerto Rico in the antiwar movement and became president of the local chapter of the Independence Party by the time he was 20 years old. He was hired as a union organizer in New York in 1976 and eventually worked his way up to the presidency.

Sources: Hispanic, March 1994, pp. 14–18.

María Elena Durazo

1989 ♦ Mexican American labor leader María Elena Durazo (1953–) became the first woman to head a major union in Los Angeles, the Hotel and Restaurant Employees Local 11, a union with a 70 percent Hispanic membership. She presides over an organization of 13,000 members and a staff of 35.

Sources: Tardiff and Mabunda, *Dictionary of Hispanic Biography*, pp. 301–302.

1993 ♦ Farm worker union leader Dolores Huerta became the first Latina inducted into the National Women's Hall of Fame. She is a Presidential Medal of Freedom awardee.

Sources: Kanellos, *Latino Almanac*, p. 125.

1995 ♦ Linda Chávez-Thompson (1944–) became the highest-ranking Latino when she assumed the position of executive vice president of the combined AFL (American Federation of Labor) and CIO (Congress of Industrial Organizations), the AFL-CIO. She had been elected national vice president in 1993 and became the first Latina to serve on the executive council of the union. She served in that position until 2007.

Linda Chávez-Thompson

Sources: Kanellos, *Latino Almanac*, p. 122.

1997 ♦ Labor leader Linda Chávez-Thompson (1944–) was elected vice chair of the Democratic National Committee. She was reelected in 2007 and served until 2012.

Sources: Kanellos, *Latino Almanac*, p. 122.

2012 ♦ New York–born Puerto Rican labor leader Ida Torres (?–2016, born Ida Inés Berrocal-Torres) was the first Latina to receive the Clara Lemlich Award for Social Activism. Starting off as a telephone operator for the United Office and Professional Workers of America, Torres rose through union ranks to become vice president in 1977, secretary-treasurer in 1984, and president in 1998 of the United Storeworkers in New York. She was also a founder of the Coalition of Labor Union Women and the National Conference of Puerto Rican Women; her activism included work with the NAACP and Labor Council for Latin American Advancement, along with leadership in the civil rights struggle and many community causes.

Sources: "Remembering Sister Ida Torres," CUNY School for Labor and Urban Studies: https://slublog.org/2016/06/08/remembering-sister-ida-torres/.

2012 ♦ Puerto Rican–born labor leader Héctor Figueroa (1962–2019) was elected president of the SEIU, one of the most powerful labor unions on the east coast of the United States. The union represents more than 170,000 building cleaners, security guards, doormen, airport workers, and others in service jobs. In his seven years of leadership, his local added some 50,000 members. He was reelected in 2018.

Sources: Kanellos, *Latino Almanac*, p. 123.

2018 ♦ Under President Héctor Figueroa's (1962–2019) leadership of the SEIU, a historic contract was signed with the Port Authority of New York and New Jersey to raise the minimum wage to $19/hour for some 40,000 workers.

Sources: Kanellos, *Latino Almanac*, p. 123.

EDUCATION

1505 ♦ The first elementary school was established in the Americas, in Santo Domingo, for the children of the Spaniards. From then on, elementary schools were included in convents, teaching children reading, writing, arithmetic, and religion. Later, the mission system in the Americas functioned to instruct the children of Indians and *mestizos.*

Sources: Kanellos, *Chronology of Hispanic American History*, p. 24.

1513 ♦ The first school in an area that would become part of the United States was established. The *Escuela de Gramática* (Grammar School) in Puerto Rico was established at the Cathedral of San Juan by Bishop Alonso Manso (1460–1539). This secondary school, in which the Latin language, literature, history, science, art, philosophy, and theology were taught, was free of charge to the students. Primary education was soon offered at schools connected to churches.

Sources: Dolan and Deck, *Hispanic Catholic Culture in the United States*, p. 296; Kanellos, *Chronology of Hispanic American History*, p. 30.

1513 ♦ The king of Spain issued an edict ordering the teaching of Latin to select Indians. After that, schools for Indians developed and became important, especially in Mexico and Peru, where painting, sculpture, and other trades were taught in addition to Latin and religion. Education for the Indians became an important function of the missions from the Floridas to California.

Sources: Kanellos, *Chronology of Hispanic American History*, p. 30.

1538 ♦ The first university in the Americas—Saint Thomas Aquinas in the city of Santo Domingo—was founded by the Dominican Order. It became a university after having functioned as a Dominican college for years. It is still functioning today as the Autonomous University of Santo Domingo.

Sources: Kanellos, *Chronology of Hispanic American History*, p. 38.

1551 ♦ The University of Mexico in Mexico City, the first university in North America, was founded by the Spaniards. The University of San Marcos in Lima, Peru, was founded in the same year. The universities were chartered by the king of Spain in 1551, but the University of Mexico did not actually open its doors until 1553 and the University of San Marcos until 1572. The latter never had an interruption in its existence and is thus considered the oldest university on the continent.

At that time, the universities followed the general models of the University of Salamanca and the University of Alcalá de Henares in Spain, offering humanities, theology, law, and medicine. Latin was the official language used in classes. Some universities taught indigenous languages for a while. Later, they also taught mathematics and physics. The degrees that were offered were bachelor's, master's (or licentiate), and doctorate.

The Jesuits were the most important teaching order in the Americas. During the colonial period, some 25 universities, in addition to numerous theological seminaries, were founded by the Spaniards in the Americas. During the 17th century, the University of Mexico had achieved the greatest distinction in the Americas, boasting 23 chairs, most of which were in canon law and theology, but others were in medicine, surgery, anatomy, astrology, rhetoric, and the Aztec and Otomi languages.

Carlos de Sigüenza y Góngora

In the last quarter of the 17th century, the university held the distinction of being home to the greatest intellectual of the period: mathematician and historian Carlos de Sigüenza y Góngora (1645–1700).

Sources: Kanellos, *Chronology of Hispanic American History*, p. 42.

1600 ♦ By 1600, the Spaniards had established the first schools in what later became the United States at missions in Florida, New Mexico, and Georgia. Later, almost all of the missions in the Southwest would operate schools into the period of U.S. rule.

Sources: Kanellos, *Chronology of Hispanic American History*, p. 48.

1612 ♦ A Franciscan missionary by the name of Francisco Pareja (1570–1628) was the first to translate books from a European language (Spanish) into an Indian language in what was to become the United States. Pareja translated books into the Timucua language from about 1612 to 1627 in what is the present state of Georgia.

Sources: Kanellos, *Chronology of Hispanic American History*, p. 48.

1746 ♦ The first effort to provide a public school outside of the walls of missions took place in Bexar (present-day San Antonio, Texas) in an effort to provide religious education to the children of the villa of San Fernando. This school was short-lived.

Sources: Chipman, *Spanish Texas, 1519–1821*, p. 256.

1793 ♦ Although schooling at missions was firmly established throughout the Spanish colonies, public education was not promoted until almost the 19th century. The king of Spain first mandated public education in the Spanish colonies in 1793. High illiteracy among soldiers prompted the king to issue the mandate. The implementation of the mandate did not reach the far northern provinces until the 1800s.

Sources: Berger, Max. "Education in Texas during the Spanish and Mexican Periods," *The Southwestern Historical Quarterly*, Vol. 51, No. 1 (July 1947), pp. 41–53.

1794 ♦ The first public schools in California were established under orders from Spanish governor Diego de Borica (1742–1800). Ten schools in five different cities were built during his term from 1794 to 1800. The successive governors established more schools during their terms. Most of the schools established during the Spanish period failed, however, for many reasons, including the lack of public education tradition among the settlers, the isolation and sparsity of the population, general indifference, and financial problems.

Sources: MacDonald, Victoria-María, "Demanding Their Rights: The Latino Struggle for Educational Access and Equity," *American Latino Theme Study: Education*, National Park Service: https://www.nps.gov/articles/latinotheme education.htm.

1802 ♦ Spanish governor Juan Bautista Elguezábal (1741–1805) of Texas issued the first compulsory school attendance law for children up to the age of 12. Elguezábal stipulated heavy fines for parents who did not comply. He ordered schools built and had teachers brought in from New Spain to educate the province's children.

Sources: Chipman, *Spanish Texas, 1519–1821*, p. 257.

1811 ♦ The first Spanish-language reading textbook for elementary school was published in the United States: *El Director de los niños para aprender a deletrear y leer: método para facilitar los progresos de los niños cuando se mandan por primera vez a la escuela* (The Children's Directory for Learning to Spell and Read: Method to Facilitate the Progress of Children When They Are First Sent to School). It was issued in Philadelphia by Mathew Carey.

Sources: Online Computer Library Center.

1812 ♦ The first elementary school textbook for learning the Spanish language was published: *El libro primero de los niños, o Nueva cartilla española* (The First Book for Children, or New Spanish Primer), written by Mariano Velázquez de la Cadena (1778–1860) and published by La Imprenta Española (The Spanish Press) in New York. Evidently, the book was in widespread use, for it had a new edition as late as 1823 and, presumably, numerous reprints before that date.

Sources: Online Computer Library Center.

1825 ♦ Mexican government officials were successful in establishing the first public schools in New Mexico between 1825 and 1827. Eight schools were opened.

Sources: Martínez, Rob, "Education in New Mexico Has Long, Tenuous History," The New Mexican, 4 June 2021: https://www.santafenewmexican.com/news/local_news/education-in-new-mexico-has-long-tenuous-history/article_f9621b04-c3ec-11eb-b8cd-9f0bfdb1bc48.html.

1827 ♦ Under Mexican rule, the State of Coahuila-Texas formulated a constitution that required all municipalities to establish public schools at the primary level. From 1828 to 1833, many decrees were issued encouraging local authorities to establish schools. Local officials, however, faced many obstacles in establishing schools, including individual and municipal poverty, lack of qualified teachers, and lack of commitment and tradition of education among the common people.

Sources: "El origen de la instrucción elemental en la frontera norte de Coahuila," *El periódico de Saltillo,* April 2014: http://www.elperiodicodesaltillo.com/2014/abril%2014/origen.html.

1850 ♦ The Territory of New Mexico established bilingual education in English and Spanish when it enacted a school ordinance. As early as 1839, Ohio led the way with English-German bilingual education, and by the 20th century, hundreds of thousands of children were receiving bilingual education in various languages in public schools throughout the nation. In 1851, Los Angeles schools provided that "all the rudiments of the English and Spanish languages should be taught" in all the schools subsidized by public funds.

Sources: "History of Bilingual Education," *Rethinking Schools*: https://rethinkingschools.org/articles/history-of-bilingual-education/.

1853 ♦ From 1853 to 1874, four Catholic religious orders came to New Mexico Territory to establish and run parochial schools for the predominantly Hispanic population. The Sisters of Loretto, the Christian Brothers, the Sisters of Charity, and the Jesuits established as many as 20 schools in as many towns and cities. The first school the Sisters of Loretto opened was the Academy of Our Lady of Light in Santa Fe. The order went on to establish several other schools throughout the territory. Similar growth took place in Texas and California.

Sources: Rosaldo et al., *Chicano*, p. 89.

1856 ♦ Political leader Antonio F. Coronel (1817–1894) became the first Hispanic to petition a local school board for bilingual education; previously, the board had approved teaching English and Spanish languages, which was not the same as "bilingual education," in all subjects. Coronel promoted the Spanish language because of the economic interests and the public service that could be rendered through its use. Although the petition failed and the Los Angeles school board did not implement bilingual education, his action set an important precedent. Coronel's considerable political and intellectual leadership as an entrepreneur and newspaper publisher contributed to his influence.

Antonio F. Coronel

Sources: Gómez-Quiñones, *Roots of Chicano Politics, 1600–1940*, pp. 231–232.

1859 ♦ The Christian Brothers established the College of San Miguel in Santa Fe, the first college in the Territory of New Mexico, principally for the higher education of Hispanics and to produce seminarians from their ranks. They also founded other schools in Las Vegas and Bernalillo, New Mexico, which by 1892 had 350 children enrolled. The college and the schools attracted students from throughout the territories of Arizona, Colorado, and Texas as well as from northern Mexico.

Sources: Rosaldo et al., *Chicano*, p. 89.

1867 ♦ The establishment of bilingual education in every school with at least 25 non-English-speaking children was first mandated in the Colorado Territory.

Sources: Kloss, *The American Bilingual Tradition*, p. 25.

1867 ♦ Francisco Solano León (1818–1891) was one of a committee of three (along with two Anglos) to organize Tucson's first public school district. The Mexican community supported the establishment and funding of public education in Arizona. The community believed that education was indispensable for Mexicans in the United States and that first and foremost for them was the learning of English. They felt that only through mastering English could they compete with Anglos in society. Three years later, Solano León was one of a committee of 17 Mexicans who lobbied the governor of Arizona, Richard McCormick, to establish a public school system. The committee comprised wealthy Mexican entrepreneurs, including Estevan Ochoa (1831–1888), who supported McCormick, and he, in turn, pushed for public education and other legislation against discrimination.

Sources: Sheridan, *Los Tucsonenses*, pp. 46–47.

1870 ♦ The elites in the Mexican community of Tucson pioneered private parochial education for their children when wealthy Mexican women were finally successful in convincing the Catholic Church to send the Sisters of Saint Joseph to open a Catholic school in Tucson, Arizona: the Academy for Young Ladies. Four years later, the male children of the elite were also able to attend their own school: Saint Augustine's Parochial School for Boys.

Sources: Sheridan, *Los Tucsonenses*, p. 47.

1872 ♦ A prominent businessman and chairman of the Committee on Public Education of the territorial legislature of Arizona, Estevan Ochoa (1831–1888) introduced the first bill to levy a compulsory property tax to support the first public schools in the territory. Thus, Tucson's first solvent public school was opened in March 1872. By 1875, enrollment had increased so much that a new building was needed; Ochoa donated the lot and supplemented the financing for construction of the new school building.

Sources: Sheridan, *Los Tucsonenses*, p. 46.

1886 ♦ Mariano Samaniego (1844–1907) was appointed a member of the first board of regents for the University of Arizona; he may have been the first Latino regent appointed in the United States. Following his appointment, no other Latino regent served until modern times. Samaniego was a wealthy businessman and politician and one of the few college graduates on the frontier. He graduated from Saint Louis University in Missouri in 1862.

Sources: Sheridan, *Los Tucsonenses*, pp. 47–48.

1891 ♦ Alado Chávez (1851–1930), the first Hispanic ("Hispano," as the *nuevomexicanos* preferred to be called) state superintendent of education, was elected in New Mexico. He had been speaker of the state legislature in 1884. From 1901 to 1903, he served as the mayor of Santa Fe.

Sources: Gómez-Quiñones, *Roots of Chicano Politics, 1600–1940*, p. 258.

1891 ♦ The first Hispanic-appointed superintendent of the Tucson, Arizona, schools was Carlos Tully (1848–1923), the only Mexican American ever to hold that office. His tenure lasted from 1891 to 1895.

Sources: Sheridan, *Los Tucsonenses*, p. 217.

1945 ♦ Mexican American–Puerto Rican parent plaintiffs filed suit against segregation in California in *Mendez et al. v. Westminster School District et al.* The suit, which was won on April 14, 1947, had been filed against four Orange County school districts based not on racial discrimination but on ethnicity and supposed "language deficiency," the excuses used by school systems to send Latino children to "Mexican schools" and deny them their 14th Amendment rights to equal protection under the law.

1930: *Salvatierra v. Del Rio Independent School District*

In 1930 Mexican American parents won their first discrimination lawsuit attacking segregation in the Texas schools in the case of *Salvatierra v. Del Rio Independent School District*. Supporting the parents in the suit was the League of United Latin American Citizens, a civil rights organization that had been formed in 1929. However, despite prominent lawyers, such as Alonso S. Perales (1898-1960) and J. T. Canales (1877-1976), joining the parents on the Del Rio ISD appeal of the decision, the parents ultimately lost to the school board's appeal, and the segregation of Mexican children in Texas public schools was upheld. *Sources:* "Del Rio ISD v. Salvatierra," Texas State Historical Association: https://www.tshaonline.org/handbook/entries/del-rio-isd-v-salvatierra.

Sources: Meier and Rivera, *Dictionary of Mexican American History*, p. 218; "A Latinx Resource Guide: Civil Rights Cases and Events in the United States," *Library of Congress Research Guides*: https://guides.loc.gov/latinx-civil-rights/mendez-v-westminster.

1946 ♦ University of New Mexico professor George I. Sánchez (1906–1972), Carlos Castañeda (1896–1958), and Alonso S. Perales (1898–1960) organized the First Regional Conference on the Education of Spanish-Speaking People in the Southwest, which focused on school segregation and bilingual education.

Sources: Calderón, Roberto, "Tejano Politics," *Texas State Historical Association*: https://www.tshaonline.org/handbook/entries/tejano-politics.

1958 ♦ Folklorist Américo Paredes (1915–1999) published his landmark study, *With His Pistol in His Hand: A Border Ballad and Its Hero*, which became the model for Chicano scholarship for more than 20 years. In his study of the folk ballad, Paredes showed how the analysis of popular culture can lead to the reconstruction of history. His book was also the first Chicano work to become the basis for a film, *The Ballad of Gregorio Cortez*, which was a landmark in the history of Chicano cinema.

Sources: Paredes, Américo, *With His Pistol in His Hand*; Kanellos, *Latino Almanac*, pp. 303–304.

1961 ♦ The first organization promoting higher education and providing counseling services for Puerto Ricans in the United States, Aspira, Inc., was founded. In 1958, educator and social worker Antonia Pantoja (1922–2002) and others founded the Puerto Rican Forum, the oldest and largest Puerto Rican social service agency in the country. The founding pioneered the Aspira Clubs, which grew into the counseling agency.

Sources: Tardiff and Mabunda, *Dictionary of Hispanic Biography*, pp. 652–653; Pantoja, Antonia, *Memoir of a Visionary*, Arte Público Press, 2002.

1963 ♦ The first bilingual education program in public schools during modern times was started in Miami's Coral Way Elementary School with a grant from the Ford Foundation. The experimental program led to Dade County public schools instituting a pioneering bilingual education program, which served as a model for Congress in its 1968 passage of the Bilingual Education Act.

Sources: Meier and Rivera, *Dictionary of Mexican American History*, pp. 39–42.

1968 ♦ The first federally mandated bilingual education programs were established with the passage by U.S. Congress of the Elementary and Secondary Education Act, Title VII, on January 2, 1968. The law mandates that children who speak languages other than English be instructed in two languages and that teachers be trained, materials developed, and research conducted to assist these children in making a rapid transition from the native language to English. Congress appropriated $7.5 million in 1969 to support 76 pilot projects serving 27,000 students. Appropriations for bilingual education expanded rapidly, surpassing the $100 million mark per year by 1978. Lobbied for and supported by Latinos from throughout the country, bilingual education has survived in the United States, despite such movements as "English-Only" and prejudice against immigrants.

Sources: Meier and Rivera, *Dictionary of Mexican American History*, pp. 42–46.

1968 ♦ Mexican American students and faculty, led by historian Rodolfo Acuña (1932–), founded the first department of Chicano studies in the nation at California State University at Los Angeles. It has since grown to become the largest department of its kind.

Sources: Tardiff and Mabunda, *Dictionary of Hispanic Biography*, p. 4.

1968 ♦ Marta P. Cotera (1938–) became the founding director of the Southwest Educational Development Laboratory in Austin, Texas. A teacher and librarian, Cotera was an activist in the Chicano Movement, one of the first to conduct educational research from a political perspective and promote feminism.

Sources: Tardiff and Mabunda, *Dictionary of Hispanic Biography*, p. 252.

1969: Dr. Américo Paredes Becomes Editor of the *Journal of American Folklore*

In 1969 Dr. Américo Paredes (1915–1999) became the first Latino to serve as editor of the most important scholarly journal of folklore in the United States: the *Journal of American Folklore*. He served as editor until 1973. During this time, Paredes was also one of the first directors of a Mexican American studies program in the United States at the University of Texas. *Sources:* Tardiff and Mabunda, *Dictionary of Hispanic Biography*, pp. 654–655; Kanellos, *Latino Almanac*, pp. 303–304.

1970 ♦ At the University of Pittsburgh, scholar Carmelo Mesa Lago (1934–) founded the *Cuban Studies Newsletter,* which marked the emergence of Cuban studies as an academic discipline.

Sources: García, *Havana USA*, p. 204.

1970 ♦ Marta P. Cotera (1938–) and her husband established the first Mexican American college, Jacinto Treviño College, in Mercedes, Texas, in the Lower Rio Grande Valley. The school, which was affiliated with the Antioch College Graduate School of Education, eventually split off to become Juárez-Lincoln University. The purpose of the now-defunct college was to prepare teachers for bilingual education.

Marta P. Cotera

Sources: Tardiff and Mabunda, *Dictionary of Hispanic Biography*, p. 252.

1970 ♦ The first university-based Latino research center was the Chicano Studies Research Center at the University of California at Los Angeles. The center conducts research and administers a library and a publications program, including the longest-running Latino academic journal, *Aztlán.*

Sources: Furtaw, *Hispanic Americans Information Directory*, p. 142.

1971 ♦ Alfredo D. de los Santos Jr. became the first Mexican American to serve as the president of a community college, the El Paso Community College in Texas. He served in that capacity until 1976, then went on to other positions in higher education at Maricopa Community College in Arizona and the University of Arizona. He was also a founding board member of the American Association of Hispanics in Education; the association confers an annual Alfredo de los Santos Jr. Distinguished Leadership in Higher Education Award each year. Among his many awards were the 2005 Leadership Award from the National Council of Instructional Administrators, the 2004 Leadership Award from the American Association of Community Colleges, the 2001 Reginald Wilson Award from the American Council on Education, and the 1998 Harold W. McGraw Jr. Prize in Education.

Sources: "Alfredo G. de los Santos, Jr.," ASU Retirees Association: https://asura.asu.edu/alfredo-de-los-santos

1971 ♦ The first Latino ethnic studies program in the Midwest was the Center for Chicano-Boricua Studies at Wayne State University in Detroit.

Sources: Furtaw, *Hispanic Americans Information Directory*, p. 150.

1971 ♦ Deganawidah-Quetzalcoatl University (DQU), the first Native American and Chicano university, was founded on April 2, 1971, near Davis, California, after a protracted struggle to have the deed transferred from an old army communications center.

Sources: Meier and Rivera, *Dictionary of Mexican American History*, p. 117.

1971 ♦ Latinos won the first suit against school financing through property taxes. In *Serrano v. Priest*, John Serrano sued the California state treasurer, alleging that his son was receiving an inferior education in East Los Angeles because schools were financed by local property taxes. The California courts found that financing schools through local property taxes did not provide equal protection of the law and, therefore, the financing system had to be changed. Lawsuits that came before the California Supreme Court in 1974 and 1977 resulted in similar findings.

Sources: Jiménez-Castellanos, Oscar, and Lawrence O. Picus, "Serrano v. Priest 50th Anniversary: Origins, Impact and Future," *BYU Education & Law Journal*: https://scholarsarchive.byu.edu/cgi/viewcontent.cgi?article=1057&context=byu_elj.

1972 ♦ The National Association for Chicana and Chicano Studies was founded to provide services and an annual convention for professors who teach courses related to Chicano themes. Its example was followed in the subsequent founding of similar associations for Puerto Rican and Cuban American studies.

Sources: Furtaw, *Hispanic Americans Information Directory*, p. 24.

1972 ♦ Aspira, Inc. and the Puerto Rican Legal Defense and Education Fund brought the first suit against a school district to force it to follow federal guidelines for instituting bilingual education. The suit claimed that tens of thousands of Latino students in the New York City school system were receiving inadequate instruction in their native language. The suit was resolved in 1974 with a consent decree forcing New York City schools to implement bilingual education.

Sources: "Aspira's Legal Landmark Cases," Aspira: https://aspira.org/about-us/aspiras-legal-landmark-cases/.

Rodolfo Acuña

1972 ♦ Professor Rodolfo Acuña (1932–) of California State University at Los Angeles wrote and published the first comprehensive history of the Chicano people. The text, which presented the model of Mexican Americans as an internal colony of the United States, became the most widely used Chicano history book ever in colleges and is now in its ninth edition.

Sources: Acuña, Rodolfo F., *Occupied America: A History of Chicanos*, 9th edition, Pearson, 2019.

1973 ♦ Educator and social worker Antonia Pantoja (1922–2002) founded the first university created specifically to serve Puerto Ricans in the United States: Universidad Boricua. Founded in Washington, D.C., with foundation grants that Pantoja had solicited, the university was designed to provide innovative, bilingual, career-oriented programs for professionals, technicians, and other workers. Pantoja served as the institution's first chancellor.

Sources: Tardiff and Mabunda, *Dictionary of Hispanic Biography*, p. 653.

1973 ♦ The first Center for Puerto Rican Studies was founded at Hunter College of the City University of New York (CUNY). In addition to coordinating Puerto Rican studies courses for the CUNY system, the center provides seminars and technical services, publishes a journal, and maintains a library and archives. Today, it is "the largest university-based research institute, library, and archive dedicated to the Puerto Rican experience in the United States."

Sources: Centro de Estudios Puertorriqueños: https://centropr.hunter.cuny.edu/; Furtaw, *Hispanic Americans Information Directory*, p. 134.

1974 ♦ In *Lau v. Nichols*, the U.S. Supreme Court held that the San Francisco Unified School District discriminated against a non-English-speaking student, Kinney Lau, by not providing a program to deal with his language problem, thereby depriving him of meaningful participation in school. This decision served as a cornerstone for the creation and maintenance of bilingual education programs across the country. The *Lau* decision laid the basis for a new interpretation of equal education opportunity, an interpretation that takes into consideration the linguistic differences of some students and then compares their opportunities to the opportunities given to English-speaking students.

Sources: "Lau v. Nichols—The Law in Education," Intercultural Development Research Association: https://www.idra.org/education_policy/lau-v-nichols-the-law-in-education/.

1975 ♦ With the support of the Catholic Church, the National Hispanic Scholarship was established. It was the first national scholarship fund to send Latino high school graduates to college.

Sources: Dolan and Deck, *Hispanic Catholic Culture in the United States*, p. 150.

1975 ♦ The National Association for Bilingual Education (NABE) was founded to recognize, promote, and publicize bilingual education. Its most important event is its annual convention, which provides seminars, research, and workshops for bilingual teachers throughout the United States. NABE has state and local affiliates that extend its services to teachers, administrators, and communities.

Sources: Furtaw, *Hispanic Americans Information Directory*, p. 24.

1975 ♦ The *Cuban Studies Newsletter*, edited at the University of Pittsburgh by Carmelo Mesa Lago, became *Cuban Studies/Estudios Cubanos*, the first journal serving the new academic field of Cuban studies.

Sources: García, *Havana USA*, p. 204.

1978 ♦ Dr. Tomás Rivera (1935–1984), the renowned scholar and creative writer, became the first Latino chancellor in the University of California System. He served as chancellor of the University of California at Riverside until his death in 1984.

Sources: Kanellos, Nicolás, "Tomás Rivera and the Creation of Nationhood," *Latinos and Nationhood: Two Centuries of Intellectual Thought*, University of Arizona Press, 2023, pp. 127–138.

1980 ♦ Sylvia L. Castillo (1952–) founded the first Latina feminist newsletter, *Intercambios Femeniles* (Feminine Exchanges), at Stanford University. Each issue was designed around a theme, such as health or careers in science, and contained statistics, networking lists, and information. The newsletter also profiled successful women and reported on the latest studies of Latinos. The newsletter led to the formation of the National Network of Hispanic Women (initially named Hispanic Women in Higher Education), which provided networking and mentoring opportunities for Latinas of all ages. The newsletter and the network eventually became independent of Stanford and relocated to Los Angeles.

Sources: Tardiff and Mabunda, *Dictionary of Hispanic Biography*, pp. 197–198.

1980 ♦ Texas Tech University broke its long tradition and hired one of its own alumni as president. Lauro F. Cavazos (1927–2022), a medical doctor and researcher, assumed the presidency of the university and of its Health Sciences Center. Cavazos later became the first Hispanic to be named secretary of education.

Sources: Tardiff and Mabunda, *Dictionary of Hispanic Biography*, p. 205.

1981 ♦ Former school principal and supervisor for state and federal education projects Rita Esquivel (1932–2019) became the first woman assistant superintendent of education for the state of California.

Sources: Tardiff and Mabunda, *Dictionary of Hispanic Biography*, p. 314.

1983 ♦ Educator Roberto Cruz (1941–) founded the first Hispanic university, the National Hispanic University (NHU), which catered to students of diverse Latino ethnicities, in San Jose, California. The four-year, 300-student institution offered some five majors, including international business and computer science. Graduates of NHU have a higher-than-average job placement rate and rate of attending graduate school.

Sources: "Founder Dr. Roberto Cruz Bio," The Foundation for Hispanic Education: https://www.tfhe.org/apps/pages/index.jsp?uREC_ID=378967&-type=d&pREC_ID=2030062.

Ramón C. Cortines

1984 ♦ Ramón C. Cortines (1932–) became the first Latino to serve as the superintendent of the San Francisco schools. He later served as an assistant secretary in the U.S. Department of Education (1993) and in 1993 became the second Latino in history to serve as the chancellor of the New York City public school system.

Sources: Tardiff and Mabunda, *Dictionary of Hispanic Biography*, pp. 250–251.

1985 ♦ The Tomás Rivera Center for Hispanic Studies was the first national Latino think tank that worked on diverse policies related to Latinos, foremost education policies. Named for the pioneering educational administrator and writer Tomás Rivera (1935–1984), it initially had offices in Claremont, California, and later moved to San Antonio, Texas. Established in 1985, the center's mission was to improve public and corporate policies, specifically in education, affecting the "Mexican-origin and Latino population of the United States." The center, beginning with its founding president, Arturo Madrid

(1930–), conducted and published numerous studies. The center closed its operations at Trinity University in San Antonio in 1996.

Sources: "Tomás Rivera Center Collection," Trinity University: https://archives.trinity.edu/tomas-river-center.

1986 ♦ Modesto A. Maidique (1940–) became the first Cuban American president of a major university: Florida International University in Miami. The Cuban-born immigrant received his Ph.D. in engineering from the Massachusetts Institute of Technology in 1970.

Modesto A. Maidique

Sources: "Modesto A. Maidique," FIU/Business: https://business.fiu.edu/about/directory/profile/maidiquem.

1986 ♦ Mari-Luci Jaramillo (1928–2019) became the first Latino to receive the Harvard Graduate School of Education's Anne Roe Award honoring leading educators who have contributed to women's professional growth.

Sources: Telgen and Kamp, *Latinas! Women of Achievement*, p. 205.

1987 ♦ Angela Beatriz Ginorio (1947–) became the first Latina to direct a national center for research on women: the Northwest Center for Research on Women at the University of Washington in Seattle. Born in Hato Rey, Puerto Rico, Ginorio received her Ph.D. in psychology from Fordham University, New York City, in 1979 and taught at Bowling Green State University in Ohio and the University of Washington.

Sources: "Angela Ginorio," University of Washington: https://gwss.washington.edu/people/angela-ginorio.

1988 ♦ President Ronald Reagan appointed a former president of Texas Tech University, Lauro F. Cavazos (1927–2022), as the first Latino secretary of education. In 1989, President George H. W. Bush reappointed Cavazos to the post. Cavazos was instrumental in having President Bush sign the executive order creating the President's Council on Educational Excellence for Hispanic Americans. Cavazos resigned in December 1990 when he was unable to support many of the president's educational policies.

Lauro F. Cavazos

Sources: Kanellos, *Latino Almanac*, p. 152.

Jaime Escalante

1988 ♦ Jaime Escalante (1930–2010) became the first Latino teacher to be the subject of a Hollywood feature film. *Stand and Deliver* tells the story of how Escalante was able to teach advanced mathematics at Garfield High, an impoverished inner-city school in East Los Angeles, and prepare its students so well that they were admitted to some of the most elite universities in the country to major in math and science. Escalante taught at Garfield from 1974 to 1990. Known as one of the nation's top educators, Escalante received the White House's Hispanic Heritage Award in 1989 and the American Institute for Public Service's Jefferson Award in 1990. In 1988, Escalante was the subject of a book that proclaimed his excellence on a national level: *Escalante: The Best Teacher in America* by Jay Mathews.

Sources: Mathews, *Jaime Escalante.*

1989 ♦ Folklorist Dr. Américo Paredes (1915–1999) became the first Latino scholar to be awarded the prestigious Charles Frankel Prize for his career-long contribution to the humanities by the National Endowment for the Humanities. This is the nation's highest recognition for a humanist. The famed folklorist, writer, and teacher was born in Brownsville, Texas. He received his B.A., M.A., and Ph.D. degrees from the University of Texas in 1951, 1953, and 1956, respectively. After working at a variety of jobs—including journalist—and serving in the armed forces, Paredes received an advanced education and became one of the most distinguished Latino scholars in U.S. history. Paredes taught at the University of Texas for his entire career. There, he was instrumental in the development of the field of folklore in academia as well as of the field of Mexican American studies. He served as president of the American Folklore Society and was recognized for his leadership internationally. Besides publishing numerous research articles, Paredes was the author of *With His Pistol in His Hand: A Border Ballad and Its Hero* (1958), *Folktales of Mexico* (1970), *A Texas Mexican Cancionero* (1976), and *Uncle Remus con chile* (Uncle Remus with Chile) (1992). He is also the author of two novels, *George Washington Gomez* (1990) and *The Shadow* (1998); two books of poems, *Cantos de adolescencia* (1937) and *Between Two Worlds* (1991); and a collection of short stories, *The Hammon and the Beans* (1994).

Sources: "Américo Paredes," Humanities Texas: https://www.humanitiestexas.org/programs/tx-originals/list/americo-paredes.

1989 ♦ Elsa Gómez (1938–) became the first Latina to be named president of a four-year liberal arts college when she assumed the position of president of Kean College in New Jersey. The New York City native received her Ph.D. in Italian from the University of Texas in 1971. Before becoming president of Kean, she served as dean of arts and sciences at Lock Haven University, Lock Haven, Pennsylvania.

Sources: Gulvas Swarden, Carlotta. "College Head Leaving After a Turbulent Year," *New York Times*, 4 September 1994.

1989 ♦ Educator Rita Esquivel (1932–2019) became the first Mexican American woman to head the Office of Bilingual Education and Minority Language Affairs in the U.S. Department of Education. Appointed by President George H. W. Bush, she had previously been the first assistant superintendent of education for the state of California.

Sources: Tardiff and Mabunda, *Dictionary of Hispanic Biography*, p. 314.

1990 ♦ The first endowed chair named for a U.S. Hispanic was instituted in the Department of Spanish and Portuguese at the University of Texas. The chair for the study of literature was named for the Texas-born author and academic administrator Tomás Rivera (1935–1984), who died while serving as the chancellor of the University of California at Riverside. (The same department that houses this chair had refused to hire him to teach there early in his career.)

Sources: Olivares, Julián, ed., *International Studies in Honor of Tomás Rivera*, Houston: Arte Público Press, 1985.

1990 ♦ Ricardo Fernández (1940–) became the first president of a college of the City University of New York, Lehman College. The Puerto Rican–born educator had served in a number of administrative positions with the University of Wisconsin and had also served as president of the National Association for Bilingual Education from 1980 to 1981.

Sources: Tardiff and Mabunda, *Dictionary of Hispanic Biography*, pp. 335–336.

1990 ♦ Joseph A. Fernández (1935–) became the first Puerto Rican and the first Latino to head New York Public Schools, one of the nation's largest school systems. Born and raised in New York, Fernández received his B.A., M.A., and Ph.D. degrees from the University of Miami. Before becoming the New York superintendent, he served in a similar capacity for the extensive Dade County Public Schools. He served as head of the school system until 1994.

Sources: Tardiff and Mabunda, *Dictionary of Hispanic Biography*, pp. 330–331.

1991: First Mexican Americans to Be Awarded the Aztec Eagle Medal

In 1991 the renowned folklorist Dr. Américo Paredes (1915–1999), labor organizer César Chávez (1927–1993), literary critic Dr. Luis Leal (1907–2010), and sociologist Dr. Julián Samora (1920–1996) became the first Mexican Americans to be awarded the Aztec Eagle medal by the president of Mexico. The medal is the highest award given by Mexico to a foreigner for contributions to Mexico. *Sources:* Kanellos, *Chronology of Hispanic American History*, p. 277.

1991 ♦ Professor Julián Samora (1920–1996) became the first U.S. Latino to have a university research center named in his honor: the Julián Samora Center at Michigan State University. The famous sociologist was responsible for preparing a whole generation of Mexican American sociologists at the University of Notre Dame and was one of the first Chicano scholars to conduct research on Mexicans in the Midwest.

Sources: "Julian Samora," Institute for Latino Studies, University of Notre Dame: https://latinostudies.nd.edu/about/history/julian-samora/.

1991 ♦ Manuel Trinidad Pacheco (1941–) became the first Latino to serve as president of a major research university in the United States when he was sworn in to that position at the University of Arizona. Born on May 30, 1941, in Rocky Ford, Colorado, Pacheco has dedicated his life to education. He obtained a B.A. degree from New Mexico Highlands University (1962) and M.A. and Ph.D. degrees from Ohio State University (1966 and 1969). Pacheco served as a professor of education and Spanish and as an administrator at various universities and colleges, including as president of the University of Missouri System from 1997 to 2002.

Sources: "Manuel Trinidad Pacheco," The University of Arizona: https://president.arizona.edu/person/manuel-trinidad-pacheco.

1994 ♦ The four-volume reference work *Handbook of Hispanic Cultures in the United States*, edited by scholars Nicolás Kanellos (1945–) of the University of Houston and Claudio Esteva-Fabregat (1918–2017) of the University of Barcelona, became the first book by a Latino publisher, Arte Público Press, to be named to the list of Outstanding Academic Books by *Choice* magazine.

The handbook, which compiles articles by scholars in four areas—literature and art, history, sociology, and anthropology—also became the first Latino book to win the American Library Association's Denali Award for Best Reference Work in 1995, as well as being named to the American Library Association's list of Outstanding Reference Sources and the New York Public Library's list of Outstanding Reference Works.

Sources: Pérez, Janet, "Reviewed Works: *Handbook of Hispanic Cultures in the United States* by Nicolás Kanellos, Claudio Esteva-Fabregat; *Literature and Art* by Francisco Lomelí; *History* by Alfredo Jiménez; *Sociology* by Félix Padilla; *Anthropology* by Thomas Weaver." *Hispania*, Vol. 79, No. 4 (Dec. 1996), pp. 810-812.

1996 ♦ The first Hispanic to direct an academic library in a Texas state university was Gilda Baeza Ortega (1952–). Ortega is the director of the Sul Ross University Library in Alpine, Texas. With the completion of her Ph.D. degree in library science, she became only the second Hispanic woman in the United States to obtain such a degree in library and information science.

Sources: "News and Notes," *Texas Library Journal*, Vol 12, no. 2 (summer 1996), p. 100.

2004 ♦ Raymund Paredes (1942–) became the first Latino to serve as commissioner and CEO of the Texas Higher Education Coordinating Board, which oversees all public universities in the state of Texas. He served until 2019. Before returning home to Texas, he was a professor and administrator in the University of California System and had also served in the education department of the Rockefeller Foundation. He served as the Texas education commissioner until 2019.

Sources: Paredes, Raymund, "Texas' Higher Education Commissioner, Will Step Down Aug. 31," *Texas Tribune*: https://www.texastribune.org/2019/01/24/raymund-paredes-states-higher-education-commissioner-will-step-down-au/.

2005 ♦ Mexican American scholar Vicki Ruiz (1955–) became the first Latino educator to be elected president of the Organization of American Historians. Ruiz specializes in Latina women's working-class history; she is the author of eight books and more than 60 articles. Ruiz has also served as president of the American Historical Association, the American Studies Association, and the Berkshire Conference of Women Historians. In 2015, she received the National Humanities Medal from President Barack Obama.

Sources: Matsumoto, Valerie J. "Vicki L. Ruiz Biography," American Historical Association: https://www.historians.org/about-aha-and-membership/aha-history-and-archives/presidential-addresses/vicki-l-ruiz/vicki-l-ruiz-biography.

2007 ♦ Robert R. Dávila (1932–), the son of Mexican American farm workers from southern California, became the first Latino deaf president of a university. After contracting spinal meningitis, he became deaf and was sent alone by his parents to a northern California state school for the deaf. There, he learned English and American Sign Language, prospered educationally, and eventually was able to achieve a master's degree in special education from Hunter College (1963) and a Ph.D. in educational technology from Syracuse University (1972). Dávila taught at various K-12 and college levels and worked in special education for the U.S. Department of Education. In 2007, he was promoted from vice president to president at Gallaudet University, the only university designed for the deaf and hard of hearing. He served as president until 2009.

Sources: "About Robert R. Dávila," Gallaudet University: https://web.archive.org/web/20070512204324/http://www.gallaudet.edu/x3566.xml.

Francisco G. Cigarroa

2009 ♦ Laredo native, pediatric transplant surgeon, and educator Dr. Francisco G. Cigarroa (1957–) became the first Latino to serve as chancellor of the vast University of Texas System, one of the largest in the nation. Prior to his naming, he had also served as the first Latino president of the University of Texas Health Science Center at San Antonio. After receiving his bachelor's degree from Yale University, Cigarroa received his M.D. from the University of Texas Southwestern Medical Center at Dallas in 1983. He continued as president until 2011 and became chair of the Ford Foundation Board of Trustees.

Sources: "Francisco Cigarroa, Chair, Board of Trustees," Ford Foundation: https://www.fordfoundation.org/about/people/francisco-g-cigarroa/.

2011 ♦ Law professor Michael A. Olivas (1951–2022) became the first Latino educator to be named president of the Association of American Law Schools. In 2018, the same association conferred on Olivas its Triennial Award for Lifetime Service to Legal Education and the Law. Olivas was elected to the American Law Institute, one of the most prestigious organizations of lawyers, judges, and law professors, and also to the National Academy of Education; he was the only person ever elected to both honor academies.

2014: Latina/o Studies Association Founded

The Latina/o Studies Association was founded in 2014 by scholars from universities throughout the United States explicitly "to engage current scholarship, exchange pedagogical models, improve mentoring structures, and increase opportunities for professional development." Its implicit purpose was to bring together the scholars and programs previously studying one's Latino ethnicity, i.e., Chicano or Puerto Rican or Cuban studies, into a national organization that would cut across ethnic disciplines and foment a national identity. The association has since sponsored a biennial conference at different sites around the nation and publishes the *Latina/o Studies Journal*. *Sources:* Latina/o Studies Association: https://latinxstudiesassociation.org/about/.

Sources: Tallet, Olivia P., "A Giant and Legend: UH Community Mourns the Loss of Professor Emeritus Michael Olivas," *Houston Chronicle*, 27 April 2022: https://www.houstonchronicle.com/news/houston-texas/houston/article/Scores-of-people-mourn-the-loss-of-a-University-of-17126210.php.

2014 ♦ Scholar Nicolás Kanellos, the Brown Foundation Professor of Hispanic Studies at the University of Houston, was the first U.S. Latino to receive the "Enrique Anderson Imbert" Prize of the North American Academy of the Spanish Language for Lifetime Achievement for contributing to the knowledge and dissemination of the Spanish language and Hispanic culture in the United States. Kanellos has won numerous awards as a scholarly author, director of research programs, and founder of Arte Público Press. In 2009, he was the first U.S. Latino to be inducted into the Spanish American Royal Academy of Literature, Arts, and Science, Cadiz, Spain. In 2014, he was awarded the Anderson Imbert Lifetime Achievement Award by the North American Academy of the Spanish Language. In 2016, he was awarded the Cross of the Order of Isabella the Catholic Queen, the highest decoration given to a civilian by the Spanish government. In 2024, President Joe Biden conferred on him the National Humanities Medal.

Sources: "A Writer's Hidden Gem in Houston: Arte Público Press," *Houston History Magazine,* Vol. 20, Fall 2022.

2016 ♦ MacArthur fellow Mónica Muñoz Martínez (1984–), an associate professor of history at the University of Texas, founded the Refusing to Forget project, which documents the history of violence against Mexican

Mónica Muñoz Martínez

and Mexican Americans in Texas over two centuries. Since its founding, the organization has created numerous museum exhibitions, fostered the creation of state historical markers, and provided information and interviews to media around the country on the history of racial violence. In 2016, Refusing to Forget was awarded the Leadership in History Award by the American Association for State and Local History. Its award-winning exhibition at the Bullock Texas State History Museum in 2016 represented the first time in history that a state cultural institution acknowledged state responsibility for racial terror.

Sources: Mónica Muñoz Martínez: https://monicamunozmartinez.com/about/.

2017 ♦ Mexican novelist Cristina Rivera Garza (1964–) became the founding director of the first Ph.D. program in Spanish Creative Writing in the United States. Rivera Garza, the winner of six of Mexico's highest literary awards, successfully launched the program at the University of Houston by recruiting a large group of recognized writers of literature in Spanish from throughout Spanish America, Spain, and the United States. A MacArthur Fellow (2020), Rivera Garza has taught at universities in both Mexico and the United States and has numerous highly acclaimed books to her name.

Sources: "Cristina Rivera Garza," Hispanic Studies, University of Houston: https://uh.edu/class/spanish/faculty/rivera-garza-c/.

2020 ♦ Mexican American Rey Saldaña (1991–) became the first Latino to be appointed president and CEO of Communities in Schools, the national organization that surrounds students with a community of support, empowering them to stay in school and achieve in life. The Stanford grad in education policy had previously served as the regional advocacy director for the Raise Your Hand Texas Foundation and was the chair of the San Antonio Metropolitan Transit Agency. He also served four terms on the San Antonio City Council.

Sources: "Rey Saldaña," Communities in Schools: https://www.communitiesinschools.org/about-us/our-leadership/profile/rey-saldana?_z=1718051324882.

Miguel Cardona

2021 ♦ Connecticut-raised Miguel Cardona (1975–) became the first U.S. secretary of education of Guatemalan heritage. Cardona was also the first Latino to serve as commissioner of public education in Connecticut. Before taking on these administrative duties, Cardona taught for two decades in the Meridian, Connecticut, school that he attended as a child.

Sources: "Dr. Miguel Cardona, Secretary of Education—Biography," U.S. Department of Education: https://www2.ed.gov/news/staff/bios/cardona.html.

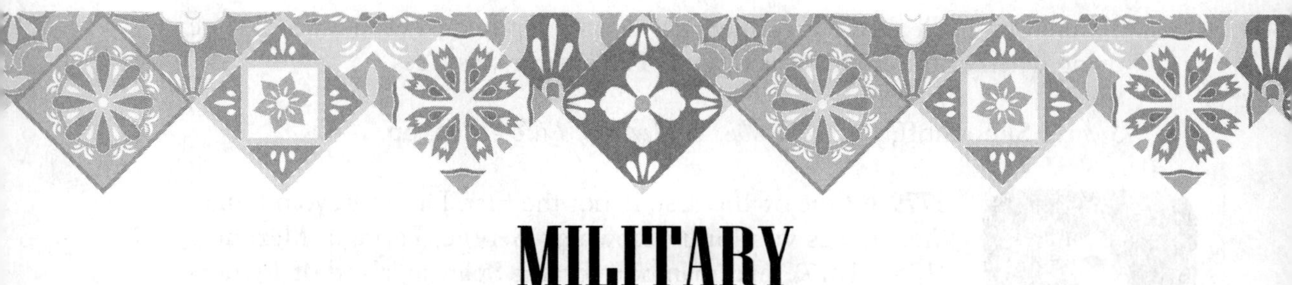

MILITARY

1600 ♦ The first black militia was formed in what later became the United States. Many of the colonists of Florida were free black craftsmen and black soldiers in the Spanish army; under Spanish law and practice, slaves had certain rights, and Spanish culture and the Catholic Church were more encouraging to releasing slaves than were British culture or Protestant religions. A black militia was present in Florida by the 17th century, with both free and enslaved blacks serving as soldiers and officers.

Sources: Henderson and Mormino, *Spanish Pathways in Florida*, p. 192.

1738 ♦ The first black commander of a Spanish regiment in lands that would become part of the United States was a runaway slave by the name of Francisco Menéndez (c. 1704–c. 1779s). Originally a Mandingo from West Africa, Menéndez escaped from English slavery in the Carolinas. After he assisted Yamassee Indians in battle, they helped him to reach the sanctuary for runaway slaves in Saint Augustine, Florida. He was betrayed by an Indian and sold into Spanish slavery as a soldier. He became an officer while still a slave, and in 1738, he was freed and made commander of the all-black regiment of soldiers at Fort Mose, just north of Saint Augustine. Captain Menéndez held the position until 1763, when Florida became a British colony and the inhabitants of Fort Mose were evacuated to Cuba.

Sources: Henderson and Mormino, *Spanish Pathways in Florida*, pp. 118–200.

1776 ♦ The first Sephardic Jewish hero of the American Revolution was Francis Salvador (1747–1776), a Charleston, South Carolina, financier. Salvador, who was from a refugee family that abandoned Spain because of persecution by the Inquisition, led his men against Tories and their Indian allies in

1776. Found still alive but scalped, Salvador is reputed to have asked before dying whether the enemy was beaten. The answer was "Yes."

Sources: Simonhoff, *Jewish Notables in America, 1776–1865*, pp. 1–4.

Jordi Farragut Mesquida

1779 ♦ One of the first, if not the first, Latino Revolutionary War heroes was Jordi (known as George) Farragut Mezquida (1755–1817), a seaman born on the Spanish island of Menorca who joined the South Carolina navy as a lieutenant and fought at the battle of Savannah (1779) and at the second defense of Charleston (1780), where he was captured. After being freed, Farragut joined the Continental Army and earned the rank of major. He was the father of the first Latino U.S. admiral, David G. Farragut.

Sources: Hispanics in U.S. History, pp. 54, 56; Secretary of Defense, *Hispanics in America's Defense*, p. 9.

1779 ♦ One of the first Hispanic Revolutionary War heroes was Louisiana governor Bernardo de Gálvez (1746–1786), who engaged British forces repeatedly for three years along the Gulf of Mexico, destroying their forts, capturing Mobile and Pensacola, and rendering great support to the Continental Army. Gálvez's victory at Pensacola in particular made the American victory at Yorktown possible. His most important feat took place in 1781, when as brigadier general, he took Mobile and Pensacola from the English to return these territories to Spanish dominion and to assist George Washington's forces in the War of Independence from England. This strategy forced the British army to fight on two fronts. The Spanish also opened a route to supply Washington's army with money, food, and weapons. As a result of this support of the Americans, Western Florida came under the dominion of Spain again through the Treaty of Versailles.

Bernardo de Gálvez

Sources: Hispanics in U.S. History, p. 54.

1780 ♦ One of the first Hispanic heroes of the American Revolution was Francisco de Miranda (1756–1816), who fought against the British at Pensacola, Florida. Miranda was an early activist for independence of the Spanish American colonies. Born in Venezuela, Miranda became a soldier in the Spanish army and later participated in the War of Independence of the thirteen British colonies in North America; he had also

Francisco de Miranda

participated in the French Revolution. Inspired by all of those ideas associated with "liberty, fraternity, equality," Miranda in 1797 founded the American Lodge in London, whose members swore their allegiance to democracy and were to work for the independence of the Spanish American colonies. In 1806, Miranda tried to liberate Venezuela by embarking from New York with a group of 200 soldiers. When they disembarked in Coro, Venezuela, they did not find the necessary support, and the mission failed. Miranda returned to England and from there prepared the liberation of his country with Simon Bolivar. When Miranda returned to Venezuela in 1810, he was arrested and sent to Spain, where he died in jail on July 14, 1816, in Cadiz.

Sources: Racine, Karen, *Francisco de Miranda: A Transatlantic Life in the Age of Revolution.* Wilmington, DE: Scholarly Resources Inc., 2003.

1811 ♦ The first martyr for Mexican independence from Spain in areas that would become the United States was Juan Bautista de las Casas (1757–1811), a captain in the militia who led a revolt in San Antonio, Texas, against the Spanish governor, Colonel Manuel de Salcedo. Casas seized the governor and officials, proclaiming support for Mexico's revolution and appointing himself as the Mexican governor of Texas. Casas was captured and executed by Spanish soldiers, and his head was exhibited at the central plaza as a warning to other sympathizers of the revolution, led by Miguel Hidalgo in Central New Spain (what would become an independent Mexico). Texas submitted to the Spanish throne again by March 1811.

Sources: Gómez-Quiñones, *Roots of Chicano Politics, 1600–1940*, pp. 48, 77–79.

1812 ♦ The first hero in the struggle for Mexican independence from Spain in areas that would become the United States was José Bernardo Gutiérrez de Lara (1774–1841), who in June 1812 led his men in taking the towns of Nacogdoches and Salcedo from the royalist garrison. Gutiérrez de Lara also sent emissaries to other parts of Texas and to the Rio Grande Valley to spread the word of the revolution.

Sources: Gómez-Quiñones, *Roots of Chicano Politics, 1600–1940*, pp. 81–83.

1840 ♦ The first Latino to lead a secessionist movement in the recently declared Republic of Texas (1836) was Texan Antonio Canales. On January 14, 1840, in San Patricio, Texas, General Canales and a mixed bag of Texas-Mexico forces, including Juan Nepomuceno Seguín (1806–1890), proclaimed the independence of the Republic of the Rio Grande, to be made up of southern Texas and the Mexican state of Tamaulipas. In the following months, Canales's forces were successful in capturing Laredo, a number of border towns, and Ciudad Victoria, the capital of Tamaulipas. In Canales's attempts to capture Saltillo, most of his troops went over to the Mexican government side, and the remaining soldiers were forced to withdraw to Texas. Canales finally surrendered to the government in November and thus ended the northern secessionist effort.

Sources: Garza, Beatriz de la, *From the Republic of the Rio Grande: A Personal History of the Place and the People*, University of Texas Press, 2013.

Juan Nepomuceno Cortina

1859 ♦ The first man to organize an armed protest by Texas Mexicans against the abuses of Anglos and the power structure they had instituted after the Mexican War (1846–1848) was Juan Nepomuceno Cortina (1824–1894), who was a military man most of his life and precipitated the "Cortina War." He was at one time or another a rancher, social bandit, and Mexican governor.

Cortina was born in Camargo, on the Mexican side of the Rio Grande River, on May 16, 1824. He was raised in a family of Mexican landowners, but after fighting against the United States in the Mexican War, he purchased and settled on a ranch near Brownsville, Texas. Recognizing the discrimination that Mexicans faced after the war, Cortina struck out against injustice when he wounded a Brownsville deputy sheriff who was mistreating a Mexican vagrant. He escaped across the border to avoid arrest and possibly death, whereupon he became a folk hero to the oppressed Mexican population in Texas. He soon led a large force of rebels who crossed the border at Matamoros and took over the city of Brownsville, raising the flag of Mexico over it. As a result of this and other actions, Cortina faced responses from local militia, the Texas Rangers, and the U.S. Army.

In mid-1860, Cortina was again forced to retreat across the border. In Mexico, he distinguished himself as an officer in Tamaulipas fighting against the French intervention. During this time, he became acting governor of Tamaulipas for a short term, and he was promoted by President Benito Juárez to general. During the American Civil War, he fought on the side of the North.

In the mid-1870s, he incurred political disfavor in Mexico and was arrested for cattle rustling. After a pardon, under General Porfirio Díaz, he returned to the border for a short period but was arrested again and spent most of his remaining years under arrest in Mexico City. He died in 1892.

Sources: Rosales, *Chicano! History of the Mexican American Civil Rights Movement*, pp. 8–10.

1862 ♦ The first Latino spy for the United States was Captain Román Antonio Baca (1834–1899), an officer in the New Mexico Volunteers, a unit that was incorporated into the Union forces during the Civil War.

Sources: Crocchiola, *The Civil War in New Mexico*; Secretary of Defense, *Hispanics in America's Defense*, p. 16.

1863 ♦ The U.S. government authorized the formation of the first Latino battalion during the Civil War. The First Battalion of Native Cavalry was formed to take advantage of the extraordinary horsemanship of the Mexican Americans of California under the command of Major Salvador Vallejo (1813–1876). Approximately 470 Mexican Americans served in the four companies of the battalion throughout California and Arizona.

Sources: Crocchiola, *The Civil War in New Mexico*; Meier and Rivera, *Dictionary of Mexican American History*, p. 93; Secretary of Defense, *Hispanics in America's Defense*, p. 14.

Diego Archuleta

1864 ♦ Diego Archuleta (1814–1884) became the first Latino brigadier general of the United States, commanding the New Mexico militia (not the U.S. Army) during the Civil War. Archuleta was born into a prominent New Mexico family and was educated in Durango, Mexico. From 1843 to 1845, he served in the Mexican National Congress as a delegate from New Mexico. After the conquest of New Mexico by the United States, Archuleta took part in two unsuccessful rebellions in 1846 and 1847. After the Mexican–American War (1846–1848), Archuleta took the oath of allegiance to the United States, served in the state assembly, and became a brigadier general for the Union. In 1857, he was appointed a U.S. Indian agent, a position to which he was reappointed by President Abraham Lincoln after the Civil War.

Sources: "From Mexican Army Colonel to Union Brigadier General," American Civil War Forum: https://www.americancivilwarforum.com/from-mexican-army-colonel-to-union-brigadier-general-556.html.

David Camden DeLeón

1864 ♦ The first surgeon general of the Confederate States was Sephardic Jew David Camden DeLeón (1816–1872) of Charleston. Known as the "Fighting Doctor," DeLeón enlisted in the army after graduating with a degree in medicine from the University of Pennsylvania in 1836. He was sent to the Florida tropics to treat the sick and wounded soldiers of the

Seminole Wars. Later, he became a hero at the Battle of Chapultepec in the Mexican War when, without any military training, he jumped into the trenches and turned the tide of battle in favor of the United States. When the Confederacy seceded from the Union, Major DeLeón left the Union to join the Confederate Army despite the pleading of his former commander, Zachary Taylor. President Jefferson Davis assigned DeLeón the important task of organizing the medical department of the Confederate Army. DeLeón became the first surgeon general of the Confederacy. He also served in the field and in hospitals in various capacities until the end of the war. After the defeat of the Confederacy, DeLeón moved to Mexico. At the request of President Ulysses S. Grant, he eventually returned to the United States and settled in New Mexico to practice medicine.

Sources: Simonhoff, *Jewish Notables in America, 1776–1865*, pp. 297–300.

1864 ♦ According to her own autobiography, Loreta Janeta Velásquez (1842–1923) was the first Latina spy in U.S. history. The Cuban-born Velásquez supposedly disguised herself as a Confederate soldier and served as Lieutenant Harry Buford. She left her married domestic life in San Antonio, Texas, without her husband's knowledge and fought at such battles as Bull Run, Ball's Bluff, and Fort Donelson. After her female identity had been detected twice and she was discharged, she began her life as a spy for the Confederacy, working in both male and female guise. The real-life existence of Velásquez has been researched, and a number of scholars conclude that much of her autobiography is fraudulent.

Loreta Janeta Velásquez (left) and disguised as Lieutenant Harry T. Buford (right).

Sources: Davis, William C. *Inventing Loreta Velasquez: Confederate Soldier Impersonator, Media Celebrity, and Con Artist.* Carbondale: Southern Illinois University Press, 2016.

1865 ♦ The first Latino Medal of Honor winner was Philip Bazaar (c. 1830–1923), a seaman born in Chile who, on January 15, 1865, courageously engaged in an assault on a fort from a six-man boat.

Sources: Secretary of Defense, *Hispanics in America's Defense*, p. 50.

1866 ♦ The first admiral of the U.S. Navy, David G. Farragut (1801–1872), was commissioned on July 26, 1866. The son of a Spanish immigrant who served in the South Carolina navy during the War of Independence, Farragut was appointed a midshipman at the age of 9. As a commander during the Civil War, Farragut was engaged in numerous battles, including the capture of New Orleans, Vicksburg, and Mobile. It was after the tremendous victory that he had led at Mobile Bay—where he is reported to have said, "Damn the torpedoes! Full speed ahead!"—that he was commissioned admiral. In today's navy, the guided missile destroyer USS *Farragut* bears his name.

Admiral David G. Farragut

Sources: Gleiter and Thompson, *David Farragut*; Secretary of Defense, *Hispanics in America's Defense*, pp. 17–18, 86.

1899 ♦ U.S. Congress authorized the establishment of the Army's 65th Infantry Regiment, the only Puerto Rican unit in U.S. military history. Known as "The Borinqueneers" (after the Taíno name for the island: Boriken), the regiment fought fiercely in both world wars and the Korean War; it became one of only four units to receive the Congressional Gold Medal.

Sources: Aikins-Núñez, Talia, *Men of the 65th: The Borinqueneers of the Korean War*, Wisconsin Rapids: Zest, 2023.

Luis R. Esteves

1915 ♦ Luis R. Esteves (1893–1958) was the first Puerto Rican and first Latino to graduate from the U.S. Military Academy at West Point. Born in Aguadilla, Puerto Rico, in 1893, before the American occupation, he obtained his elementary and secondary education under American military rule of the island and, without his parents' knowledge, took the test and was admitted to West Point. After graduating, Esteves rose through the ranks to become a brigadier general in 1937. In 1919, he organized the first Puerto Rican National Guard, commanding its first battalion and its first regiment.

Sources: Secretary of Defense, *Hispanics in America's Defense*, p. 93.

Marcelino Serna

1918 ♦ The first Latino soldier to be awarded the Distinguished Service Cross was Private Marcelino Serna (1896–1992) of Albuquerque, New Mexico, who on September 12, 1918, single-handedly captured 24 German soldiers. The Albuquerque native was not recommended for a Medal of Honor because he was only a "buck" private and could not read or write English well enough to sign reports.

Sources: Secretary of Defense, *Hispanics in America's Defense*, p. 25.

Joe P. Martínez

1943 ♦ The first Latino Medal of Honor winner of World War II was Private Joe P. Martínez (1920–1943), who took part in the American invasion of the Aleutian Islands in May 1943. The Taos, New Mexico, native led his outnumbered platoon in fighting Japanese soldiers in their trenches and was finally mortally wounded in his valiant attacks. A Disabled American Veterans chapter in Colorado and an American Legion post in California are named in his honor.

Sources: Secretary of Defense, *Hispanics in America's Defense*, p. 28.

Guy Gabaldón

1944 ♦ Guy Gabaldón (1926–2006), a Mexican American born in Los Angeles who was adopted by a Japanese American family, became a war hero at the battle for Saipan Island. He is the first Latino whose military heroism became the subject of a Hollywood film, *Hell to Eternity*. In 1970, Gabaldón returned his Navy Cross and Purple Heart to the government in protest of discrimination against minorities in the United States.

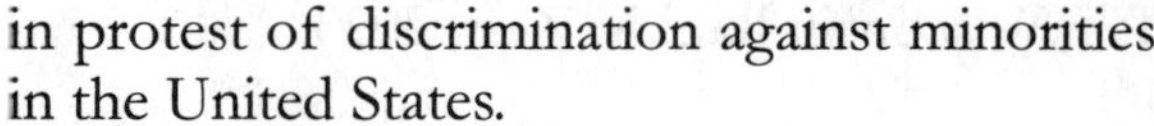

Sources: Meier and Rivera, *Dictionary of Mexican American History*, pp. 139–140.

Manuel J. Fernández Jr.

1952 ♦ The first Latino flying ace was Colonel Manuel J. Fernández Jr. (1925–1980), who from September 1952 to May 1953 during the Korean War flew 125 combat missions in the F-86, engaging communist MIG aircraft. On his fifth victory, he became an "ace" and ended the war with 14.5 "kills" to his credit. His 14.5 air victories placed him 60th among the top U.S. Air Force aces of the two world wars and the Korean War combined.

Sources: Secretary of Defense, *Hispanics in America's Defense*, p. 35.

1963 ♦ *Among the Valiant* became the first book to document the heroism and valor of Mexican Americans in the armed services during World War II. Its author, Raúl Morín (1913–1967), a commercial artist from Lockhart, Texas, was denied publication of the book for 10 years until the American G.I. Forum backed its publication and distribution. After the book's successful publication, Morín remained active in Mexican American and Democratic political organizations and in veterans affairs. In 1968, a veterans' memorial site in East Los Angeles was officially named Raúl Morín Memorial Square.

Sources: Meier and Rivera, *Dictionary of Mexican American History*, p. 239.

1964 ♦ Horacio Rivero Jr. (1910–2000) became the first Latino four-star admiral in the U.S. Navy. Born in Ponce, Puerto Rico, on May 16, 1910, Rivero graduated from the U.S. Naval Academy in 1931 and began serving on a variety of cruisers and battleships. During World War II, he saw considerable action in the Pacific and participated in the Iwo Jima and Okinawa campaigns and the first carrier raids on Tokyo. He was awarded the Legion of Merit for saving his ship and preventing loss of life during a fierce typhoon in 1945. In 1955, he was promoted to rear admiral and to vice admiral in 1962. In 1964, he was promoted to admiral and became vice chief of naval operations. In 1968, he commanded NATO forces as commander in chief of Allied Forces, Southern Europe. He retired in 1972 and was later named ambassador to Spain.

Admiral Horacio Rivero Jr.

Sources: Secretary of Defense, *Hispanics in America's Defense*, p. 89.

1974 ♦ The U.S. Navy named a ship for a Latino Vietnam hero, who was also awarded the Navy Cross. The 4,200-ton antisubmarine escort ship USS *Valdez* was named for the New Mexico native Phil Valdez (1946–1967), who was killed while saving two marines on January 29, 1967.

Sources: Meier and Rivera, *Dictionary of Mexican American History*, p. 361.

1976 ♦ Richard E. Cavazos (1929–2017) became the first Mexican American brigadier general in the U.S. Army in modern times (Diego Archuleta was

Gen. Richard E. Cavazos

a U.S. brigadier general in New Mexico during the Civil War; he was a Mexican native who was a colonel in the New Mexico militia). Born in Kingsville, Texas, on January 31, 1929, Cavazos received a B.S. degree in geology at Texas Tech University and was commissioned a second lieutenant in 1951. After graduating and becoming a second lieutenant, Cavazos deployed to Korea, where he was assigned as the platoon leader of E Company, 2nd Battalion, 65th Infantry Regiment, which was known as "The Borinqueneers," the famed 65th Infantry unit made up primarily of Puerto Rican soldiers, many of whom only spoke Spanish. After ready acceptance by them of a Mexican American leader, Cavazos went on to a distinguished career of 30 years of military service. Cavazos engaged in many battles in Korea and Vietnam and, unlike many commanders who directed operations from a rear post or from a helicopter, Cavazos was known to be on the ground serving alongside his men. He attended various military training schools and commanded forces in Vietnam as well as served in the Pentagon. In 1976, he became commanding general of the 9th Infantry division and post commander of Fort Lewis, Washington. In 1982, Cavazos was promoted to four-star general. From 1982 to 1984, the year of his retirement, General Cavazos was commander of the U.S. Armed Forces Command, Fort McPherson, Georgia.

Sources: Secretary of Defense, *Hispanics in America's Defense*, p. 91.

1979 ♦ Edward Hidalgo (1912–1995) became the first Latino to serve as secretary of the U.S. Navy. His two-year stint followed a career in which he had served as special assistant to the secretary of the Navy, special assistant for economic affairs to the director of the U.S. Information Agency (USIA), and general counsel and congressional liaison for the agency. From 1977 to 1979, he served as assistant secretary of the U.S. Navy. Hidalgo was born in Mexico City and immigrated to the United States as a child.

Edward Hidalgo

Sources: Meier and Rivera, *Dictionary of Mexican American History*, p. 161; Secretary of Defense, *Hispanics in America's Defense*, p. 217.

1980 ♦ The U.S. government commemorated the Hispanic contribution to the American War of Independence by issuing a stamp recognizing General Bernardo de Gálvez's 1780 victory at the Battle of Mobile Bay.

Sources: Secretary of Defense, *Hispanics in America's Defense*, p. 8.

1981 ♦ Puerto Rican Olga E. Custodio became the first Latina to complete the U.S. Air Force military pilot training: the first Latina fighter pilot. Most of her career in the Air Force was subsequently spent training future military pilots at various bases. She retired as a lieutenant colonel in 2003 and became a commercial pilot for American Airlines, one of the first Latinas to be a commercial airline captain. She retired from American Airlines in 2008 with more than 11,000 flight hours. In 2017, Custodio was inducted into the San Antonio Aviation and Aerospace Hall of Fame.

Sources: "National Hispanic Heritage Month: Olga E. Custodio," Transportation History: https://transportationhistory.org/2017/09/22/national-hispanic-heritage-month-olga-e-custodio/.

1982 ♦ Brigadier General Richard E. Cavazos (1929–2017) was promoted to become the first Latino four-star general in the U.S. Army.

Sources: "Richard E. Cavazos," National Museum of the United States Army: https://www.thenmusa.org/biographies/richard-e-cavazos/.

Gen. Carmelita Vigil-Schimmenti

1985 ♦ Carmelita Vigil-Schimmenti (1936–) became the first Latina to be promoted to brigadier general in the U.S. armed forces. Starting out as a nurse, she worked her way up the ranks and, as brigadier general, commanded the U.S. Air Force Nurse Corps, Office of the Surgeon General, Headquarters U.S. Air Force, Washington, D.C.

Sources: Kanellos, *Latino Almanac*, p. 204.

Vice Admiral Diego E. Hernández

1986 ♦ Vice Admiral Diego E. Hernández (1934–2017), a Puerto Rican native, became the deputy commander in chief of the U.S. Space Command, serving until 1989; he was also the deputy commander of the North American Aerospace Defense Command.

Sources: Kanellos, *Latino Almanac*, p. 201.

2003 ♦ Kingsville, Texas, native General Ricardo Sánchez (1953–) held the top military position in Iraq during the most critical period of the war when he became commander of Joint Task Force 7, the coalition ground forces in the U.S.-led occupation of Iraq.

Sources: Kanellos, *Latino Almanac*, p. 203.

Maj. Gen. Angela Salinas

2006 ♦ Angela Salinas (1953–) became the first Latino to hold the rank of brigadier general of the U.S. Marine Corps when she assumed the command of the Marine Corps Recruit Depot in San Diego. In 2012, she was promoted to major general. She retired in 2013 as the highest-ranking Latina in the Marines.

Sources: Kanellos, *Latino Almanac*, pp. 202–203.

2023 ♦ On May 9, 2023, the first military fort was named for a Latino soldier when Fort Hood was renamed Fort Cavazos in honor of Richard E. Cavazos (1929–2017). Speaking at the ceremony, Lieutenant General Sean Bernabe, III Armored Corps Commanding General, stated, "We are proud to be renaming Fort Hood as Fort Cavazos in recognition of an outstanding American hero, a veteran of the Korea and Vietnam wars and the first Hispanic to reach the rank of four-star general in our Army. General Cavazos' combat-proven leadership, his moral character and his loyalty to his soldiers and their families made him the fearless yet respected and influential leader that he was during the time he served, and beyond."

Sources: "Richard E. Cavazos," National Museum of the United States Army: https://www.thenmusa.org/biographies/richard-e-cavazos/.

Business and Commerce

1508 ♦ The first agricultural product introduced to the Americas by the Spaniards was sugarcane. Originally from India, the plant was taken first to Hispaniola and then to the rest of the Americas for its cultivation. The first sugar mill was built in 1508 or 1509 on Hispaniola. The first samples of sugar were sent to Spain in about 1515. By 1523, there were 24 mills operating on the island. The Hispanic settlers of Florida, Louisiana, and Texas also introduced sugarcane to those areas.

Sources: Kanellos, *Chronology of Hispanic American History*, pp. 24, 65.

1565 ♦ Stock raising and ranching became established under the Spanish around Saint Augustine and Tallahassee, Florida. Most of the cattle were raised for local consumption, but there was enough surplus to make cattle the basis of trade, and smuggling to Cuba began to be instituted. Ranching did not flourish in Florida as it would later in California and Texas, however. By 1800, the tax rolls showed only 34 ranches with some 15,000 to 20,000 cattle.

Sources: Slatta, *Cowboys of the Americas*, pp. 19, 22.

1598 ♦ The leading Spanish colonizer and future governor of the province of New Mexico, Don Juan de Oñate (c. 1550–1630), introduced livestock breeding to what would become the American Southwest. He established a livestock industry that would supply the burgeoning silver mining industry in northern New Spain (Mexico), especially around Zacatecas and Guanajuato. There was an intense demand for cattle, horses, and mules, as well as tallow for candles, hides for water and ore bags, clothing, harnesses, hinges, and numerous other items. From New Mexico and western Texas, cattle and livestock ranching spread into the Great Plains and became the basis of much of today's livestock industry. Spain had one of the oldest sheep cultures in the Old World, and it introduced the churro sheep—a small, lean animal that produced coarse wool and could endure long marches and all types of weather. The churro became so acclimated to New Mexico and the Southwest that it became the basis for the large sheep industry that would develop over the centuries. In about 1876, fine merino sheep were brought by Anglos from the eastern seaboard and crossed with the churros to produce a hybrid animal that provided a better quality wool while being ideally acclimated to the environment. By 1880, the Southwest was producing four million pounds of wool per year. In New Mexico, as elsewhere in the Southwest and the rest of Spanish America, it was the Hispanicized Indians who became the cowboys and shepherds over the centuries, especially since much of ranching originated in and around the missions. The Spaniards also taught the Indians to weave wool, and the Indians—especially Navajo women in the early 19th century—labored in the textile industry in New Mexico. Land grants to individuals, along with grazing rights, also facilitated the development of large cattle and sheep ranches. This was a particular inheritance from the Spaniards and Mexicans for Anglos when they came into the Southwest. A Mexican homestead in the Southwest consisted of 4,470 acres, 28 times the size of an Anglo-American homestead in the Ohio Valley. The Spanish and Mexican land-use system was much better adapted to an arid environment and facilitated the growth of the cattle industry on the open range within that environment.

Sources: Rosaldo et al., *Chicano*, pp. 5–8, 13; Slatta, *Cowboys of the Americas*, pp. 20–22.

1663 ♦ Florida-born Tomás Menéndez Márquez (1643–1706) inherited his father's cattle ranch in central Florida and built it up over the years into the largest ranch and provider of hides, dried meat, and tallow to the Spanish colonies in Florida. Menéndez Márquez's products were also exported through shipping to Havana via the Florida port of San Martín. Menéndez Márquez owned his own frigate, with which he brought some of his own goods to market in Havana, returning with extensive trade items to be sold in Florida; his business interests expanded into areas far beyond ranching, including the import of Cuban rum. His fortunes increased further when, in 1684, he was appointed royal *contador*, or accountant-treasurer, for Florida. La Chúa Ranch became the largest cattle ranch on lands that would become the United States, extending from the Saint Johns River westward to the Gulf of Mexico and from Lake George northward to the Santa Fe River. Within its boundaries were contained what is today Ocala, Payne's Prairie, Alachua, Palatka, and Gainesville. The ranch produced more than one-third

Mission San Xavier del Bac, founded in 1692 near Tucson, was one of 20 missions in modern Arizona established by Father Eusebio Kino.

of Florida's cattle and horses in the late 17th century. The ranch met its end when James Moore, with Carolinians and Creek Indians, invaded the Florida peninsula and overran La Chúa in 1702, causing the ranch hands to flee and the cattle to become feral.

Sources: Henderson and Mormino, *Spanish Pathways in Florida*, pp. 118–139.

1687 ♦ Father Eusebio Kino (1645–1711) established the mission of Nuestra Señora de los Dolores in Arizona, through which he introduced livestock to the Pimería Alta region of northern New Spain. From there, he went on to establish at least 20 other missions in what is today Arizona. His first mission in what became Arizona was San Xavier del Bac, founded in 1692. Kino introduced and promoted livestock tending as essential in converting and feeding the Pima Indians. Franciscan missionaries continued to spread ranching and livestock tending throughout missions in Arizona, New Mexico, and California. Under the Spanish and the Mexicans, ranching grew into an important and lucrative business, especially in California.

Sources: Slatta, *Cowboys of the Americas*, p. 22.

1690 ♦ An expedition headed by Captain Alonso de León (c. 1639–1691) brought livestock to the first Spanish mission in east Texas: San Francisco de los Tejas. This was the beginning of the cattle industry in east Texas, as they continued to stock this and other missions as well as raise their own livestock. By 1800, cattle ranching had spread along the Neches and Trinity rivers.

Sources: Slatta, *Cowboys of the Americas*, p. 21.

1721 ♦ José de Azlor y Virto de Vera, the Marquis of San Miguel de Aguayo (1677–1734), laid the groundwork for ranching along the northern Rio Grande when he brought 400 sheep and 300 cattle into south Texas from Nuevo León, Mexico. In about 1722, he also introduced large numbers of horses, mules, cattle, and sheep to be ranched at the missions in the San Antonio area. In 1748, José Escandón (1700–1770) brought 4,000 colonists into the area, and the expanded population base made livestock raising even more important. In 1757, one José de la Tienda reported more than 80,000 head of cattle, horses, and mules and more than 300,000 sheep and goats in the area. By 1781, nearly all available land grants in southern Texas had been assigned, and nearly all of the lands were in use as ranches.

Sources: Chipman, *Spanish Texas, 1519–1821*, pp. 246–247; Simons and Hoyt, *Hispanic Texas*, p. 60.

1750 ♦ The Spanish governor of Texas attempted in vain to license and regulate the illegal trade in cattle between Spanish Texas and French Louisiana; these were the first cattle drives on record. *Vaqueros*, Hispanic cowboys, had been illegally driving cattle from Texas to market in French Louisiana for decades. When Spain acquired Louisiana in 1763, this trade was no longer illegal; however, when the Louisiana Territory passed to the United States in 1803, cattle driving from Texas to Louisiana once again constituted a lucrative smuggling trade. By the late 18th century, some 15,000 to 20,000 head of cattle moved eastward to Louisiana each year. By the early 1800s, illegal horse and mule trading also became a lucrative business, and Anglo settlers in the Mississippi Valley provided an expanded market for all Texas livestock.

Sources: Slatta, *Cowboys of the Americas*, pp. 19, 22.

1760 ♦ Captain Blas María de la Garza Falcón (1712–1767) obtained a grant to 975,000 acres of land in southern Texas, which he called Rancho Real de Santa Petronila. In time, it would become the largest cattle ranch in the United States: the King Ranch.

Sources: Kanellos, *Chronology of Hispanic American History*, p. 57.

1762 ♦ Trade between the British colonies and Cuba was initiated, leading to the establishment of the first communities of Cubans in the United States. During the Seven Years' War, the British occupied Havana, Cuba, for 10 months. During that time, Cubans came into contact with soldiers and traders from the British North American colonies, and they discovered the benefits of commercial relations outside of the Spanish Empire. This was to have great influence on the future relations of Cuba and the United States, especially as trading partners. During the first half of the 19th century, commercial relations expanded dramatically, leading to the beginnings of Cuban communities in New Orleans, New York, and Philadelphia. Many Cubans immigrated to the United States to pursue higher education. The United States also became a refuge for Cuban dissidents, exiles, and revolutionaries plotting the independence of their homeland. These close relations with the United States led to a strong movement among many Cubans—and even among U.S. politicians—to annex the island to the United States.

Sources: Kanellos, *Chronology of Hispanic American History*, p. 57.

1763 ♦ The first successful large-scale merchant and entrepreneur to be born in a mainland area that would become part of the United States was Francisco Javier Sánchez (1736–1807). He became the owner of vast cattle ranches in Florida that stocked the Spanish and British military and governments in Florida as well as the civilian population of Saint Augustine. He also became the owner and operator of stores, plantations, and ships and engaged in the slave trade, despite having been married to a mulatto and having cared for his mulatto offspring.

Sources: Henderson and Mormino, *Spanish Pathways in Florida*, pp. 168–187.

Father Junípero Serra

1769 ♦ Cattle ranching was first introduced to California by Franciscan missionary Father Junípero Serra (1713–1784) with the founding of the mission at San Diego. He proceeded to establish missions and their reliance on livestock tending, ranching, and farming all along the California coast. In 1775 and 1776, Juan Bautista de Anza (1736–1788) brought settlers and trailed livestock from Arizona to Monterey and San Francisco in northern California.

Sources: Slatta, *Cowboys of the Americas*, p. 22.

1789 ♦ The small-farm land grant in Tubac, Arizona, received from Spain in 1789 by Toribio Otero (1761–?), became the basis generations later for the making of "the cattle king of Tubac," Toribio Otero's great-grandson, Sabino Otero. On the basis of this initial inherited ranch, Sabino Otero (1846–1914) built the largest ranching operation in southern Arizona during the 1870s and 1880s.

Sources: Sheridan, *Los Tucsonenses*, pp. 52–53.

1800 ♦ The first major livestock economies flourished in Texas: horse ranching in Nacogdoches and cattle and horse ranching along the Rio Grande Valley and around San Antonio and further south. Cattle ran free on the open range and were herded and driven to market and slaughtered. The Anglo immigrants who settled in Texas considered these cattle wild and simply appropriated them, although they belonged to the Hispanic ranchers and were tended by *vaqueros* (cowboys). They did not create a cattle industry but simply took it over.

Sources: Slatta, *Cowboys of the Americas*, p. 19.

1810 ♦ Hispanic ranchers in California began shipping hides, tallow, and dried beef to South America, providing an impetus for an expansion of the cattle business. The hide and tallow trade also expanded beginning in 1822, when the Boston markets opened to the Californios; thus, the trade with markets on the East Coast far antedates U.S. expansion into California.

Sources: Rosaldo et al., *Chicano*, p. 9.

1821 ♦ Under the Republic of Mexico, many more land grants were issued for California lands than under Spanish rule; many of these grants became the basis of an ever-expanding ranching industry. More than 400 land grants were issued between 1833 and 1846 for tracts of land ranging from 4,000 to

1817: A Big Step Toward Ending Slavery

Spain became the first European colonial power to outlaw the slave trade in all of its colonies north of the equator in 1817. Spain signed a treaty with England providing for the suppression of the slave trade. This included the selling of slaves in areas that eventually became part of the United States. However, Spain did not outlaw slavery itself, just the commercial trade in slaves. *Sources:* Kanellos, *Chronology of Hispanic American History*, p. 73.

100,000 acres. By the time of the U.S. takeover, there were more than eight million acres held by some 800 ranchers. Under the United States, the ranching way of life soon succumbed. Most of the large tracts of land fell into the hands of speculators, land plungers, and railroad right-of-way seekers and prepared the way for the concentration of large land holdings in the hands of a few owners who would become the builders of California's giant agribusiness. By 1889, one-sixth of the farms in the state produced more than two-thirds of the crops.

Sources: Rosaldo et al., *Chicano*, p. 159.

1822 ♦ Hispanic ranchers and missions began exporting hides and tallow to the east coast of the United States after a deal was struck between a British company and Father President Mariano Payeras (1769–1823) of La Purísima Concepción Mission to make contracts with individual missions for their hides and tallow. (In the Franciscan missions of California, as well as Arizona, New Mexico, and Texas, Indians herded and slaughtered the cattle and prepared the meat and by-products.) Demand in New England and England for these products became so intense that by the 1830s, they became California's principal exports. It is estimated that Boston traders alone may have handled some six million hides and 7,000 tons of tallow from 1826 to 1848.

Sources: Fontana, *Entrada*, p. 217.

1825 ♦ One of the first women entrepreneurs on the frontier, María Gertrudis Barceló (1800–1852), began operating a game of chance in the Ortiz Mountains of New Mexico. She later opened a gambling casino in Santa Fe; it became one of the most famous establishments of its kind, serving the elite. She invested her profits in trade and merchandise and became very wealthy, even prospering under American occupation.

Sources: Tardiff and Mabunda, *Dictionary of Hispanic Biography*, p. 99.

1829 ♦ The new Republic of Mexico under Afro-Mexican president Vicente Guerrero (1782–1831) abolished slavery. This abolition also affected the Mexican lands to the north, which would eventually become part of the United States.

Vicente Guerrero

Sources: Kanellos, *Chronology of Hispanic American History*, p. 84.

1830 ♦ The first Longhorn cattle appeared, resulting from the crossbreeding of the Spanish Retinto and animals imported to Texas by Anglo settlers. Immune to tick fever and accustomed to the tough brush country of southern Texas, the Longhorn became the basis for the western livestock industry. After the Civil War, cattle ranching became especially important to the nation; Texas cowboys drove some 10 million head of Longhorn north to railheads and markets. Over time, the Longhorn was replaced by many other breeds, but in the initial stages of this important industry, it was the mainstay. Along with the trade in beef, an industry in hides, tallow, and other by-products flourished in the coastal "factories" of Texas.

Sources: Slatta, *Cowboys of the Americas*, pp. 19–20.

King Kamehameha III

1832 ♦ King Kamehameha III of Hawaii arranged for Mexican *vaqueros* to come to Hawaii from California to teach ranching skills to the Hawaiians; thus, the cattle industry was born on the Hawaiian Islands. Cattle had actually been introduced by George Vancouver in 1793 and horses—California mustangs—by Richard J. Cleveland in 1803. The cattle had been allowed to run wild, however, and only in the 1820s had they begun to be hunted for their hides, tallow, and meat. The Hawaiian word for cowboy, *pianolo*, derives from *español.* Many of the techniques and traditions of the Hawaiian ranching industry are owed to the Hispanic cowboy.

Sources: Slatta, *Cowboys of the Americas*, pp. 23–24.

1837 ♦ Philip Edwards (1812–1869) drove cattle from California north to Oregon, thus opening up the Northwest for ranching, with the help of California *vaqueros*. Ranchers in Oregon established the tradition of employing Mexican American cowboys in the late 19th and early 20th centuries; they came to compose up to half of the cowhands. In 1869, six Mexican American cowboys, led by Juan Redón, drove 3,000 head of cattle for John Devine, who established the largest ranch in Oregon. Redón stayed on to work as Devine's foreman.

Sources: Slatta, *Cowboys of the Americas*, p. 167.

1842 ♦ The first real estate mogul in Texas was a Sephardic Jewish banker who brought European immigrants to Texas following the establishment of the Republic of Texas. Henry Castro (1786–1865) was a banker in Alsace's Spanish Sephardic community who lent Texas president Sam Houston money for the development of the new republic. In addition, Castro entered into a five-year agreement with Houston in 1842 to

Henry Castro

colonize a land empire west of San Antonio (his contract was later extended another three years). From 1842 to 1847, Castro relocated more than 5,000 immigrants, mostly from France and the Rhineland, in 27 ships. Castro received land grants that included Medina County and parts of Frio, McMullen, Zavala, Uvalde, Bexar, and Bandera counties. He was the founder of the towns of Quihi, Vandenberg, and D'Hanis. The settlers of Castroville named their town in his honor; this was the county seat of Medina County. Fifteen years after Castro's death (in Monterrey, Mexico), the State of Texas named a stretch of land in the panhandle Castro County in his honor. Another Sephardic Jew who became a real estate mogul was Jacob de Cordova (1808–1868), who founded the De Cordova Land Agency and assisted people from the Northeast in relocating to Texas after it had become a state. The largest number of land patents issued by the State of Texas were certificates held or controlled by de Cordova. It was de Cordova and two of his partners who founded and laid out the city of Waco, Texas. To entice northerners to move to Texas, de Cordova lectured throughout the Northeast. When laying out plots of land for towns, de Cordova's custom was to present free of charge a lot for each religious denomination's construction of a house of worship.

Sources: Simonhoff, *Jewish Notables in America, 1776–1865*, pp. 288–291.

1856 ♦ Joaquín Quiroga laid the foundations for the lucrative freighting business in Arizona by carrying the first load of goods from Yuma to Tucson in his 14-mule pack train. In the next decades, Mexican entrepreneurs would become the major owners of freighting companies, linking the California coast with the Arizona and New Mexico territories, Baja California, and northern Mexico. They even reached as far east as Missouri. The importance of the freight-hauling business by mule and wagon train only subsided with the introduction of the railroads, and then, some of these same entrepreneurs made the transition to hauling freight and people by wagon and stagecoach to secondary and outlying communities. Although Hispanics had followed trails blazed and used by Indians for centuries, they also pioneered most of the techniques and opened most of the trails that would later be used for trade and communication during the territorial and early statehood periods. In fact, some of today's major highways run along those routes pioneered for trade by Hispanics and Mexicans.

Sources: Sheridan, *Los Tucsonenses*, pp. 43–45.

1870 ♦ The first Hispanic urban real estate mogul in Tucson under U.S. rule, and possibly in the entire Southwest, was Leopoldo Carrillo (1836–1890), who the 1870 census shows to have been the wealthiest man in Tucson, Arizona. Besides owning rental homes, commercial properties, and farmland, he also owned and operated ice cream parlors, saloons, and even Tucson's first bowling alley. By 1881, he owned nearly 100 houses in Tucson, making him one of the most prominent local landlords.

Leopoldo Carri o

Sources: Sheridan, *Los Tucsonenses*, pp. 50–51.

1875 ♦ Estevan Ochoa (1831–1888) developed his freight business into the largest Hispanic-owned company in Tucson, second only in the overall community to E. N. Fish and Company, handling some $300,000 in transactions per year. By 1880, Ochoa and Company was the largest taxpayer in Pima County. Expanding from the long-distance hauling of freight by mule train, he and his partner, Pickney Randolph Tully, went into the mercantile business with stores that depended on freight hauling. Thus, he and his partners were among the first businessmen on the frontier to implement vertical integration. They also invested in mining and raising sheep. At the beginning of the 1880s, they were grazing 15,000 sheep and operating a wool factory; a settlement started at a camp where they raised sheep and eventually became the town of Ochoaville, named in his honor. Ochoa is credited with having introduced to Tucson and its surrounding communities a number of industrial technologies for turning out woolen blankets that had been developed in factories in the eastern United States.

Sources: Sheridan, *Los Tucsonenses*, pp. 42–49.

1879 ♦ Estevan Ochoa became the first Arizona pioneer to plant cotton for commercial purposes. He investigated its potential by planting an acre of Pima cotton and then sending samples back to the eastern United States for testing.

Sources: Sheridan, *Los Tucsonenses*, p. 45.

1882 ♦ Bernabé S. Robles (1857–1945) was the first Latino to become a millionaire by taking advantage of the Homestead Act. He and his brother, Jesús, applied for and received two homesteads in southern Arizona and opened a stagecoach station there in 1882. He then founded what became the famous Three Points Ranch. He expanded his holdings and eventually controlled more than one million acres between Florence and the Mexican border. He was one of the most successful cattlemen in Arizona. In 1918, he invested the profits from ranching in urban real estate in the Tucson area. Part of the inheritance he left his children was 65 parcels of the most valuable Tucson properties.

The first cigar factory in Ybor City still stands today. If you visit Tampa, Florida, you can book a tour of the old factories.

Sources: Sheridan, *Los Tucsonenses*, p. 97.

1886 ♦ The first transfer of a whole industry from Latin America to the United States and the subsequent building of a company town occurred when Spanish and Cuban entrepreneurs acquired Florida swampland near Tampa and built a cigar-producing town, Ybor City. In 1880, the population of Tampa was only 721; a decade later, the combined population of Tampa and Ybor City was 5,500, and that number tripled by 1900. The first of the entrepreneurs to establish their cigar factories, Vicente Martínez Ybor (1818–1896) and Ignacio Haya (1842–1906), hoped to attract a docile workforce (unlike the labor union activists in Cuba), avoid U.S. import tariffs, and get closer to their markets in the United States. Also, the Cuban wars for independence were raging and continually disrupting business. Martínez Ybor, Spanish by birth, had immigrated to Cuba when he was 14; after working in cigar factories in Key West and New York, he settled in Tampa and built the world's largest cigar factory there. Ybor City became the principal cigar-producing area in the United States when cigar smoking was at its peak. By 1900, there were about 150 cigar factories in West Tampa and Ybor City, producing more than 111 million cigars annually.

Sources: Florida Department of State, *Florida Cuban Heritage Trail,* p. 34; Henderson and Mormino, *Spanish Pathways in Florida,* pp. 40–45, 262.

1889 ♦ Mexican immigrant Federico Ronstadt (1868–1954) founded a carriage business that became the largest of its kind in Tucson, Arizona, and the surrounding region, including Sonora, Mexico. At its height, Ronstadt's wagon shop and hardware store employed 65 people, who, besides repairing vehicles of all kinds, manufactured wagons, buggies, harnesses, and saddles. Ronstadt executed most of the iron forging himself and became known as one of the finest wagon and carriage makers in the Southwest. Ronstadt's business territory extended from California to Sonora, Mexico, where he had agents in Cananea, Nogales, Hermosillo, and Guaymas. By 1910, approximately one-third of his business was transacted south of the border. Ronstadt also marketed nationally known brands of wagons and farm machinery.

Sources: Sheridan, *Los Tucsonenses,* pp. 94–95.

1949 ♦ Romana Acosta Bañuelos (1925–2018) opened her tortilla factory in downtown Los Angeles with the $500 she had made washing dishes and making tortillas for other establishments. This humble beginning grew into Ramona's Mexican Food Products, a multimillion-dollar business headquartered in Gardena, California. Her business acumen transferred into her becoming a cofounder of the Pan-American National Bank in East Los Angeles in 1963. In 1971, she became the first Latina to serve as treasurer of the United States under President Richard Nixon. Her rise to national prominence was preceded by hardship as a child born in Miami, Arizona, in 1925 to Mexican immigrant parents; despite her being an American citizen, she was deported during the Depression to Sonora, Mexico, with her family. It was here that she was initiated in food preparation and service by assisting her mother in cooking empanadas and delivering them to local restaurants and bakeries.

Sources: Reyes-Velarde, Alejandra, "Romana Acosta Bañuelos, First Latina U.S. Treasurer and Mexican American Pioneer, Dies at 92," *Los Angeles Times,* 22 January 2018.

1968 ♦ Cuban American businesswoman Remedios Díaz-Oliver (1938–) became the first woman to earn the E Award—Excellence in Export—given by President Lyndon B. Johnson. Díaz-Oliver was head of the exporting division of the Emmer Glass container business in Miami. Díaz-Oliver went on to found her own company, American International Container, in 1976, and another company, All American Container, in 1991. In 1984, she was named Woman of the Year by the Latin Business and Professional Women Association, and in 1987, she was named Woman of the Year by the U.S. Hispanic Chamber of Commerce.

Sources: Tardiff and Mabunda, *Dictionary of Hispanic Biography*, pp. 286–288.

1972 ♦ The American Association of Hispanic Certified Public Accountants was founded to maintain and promote professional and moral standards of Hispanics in the accounting field. The organization assists members in practice development and develops business opportunities in securing government contracts for members. It also sponsors seminars and bestows scholarships.

Sources: Furtaw, *Hispanic Americans Information Directory*, p. 1.

1975 ♦ Katherine D. Ortega (1934–) became the first woman to serve as president of a California bank when she accepted the position of director and president of the Santa Ana State Bank. In 1963, she became vice president of the Pan-American National Bank, cofounded by Romana Acosta Bañuelos. In 1977, she returned to her native New Mexico to lead her family's accounting firm, which grew into the Otero Savings and Loan Association. Ortega later became treasurer of the United States under President Ronald Reagan.

Katherine D. Ortega

Sources: Vicki Ruíz and Virginia Sánchez Korrol, "Latina U.S. Treasurers," *Latinas in the United States: A Historical Encyclopedia,* Volume I, Indiana University Press, 2006, pp. 374–375.

1977 ♦ Carlos José Arboleya (1929–) became the first Cuban president and CEO of a major bank in the United States, Barnett Bank of Miami. Prior to tat appointment, he had been co-owner, president, and director of Flagler Bank in Miami. Since 1983, he has served as vice chairman of the Barnett Bank of South Florida. Thanks to Arboleya and other Cuban American businessmen and bankers, Miami has become a major banking center for Latin America.

Sources: Kanellos, *Latino Almanac*, pp. 92–93.

Hector Barreto Jr.

1979 ♦ Mexican native Hector Barreto Jr. (1961–) founded the U.S. Hispanic Chamber of Commerce (USHCC). Barreto worked his way up from digging potatoes and packing meat to running his own companies in Kansas City, including restaurants and import and construction businesses. As president of the USHCC, Barreto worked for greater representation of Hispanics in government and business.

Sources: Hispanics in U.S. History, p. 66.

1979 ♦ Humberto Cabañas (1947–) became the first Hispanic CEO of a major corporation in the hospitality industry when he assumed the position of CEO and founding president of Benchmark Hospitality Group in The Woodlands, Texas. He was also the first U.S. Hispanic president of the International Association of Conference Centers, from which he received a distinguished service award in 1988.

Sources: Kanellos, *Latino Almanac*, p. 93.

Frank A. Lorenzo

1980 ♦ Frank A. Lorenzo (1940–) became the first Latino to serve as the president of a major national and international airline: Continental Airlines, headquartered in Houston, Texas. From 1986 to 1990, Lorenzo served as chairman and CEO of Continental. A graduate of the Harvard M.B.A. program, Lorenzo served as president and chairman of the board of Texas International Airlines (TIA) from 1972 to 1980; TIA became the holding company for Continental Airlines. Lorenzo was eventually embattled by strikes and financial problems and was forced to resign.

Sources: Boyer, Peter J., "The Double Life of Frank Lorenzo," *Vanity Fair* (December 1989): https://archive.vanityfair.com/article/1989/12/the-double-life-of-frank-lorenzo.

1981 ♦ Roberto C. Goizueta (1931–1997) became the first U.S. Hispanic to lead one of the largest corporations in the world, Coca-Cola, when he became the company's CEO and chairman of the board. One of the highest-paid CEOs in the United States, the native Cuban started out as a Coca-Cola bottler in Miami after receiving his B.S. degree in engineering from Yale University in 1953. Goizueta also sat on the boards of Ford Motor Company, Eastman Kodak, and many other major companies. He was recognized as an immigrant making an outstanding contribution to American society with the Ellis Island Medal of Honor in 1986. In 1984, Goizueta also received the Herbert Hoover Humanitarian Award from the Boys Clubs of America.

Sources: Greising, David, *I'd Like the World to Buy a Coke: The Life and Leadership of Roberto Goizueta,* John Wiley & Sons, 1989.

1983 ♦ California native Luis Nogales, known as one of the most outstanding Hispanic businessmen in the United States, assumed the position of executive vice president for United Press International (UPI), the second largest news agency in the world, and became president of the corporation in 1984. He thus became the highest-placed Hispanic in the news profession in the United States. Nogales resigned from UPI in 1985 and took the company through bankruptcy proceedings until 1986. In 1987, he became president of the Univision television network, a position he kept for only one year.

Sources: Gordon, Gregory, and, Ronald E. Cohen. *Down to the Wire: UPI's Fight for Survival.* McGraw-Hill, 1989.

1983 ♦ Banker Katherine D. Ortega became the first Hispanic to serve as a commissioner of the Copyright Royalty Tribunal, which determines what royalty fees cable companies and jukebox operators pay throughout the nation.

Sources: Telgen and Kamp, *Latinas! Women of Achievement*, p. 293.

1990 ♦ Sosa, Bromley, Aguilar & Associates (now Bromley Communications), the San Antonio advertising agency founded and headed by Lionel Sosa (1939–), became the first Latino concern to be named Agency of the Year and the Hottest Agency in the Southwest by *Adweek* magazine. In 1989, Sosa & Associates had billings of $54.8 million. Included among Sosa's clients were American Airlines, Coca-Cola USA, Montgomery Ward, and Western Union. Lionel Sosa has won many other awards, such as the 1988 Gold ADDY from the American Advertising Federation, the 1989 Marketing Person of the Year award, the 1989 Silver Award from the Public Relations Society of America, and the 1990 Entrepreneur of the Year award. In 2005, *Time* magazine named Sosa to its "25 Most Influential Hispanics in America."

Sources: Sosa, Lionel. *Think & Grow Rich: A Latino Choice.* Napoleon Hill Foundation, 2006.

1990 ♦ Ramona's Food Products, owned by the former U.S. treasurer Romana Acosta Bañuelos, became the largest Mexican food-processing company in the state of California.

Sources: Tardiff and Mabunda, *Dictionary of Hispanic Biography*, p. 97.

1991 ♦ Ignacio Lozano Jr., publisher of Los Angeles's Spanish-language daily newspaper *La Opinión*, became the first Hispanic to receive the Lifetime Achievement Award from the U.S. Small Business Administration. In addition to serving as publisher for the widely circulating newspaper that he inherited from his father, Lozano also served as U.S. ambassador to El Salvador from 1976 to 1977.

Sources: Tardiff and Mabunda, *Dictionary of Hispanic Biography*, p. 496.

1991 ♦ Roberto C. Goizueta, CEO of Coca-Cola, earned a bonus of nearly $83 million in stock, one of the largest ever.

Sources: Grant, Linda," "Coke Chairman's Pay Is Called Hard to Swallow," *Los Angeles Times* 20 March 1992.

1992 ♦ Goya Foods became the largest Hispanic-owned company in the United States. After the death of its founder, Prudencio Unanue Ortiz, in 1976, his son, Joseph A. Unanue, took over the chain that his father had built from an importing business. Under Joseph A. Unanue's guidance, the company grew to sell more than 800 products. Its revenue rose to $453 million by 1992, a growth rate of some 12 percent annually. Unanue accomplished this feat mainly by expanding the products offered from those specifically catering to Puerto Ricans and Cubans to include food products appealing to Mexicans and Central Americans precisely at the time that their populations were growing significantly within the United States.

Goya food products are sold in supermarkets all across the United States.

Sources: Tardiff and Mabunda, *Dictionary of Hispanic Biography*, p. 907.

1993 ♦ Linda G. Alvarado (1952–), president of her own Alvarado Construction company, became the first Latino, male or female, to own a Major League Baseball team: the Colorado Rockies. She was also one of four women to win the Sara Lee Corporation's Frontrunner Award. She was the first Hispanic to receive the honor. She is also president of Palo Alto, Inc., and the Alvarado Restaurant Entities, which owns and operates YUM! Brands restaurants in multiple states. In addition, Alvarado is a corporate director at 3M Company, Mayo Clinic,

Linda G. Alvarado

Pepsi Bottling Group, Pitney Bowes, Qwest Communications, the Taco Bell Foundation, and others.

Sources: "Linda Alvarado." https://americanhistory.si.edu/profile/3104.

1995 ♦ Martha S. Tabio became the first Hispanic to be named president of Financial Women International, an organization of 10,000 members worldwide. Since 1987, Tabio has been a senior vice president of Barnett Bank of South Florida.

Sources: "About People," *Hispanic Business*, April 1996, p. 68.

1995 ♦ Arthur C. Martinez became the first Latino to lead one of the nation's largest merchandisers: Sears. In August, he became chairman and CEO. Martinez traces his Hispanic heritage to ancestors who immigrated to New Orleans from Spain.

Sources: Hispanic Link Weekly Report, 14 August 1995, p. 3.

1996 ♦ *Hispanic Business* magazine published its first Hispanic Business Rich list, which documented that there were at least 11 Hispanic entrepreneurs and corporate leaders whose net worth was $100 million or more. At the top of the list as the nation's wealthiest corporate leader was Coca-Cola CEO Roberto C. Goizueta, whose net worth was placed at $574 million. Behind him was Joseph A. Unanue and family, owners of Goya Foods, with a net worth of $444 million. Of the 11, one was of Mexican origin, two of Puerto Rican origin, two of Spanish origin, and the rest of Cuban origin.

Sources: Hispanic Business, March 1996, p. 18.

1996 ♦ Eduardo Sánchez became the first Latino vice president of international relations for one of the world's largest corporations, McDonald's. Sánchez began as a kitchen crew member mopping floors in Tampa, Florida, in 1976. As vice president, he became responsible for McDonald's in all 21 Latin American countries.

Sources: Hispanic Link Weekly Report, 22 January 1996, p. 1.

1996 ♦ Enrique Hernández Jr. (1958–) was the first Latino to be named to the board of directors of the McDonald's Corporation, one of the world's largest corporate entities. Hernández is currently president and CEO of Inter-Con Security Systems, Inc., and principal partner and cofounder of Interspan Communications.

Sources: "McDonald's Board of Directors Names Enrique Hernandez, Jr. Non-Executive Chairman," *Reuters* (26 May 2016): https://www.reuters.com/article/idUSASC08RIS/.

Marcelo Claure

1997 ♦ Marcelo Claure (1970–) founded Brightstar as a small, Miami-based wireless distributor and transformed it into the world's largest global wireless distribution and services company; its revenues exceeded $10 billion and became a presence in more than 50 countries when Claure sold the company to Sprint. Brightstar was recognized as the largest Hispanic-owned business in U.S. history. He later became CEO of Sprint.

Sources: Wile, Rob, "From 'Unknown' to Wealthiest Hispanic-American—and Now, He's Moving Back to Miami," *Miami Herald*, 15 October 2018.

1997 ♦ The Gambrinus Company, founded by Mexican Carlos Alvarez (1950–2024) to distribute the Modelo brands of Mexican beer, experienced its Corona beer becoming the number-one imported beer in the United States, surpassing Heineken. Having obtained the license to distribute the beers in Texas and the eastern part of the United States, Alvarez grew the company into becoming its largest importer.

In the mid-1980s, Alvarez expanded his export business into Canada, Japan, Australia, and New Zealand; today, Corona is available in over 150 countries around the world. In 1989, he purchased the flagging Spoetzl Brewery in Shiner, Texas, and built its Shiner Bock into an iconic Texas brew, now enjoyed around the United States. For an encore, he became a brewer, establishing the Trumer Pils brewery in Berkeley, California, after forging a partnership with the Trumer brewery in Salzburg, Austria. He has been acknowledged as a business and charitable leader repeatedly, and his name is immortalized in the Alvarez College of Business of the University of Texas at San Antonio. In 2010, he was inducted into the Texas Business Hall of Fame.

Sources: "Carlos Alvarez," Texas Business Hall of Fame: https://texasbusiness.org/wp-content/uploads/2019/07/TBHF_2010_Legend_Bios.pdf.

1998 ♦ Salvadoran immigrant María Ríos founded Nation Waste, Inc., which has become the first multimillion-dollar, Latina-owned waste removal company in U.S. history and one of the largest minority-owned companies in the state of Texas. NWI is a waste disposal company specializing in construction, demolition, commercial/industrial non-hazardous waste removal, portable toilets, and recycling services.

Sources: "Top Women: María Ríos": https://top30women.com/maria-rios/.

1999 ♦ Carlos Miguel Gutiérrez (1953–) was appointed president and CEO of Kellogg Company, becoming one of two Latino CEOs of a Fortune 500 company—the other was Roberto C. Goizueta. Gutiérrez was also the youngest CEO in the company's nearly 100-year history. In 1975, Gutiérrez became a sales representative for Kellogg Corporation in Mexico. From that humble position, he worked his way up to top management. In 2004, President George W. Bush nominated Gutiérrez as secretary of commerce. After the U.S. Senate confirmed him for secretary, the board of Kellogg accepted his resignation as CEO.

Carlos Miguel Gutiérrez

Sources: Gutiérrez, Carlos, "Carlos Gutiérrez: Business Man and US Secretary of Commerce," *Latino Leaders Speak: Personal Stories of Struggle and Triumph*, eds. Mickey Ibarra and Maria Pérez-Brown, Arte Público Press, 2017.

2003 ♦ Linda Alvarado (1951–), president of her own Alvarado Construction company and co-owner of the Colorado Rockies baseball team, was inducted into the National Women's Hall of Fame. She was cited for changing the "male only" image of construction contractors across the country and for opening doors for women to enter construction and non-traditional business fields. She was only 27 years old when she became a member of the board of United Bank; today, she serves on the boards of five public companies.

Sources: "Linda G. Alvardo," National Women's Hall of Fame: https://www.womenofthehall.org/inductee/linda-g-alvarado/.

2004 ♦ Eduardo Sánchez, who started out mopping floors at McDonald's in Tampa, Florida, became CEO of Lopez Foods, a major supplier for McDonald's, headquartered in Oklahoma City. Lopez Foods is a major supplier of meat to the McDonald's Corporation; under his watch, the tremendously successful McRib was introduced. Now, under the name of Lopez-Dorada Foods, the company is the largest food-processing company owned by a Latino in the United States, with 2,000 employees and revenues of over $1 billion. He was succeeded as CEO by Francisco "Pancho" González in 2022; Eduardo Sánchez continued to serve as chairman of the board of directors.

Sources: "Conoce a uno de los hispanos que están detrás del famoso McRib de McDonald's," *People en Español*, December 12, 2022: https://peopleenespanol.com/noticias/familia-hispana-produce-carne-para-mcrib-mcdonalds-dueno-eduardo-sanchez/.

2004: Largest Hispanic-owned IT Integration Company

Anthony R. Jiménez (1961–) literally founded MicroTech on his kitchen table in 2004 as a one-man operation. Today, he is the award-winning chairman and CEO of the company, one of the largest Hispanic-owned IT integrators in the nation. Under his leadership, MicroTech is focused on technology services, cloud computing, product solutions, network systems integration, cybersecurity, telecommunications, mobility, and managed services and solutions. Today, MicroTech is a profitable half-billion-dollar company with skilled professionals in more than 40 states supporting more than 100 prime contracts throughout the federal government and providing IT, network, and telecom support to numerous Fortune 500 companies around the globe. *Hispanic Business* magazine selected MicroTech as one of the 25 largest Hispanic-owned businesses in the nation in 2011. *Sources:* "Tony Jimenez Finds Success through Calculated Risks," *Hispanic Executive*, 8 August 2022: https://hispanicexecutive.com/tony-jimenez-microtech-2/.

2006 ♦ Cuban-born Ralph Alvarez (1955–) was named president and COO of McDonald's North America, one of the largest corporations in the United States; he served until his retirement in 2009. He had previously served as president of McDonald's Mexico. The University of Miami–educated business leader joined the board of Eli Lilly in 2009 and in 2017 became a partner in Advent International Corporation.

Sources: "Ralph Alvarez," Lilly: https://www.lilly.com/leadership/board-of-directors/ralph-alvarez.

2007 ♦ Richard A. Gonzalez was named CEO of Abbot Laboratories after working his way up to the position at Abbot for some 30 years. Gonzalez stepped down in 2010 after it was revealed that he had not earned a college degree but had included this credential in his resumé. When AbbVie split off from Abbot in 2013, Gonzalez was named CEO of the new corporation and has remained there as one of the longest-lasting CEOs in Big Pharma. AbbVie is a global biopharmaceutical company that employs more than 50,000 people worldwide.

Sources: Parker, Garrett, "Ten Things You Didn't Know about R-chard Gonzalez," *Money Inc.*: https://moneyinc.com/abbvie-ceo-richard-gonzalez/.

2008 ♦ The National Council on Economic Education presented Julie Stav with its Visionary Award, an accolade "that honors champions of economic empowerment in all of its many forms, from those who have raised awareness about the need for economic and financial literacy, to those who, having succeeded in their chosen field by using sound economic decision-making, have turned that success into good public works." Stav is the founder and owner of a multimedia communications platform that includes a national radio show, "Tu Dinero con Julie Stav," her *New York Times* bestselling books, online classes on investing and money management, and hundreds of appearances on Univision as an on-air financial expert. Beginning as a child refugee from Cuba, Stav did not speak English when she enrolled in Los Angeles schools and was tested as mentally deficient; she quickly learned the language but struggled to get into college, eventually obtained her teaching degree from Loyola Marymount University, and, recently divorced and the mother of a four-year-old, decided to take control of her finances, teaching herself about investing and managing finances. She made her way into becoming a national expert on finances, especially appealing to Spanish-language audiences, and becoming a wealthy entrepreneur herself.

Sources: "Julie Stav," *Latino Leaders Speak*, pp. 255–260.

2009 ♦ Matías de Tizanos (1979–) was honored as a Young Global Leader by the World Economic Forum and one of the top 10 Latino entrepreneurs by *Inc.* magazine in 2011–2012. Tizanos is the founder and leader of diverse businesses, launching a variety of IT firms in Central America, Mexico, and the United States. In the United States, he established 11 different companies, including Autoweb.com, Inc., Click Diario Network, and HealthCare.com; currently, he is CEO of Kaptyn, Inc., and PF Holdings, LLC. He is also the founder of Hotels.com.

Sources: Kanellos, *Latino Almanac*, p. 101.

2013 ♦ María Ríos, CEO of Nation Waste, Inc., the first multimillion-dollar, Latina-led waste removal company and one of the largest minority-owned companies in Texas, was included among the Most Powerful Women Entrepreneurs by *Fortune*, and Goldman Sachs honored her as one of its 100 Most Intriguing Entrepreneurs.

Sources: Kanellos, *Latino Almanac*, pp. 99–100.

2014 ♦ Marcelo Claure became CEO of Sprint, one of the world's largest telecommunications companies, providing service to 54.6 million customers in nearly 200 countries around the world. When Claure joined the company, he took it through a significant transformation: growing revenue and reducing expenses by more than $6 billion while massively improving the quality of its products and services. During his four years as CEO, Sprint revitalized its brand and went from losing millions of customers to gaining more than 2.1 million. The company achieved its best financial results in company history. Claure was subsequently named a Young Global Leader of the World Economic Forum and named a member of Ernst & Young's Entrepreneur of the Year Hall of Fame. In 2023, *Forbes* placed his net worth at $2 billion.

Sources: Wile, Rob, "From 'Unknown' to Wealthiest Hispanic-American—and Now, He's Moving Back to Miami," *Miami Herald*, 15 October 2018.

María Contreras-Sweet

2014 ♦ María Contreras-Sweet (1955–) became the first Latina to lead the U.S. Small Business Administration. At the SBA, from 2014 to 2017 she oversaw the world's largest business counseling network, the federal small business contracting program, and a $120 billion loan program. After immigrating from Mexico as a child, she developed a career in business and government. In 1999, she became the state's first Latina cabinet official, serving five years as secretary of the Business, Transportation, and Housing Agency. Subsequently, she served as vice president of public affairs for the 7-Up/RC Bottling Company, where she was a leading corporate negotiator for the creation of the Beverage Container Recycling and Litter Reduction Act, expanding California law's recycling system. From 1999 to 2003, she served as the California cabinet secretary of the Business, Transportation, and Housing Agency, managing 44,000 employees and a $14 billion budget.

Sources: Fox, Tom, "Maria Contreras-Sweet on Running the Small Business Administration," *Washington Post,* 30 January 2015.

2014 ♦ *El Clasificado*, founded and owned by Martha de la Torre (1957–), was recognized as "Best Classified Website" by *Editor and Publisher* in 2014. *El Clasificado* is the largest Hispanic classified ad platform, ranked among the top 115 classified marketplaces in the world, according to Similarweb.com. Today, yearly revenues are approximately $20 million. Besides *El Clasificado*, included in her conglomerate EC Hispanic Media are *Quinceanera.com, Su Socio de Negocios, EmpleosLatino.com, Al Borde*, Pantera Digital, and Twyzle, which specializes in the Latino market and offers print, digital, social media, and event advertising and marketing solutions to its clients. In 2010, CNBC named de la Torre one of the top 10 Hispanic entrepreneurs.

Martha de la Torre

Sources: "Marta de la Torre, CEO & Founder," *Hispanic Media:* https://www.echispanicmedia.com/martha-de-la-torre-biography/.

2015 ♦ Mexican-born Mauricio Gutiérrez (1970–) became CEO of NRG Energy, one of the largest power companies in the United States, and took the regional company (headquartered in Texas) into a Fortune 500 company. Gutiérrez started as an energy trader at the Houston-based Dynegy and then joined NRG in 2004. Under his leadership, by 2021, the company doubled its customer base to roughly six million residential and business clients and nearly tripled the company's market capitalization to $9.5 billion. He stepped down from NRG in 2023.

Sources: "Mauricio Gutierrez, One of 16 Hispanic CEOs in the Fortune 500," *Business Insider.* https://www.businessinsider.com/mauricio-gutierrez-nrg-ceo-interview-diversity-sustainability-2021-12.

2016 ♦ Enrique Hernández Jr. (1955–) was named non-executive chairman of the board of McDonald's Corporation. He is president and CEO of Inter-Con Security Systems, Inc., one of the largest security system providers worldwide.

Sources: "Brief—McDonald's Board of Directors Names Enrique Hernandez Jr. Non-Executive Chairman," *Reuters,* 26 May 2016.

Oscar Muñoz

2016 ♦ Oscar Muñoz (1959–) became CEO of United Airlines, one of the largest airline companies in the world. Muñoz's tenure as CEO ended in 2020 when he transitioned to the role of executive chairman of the board. Prior to his leadership at United Airlines, Muñoz had worked his way up in corporate America at Qwest, AT&T, Coca-Cola, and PepsiCo until he became the president and COO at CSX Corporation in 2012.

Sources: Kuehner-Hebert, Katie. "Under CEO Oscar Munoz, United Airlines Holdings Inc. Ups Its 2019 Guidance." *Chief Executive*, 18 November 2019.

2016 ♦ Nina Vaca (1971–), founder and CEO of Pinnacle Group, an IT consulting firm, was inducted into the Minority Business Hall of Fame and Museum and also received an *Enterprising Women*'s Woman of the Year Award. In 2013, she had been named to the list of 100 Most Intriguing Entrepreneurs by Goldman Sachs. In 2019, she joined the Forbes Technology Council.

Nina Vaca

Sources: Kanellos, *Latino Almanac*, p. 102.

2017 ♦ Geisha Williams (c. 1961–) became the first Latina to serve as a CEO of a Fortune 500 company when she was named president and CEO of the Pacific Gas and Electric Company. The Cuban American, whose maiden name was Jiménez, lasted in the job until January 2019. The daughter of Cuban political refugees, Williams had started at PG&E in 2017 and climbed the ladder to leadership.

Sources: Zarya, Valentia, "PG&E's Bolt of Energy," *Fortune,* 15 June 2017: https://fortune.com/2017/06/15/fortune-500-pge-geisha-williams/.

2019 ♦ Cheryl Miller, born in Puerto Rico in 1972, became CEO of AutoNation, the country's largest automotive retailer and No. 129 on that year's Fortune 500. Miller was the first female CEO of a publicly traded automotive retailer. She had already served as CFO for the auto retailer in 2014.

Sources: Punds, Marcia Heroux, "How Deal-Maker Cheryl Miller Rose to Become AutoNation's New CEO," *Seattle Times* 11 August 2019: https://www.seattletimes.com/business/how-deal-maker-cheryl-miller-rose-to-become-autonations-new-ceo/.

Jorge M. Pérez

2020 ♦ Jorge M. Pérez (1949–) retired as president and CEO of Related Group after building the firm into one of the most prolific high-rise condo builders in the southern United States. Pérez has owned numerous condo towers around the country and has built apartments and condos in Atlanta, south Florida, Fort Myers, Tampa, Dallas, Denver, Phoenix, and Las Vegas. During his career, Pérez developed or managed more than 90,000 residences. In addition, he built projects in Argentina, Brazil, Panama, Uruguay, and Mexico.

Sources: "Billionaires: Jorge Perez," *Forbes* 8 October 2023: https://www.forbes.com/profile/jorge-perez/?list=forbes-400&sh=a8a9542100b2.

2022 ♦ Joseph Domínguez (1965–) was named president and CEO of Constellation, which employs 13,000 workers and has a generating capacity of more than 32,400 megawatts, producing 10 percent of the nation's clean energy for more than 20 million homes and businesses. From 2018 to 2021, Domínguez served as CEO of ComEd, an Exelon company, which powers the lives of more than four million residential and business customers, or 70 percent of Illinois's population. He is cofounder of the Association of Latino Energy and Environmental Professionals, a national association dedicated to ensuring that Latinos have a voice in the discussion and development of energy policies, regulations, R&D technologies, and environmental issues.

Sources: "Joseph Domínguez," Constellation Energy: https://www.constellationenergy.com/our-company/leadership/executive-profiles/joseph-dominguez.html.

2022 ♦ Francisco "Pancho" González was named CEO of Lopez-Dorada Foods, the nation's largest Latino-owned meat manufacturing company and a subsidiary of Tyson Foods, Inc. González previously served as vice president of the Americas for Inspire Brands, where he was responsible for all brands, including Arby's, Baskin-Robbins, Buffalo Wild Wings, Dunkin', Jimmy John's, and Sonic, in 16 countries. He also spent eight years as a multi-unit franchisee for McDonald's in Mexico. While there, he served as president for the Mexican Co-op and eventually as managing director of McDonald's Mexico for McDonald's Corp.

Sources: "Lopez-Dorada Foods Names González CEO," *The Journal Record*, June 1, 2022: https://journalrecord.com/2022/06/01/lopez-dorada-foods-names-gonzalez-ceo/.

2022 ♦ Jesús "Jay" Malave (1969–) was named CFO of Lockheed Martin, one of the world's largest aerospace companies and the largest U.S. defense contractor. In addition to his oversight of all internal and external financial reporting, he is responsible for investor relations and plays a key role in the development of the corporation's strategic growth plan and the evaluation, execution, and integration of mergers and acquisitions. He previously served as CFO at L3 Harris Technologies, UTC Aerospace Systems, and Carrier. Malave, a Connecticut native and son of Puerto Rican parents of modest means, earned a bachelor's degree in mathematics from the University of Connecticut, a master's in accounting from the University of Hartford, and a J.D. from the University of Connecticut School of Law.

Sources: Soule, Alexander. "CT Native Tasked with Leading the Finances of Nation's Largest Defense Conglomerate," *CT Insider,* 24 September 2022: https://www.ctinsider.com/business/article/CT-native-leads-finances-for-Lockheed-Martin-17457260.php.

Richard Montañez

2023 ♦ Amazon Prime began streaming *Flamin' Hot*, the story of how Richard Montañez (c. 1958–) came up with the idea for the PepsiCo snack product Flamin' Hot Cheetos. Montañez began work as a janitor in the Frito-Lay plant in Cucamanoga, California, and rose to become a Hispanic market executive at Frito-Lay and eventually vice president of multicultural sales and community promotions for PepsiCo North America. Since the early 2000s, Montañez has been a popular speaker around the country, claiming to have invented Flamin' Hot Cheetos and brought it to market in 1990. Flamin' Hot Cheetos has been one of PepsiCo's greatest snack food successes and opened the path to numerous spicy products aimed at the Latino market and beyond. This story has been disputed by various Frito-Lay sources and a *Los Angeles Times* exposé, but the rise of Montañez to an important executive position and his successful marketing of this and other products is undisputed.

Sources: Montañez, Richard, "Richard Montañez," *Latino Leaders Speak*, pp. 149–160; "The man who didn't invent Flamin' Hot Cheetos," *Los Angeles Times* 16 March 2021: https://www.latimes.com/business/story/2021-05-16/flamin-hot-cheetos-richard-montanez.

RELIGION

1509 ♦ Pope Julius II authorized the Catholic kings of Spain to administer the Catholic Church in the Americas in exchange for underwriting the costs of evangelization in the New World. In 1511, he issued a bull, the Pontifex Romana, which established various dioceses in the New World. This was the official introduction of Christianity to the New World.

Sources: Kanellos, *Chronology of Hispanic American History*, p. 26.

1511 ♦ The Diocese of San Juan Bautista (Puerto Rico) was established by Pope Julius II. The first bishop for Puerto Rico, Alonso Manso (1460–1539), was named that year; in effect, he became the first bishop to be named in the Americas and the first bishop in lands that are now part of the United States. He said his first Mass in Puerto Rico in 1513. He also became the first inquisitor in the Americas and functioned as such until he was replaced by Rodrigo Bastidas (?–1570) in 1539.

Sources: Kanellos, *Chronology of Hispanic American History*, p. 27.

1512 ♦ The first cathedral, Santo Domingo, and the first hospital that belonged to the Dominicans, also named Santo Domingo, were built by the Spaniards on the island of Española (now Hispaniola). The first school was also located there.

Sources: Kanellos, *Chronology of Hispanic American History*, p. 27.

1521 ♦ The first Catholic priests to set foot in what would later become the United States were the missionaries in Juan Ponce de León's (1474–1521) abortive mission to colonize Florida. Subsequent expeditions to colonize Florida during the 16th century also had missionaries with them; for the most part, they were Dominicans and Franciscans. In 1567, Jesuit missionaries arrived to reinforce the efforts to Christianize the Indians.

Sources: Fontana, *Entrada*, p. 47.

1531 ♦ The first appearance of the Virgin Mary in the New World reportedly took place in Mexico. According to the Catholic faithful, on December 12, the Virgin Mary, Our Lady of Guadalupe, a version of the Spanish Virgin of Guadalupe, appeared to the Indian Juan Diego (1474–1548) on the hill of Tepeyac, just outside Mexico City. She appeared to Juan Diego with Indian features on the site of a temple devoted to the Aztec goddess Malintzin and miraculously caused her image to be emblazoned on his *tilma*, a type of poncho. This image is the one guarded at today's Shrine of the Virgin of Guadalupe, built on the original site, and duplicated in the thousands of churches bearing the Virgin's name wherever Mexicans live. The Virgin of Guadalupe was named the patron saint of Mexico and the Americas and has become a symbol of the Catholic Church in those countries, a church for Indians, *mestizos*, and Creoles. The miraculous appearance led to the rapid and massive conversion of many of the Amerindian peoples in Mexico and the other Indian lands being conquered and incorporated by the Spaniards. By the time of Father Miguel Hidalgo's shout for independence from Spain in 1810, the cult of the Virgin of Guadalupe had become so strong among Indians, *mestizos*, and Creoles that he invoked her name as a rallying cry. From then on, she became a symbol of Mexican nationalism.

Sources: Kanellos, *Chronology of Hispanic American History*, p. 34.

1565 ♦ The first sustained religious conversion and ministering to the Indians in what would become the United States began with Pedro Menéndez de Avilés's (1519–1574) colonization of La Florida. In 1566, the Nombre de Dios Mission was established at what is today the northern edge of Saint Augustine, Florida. It was the longest-surviving mission in La Florida, the only one existing beyond 1706 in its original location. In all, there were more missions established in Florida (some 100) than in California (40), the latter being built much later. The Florida missions stretched from the coast of what became South Carolina across north Florida to the vicinity of Marianna. Jesuits made the initial inroads among the Calusa and Tequesta Indians of south Florida and the Guale and Escamacu Indians of Georgia and South Carolina. The Franciscans began working these areas in 1753, especially among the Timucua Indians.

Our Lady of La Leche Shrine in St. Augustine, Florida, was founded in 1609 and is the oldest Catholic shrine in the United States.

Sources: Fontana, *Entrada*, pp. 47, 71; Henderson and Mormino, *Spanish Pathways in Florida*, pp. 140–142.

1565 ♦ Some historians claim that the first Thanksgiving held in what would become the United States was that celebrated by priests and Timucua Indians sharing a feast after Mass was said by the priests in Pedro Menéndez de Avilés's (1519–1574) colonizing mission. Today, a stainless steel cross and a chapel mark the site of these events, which led to the establishment of the first Catholic parish, Nuestra Señora de la Leche (Our Lady of Milk), in what would become part of the continental United States.

Sources: Florida Department of State, *Florida Cuban Heritage Trail*, p. 56.

1566 ♦ Father Pedro Martínez (1533–1566) became the first Jesuit missionary to be martyred by the Indians; he was clubbed to death near present-day Cumberland Island.

Sources: Fontana, *Entrada*, p. 48.

1573 ♦ The Franciscan order arrived in Florida to establish the first missions in lands that would later become the United States. A century later, their missions would extend along the east coast of North America from Saint Augustine, Florida, to North Carolina. The Franciscans also established a string of missions from Saint Augustine westward to present-day Tallahassee. In the 17th century, the Franciscans established more missions and acculturated more Indians in northern New Spain—what would become the Southwest of the United States—than any other order.

Sources: Kanellos, *Chronology of Hispanic American History*, p. 46.

1602 ♦ The first Christian parish in the United States was founded in Saint Augustine. The Cathedral of Saint Augustine today houses a replica of the chapel of the church first founded on that site in 1602.

Sources: Fontana, *Entrada*, p. 49.

1690 ♦ On May 24, 1690, the first permanent Spanish settlement in Texas, San Francisco de los Tejas, was founded near the Neches River by two Spanish priests, Father Damián Massanet and Father Miguel de Fontcuberta (?–1691).

Sources: Kanellos, *Chronology of Hispanic American History*, p. 52.

1691 ♦ Father Eusebio Kino (1645–1711), an untiring Jesuit missionary, made the first inroads into Arizona. By 1700, Kino had established a mission at San Xavier del Bac, near present-day Tucson; he later established other missions in Arizona, including Nuestra Señora de los Dolores, Santa Gertrudis de Saric, San José de Imuris, Nuestra Señora de los Remedios, and San Cayetano de Tumacacori.

Sources: Kanellos, *Chronology of Hispanic American History*, p. 52.

1699 ♦ The first religious book in the Spanish language to be published in the United States was Cotton Mather's *La fe del Christiano: en veinticuatro articulos de la institutción de Christo embiada a los españoles, para que abran sus ojos, para que se conviertan de las Tinieblas a la luz, y de la potestad de Satanás a Dios: para que reciban por la fe que es en Jesus Christo, remisión de pecado, y suerte entre los santificados* (The Faith of the Christian: In Twenty-four Articles on the Christian Institution Sent to the Spanish So That They Might Open Their Eyes in Order for Them to Convert from Darkness to Light, and from the Power of Satan to God: So That They Receive Through Faith in Jesus Christ the Remission of Their Sins and the Fortune of the Sanctified). This was the first publication in what would become a large industry in the United States: the publication of religious books in Spanish, especially by Protestant denominations wishing to convert Hispanics.

Sources: Online Computer Library Center.

1769 ♦ On July 3, 1769, Fray Junípero Serra (1713–1784) established the first mission in Alta California at the site of present-day San Diego. Serra eventually founded 10 missions, traveled more than 10,000 miles on foot, and converted close to 6,800 Amerindians.

Sources: Kanellos, *Chronology of Hispanic American History*, p. 58.

c. 1790 ♦ The Brotherhood of Penitentes, a mystic lay order, was first introduced to New Mexico from New Spain (Mexico). In a province far from the metropolitan centers and the reach of the established Church, the Penitentes took on many of the responsibilities of priests and of government,

Founded in 1769 by Fray Junípero Serra, Mission San Diego de Alcalá was the first mission established in California.

enforcing law, order, and religiosity on the frontier. Although some of their practices, such as flagellation, harkened back to medieval Christianity, the Penitentes were responsible for the survival of the faith and the conservation of many religious and cultural practices on the frontier.

Sources: Rosaldo et al., *Chicano*, pp. 137–145.

1812 ♦ The first book by a Hispanic promoting freedom of religion was written anonymously and published in Philadelphia. It was entitled *A todos los que habitan las islas y el vasto continente de la América española: obrita curiosa, interesante, y agradable seguida de un discurso sobre la intolerancia religiosa* (To All Who Inhabit the Islands and the Vast Continent of Spanish America: A

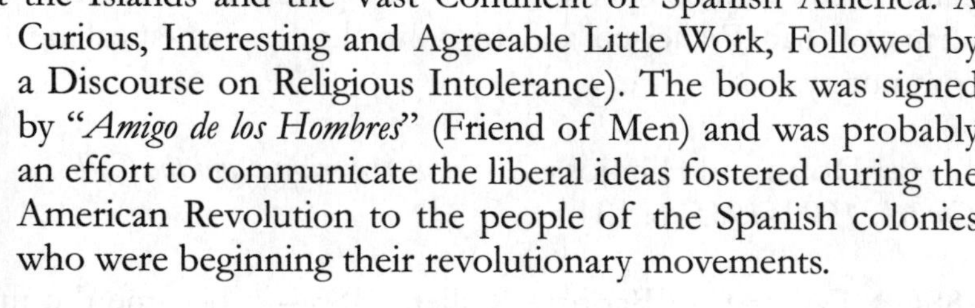

Curious, Interesting and Agreeable Little Work, Followed by a Discourse on Religious Intolerance). The book was signed by "*Amigo de los Hombres*" (Friend of Men) and was probably an effort to communicate the liberal ideas fostered during the American Revolution to the people of the Spanish colonies who were beginning their revolutionary movements.

Sources: Online Computer Library Center.

Francisco García Diego y Moreno

1840 ♦ Francisco García Diego y Moreno (1785–1846) became the first Catholic bishop of California. The seat of the first bishopric was San Diego, and the diocese included both California and Baja California. García Diego y Moreno ordained the first priests in California in June 1842 at Mission Santa Barbara.

Sources: Meier and Rivera, *Dictionary of Mexican American History*, p. 143.

1844 ♦ The first Catholic seminary was founded in California near Mission Santa Inés. Bishop Francisco García Diego y Moreno founded the seminary to prepare priests for service in California and Baja California.

Sources: Meier and Rivera, *Dictionary of Mexican American History*, p. 143.

1857 ♦ Father Antonio José Martínez (1793–1867) became the first priest to be excommunicated by the Catholic Church in the United States. After repeated battles with the new bishop of New Mexico, John Baptiste Lamy, who Martínez believed was prejudiced against New Mexicans, Bishop Lamy excommunicated the priest for insubordination. Martínez formed his own schismatic church, which he led until his death on July 28, 1867.

Sources: Meier and Rivera, *Dictionary of Mexican American History*, p. 10.

1865 ♦ Bishop José Sadoc Alemany (1814–1888) appointed the first pastor in the United States to specifically serve a Hispanic community. He named Father Gabriel Serrano *pastor hispanorium*. Serrano was appointed to work with the Spanish-speaking community in San Francisco.

Sources: Dolan and Hinojosa, *Mexican Americans and the Catholic Church, 1900–1965*, p. 134.

1875 ♦ Bishop José Sadoc Alemany (1814–1888) established the Our Lady of Guadalupe parish as the first national Hispanic parish to tend specifically to the Spanish-speaking residents of San Francisco and to unite the Spanish-speaking community.

José Sadoc Alemany

Sources: Dolan and Hinojosa, *Mexican Americans and the Catholic Church, 1900–1965*, p. 134.

1884 ♦ Father Jean Baptiste Ralliere (1834–?) became the first person to collect the Spanish religious songs of New Mexico and publish them for use by local churches in New Mexico. Entitled *Cánticos espirituales recogidos por el Padre Juan B. Ralliere* (Spiritual Canticles Collected by Father Juan B. Ralliere), the successful hymnal was used well into the 20th century.

Sources: Dolan and Hinojosa, *Mexican Americans and the Catholic Church, 1900–1965*, p. 29.

1897 ♦ A group of Los Angeles Catholic churchwomen established the first Latino settlement house in the United States, El Hogar Feliz (The Happy Home), to serve the Mexican community. The house included a clinic and a school. After operating at various sites, the school finally settled next to the Plaza Church in the heart of the Mexican community.

Sources: Dolan and Hinojosa, *Mexican Americans and the Catholic Church, 1900–1965*, p. 156.

1917 ♦ Brother Angélico Chávez (1910–1996) became the first native New Mexican to become a Franciscan friar. From the time of his ordination in 1917, at the age of 27, until the age of 62, he served as pastor in several towns and Indian pueblos in New Mexico. Chávez is also known as the greatest religious poet of U.S. Hispanic origin.

Sources: "Angélico Chávez," *Dictionary of Literary Biography, Vol. 82: Chicano Writers*, pp. 86–90.

1933 ♦ The first group of nuns whose mission was to work exclusively with Latinos in the United States was founded. The Missionary Catechists of Divine Providence worked among the poor Mexicans and Mexican Americans in south Texas. In 1946, the group was approved as an official branch of the Sisters of Divine Providence for Mexican Americans.

Sources: Dolan and Deck, *Hispanic Catholic Culture in the United States*, p. 188; Dolan and Hinojosa, *Mexican Americans and the Catholic Church, 1900–1965*, pp. 66–67.

1936 ♦ Mariano S. Garriga (1886–1965) was appointed bishop of the diocese of Corpus Christi, thus becoming the first Latino and first Mexican American to be named a Catholic bishop in modern times. No other Latino Catholic bishop was named until the appointment of Patricio Flores (1929–2017) to the diocese of San Antonio in 1970. Before the 1970s were over, eight other Hispanics had been named to bishoprics, thus serving the needs of the burgeoning Latino population in the Church.

Sources: Meier and Rivera, *Dictionary of Mexican American History*, pp. 86, 144.

1944 ♦ The first seminar on the Spanish-speaking community within the Catholic Church in the United States was held in San Antonio, Texas, under

1945: The Bishop's Committee for the Spanish-Speaking

In 1945 the Bishop's Committee for the Spanish-Speaking was founded by the Catholic Church to care for the spiritual and social welfare of Latino Catholics, at first in the four episcopal provinces of Los Angeles, Santa Fe, Denver, and San Antonio. In 1964, the committee became national, extending everywhere in the United States where there were considerable concentrations of Latinos. The Bishop's Committee was extended through diocesan-level councils in these Latino population centers. Most of the leaders of these councils were Latino laypersons. The first projects undertaken included the construction of clinics, settlement houses, and community and catechetical centers. Later phases extended programs to migrant workers and provided education and recreation for the young. By the early 1960s, representatives of some 70 dioceses worked with the committee. *Sources:* Dolan and Deck, *Hispanic Catholic Culture in the United States*, pp. 134–135, 234–236; Dolan and Hinojosa, *Mexican Americans and the Catholic Church, 1900–1965*, pp. 113–116.

the sponsorship of Archbishop Robert E. Lucey. Fifty delegates from western and southwestern states met for three days to discuss the condition of Latinos within the Church. This and following meetings led to the formation of Catholic councils for the Spanish-speaking in 1945.

Sources: Dolan and Deck, *Hispanic Catholic Culture in the United States*, pp. 133–134.

1953 ♦ Spanish American Catholic Action was founded in New York City under Francis Cardinal Spellman, mostly to deal with Puerto Ricans and their culture within the Catholic Church. Under its auspices, the famed priest Ivan Illich (1926–2002) set up his Institute for Intercultural Communication in Ponce, Puerto Rico.

Sources: Dolan and Deck, *Hispanic Catholic Culture in the United States*, p. 137.

1957 ♦ The first *cursillo*, or short course on Christianity, given by Latino laymen in order to reenergize Latino Catholics was given in Waco, Texas. The *cursillo* grew into a dynamic movement within Latino Catholic communities in the United States, building community solidarity and lay leadership. The *cursillo* movement even became one of the bases on which the United Farm Workers began its union in 1965.

Sources: Dolan and Deck, *Hispanic Catholic Culture in the United States*, pp. 216–220; Dolan and Hinojosa, *Mexican Americans and the Catholic Church, 1900–1965*, pp. 116–119, 222–224.

1958 ♦ The Caballeros de San Juan (Knights of Saint John), an organization under the auspices of the Catholic Church, became the largest society of Spanish-speaking people in the Midwest as the number of Puerto Ricans migrating there exploded.

Sources: Dolan and Hinojosa, *Mexican Americans and the Catholic Church, 1900–1965*, p. 291.

1959 ♦ The Catholic Church in Miami established the first center to assist Cuban refugees, the Centro Hispano Católico. The center offered such services as housing and job referrals, English classes, a day nursery, educational programs for children, an outpatient clinic, small loans, and used clothing, among other items.

Sources: García, *Havana USA*, p. 19.

1963 ♦ Saint Vincent de Paul Seminary in Boynton Beach, Florida, became the nation's first bilingual, multicultural seminary in order to deal with the explosion of the Latino population that resulted from the number of Cubans coming into exile in the United States.

Sources: Dolan and Deck, *Hispanic Catholic Culture in the United States*, p. 193.

1965 ♦ The Migrant Ministry of the National Council of Churches, a Protestant organization, became the first religious group in the history of labor organizing to support the formation of a union among farm workers and to offer long-term support for their efforts. From the beginning of the United Farm Workers Union, led by César Chávez (1927–1993), members of the Migrant Ministry walked alongside the workers on the picket lines. This support came from a Protestant organization, whereas Catholic parish priests refused to support the predominantly Catholic farm workers at first.

Sources: Dolan and Deck, *Hispanic Catholic Culture in the United States*, p. 147.

1969 ♦ Padres Asociados para Derechos Religiosos, Educativos y Sociales (Priests United for Religious, Economic and Social Rights; PADRES) was the first organization of Mexican American priests to press for services to the Spanish-speaking within the Catholic Church. Some 50 Mexican American priests met on October 7–9, 1969, in San Antonio, Texas, to found the organization and draft 27 resolutions, one of which called for the naming of native Latino bishops. From its inception, the organization participated in civil rights and labor movement struggles of Mexican Americans in the Southwest and pushed for reforms in the Church. By the time of its 1975 national convention, PADRES counted four Hispanic bishops in its membership.

Sources: Dolan and Deck, *Hispanic Catholic Culture in the United States*, p. 154.

1970 ♦ Patricio Flores (1929–2017) became the first native-born Latino bishop of the Catholic Church in the United States when Archbishop Francis J. Furey named him auxiliary bishop. During his first few years after elevation to bishop, Flores functioned as the unofficial shepherd of Hispanics in the United States, lending his support to the important causes of Hispanics, including the farm workers' union and the National Chicano Moratorium on the Vietnam War. He also served for a number of years as chair of the Texas Advisory Committee to the U.S. Commission on Civil Rights. Flores later rose to archbishop. Between 1970 and 1992, 22 other Latino bishops were named.

Sources: Dolan and Deck, *Hispanic Catholic Culture in the United States*, pp. 149–150.

1971 ♦ The Catholic Church established the first institute for training Latinos for the ministry, the Mexican American Cultural Center in San Antonio, Texas. Serving as an entry point for Latin American liberation theology, the center administered courses to some 9,000 laypersons and clergy, half of whom were Anglos. The courses dealt with everything from culture and pastoral service to research and leadership development.

Sources: Dolan and Deck, *Hispanic Catholic Culture in the United States*, p. 156.

1971: Las Hermanas

Las Hermanas, an organization of 50 Latina Catholic nuns, was formed in 1971 to promote "effective and active service to the Hispanic people" in the fields of education, health, pastoral work, and sociology. As one of its first issues, Las Hermanas addressed the cause of more than 1,000 Mexican nuns working in seminaries, retreat houses, and convents in the United States doing domestic work rather than ministering to the needs of the Hispanic lay community in the United States. Las Hermanas also lobbied for the naming of Hispanic bishops and for direct services to Latino communities. *Sources:* Dolan and Deck, *Hispanic Catholic Culture in the United States*, pp. 152–153, 261–266.

1972 ♦ The First National Hispanic Pastoral Encounter (*Encuentro*) took place in Washington, D.C. It was designed to assess the relationship of the Catholic Church with Latinos in the United States. Demands were made for representation of Latinos in the Church and appropriation of resources. The second pastoral encounter met in 1977, and subsequent meetings have been held every few years.

Sources: Dolan and Deck, *Hispanic Catholic Culture in the United States*, pp. 111, 142–144.

1973 ♦ New Mexico–born teacher and clergyman Robert Sánchez (1934–) became the first Mexican American archbishop of the Catholic Church chosen by the pope to be the archbishop of Santa Fe.

Sources: Meier and Rivera, *Dictionary of Mexican American History*, p. 318.

1973 ♦ The first wholesale institutional support by the Catholic Church for the union effort of farm workers came with the vote of the Catholic bishops to support the national grape and lettuce boycotts. The bishops requested the legislature and the governor of California to authorize secret, free elections for the farm workers to choose the union that would represent them. The bishops supported the establishment of the Agricultural Labor Relations Board to mediate disputes between the union and the growers.

Sources: Dolan and Deck, *Hispanic Catholic Culture in the United States*, p. 148.

1973 ♦ San Antonian Carlos Rosas (1939–2020) became the first person to compose Mexican American songs to be sung at Catholic Mass. Among his most popular compositions for Mass, many of which are still sung, are "*Virgencita, Bendice Estos Dones*" (Little Virgin, Bless These Gifts), "*Misa de San Juan*" (Saint John's Mass), and "*Rosas de Tepeyac*" (Roses of Tepeyac).

Sources: Dolan and Deck, *Hispanic Catholic Culture in the United States*, p. 385.

1974 ♦ Under the leadership of Pablo Sedillo, the National Conference of Catholic Bishops' (NCCB) Committee for the Spanish-Speaking for the first time rises to the top of the Church hierarchy in the United States, becoming the secretariat for the Spanish-speaking.

Sources: Dolan and Deck, *Hispanic Catholic Culture in the United States*, p. 139.

1974 ♦ Allan Figueroa Deck, S.J. (1945–), became the first Latino to earn a doctorate in theology. He obtained his degree from Fordham University in

New York City. Today, Father Figueroa Deck is a lecturer and Distinguished Scholar of Pastoral Theology and Latino Studies at Loyola Marymount University in Los Angeles. He is also the editor of the book *Frontiers of Hispanic Theology in the United States.*

Sources: Dolan and Deck, *Hispanic Catholic Culture in the United States*, p. 192.

1977 ♦ The first national meeting of Latino catechists took place in Corona, California, in December 1977. Its purpose was to identify catechetical needs of the Latino community. The meeting was made possible with a grant from the American Board of Catholic Missions.

Sources: Dolan and Deck, *Hispanic Catholic Culture in the United States*, p. 190.

1977 ♦ The Catholic Church established the first National Hispanic Youth Task Force in response to initiatives by Latino youth in the Northeast, who had earlier established Concilio Pastoral Juvenil (Youth Pastoral Council).

Sources: Dolan and Deck, *Hispanic Catholic Culture in the United States*, p. 295.

1979 ♦ Patricio Flores (1929–2017) became the first Mexican American to be named an archbishop of the Catholic Church. Born Patricio Fernández Flores in Ganado, Texas, the seventh of nine children, Flores attended Saint Mary's Seminary in La Porte, Texas, and Saint Mary's Seminary in Houston. He was ordained a Catholic priest on May 26, 1956, and served in a variety of functions in the diocese of Galveston-Houston.

He became the director of the Bishop's Committee for the Spanish-Speaking, serving until March 18, 1970, when Pope Paul VI appointed him to serve as auxiliary to the archbishop of San Antonio. On May 5, 1970, he was consecrated a bishop. Bishop Flores was the first Mexican American elevated to the hierarchy of the Catholic Church in the United States since 1936. On May 29, 1978, Bishop Flores was installed as the bishop of the diocese of El Paso, where he served until he was installed as the archbishop of San Antonio on October 13, 1979.

Flores pioneered programs within the Church and in government on behalf of the civil rights of Hispanics and immigrants. In 1983, he was one of four bishops elected to represent the hierarchy of the United States at the Synod of Bishops in Rome; he was the first U.S. Hispanic ever selected. In 1986, he was awarded the Ellis Island Medal of Honor in honor of the Statue of Liberty's 100th birthday.

Sources: Kanellos, *Chronology of Hispanic American History*, pp. 195, 256.

1979 ♦ The Instituto de Liturgia Hispana (Hispanic Liturgy Institute) was founded as the first Catholic liturgy center to specifically serve the liturgical needs of the Latino Catholic community.

Sources: Dolan and Deck, *Hispanic Catholic Culture in the United States*, pp. 372–373.

1980 ♦ Cuban Catholic priest Father Felipe J. Estévez (1946–) became the first Latino rector of a seminary in the contemporary United States, serving at Saint Vincent de Paul Seminary in Boynton Beach, Florida.

Sources: Dolan and Deck, *Hispanic Catholic Culture in the United States*, p. 193.

1980 ♦ The first journal attending to Latino religious issues, *Apuntes: Reflexiones Teológicas Desde el Contexto Hispano-Latino* (Notes: Theological Reflections from the Hispanic-Latino Context), was founded as an ecumenical, bilingual journal providing theological, biblical, and historical reflection to Latinos and enriching the pastoral ministry and understanding of the Church. It was established under the aegis of the Mexican American Program (now called the Hispanic/Latino Ministries) of the United Methodist Church. The founding editor was Dr. Justo L. González (1937–), a prolific author on Latino religious history and theology. It was published at Southern Methodist University.

Sources: "Apuntes," SMU Scholar: https://scholar.smu.edu/apuntes/about.html.

1986 ♦ Minerva G. Carcaño (1954–) became the first Latina to be a United Methodist district superintendent, serving in West Texas, New Mexico, and Oregon. She had served as a pastor in churches in California and Texas. The United Methodist Church is the second largest Protestant denomination in the United States.

Sources: Kanellos, *Latino Almanac*, pp. 194–195.

1988 ♦ The first school to train Latino theologians in the United States was founded by Jesuit Father Allan Figueroa Deck (1945–) at Berkeley. The Academy of Hispanic Theology membership was limited to Latino clergy with a doctoral degree. The major objective of the academy was the development of an indigenous Latino theology in the United States.

Sources: Dolan and Deck, *Hispanic Catholic Culture in the United States*, p. 158.

1983: First Pastoral Letter on Latino Catholics

In 1983 the National Council of Catholic Bishops published its first pastoral letter dealing with Latino Catholics. Whereas previously, Latinos in the United States were seen by the Catholic Church as a problem, the letter signaled a turning point in the view of the Catholic hierarchy toward the Church's Latino constituency. Entitled "The Hispanic Presence; Challenge and Commitment," the letter stated, "We recognize the Hispanic community among us as a blessing from God." The letter recognized the particular history and culture of Latinos within the church and pledged that the church would accommodate and learn from them; "this Hispanic presence challenges us all to be more catholic, more open to diversity of religious expression." *Sources:* Dolan and Deck, *Hispanic Catholic Culture in the United States*, pp. 152–153.

1988 ♦ The Most Reverend Roberto O. González (1945–2024) became the youngest Catholic bishop in the United States upon being named auxiliary bishop of the archdiocese of Boston. He was also the first Latino bishop of Boston. In 1995, it was announced that González would succeed as the next bishop of Corpus Christi, Texas.

Sources: "Bishop Roberto O. González, OFM," Diocese of Corpus Christi: https://diocesecc.org/bishop-roberto-o-gonzalez-ofm.

1991 ♦ Latino ministry within the Catholic Church came of age when the first consortium of movements, institutes, regional offices for Latino ministry, and religious congregations was organized as the National Catholic Council for Hispanic Ministry (NCCHM). According to founder Father Allan Figueroa Deck (1945–), NCCHM was formed to promote the articulation of theological, pastoral, and social issues and concerns of special interest to Latinos. It conducts workshops, research, and publications and facilitates communication between grassroots communities and church, civic, and professional organizations. It held its first meeting at Mary Center in Burlingame, California, and its first major activity was the Hispanic Congress '92: Roots and Wings. Today, the council counts some 51 organizations as members, including regional offices of Hispanic ministry; professional associations of ministers, such as priests, deacons, and catechists; pastoral institutes and centers; church congregations; apostolic movements; and media and publishing organizations. Its first congress drew 750 participants in 1992.

Sources: Dolan and Deck, *Hispanic Catholic Culture in the United States*, p. 159; Rosazza, Marisa. "Distinctive Contributions of Hispanic Catholics," *Texas Catholic Herald*, pp. 20–21.

1992 ♦ Sister Anita de Luna (1935–2006) became the first Mexican American woman religious to be elected president of the Leadership Conference of Women Religious.

Sources: Dolan and Deck, *Hispanic Catholic Culture in the United States*, p. 188.

1992 ♦ María Canton became the first layperson (also the first woman and the first Latino) to be given the Pope Paul VI Award for Leadership in Evangelization by the National Council for Catholic Evangelization. Canton, a Cuban exile, started a storefront Catholic evangelization center in Miami soon after her escape from Cuba in the Mariel Boatlift.

Sources: Dolan and Deck, *Hispanic Catholic Culture in the United States*, p. 189.

1992 ♦ The Conference of Catholic Bishops was established in Washington, D.C., the first national secretariat for Hispanic affairs, with Pablo Sedillo as its first director.

Sources: Dolan and Deck, *Hispanic Catholic Culture in the United States*, p. 234.

1995 ♦ Father Leopoldo Alard (1941–2003) was the first Latino to be elected a bishop of the Episcopal Church. On September 9, 1995, Alard was consecrated suffragen bishop of the Episcopal Diocese of Texas, a diocese of 49,000 square miles. The suffragen bishop acts as an assistant to the bishop. Previously, Alard had served 15 years as a parish priest and Episcopal school headmaster in Homestead, Florida. In 1986, he became the executive director of the Center for Hispanic Ministries in Austin, Texas. After that, he served as vicar of Santa Cruz, the diocese's fastest-growing parish, located near the Port of Houston. Alard was born in Matanzas, Cuba, and immigrated to the United States at the age of 20 after becoming disillusioned with Fidel Castro's revolution. Alard received his divinity degree from the Episcopal Seminary of the Caribbean in 1967.

Sources: Hispanic, December 1995, p. 12; *Houston Chronicle*, 13 May 1995, p. 29A.

Minerva G. Carcaño

2004 ♦ Minerva G. Carcaño (1954–) became the first Latina to serve as a bishop of the United Methodist Church. The

United Methodist Church is the second largest Protestant denomination in the United States. From 2004 to 2012, Carcaño served as bishop for the Phoenix Episcopal Area; in 2012, she became the resident bishop in the Los Angeles Episcopal Area; and in 2016, she was bishop in the San Francsico Episcopal Area.

Sources: Kanellos, *Latino Almanac*, pp. 194–195.

SCIENCE AND EXPLORATION

Explorers and Adventurers

Juan Ponce de León

1509 ♦ Juan Ponce de León (1460–1520) colonized the first New World area to later become part of the United States, the island of San Juan Bautista (Puerto Rico). He was then appointed governor as a reward for his labors. Ponce de León was noted for putting down Indian uprisings in Puerto Rico. He was removed as governor of the island in 1511, and he returned to Spain in 1512.

Sources: Kanellos, *Chronology of Hispanic American History*, pp. 24, 26.

1513 ♦ On February 4, 1513, the Gulf Stream was discovered by pilot Antonio de Alaminos during Juan Ponce de León's (1460–1520) voyage to Florida. Antonio de Alaminos had served as the pilot on Christopher Columbus's fourth voyage (1502–1504). This discovery resulted in Havana's becoming a major port of assembly and Florida's becoming a strategic stopping place for voyages. The current runs from the Straits of Florida into the Bahama Channel, past the coast of the Carolinas into the open ocean, where it forks northward to Norway and east to the Azores. Spanish ships, therefore, headed for the Azores, refitted, and returned to Spain.

Sources: Kanellos, *Chronology of Hispanic American History*, p. 30.

1513 ♦ Juan Ponce de León (1460–1520) became the first European to explore the mainland of what would become the United States. In negotiations with the Spanish Crown, it was decided that Ponce de León would lead expeditions to settle Bimini (Florida). He had to cover expenses himself but would receive 10 percent of all royal revenues derived from the exploitation of Bimini. Ponce de León's expedition left Spain on March 4, 1513, and arrived at the coast of Florida on April 3. After exploring the coast, he returned to Spain to make a report to the Council of the Indies and to make new proposals to the Crown. He was granted new concessions and appointed captain general of an armada against the Carib Indians. In 1520, Ponce de León set out on his last journey to take possession of Florida for the Crown. His expedition was subsequently destroyed by the Indians of the peninsula, and Ponce de León returned to Cuba with an arrow wound that took his life.

Sources: Kanellos, *Chronology of Hispanic American History*, p. 13.

1519 ♦ Alonso Alvarez de Pineda (1494–1520) discovered the coast of the Gulf of Mexico and claimed Texas for Spain. The first map to chart the entire Gulf of Mexico was created from information from this exploration. Alvarez de Pineda's map is the first document of Southwestern history.

Sources: Chipman, *Spanish Texas, 1519–1821*, p. 243; Fontana, *Entrada*, p. 17.

1520 ♦ Explorer Alonso Alvarez de Pineda (1494–1520) settled the question of Florida's geography, proving that it is not an island but part of a vast continent. He, in effect, proved the existence of North America.

Sources: Kanellos, *Chronology of Hispanic American History*, p. 33.

1524 ♦ Esteban Gómez (1483–1538) was the first Hispanic to explore the northeastern coast of North America in search of a passage to the Orient. After leaving from La Coruña, Spain, and crossing the Atlantic, he explored from the coast of Nova Scotia down to Florida. Gómez went on to explore Hudson Bay and the Delaware and Connecticut rivers some 80 years before Henry Hudson. His exploration contributed to many of the maps of the coast that were created during the 16th century.

Sources: Fontana, *Entrada*, pp. 18–19.

1526 ♦ San Miguel de Guadalupe, the first European settlement in what is now the United States, was founded by the Spaniards on the coast of present-day Georgia near the Savannah River. Founded by Lucas Vásquez de Ayllon (1489–1526) in what was then called La Florida, the colony was abandoned in early 1592 after more than 400 people had died of disease and hunger.

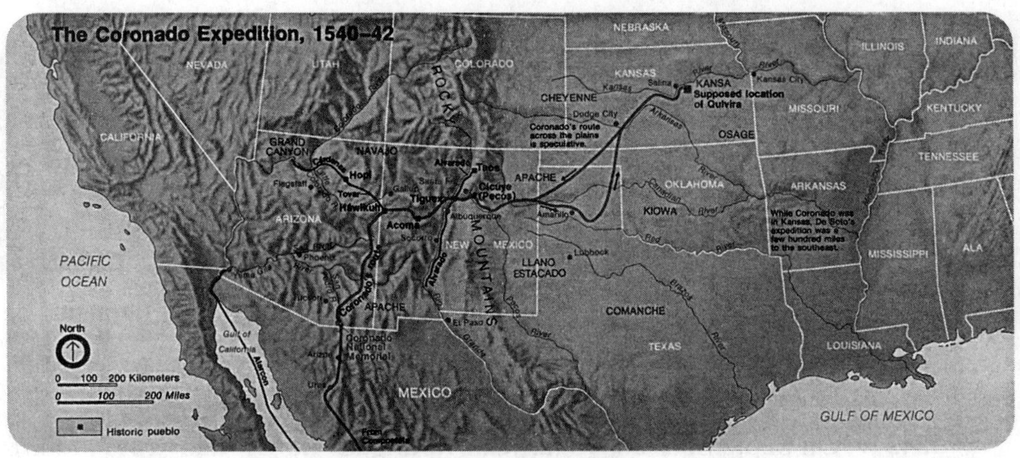

The route of the Coronado expedition (courtesy of the University of Texas Libraries, the University of Texas at Austin).

Sources: Weber, David J. *The Spanish Frontier in North America.* Yale University Press, 2014, p. 31.

1540 ♦ Francisco Vásquez de Coronado (1510–1554) and the members of his expedition became the first Europeans to explore the Grand Canyon. In 1540, Coronado set out from Mexico (New Spain) leading several hundred Spaniards and Indian allies on an expedition financed by his wife to search for Cíbola (or Quivira), where the seven cities of gold were rumored to be located. Along the way north into the present-day Southwest, Coronado conquered various Indian tribes, including Zunis, living in what were thought to be the cities of gold. On August 25, 1540, the expedition encountered the Grand Canyon; they later encountered the Rio Grande, which they named Nuestra Señora (Our Lady). All along the way, the Europeans had their first encounters, some peaceful, others violent, with many native groups; included among these were the massacres of the Tiguex and Cicuye Indians. Coronado never found the supposed cities of gold but reached as far north as today's state of Nebraska. Coronado wrote to the king that he had found lands poor in metals but rich in livestock and very suitable for farming; however, Coronado had traveled and explored more land in the shortest period of time than any other explorer to that date. In so doing, he prepared the way for the future settlement of what became the American Southwest. He returned to Nueva Galicia in 1541. He died in Mexico City in 1554.

Sources: Winship, George Parker, trans. and ed., *The Journey of Coronado 1540–1542*, Fulcrum Publishing, 1990.

1541 ♦ From 1539 to 1542, Hernando de Soto (c. 1497–1542) explored the present states of Florida, Alabama, Mississippi, Tennessee, North Carolina, Arkansas, and Louisiana. In May 1541, he arrived at the Mississippi River, the largest river he had ever seen. He named it Río Grande de la Florida (Great River of Florida). De Soto and his men were the first Europeans to see the Mississippi River. During the course of his journeys, De Soto lost 1,000 men and then also took ill and died at the age of 42.

Hernando de Soto

Sources: Fontana, *Entrada*, pp. 22–25.

1542 ♦ On September 28, 1542, Juan Rodríguez de Cabrillo (1499–1543), a Portuguese sailor commissioned by the Spanish viceroy, sailed north of Mexico's west coast in search of treasures. He entered and explored what he described as an excellent port: present-day San Diego, California.

Sources: Kanellos, *Chronology of Hispanic American History*, p. 40.

1560 ♦ The Spanish founded Santa Elena in what is today the state of South Carolina. San Miguel de Guadalupe in present-day Georgia, Santa Elena in today's South Carolina, and St. Augustine in Floria all predate Jamestown (in what is now Virginia), which was founded by the British in 1607 and the arrival of the Mayflower in 1620.

Sources: Kanellos, *Chronology of Hispanic American History*, p. 45.

1562 ♦ Diego Gutiérrez (1485–?), a pilot and a chart and instrument maker in Seville, created the largest, most complete print map of the Americas, relying on the data collected by Spain during its explorations. The map included information on the people and settlements and the fauna and flora from Tierra del Fuego all the way up to Labrador on the east coast of the hemisphere and to California on the west coast. His was the largest printed map of the hemisphere known up to that time.

Sources: Lockhart, James, "The Central Areas during and after the Conquest," in Herbert, *1492*, p. 146.

1565 ♦ The first permanent European settlement in what is now the United States was Saint Augustine, Florida, founded by Pedro Menéndez de Avilés (1519–1574) on the order of King Philip II of Spain. Menéndez de Avilés established seven settlements in all on the coast of La Florida. The Spaniards were welcomed by the Timucuan Indians, who gave the soldiers and set-

The chief of the Timucua people gave Pedro Menéndez de Avilés the tribe's great house.

tlers shelter in their huts. The site of the original village of Saint Augustine was moved a year later, in 1566, to a more strategic site. Saint Augustine became the most successful strategic post for the Spaniards in defending the Florida coast. It was the only one that endured storms, fires, famine, and raids by the French and English.

In 1586, the English privateer Francis Drake looted and burned Saint Augustine, forcing the villagers to flee to the forest. Once the privateer was gone, they returned to rebuild. During the 17th century, the city and other areas of Florida received a considerable number of emigrants from Spain and the Spanish Caribbean. The population of Saint Augustine grew to 2,000 by the turn of the 18th century. The city was afforded more security by the building of the San Marcos Fort, begun in 1672 and finished in 1756. In 1763, the region of the Florida peninsula called Eastern Florida—as opposed to Western Florida, which ranged from the Georgia coast to the Mississippi River—came under British control as a result of the Treaty of Paris. This area included Saint Augustine.

In 1783, under the Treaty of Versailles, Eastern Florida was returned to Spain. It remained a possession of Spain until 1821, when it was surrendered to the United States. Louisiana, which had been discovered by the Spanish but settled by the French from Canada, remained a French colony until 1763, when it, too, passed into Spanish possession as a result of the Treaty of Paris. Louisiana was ceded to France in 1801 but was sold to the United States by Napoleon in 1803.

Sources: Kanellos, *Chronology of Hispanic American History*, p. 45.

1590 ♦ Juan de Fuca (1536–1602) navigated his ships to the northern coast of present-day Washington State. Spanish maps from the period show the Strait of Juan de Fuca as a possible Northwest Passage.

Sources: Kanellos, *Chronology of Hispanic American History*, p. 47.

1602 ♦ With three ships, Sebastián Vizcaíno (1548–1624) explored and charted the coast of California. He identified Monterey as an ideal place for major Spanish settlement.

Sources: Fontana, *Entrada*, p. 69.

1693 ♦ A great Spanish Mexican scientist and mathematician of his time, Carlos de Sigüenza y Góngora (1645–1700) accompanied Admiral Andrés de Pez (1657–1723) on a scientific expedition into what is today the southeastern United States. Sigüenza y Góngora studied the topography, fauna, and flora and later published his findings in Mexico City, becoming the first scientist and university professor to study the region. He published his findings in his book *Descripción de la bahía de Santa María de Galve* (Description of the Bay of Santa María de Galve).

Sigüenza y Góngora authored numerous books in all the fields of his broad interests and was also one of the first to write scholarly accounts of territories that would become part of the United States. In addition to his book about the lands around the northeastern Gulf of Mexico, he also published *Historia de la provincia de Tejas* (History of the Province of Texas). Finally, his encyclopedic knowledge and study extended to include what might be considered anthropology today. He researched and wrote about the Aztecs and the Chichimecas in his books *Genealogía de los reyes mejicanos* (Genealogy of the Mexican [Mechica] Kings) and *Historia del imperio de los chichimecas* (History of the Chichimeca Empire). Sigüenza y Góngora died in 1700 in Mexico City. Unfortunately, a devastating fire in Mexico City in 1792 consumed many of his manuscripts.

Sources: Fontana, *Entrada*, p. 77.

1774 ♦ Led by a Spanish Franciscan missionary by the name of Pedro de Garcés (1780–1825), government official Juan Bautista de Anza (1735–1788) pioneered a route across the Sonora and Mohave deserts to southern California. Because of his success, he was next requested by the viceroy of Mexico to find a route to Alta California and lead soldiers and settlers there to found a colony on San Francisco Bay.

Sources: Meier and Rivera, *Dictionary of Mexican American History*, p. 17.

1775 ♦ Captain Bruno de Hezeta (1743–1807) explored and mapped the mouth of the Columbia River and its interior for 20 miles some 30 years before American explorers Lewis and Clark arrived there. A companion ship commanded by Peruvian Juan Francisco de la Bodega y Cuadra (1743–1794) got as far north as 58° 30' north latitude in Alaska.

Sources: Fontana, *Entrada*, pp. 181–182; Sánchez, Joseph P., "Hispanic American Heritage," in Viola and Margolis, *Seeds of Change*, p. 182.

1775 ♦ Retired soldier Manuel Butron (1727–1793) and his Amerindian wife received the first land grant in California, consisting of a few acres near the San Carlos Barromeo Mission close to Monterey. This land grant policy was developed in Spain to encourage settlement in its faraway lands and ensure agricultural productivity. During the Mexican regime, the number of land grants accelerated greatly so that by the time of the Anglo-American migration, most of the best land was already in the possession of Hispanic Californians.

Sources: Fontana, *Entrada*, p. 171.

1776 ♦ The first pioneers to make their way overland to California were led by Juan Bautista de Anza (1736–1788) from San Miguel de Horcasitas in Sonora, Mexico (New Spain), to the California coast, where they would establish the port and city of San Francisco, California. The pioneers founded the San Francisco Presidio on September 17, 1776, and the Dolores Mission in October. Father Pedro Font (1737–1781) was the first to give the name San Francisco to the bay. The train of wagons included some 240 persons (more colonists were picked up along the way); among them were soldiers and their families, cowboys, muleteers, and servants. They took along with them 302 head of beef cattle, 140 pack mules, and 340 saddle animals.

Juan Bautista de Anza

Sources: Fontana, *Entrada*, pp. 160–164, 172.

1777 ♦ The governor of Alta California, Felipe de Neve (1724–1784), established his capital in Monterey and also founded the village of San Jose with some of the settlers brought earlier by José Moraga (1745–1785).

Sources: Kanellos, *Chronology of Hispanic American History*, p. 58.

1779 ♦ Ignacio de Arteaga (1731–1783) sailed to the mouth of Prince William Sound in Alaska, named the port Santiago de Apostol, and claimed it for Spain; this was the northernmost point ever taken possession of by Spanish subjects.

Sources: Fontana, *Entrada*, p. 183.

1781 ♦ California governor Felipe de Neve (1724–1784) went south from Monterey with other settlers and established Nuestra Señora la Reina de los Angeles de Porciúncula (Los Angeles).

Sources: Kanellos, *Chronology of Hispanic American History*, p. 58.

Alejandro Malaspina

1790 ♦ Alejandro Malaspina (1754–1810) became the first man to explore and map the Pacific coast of North America. On a scientific expedition that included naturalists, astronomers, and artists in search of a northern route from the Pacific to the Atlantic oceans, Malaspina was finally deterred when an impassable glacier in Alaska blocked his path. That glacier is now known as Malaspina Glacier. Because of the Malaspina expedition, Spain was able to claim possessions as far north as Alaska and found settlements such as those in Valdez and Cordova. At Yakutat Bay, artists Tomás de Suria (1761–1844) and José Cardero (1766–1811) made drawings of the Tlingit people who inhabited the region. These are believed to be the first drawings by Europeans (or their Latino descendants in the New World) of Alaskan natives.

Sources: Fontana, *Entrada*, p. 186; *Hispanics in U.S. History*, p. 44.

1792 ♦ Naturalist José Mariano Mociño Suárez Losada (1857–1820), on an expedition led by Juan Francisco Bodega y Cuadra (1743–1794), was the first to study and describe the Nootka region of Alaska, leaving for posterity detailed written accounts of the native inhabitants. His companion, Atanasio Echeverría y Godoy (1771–1803), became the first artist to depict the plants, animals, people, and scenes in the Nootka region.

Sources: Fontana, *Entrada*, p. 186.

1806 ♦ When Zebulon Montgomery Pike crossed the Missouri River in his exploration of the West, he was actually following a trail blazed by Captain Facundo Melgares (1775–?) of Santa Fe, who had been trading among the Pawnees and working out peace treaties with them.

Sources: Sánchez, Joseph P., "Hispanic American Heritage," in Viola and Margolis, *Seeds of Change*, p. 182.

1842 ♦ The first man to discover and mine gold in California was a Mexican herder by the name of Francisco López. He made his find on March 19, 1842, in Feliciano Canyon near Los Angeles. Mexicans worked diggings from Los Angeles up to Santa Cruz from this time on, years prior to James Marshall's discovery at Sutter's Mill on January 24, 1848, which led to the California gold rush.

Sources: Meier and Rivera, *Dictionary of Mexican American History*, pp. 200–201.

1845 ♦ Andrés Castillero (c. 1830s–c. 1850s), a Mexican army captain, discovered mercury in red cinnabar rocks close to San Jose, California, and founded the New Almaden mine and mining town with local Indian and Mexican workers. But the outbreak of the Mexican-American War and his need for finances ended his and his workers' business. By 1850, the British company of Barron and Forbes had bought the mine, and it was later taken over by the New York Quicksilver Mining Corporation. The mine became the second largest producer of quicksilver in the world during the remainder of the 19th century.

Sources: Meier and Rivera, *Dictionary of Mexican American History*, pp. 253–255.

Space Exploration

Franklin Chang-Díaz

1986 ♦ Franklin Chang-Díaz (1950–) became the first Latino in space; the astronaut spoke to television viewers from the space shuttle *Columbia* in Spanish. Chang-Díaz was born and raised in Costa Rica, the grandchild on his paternal side of a Chinese immigrant to Costa Rica. Chang-Díaz immigrated to the United States in 1969 and studied mechanical engineering at the University of Connecticut. He received a Ph.D. in physics from the Massachusetts Institute of Technology in 1977 and three years later was chosen by National Aeronautics and Space Administration (NASA) for the space program.

Sources: "Chang-Díaz, Franklin," Internet Archive Current biography yearbook 2011: https://archive.org/details/currentbiography0000unse_z0h6/page/120/mode/2up.

1990 ♦ Mexican American Ellen Ochoa (1958–) became the first Latina to serve as an astronaut. Born in Los Angeles on May 10, 1958, Ochoa graduated as valedictorian from both high school and San Diego State University, where she majored in physics. Ochoa went on to Stanford University, where she earned both a master's degree and a Ph.D. in electrical engineering. Ochoa is also an accomplished researcher who has three patents in optical processing to her name.

Ellen Ochoa

Sources: Telgen and Kamp, *Latinas! Women of Achievement*, pp. 279–285.

1990 ♦ Adriana Ocampo (1955–), a science coordinator for the CalTech Jet Propulsion Laboratory in Pasadena, California, developed the concept for "Space Conference for the Americas: Prospects in Cooperation" in conjunc-

Adriana Ocampo

tion with the United Nations. The purpose of the conference, which was held in Costa Rica and has since been repeated in Chile, was to further cooperation among the Pan American countries in the areas of science and technology for peaceful uses of space. This conference followed in the wake of other conferences she helped to develop in Costa Rica, Colombia, Nigeria, Egypt, and Mexico to involve third world nations in the space program. In 2002, she was named one of the most important women in science by *Discover* magazine.

Sources: "Adriana Ocampo," NASA: https://science.nasa.gov/people/adriana-ocampo/.

2004 ♦ California-raised Joseph Michael Acabá (1967–) became the first U.S. astronaut of Puerto Rican heritage. He participated in his first space mission in 2009, had two more space flights, and later served as flight engineer at the International Space Station. During that time, he also had three spacewalks.

Joseph Michael Acabá

Sources: "NASA's New Astronaut Leader to Help Pick Next Moon Visitors," *Houston Chronicle,* 2 February 2023.

Frank Rubio

2023 ♦ Astronaut Frank Rubio (1975–) set the American record for the longest space flight of 371 days aboard the International Space Station. He logged more than 157 million miles during the mission and circled the globe nearly 6,000 times. Rubio is a flight surgeon and fighter pilot who had 1,100 hours of flying time. He began his career as an astronaut in 2017. The son of Salvadoran immigrants was raised in Miami, Florida, and graduated from the U.S. Military Academy.

Sources: "Record-breaking Army Astronaut Receives Rare Qualification Device," U.S. Army: https://www.army.mil/article/273930?a.

Agriculture

1493 ♦ Sugarcane was introduced to the New World by Christopher Columbus during his second voyage. Originally from India, the plant was taken first to Hispaniola and then to the rest of the Americas for its cultivation. The first sugar mill was built in 1508 or 1509 on Hispaniola. From there, New World sugar was shipped to Spain beginning in 1516. All the technology, plants, and technicians involved in sugar production were brought to the New World by the Spaniards. By 1523, there were 24 mills operating on the island.

Sources: Mintz, Sidney W., "Pleasure, Profit, and Satiation," in Viola and Margolis, *Seeds of Change*, p. 117.

1521 ♦ Spaniards Hernán Cortés (1485–1547) and Gregorio de Villalobos introduced ranching to Mexico when they imported cattle from Cuba for breeding purposes. This was the beginning of the ranching industry and culture on the mainland; it would travel north and eventually become one of the principal industries of the American Southwest. Not only were cattle introduced, but all of the components of ranch ecology, including cattle, sheep, goats, hogs, and the plant species these animals consume, were also introduced.

Sources: Bennett, Deb, and Robert S. Hoffmann, "Ranching in the New World," in Viola and Margolis, *Seeds of Change*, pp. 90–95.

1521 ♦ Spanish explorers took horses and cattle to Florida on Juan Ponce de León's (1460–1520) second trip. Hernando de Soto (1500–1542) was next to import livestock to Florida, including more than 300 horses and some cattle in 1539. It was in Florida that the Spanish established the first stock raising in what is now the United States. Missions spearheaded settlement and stock raising. By 1565, some stock raising was established around Saint Augustine and Tallahassee. The first ranchers raised cattle for local consumption but also smuggled stock to Cuba. Ranching was difficult in the swamps and tropics; it did not flourish as it later did in California and Texas. By 1800, the Spanish tax rolls showed only 34 ranches with some 15,000 to 20,000 cattle.

Sources: Slatta, *Cowboys of the Americas*, p. 10.

1535 ♦ Although horses were introduced by the Spaniards into areas that became present-day Florida as early as 1521, Antonio de Mendoza (1495–1552) was the first to bring horses to the mainland of the Americas for breeding purposes, introducing them into Mexico in 1535. By 1650, there were countless herds of mustangs in northwest Mexico, and they later made their way into the Great Plains of North America. The first breeding herds of horses were brought to Florida by Pedro Menéndez de Avilés (1519–1574) in 1565. Don Juan de Oñate's (c. 1550–1630) colonization of New Mexico brought more horses north in 1598. During the next three centuries, Santa Fe, New Mexico, served as the center for distribution of horses.

1564: Grapes Introduced to California

In 1564 Spanish Mexican missionaries introduced grapes to California, the future site of the most important wine industry in the United States. The European vine, *V. vinifera*, was introduced from Mexico and by 1600 was producing grapes principally for sacramental wine in and around San Diego and Los Angeles. In 1767, the Franciscan brothers introduced what was later called the mission grape. By the early 1800s, surplus wine was sold to consumers. *Sources:* Hobhouse, Henry, "New World, Vineyard to the Old," in Viola and Margolis, *Seeds of Change*, p. 61.

Sources: Bennett, Deb, and Robert S. Hoffmann, "Ranching in the New World," in Viola and Margolis, *Seeds of Change*, pp. 107–108.

1539 ♦ Hernando de Soto (1500–1542) drove a herd of pigs from Florida to Arkansas, with numerous pigs escaping along his path; these became the foundation for the feral populations of North America. Later populations of pigs were introduced by the Franciscan missionaries in Texas and elsewhere. The razorback, prized by hunters throughout the South, arose from these populations.

Sources: Bennett, Deb, and Robert S. Hoffman, "Ranching in the New World," in Viola and Margolis, *Seeds of Change*, p. 103.

1598 ♦ Cattle and ranching were first introduced north of the Rio Grande by Spanish Mexican colonists headed by Don Juan de Oñate (c. 1550–1630) when they crossed the river with 7,000 head of cattle somewhere near present-day El Paso into what became New Mexico. Besides cattle, Oñate brought in more than 4,000 head of shaggy sheep, which became the foundation of the churro breed of the Navajos. The first ranches along the Rio Grande in Texas were founded from 1659 to 1682. During the next century, cattle ranching flourished all along the north of the river, and by the 1830s, cattle had been driven from California to northern Oregon.

Sources: Bennett, Deb, and Robert S. Hoffman, "Ranching in the New World," in Viola and Margolis, *Seeds of Change*, pp. 98–100.

1600 ♦ The Spanish settlers along the Rio Grande Valley introduced the plow and beasts of burden to the Pueblo Indians, ushering in an agricultural technology that would endure for centuries in what would become the American Southwest. They also introduced irrigation and new craft techniques, such as those involved in carpentry and blacksmithing, and a new profit-driven economy.

Sources: Fontana, *Entrada*, pp. 80–81.

1600 ♦ A more efficient and rapid sugar mill was invented in Mexico or Peru and later disseminated throughout areas of the Americas engaged in sugar production. This was the vertical three-roller mill, which allowed for a quicker and more thorough extraction of sugar juice.

Sources: Mintz, Sidney W., "Pleasure, Profit, and Satiation," in Viola and Margolis, *Seeds of Change*, p. 120.

Ramón de la Sagra

1827 ♦ The first book on Cuban horticulture to be published in the United States, Ramón de la Sagra's (1798–1871) *Memorias para servir de introducción a la horticultura cubana* (Memories to Serve as Introduction to Cuban Horticulture), was issued in New York. This Spanish botanist also traveled widely in the United States and published a travel book, *Cinco meses en los Estados-Unidos de la América del Norte* (Five Months in the United States of North America), París (1836), which was one the first travel books on the United States written by a Hispanic author.

Sources: Online Computer Library Center.

1830 ♦ The first Longhorn cattle appeared, a result of the crossbreeding of the Spanish Retinto and animals brought to Texas by Anglo settlers. Immune to tick fever and accustomed to the tough brush country of south Texas, the Longhorn became the basis for the western livestock industry.

Sources: Slatta, *Cowboys of the Americas*, p. 19.

Medicine and Biology

1512 ♦ The first hospital in the Western Hemisphere was founded at the Cathedral of Santo Domingo in the city of that name on the island of Hispaniola. It was built by the Spaniards. The first school was also located there.

Sources: Kanellos, *Chronology of Hispanic American History*, p. 27.

The first hospital in the Southwest was located at the Alamo in San Antonio.

1536 ♦ The first social science and biological document of the indigenous peoples and the flora and fauna of the South and Southwest, particularly of the Amerindians of the region, was a report written in 1536 in Mexico City by three shipwrecked Europeans and an Afro-European, one of whom was Alvar Núñez Cabeza de Vaca (1490–1557). No other region in the present-day United States was described so early with so much detail.

Sources: Chipman, *Spanish Texas, 1519–1821*, pp. 243–246.

1805 ♦ The first hospital in the Southwest was founded in San Antonio, Texas, under Spanish rule. It was located in the Alamo. By 1806, the Alamo hospital was caring for 18 patients, with a waiting list of 20 others. It closed by 1814.

Sources: Chipman, *Spanish Texas, 1519–1821*, p. 258.

1807 ♦ The first medical publication by a Latino in the United States was Valentín de Foronda's (1751–1821) *Cartas presentadas a la Sociedad Filosófica de Philadelphia* (Letters Presented to the Philadelphia Philosophic Society), published by Duane in Philadelphia. In 1810, a Sephardic Jew, Jacob de la Motta (1789–1845), published another medical treatise: *An Investigation of the Properties and Effects of the Spiraea Trifoliata of Linnaeus, or Indian Physic.* In 1820, de la Motta gave an address to the Georgia Medical Society entitled "On the Causes of the Mortality among Strangers, during the Late Summer and Fall," which was later published.

Sources: Simonhoff, *Jewish Notables in America, 1776–1865*, pp. 189–192.

1823 ♦ The first book of prescriptions (pharmaceuticals) written and published in the Spanish language in what would become a state of the Union was published in Sonoma, California, by the Imprenta del Gobierno (Government Printing House) under the title *Botica general de los remedios experimentados; que a beneficio del Público se reimprime por su original en Cadiz* (General Collection of Proven Remedies; Reprinted from the Original of Cadiz for the Benefit of the Public).

Sources: Online Computer Library Center.

1827 ♦ The first handbook of medical treatments written by a Latino scholar was published in Philadelphia: *Compendio de la medicina: o medicina práctica ...* (Compendium of Medicine; or Practical Medicine ...) by Juan Manuel Venegas claimed to have drawn its remedies from observations of medicine in New Spain, presumably influenced by the medicine practiced by Native Americans.

Sources: Online Computer Library Center.

c. 1836 ♦ Sephardic Jew Jacob de la Motta (1789–1845) of Charleston, South Carolina, became the first Latino pharmacist on record when he bought and operated Apothecaries Hall, reputed to be the first pharmacy in the Americas, which supposedly started in 1780. The equipment, the brass scales, and the interior woodwork of this old pharmacy are housed today in the Charleston Museum.

Sources: Simonhoff, *Jewish Notables in America, 1776–1865*, p. 191.

1836 ♦ The first Latino known to have graduated from an Ivy League school (University of Pennsylvania) in medicine was David Camden DeLeón, who came from a multitalented Sephardic Jewish family in Charleston, South Carolina. After graduation in 1836, DeLeón enlisted in the army and was sent to the Florida tropics to treat the sick and wounded soldiers of the Seminole Wars. He later became a hero at the Battle of Chapultepec in the Mexican War and later a hero of the Confederacy in the U.S. Civil War. DeLeón became the first surgeon general of the Confederacy. After the defeat of the Confederacy, DeLeón moved to Mexico. At the request of President Ulysses S. Grant, DeLeón eventually returned to the United States and settled in New Mexico, where he practiced medicine and wrote for medical journals.

Sources: Simonhoff, *Jewish Notables in America, 1776–1865*, pp. 297–300.

Carlos Juan Finlay

1881 ♦ Carlos Juan Finlay (1833–1915), a Cuban doctor educated in Philadelphia, proposed that yellow fever was spread by the *Aedes aegypti* mosquito and was met with skepticism from the medical community. It was not until the American occupation of Cuba in 1900, when American soldiers were dying of the disease and Army doctor Major Walter Reed visited Finlay and observed his experiments, that the medical community took his work seriously enough to implement a program of eradication of the dreaded mosquito. Under the direction of engineer William Gorgas, the U.S. Army destroyed the swamps where the mosquito lived.

Sources: Hispanics in U.S. History, p. 8.

1900 ♦ The famous Mexican faith healer Teresa Urrea (1873–1906), known as La Santa de Cabora (The Saint from Cabora), was hired by an American medical company to make her talents available to the masses. By 1904, she had become disillusioned with the commercialism of the company and withdrew from her contract to continue working as a free agent in Clifton, Arizona.

Sources: Putnam, Frank B., "Teresa Urrea, 'The Saint of Cabora,'" *Southern California Quarterly*, 45 (September 1963), pp. 245–264.

1957 ♦ After many years of research, Mexican American virologist/bacteriologist Sarah Elizabeth Stewart (1905–1976) co-researched and published a paper, "The Induction of Neoplasms with a Substance Released from Mouse Tumors by Tissue Culture," in *Virology*, substantiating her concept that viruses can cause various types of cancer. The virus she identified turned out to cause some 20 types of tumors. Today, scientists have built on her research to identify such viruses and even develop vaccines against them, such as the human papilloma virus.

Sarah Elizabeth Stewart

Born in Jalisco, Mexico, to an Anglo-American mine owner and a Mexican homemaker, Stewart moved with her family to New Mexico during the Mexican Revolution. While working as one of the first women researchers at the National Institutes of Health, she obtained her Ph.D. from the University of Chicago in 1939. Shortly thereafter, she developed the theory that viruses could cause cancer but felt she needed a medical degree to do the research and gain credibility for her work; however, women were not yet allowed in medical schools. She thus accepted a position as an instructor of bacteriology at Georgetown University Medical School, where she was allowed to take medical courses for free and had access to the labs and facilities.

In 1947, Georgetown changed its policy and started to admit women; consequently, Stewart became the first woman, and first Latina, to earn a medical degree at that institution. She continued to overcome many barriers as a woman and as a theorist that cancer could be caused by viruses until finally publishing a series of papers resulting from experiments that proved her point and laid the groundwork for hundreds of microbiologists and oncologists in the decades to come.

Sources: McNeill, Leila, "The Woman Who Revealed the Missing Link Between Viruses and Cancer," *Smithsonian Magazine*, 17 June 2019: https://

www.smithsonianmag.com/science-nature/woman-who-revealed-missing-link-between-viruses-and-cancer-180972427/.

Severo Ochoa

1959 ♦ Biochemist and professor at New York University Severo Ochoa (1905–1993) became the first Latino to win a Nobel Prize in Physiology or Medicine. He shared the prize with his former student Arthur Kornberg for their work in discovering the enzymes that help produce nucleic acids. In effect, these two scientists had discovered how to synthesize both RNA and DNA. Ochoa was born in Spain but became a naturalized American citizen in 1956. He taught at universities in Spain, Germany, England, and the United States.

Sources: Hispanics in U.S. History, p. 83; Tardiff and Mabunda, *Dictionary of Hispanic Biography*, p. 621.

1965 ♦ California-born zoologist Evelyn Margaret Rivera (1929–2015) received the UNESCO Award from the International Cell Research Organization for her research on cancer and the biology of tumors.

Sources: "Obituary: Evelyn Margaret Rivera": https://www.dignitymemorial.com/obituaries/east-lansing-mi/evelyn-rivera-6300469.

1970 ♦ Celso Ramón García (1922–2004) became the first U.S.-born Latino to hold an endowed chair in medicine at an Ivy League medical school: the William Shippen Jr. Chair in Human Reproduction at the University of Pennsylvania Medical School. Born in New York City in 1921, García has held teaching positions at various universities from Harvard to the University of Puerto Rico.

Sources: Pearce, Jeremy, "Celso-Ramón García, 82, Helped Refine 'the Pill,'" *New York Times*, 16 February 2004.

1972 ♦ After his appointment as an assistant professor in the Wayne State School of Medicine in 1972, Puerto Rican anatomist José Alcalá (1940–) conducted the research that would make him the foremost expert on the cell makeup of the human eye lens. In his research, Alcalá developed laboratory methods to study the histology of ocular tissue, which ultimately helped to explain the development of cataracts, among other maladies of the eye.

Sources: Tardiff and Mabunda, *Dictionary of Hispanic Biography*, p. 8.

Rodolfo R. Llinás

1975 ♦ Neurobiologist Rodolfo R. Llinás (1934–) became the first Latino scientist to serve as editor of *Neuroscience Journal.* Born in Bogota, Colombia, Llinás is chairman emeritus of the Department of Physiology and Biophysiology of New York University, where he conducted structural and functional studies of neuronal systems and also studied the evolution and development of the central nervous system. He was also the chairman of NASA's Neurolab Science Working Group. In 1991, Llinás received UNESCO's Albert Einstein Medal. In 2018, he received the Ralph W. Gerard Prize in Neuroscience from the Society for Neuroscience.

Sources: Llinás, Rodolfo, ed., *Neurobiology of Cerebellar Evolution and Development.* Chicago: American Medical Association, 1969.

1975 ♦ José R. Coronado (1932–2011) became the first Latino to direct a major U.S. hospital, the Audie L. Murphy Veterans Hospital, a 704-bed tertiary facility and a 120-bed nursing home affiliated with the University of Texas Health Science Center at San Antonio. Coronado was born on April 3, 1932, in Benavides, Texas, and obtained an M.S. degree in educational administration from Texas A&I in Kingsville in 1959 and an M.S. in hospital administration from Baylor University in Waco in 1973. In 1995, he became director of the South Texas Veterans Healthcare System.

Sources: "Jose Coronado Obituary," *San Antonio Express-News:* https://www.legacy.com/us/obituaries/sanantonio/name/jose-coronado-obituary?id=10038664.

1978 ♦ Dr. Mario E. Ramírez (1926–2017) became the first Latino to be named by *Good Housekeeping* magazine as the Family Doctor of the Year. The family practitioner was born in Roma, Texas, and received his medical degree from the University of Tennessee College of Medicine in Knoxville in 1948.

Sources: "Dr. Mario E. Ramirez—Biography of a Doctor," UT Health/The Libraries: https://libguides.uthscsa.edu/c.php?g=924869&p=6704801.

1986 ♦ Antonia C. Novello (1944–) became the first Latino to serve as deputy director of one of the National Institutes of Health, the National Institute of Child Health and Human Development, where she nurtured a special interest in children with AIDS. At the time, she was also a clinical professor of pediatrics at Georgetown University Hospital. Novello became surgeon general in the George H. W. Bush and Bill Clinton administrations.

1989: First Hispanic U.S. Surgeon General

Antonia C. Novello (1944–) became the nation's first Hispanic surgeon general in 1989. Born and educated through medical school in Puerto Rico, Novello received a Ph.D. in medicine from the Johns Hopkins University School of Medicine in 1982. Prior to being named the nation's top doctor, Novello had become an international leader and respected researcher in children's health and nephrology. *Sources:* Telgen and Kamp, *Latinas! Women of Achievement*, pp. 273-278.

Sources: Telgen and Kamp, *Latinas! Women of Achievement*, pp. 273–278.

1992 ♦ One of the world's leading plant chemists, Eloy Rodríguez (1947–), reported to the American Association for the Advancement of Science that he and his colleague Richard Wrangham had identified a process for finding plants with medicinal properties by observing animal behavior and interaction with plants. Rodríguez and Wrangham coined the term "zoopharmacognosy" to describe this process, and since then, many animal behaviorists have reported on animal usage of curative plants, thus leading to a revolution in finding new medicines. In addition to identifying new medicinal plants, Rodríguez has also found plant chemicals that kill fleas and mites by observing how monkeys rub leaves with these chemicals on their fur. Rodríguez also studies how native peoples in the tropics use curative plants.

Sources: Winter, Metta, "Animals Point to Nature's Medicines," *Cornell Focus*, Vol. 5, no. 1 (1996); pp. 5–7.

1995 ♦ Lydia Aguilar-Bryan (c. 1951–) and her husband, Joseph Bryan, endocrinologists at Houston's Baylor College of Medicine, were the first researchers to solve the problem of hyperinsulinism. After a decade of research, they were able to discover how the body regulates the secretion of insulin and prepare the way for a cure or better treatment of diabetes. Thanks to their work, there may soon be a prenatal test for hyperinsulinism and, down the road, a genetic remedy. As a researcher and doctor, Aguilar-Bryan is particularly interested in diabetes because it strikes people of Mexican descent in unusually high numbers. She is a native of Mexico City who watched her grandmother and uncles die of the disease. As a graduate student at the University of Texas, she studied diabetes in Mexican American populations in Starr County, Texas, and has continued to work on the problem since joining the Baylor College of Medicine in 1985.

Sources: Thorpe, Helen. "Lydia Aguilar-Bryan and Joseph Bryan," *Texas Monthly*, September 1995, pp. 116–117, 148–149.

1995 ♦ In an undertaking reminiscent of that in the science fiction film *Jurassic Park*, Latino scientist Raúl Cano (c. 1948–) of the California Polytechnic State University was the first Latino biologist to revive several hundred specimens of bacteria from ancient bees, gnats, and beetles trapped in amber as much as 135 million years ago. Cano exerts this effort in his search for new enzymes and antibiotics that can be used in pharmaceuticals. Cano is the leading biologist in reviving ancient spores.

Sources: "Meet the Chief Scientific Officer of BiotiQuest," BiotiQuest: https://biotiquest.com/pages/dr-raul-cano.

José Hernández

1995 ♦ Engineer José Hernández (1962–) of the Lawrence Livermore National Laboratory in California was instrumental in developing a computerized digital mammography system that may improve the early detection of breast cancer. In 1995, he received the Hispanic Engineer National Achievement Award for Outstanding Technical Contribution. In 2004, Hernández was selected for the U.S. Astronaut Corps and eventually flew to the International Space Station.

Sources: Hispanic Link Weekly Report, 16 October 1995, p. 1.

2011 ♦ Dr. Alfredo Quiñones-Hinojosa (1968–) cofounded Mission: BRAIN (Bridging Resources and Advancing International Neurosurgery), a nonprofit foundation that provides neurosurgical expertise and resources to patients, caregivers, and healthcare providers in underserved areas around the world. The foundation has grown to include more than 1,000 medical/surgical members in some 23 countries, where its doctors volunteer in public hospitals in remote areas of the world and perform surgeries on patients who cannot afford to travel to any of the major care centers.

Alfredo Quiñones-Hinojosa

Quiñones-Hinojosa was born into a farm worker family outside Mexicali, Mexico, and has ascended to the ranks of the world's leading neurosurgeons and researchers. His multi-award-winning work and writing of research articles and books is reflected in his positions at the Mayo Clinic: the William J. and Charles H. Mayo Professor and Chair of Neurologic Surgery, the Monica Flynn Jacoby Endowed Chair, and the James C. and Sarah K. Kennedy Dean of Research at the Mayo Clinic in Jacksonville, Florida.

Sources: Piana, Ronald, "Alfredo Quiñones-Hinojosa, MD: From Migrant Farm Worker to Neurosurgeon in Search of a Cure for Brain Cancer," *The Ascot Post*: https://ascopost.com/issues/july-25-2023/alfredo-quiñones-hinojosa-md-from-migrant-farm-worker-to-neurosurgeon-in-search-of-a-cure-for-brain-cancer/.

Anthropology

1541 ♦ Rodrigo Rangel (1447–1530) and a soldier known only as the Gentleman of Elvas were the first to describe the culture of the Caddo Indians, which they observed on the expedition of Hernando de Soto (1500–1542) to southern Arkansas and east Texas.

Sources: Chipman, *Spanish Texas, 1519–1821*, p. 244.

1542 ♦ Alvar Núñez Cabeza de Vaca (1490–1557) can be considered the first anthropologist and ethnographer of the New World because of his accounts of the Amerindians of the South and Southwest of the present-day United States. He documented his observations and experiences in his book *La relación* (The Account), which was published in Spain in 1542 after his return from the New World. In the winter of 1528, Cabeza de Vaca was one of only 15 survivors of a shipwreck off the coast of Florida. The Indians, who were suffering from illness, forced the survivors to become "healers," and Cabeza de Vaca began his career as a renowned physician among the Indians. During the six years that he remained among the Indians along the Gulf Coast as far west as Texas, Cabeza de Vaca also became a merchant and a translator. He recorded in great detail for the first time many observations about the Indians of the South and Southwest. In 1534, he and three other marooned survivors set out on a march west in search of New Spain. They marched on foot completely across Texas and into New Mexico, going from one tribe to the next as healers and traders. They finally encountered Spaniards in what is today northwestern Mexico in 1536. Cabeza de Vaca's nine-year journey from Florida to New Mexico ended when he set sail in April 1537 for Spain. His memoir *La relación* (The Account) may be considered the first ethnographic study of the Americas as well as a literary masterpiece, possibly the first book of "American literature" written in a European language.

Alvar Núñez Cabeza de Vaca

Sources: Chipman, *Spanish Texas, 1519–1821*, pp. 243–244.

1595 ♦ The first European to study and translate the languages of Indians residing in what is today the United States was Father Francisco Pareja (c. 1570–1628), who, from 1595 until his death sometime after 1626, became an expert in the Timucua language and published four works on the language. These studies are the basic texts used by modern linguists to understand the now extinct language. Father Pareja was a missionary to the Timucua Indians at the San Juan del Puerto Mission, founded in 1587, in what is now Georgia.

Sources: Fontana, *Entrada*, p. 49.

Inventors

Rafael Guastavino

1885 ♦ Spanish immigrant Rafael Guastavino (1842–1908) obtained the first of his 25 patents, this one for new mortars he developed for tiled floor and ceiling vaults, partitions, and stairs. Over the years, this architect and contractor developed fireproofing innovations and perfected traditional cohesive masonry for modern use; he was responsible for building the tiled vaults for such New York City monuments as Grand Central Station, Carnegie Hall, the old Penn Station, the Metropolitan Museum of Art, the Plaza and Biltmore hotels, the Cathedral of Saint John the Divine, and many others. Born in Valencia, Spain, Guastavino studied architecture in Barcelona, where he built factories, houses, and theaters, incorporating many of the traditional technologies of Mediterranean architecture. Guastavino immigrated to the United States in 1881 in search of broader markets and better mortars and went on to become one of the most recognized designers and builders of vaults, domes, and tiled surfaces, promoting their acoustics, elegance, and economy. By 1891, Guastavino's company had offices in New York, Boston, Providence, Chicago, and Milwaukee. In 1892, Guastavino documented his successful system of construction in his book *Essay on the Theory and History of Cohesive Construction.* After his death, Guastavino's business was continued by his son Rafael II, who expanded the company and was responsible for numerous patents of his own. In all, the Guastavinos were responsible for domes built at state capitals, major universities, museums, and railroad stations throughout the United States, as well as the Supreme Court building and the Natural History Museum in Washington, D.C.

Sources: "Master Builders," *Humanities* 16/3 (May/June 1995), pp. 29–30.

1907 ♦ Mexican inventor Víctor Ochoa (1850–1945) invented and patented the electric brake for street cars, which he sold to the American Brake Co.

in 1907 in Seattle. Previously, he had invented a glider and then a plane with a motor in 1904. He was also the inventor of a fountain pen and sold the patent to the Waterman Co. in 1900 and patented a pen and pencil clip for holding them in the pocket, which he sold to the American Pen and Pencil Co. in 1907.

Sources: "Victor Ochoa's Biographical Sketch," Smithsonian Education: https://smithsonianeducation.org/scitech/impacto/graphic/victor/man.html.

1978 ♦ George Castro (1939–2024) discovered the mechanism of the intrinsic charge carrier of organic photoconductors. Years later, such materials in the form of organic polymeric films became the basis for flexible photoconductors that are used in photocopying machines and high-speed printers. Born in Los Angeles, California, Castro received his B.S. in chemistry from the University of California at Los Angeles in 1960 and his Ph.D. in physical chemistry from the University of California at Riverside in 1965. He began working as a researcher for IBM in 1968 and in 1986 became the manager of Synchrotron Studies for IBM at the Almaden Research Center. In 1978, he received the Outstanding Innovation Award from IBM, and in 1990, he was elected a fellow of the American Physical Society. Castro assumed the leadership of the Physical Sciences Division of the IBM San Jose Research Lab in 1975, three years after its formation. He built the organization into one that is world famous for its scientific discoveries. These include the discovery of the first superconducting polymer, novel organic metals and superconductors, high-resolution laser techniques, and new methods of investigating magnetic materials.

Sources: Kanellos, *Chronology of Hispanic American History*, pp. 211, 276.

Physics, Chemistry, and Engineering

1610 ♦ The first irrigation canals and irrigation systems north of the Rio Grande were built in Santa Fe, New Mexico, by Spanish, Indian, and *mestizo* colonizers. They dug two *acequias madres* (main ditches) on each side of the small river that passed through the center of the town they were establishing. The Spanish had strict codes and plans for the construction of irrigation systems for the towns they were founding in the arid present-day Southwest; such systems were often constructed in advance of the building of the forts, houses, and churches. The undertaking was quite often massive, calling for digging, dredging, and transporting materials and the feeding of humans and animals. This was the case in the founding of Albuquerque in 1706, of San Antonio in 1731, and of Los Angeles in 1781. The canals of San Antonio were so well planned, lined with stone and masonry as they were, that many of them are still functioning today.

Sources: Simmons, "Spanish Irrigation Practices in New Mexico," pp. 138–139.

1760 ♦ The Spanish governor of Texas proposed that the heavy traffic in cattle from Texas to French Louisiana be licensed and regulated. This proposal underscored the realization that Hispanic cowboys had been driving cattle to Louisiana for decades and that it was a lucrative trade. The first cattle drives to take place in what would become the United States had already begun. After the United States acquired the Louisiana Territory in 1803, the cattle drives continued as smuggling.

Sources: Slatta, *Cowboys of the Americas*, p. 19.

1790 ♦ The idea for a transcontinental road first occurred to the Spanish governor of California, Pedro Fages (1734–1794), who wrote his viceroy for permission to contact George Washington about constructing a continental trail from Virginia to California, with the roads meeting at the Spanish fort at Saint Louis. The idea did not take hold until 1869, when the transcontinental railroad finally linked East and West.

Sources: Sánchez, Joseph P., "Hispanic American Heritage," in Viola and Margolis, *Seeds of Change*, p. 182.

1943 ♦ Latino physicist Luis Walter Alvarez (1911–1988) left his post at the Massachusetts Institute of Technology to join the Manhattan Project to develop the first atomic bomb. He was responsible for the development of the triggering device of the first plutonium bomb, and he flew in a B-29 following the *Enola Gay* to observe the bomb's detonation over Hiroshima.

Sources: Tardiff and Mabunda, *Dictionary of Hispanic Biography*, p. 39.

1968 ♦ Luis Walter Alvarez (1911–1988) became the first U.S.-born Latino to win the Nobel Prize in Physics. Born on June 13, 1910, in San Francisco, California, Luis Alvarez was one of the United States' most distinguished and respected physicists. With B.S. (1932) and Ph.D. (1936) degrees from the University of Chicago, Alvarez also received a number of honorary degrees from universities in the United States and abroad. He developed most of his work at the University of California at Berkeley from 1936 until his death.

From 1954 to 1959 and from 1976 to 1978, he served as associate director of the prestigious Lawrence Berkeley Lab. In 1986, Alvarez was awarded the Nobel Prize in Physics in recognition of his work in the development of bubble chambers for the detection and identification of subatomic particles. He had also received the Collier Trophy (1946), the Scott Medal (1953), the Einstein Medal (1961), and the National Medal of Science (1964), in addition to many other awards. He was the first Latino to win most of these awards. Alvarez was a pioneer in particle physics, astrophysics, ophthalmic and television optics, geophysics, and air navigation. Alvarez died in 1988.

Sources: Tardiff and Mabunda, *Dictionary of Hispanic Biography*, pp. 38–40.

Luis Walter Alvarez

1980 ♦ Physicist Luis Walter Alvarez (1910–1988) became the first scientist to develop the theory that the extinction of the dinosaurs was due to the crash of a giant meteor into the earth; the meteor raised so much dust into the atmosphere that it blocked out the sun and caused the vegetation consumed by dinosaurs to die.

Sources: Tardiff and Mabunda, *Dictionary of Hispanic Biography*, pp. 38–40.

1996 ♦ Florida International University engineering professor Milton J. Torres (1931–2015) developed a liquid polymer called PantherSkin that strengthens old metal, resists fire, and even contains explosions. The polymer is applied in a foam, and it is believed that it can be used in safeguarding airplanes from explosions. He specifically set out to develop PantherSkin in 1988 in response to an airplane explosion that caused the death of a flight attendant.

Sources: "New Technologies Could Ensure Safer Flights," *Houston Chronicle*, 3 September 1996.

Awards and Honors

1966 ♦ California-born David Pimentel (1925–2019) became the first Latino to be named to the President's Science Advisory Committee. The Cornell-educated entomologist has also served UNESCO, the National Academies of Science, the U.S. Department of Energy, and the Environmental Protection Agency.

Sources: Pimentel, David, ed. *Global Economic and Environmental Aspects of Biofuels*. Routledge, 2012.

1989 ♦ Dr. Mario J. Molina (1943–2020) became the first Latino scientist to receive the NASA Medal for Exceptional Scientific Achievement. That same year, he was also the first Latino to receive the United Nations Environmental Programme Global 500 Award. Molina's research on fluorocarbon depletion of the earth's ozone shield has resulted in nations around the world taking steps to curb the use of materials that emit fluorocarbons.

Mario J. Molina

Sources: Kanellos, *Latino Almanac*, p. 214.

1989 ♦ Venezuelan-born biologist Francisco Dallmeier (1953–) became the director of the Smithsonian Institution's famous Man and the Biosphere Biological Diversity Program, which coordinates field biodiversity research and training in the United States and various Latin American countries.

Sources: Kanellos, *Latino Almanac*, p. 212.

Richard A. Tapia

1990 ♦ Dr. Richard A. Tapia (1938–), a mathematics professor at Rice University in Houston, Texas, became the first Hispanic mathematician to be named a fellow of the American Physical Society. Tapia, who has also been a leader in bringing minorities into the study of math and sciences, received the Martin Luther King Jr. Award in 1987.

Sources: Tapia, Richard A., *Losing the Precious Few: How America Fails to Educate Its Minorities in Science and Engineering*. Houston: Arte Público Press, 2022.

1991 ♦ Neurobiologist Rodolfo R. Llinás (1934–) received UNESCO's Albert Einstein Medal.

Sources: Llinás, Rodolfo R., and Churchland, Patricia S., *Mind-Brain Continuum: Sensory Processes*, Baltimore: The MIT Press, 1996.

1991 ♦ Argentine American mathematician Alberto P. Calderón (1920–1998) became the first Latino to receive the National Medal of Science, conferred by President George H. W. Bush. In large part, the distinction recognized his groundbreaking work on singular integral operators and their application to important problems in partial differential equations. Calderón had presented his first revolutionary paper on the topic as early as 1985 at the American Mathematical Society. Calderón's theory of singular operators has contributed to linking several branches of mathematics and has had practical applications in physics and aerodynamic engineering.

Sources: Tardiff and Mabunda, *Dictionary of Hispanic Biography*, pp. 152–153.

1991 ♦ Alberto Vinicio Baez (1912–2007) advanced the study of X-ray imaging optics. The SPIE conferred the Dennis Gabor Award on Baez, a Mexican-born, U.S.-trained physicist, and co-researcher Paul Kirkpatrick "in recognition of their important role in the development of X-ray imaging optics. Their early discoveries that grazing incidence optical systems could be used to focus X-rays gave birth to the field of X-ray imaging optics. Their pioneering contributions to this field include the Kirkpatrick-Baez X-ray double reflecting imaging system. The Kirkpatrick-Baez Lamar X-ray telescope has been approved for flight on the Freedom Space Station." In his research, Baez specialized in X-ray radiation, optics, and microscopy as well as science and environmental education.

Sources: Kanellos, *Chronology of Hispanic American History*, pp. 173, 277.

France A. Córdova

1993 ♦ France Anne-Dominic Córdova (1947–) became the first Latino to be named chief scientist for NASA. Córdova had published more than 150 scientific papers, especially in astrophysics. She served as president of Purdue University from 2007 to 2012 and then became president of the Science Philanthropy Alliance.

Sources: Kanellos, *Latino Almanac*, p. 212.

1994 ♦ Dr. Richard A. Tapia (1938–) became the first recipient of the National Nico Haberman Award for promoting the representation of minorities and women in the computational sciences, given by the Computer Research Association, Washington, D.C. A Los Angeles native, Tapia received his B.S., M.S., and Ph.D. degrees in mathematics from the University of California at Los Angeles and has developed his career at Rice University in Houston.

Sources: Tapia, Richard A., *Losing the Precious Few: How America Fails to Educate Its Minorities in Science and Engineering*. Houston: Arte Público Press, 2022.

Francisco Ayala

1994 ♦ Francisco Ayala (1934–2023), professor of ecology and evolutionary biology at the University of California at Irvine, became the first Latino to serve as president of the American Association for the Advancement of Science, Washington, D.C. In 2001, Ayala was awarded the National Medal of Science.

Sources: Hispanic Business, October 1994, p. 70.

1995 ♦ Mario J. Molina (1943–2020), a researcher and professor at the Massachusetts Institute of Technology (MIT), shared the Nobel Prize in Chemistry with two others for work that led to an international ban on chemicals believed to be depleting the ozone protective layer of the earth. A native of Mexico with a B.S. in chemical engineering from the National Autonomous University of Mexico (1965) and a Ph.D. in physical chemistry from the University of California at Berkeley (1972), he taught and conducted research at various universities in the United States. From 1982 until 1989, Molina was a senior research scientist at the CalTech Jet Propulsion Laboratory. In 1989, he was appointed professor in the Department of Earth, Atmospheric, and Planetary Sciences at MIT. In 1992, he became the Lee and Geraldine Martin Professor of Environmental Sciences at MIT. Molina was a world leader in developing scientific understanding of the chemistry of the stratospheric ozone layer and its susceptibility to man-made perturbations. He explained through his laboratory experiments new reaction sequences that enable the catalytic processes that account for most of the observed ozone destruction in the Antarctic stratosphere. His other awards included the NASA Medal for Exceptional Scientific Achievement (1989), the United Nations Environmental Programme Global 500 Award (1989), the appointment as Pew scholar on conservation and the environment from 1990 to 1992, and the Hispanic Engineer National Achievement Award (1992).

Sources: "Mario J. Molina–Biographical," The Nobel Prize: https://www.nobelprize.org/prizes/chemistry/1995/molina/biographical/.

1995 ♦ Senior research physicist F. J. Duarte (1954–) of Eastman Kodak Company became the first Latino to win the Engineering Excellence Award presented by the Optical Society of America. He was recognized for his work in developing systems to assess the density of photographic film, for which he and Kodak earned a patent in 1993.

F. J. Duarte

Sources: "About People," *Hispanic Business*, April 1996, p. 68.

1995 ♦ U.S. Surgeon General Antonia C. Novello (1944–) became the first Hispanic to win the Ronald McDonald Children's Charities Award of Excellence of $100,000 for her work in fighting preventable diseases. Her work led to an overhaul of the nation's immunization programs.

Sources: Hispanic Link Weekly Report, 16 October 1995, p. 1.

1996 ♦ There were finally enough Latino representatives in the sciences in the United States to be featured in a documentary series for television, *The Changing Face of Science*, focusing on minorities in American science. Mathematician Richard A. Tapia (1938–), a professor at Houston's Rice University, and engineer–entrepreneur Israel Galván, also of Houston, were among the 20 minority scientists and technologists featured. Tapia, a Los Angeles native, joined the faculty at Rice University in 1970 and has helped to make his department the number-one department in the United States for graduating women and minority Ph.D. degrees. He was also the first native-born Mexican American to be elected into the National Academy of Engineering.

Sources: Tapia, Richard A., *Losing the Precious Few: How America Fails to Educate Its Minorities in Science and Engineering*. Houston: Arte Público Press, 2022.

1996 ♦ The National Society for Hispanic Physicists (NSHP), boasting more than 100 members, was founded by David Ernst and Carlos R. Ordóñez (1957–). The NSHP operates an electronic bulletin board and mentoring and outreach programs to recruit Latino students into the physical sciences and help them attain post-graduate degrees. In 2022, the American Physical Society awarded Ordóñez the Edward A. Bouchet Award for diversifying the study of physics.

Sources: Hispanic Link Weekly Report, 9 September 1996, p. 4.

1996 ♦ President Bill Clinton named Joaquín Bustoz Jr. (1939–2003), a mathematics professor at Arizona State University (ASU), as one of 10 teachers in the nation to receive the first Presidential Awards for Excellence in Science, Mathematics, and Engineering Mentoring. The award comes with a grant of $10,000. Professor Bustoz founded ASU's science honors program in 1986, which in 10 years of existence brought more than 1,000 minority students to campus for intensive summer instruction and mentoring.

Sources: Hispanic Business, December 1996, p. 58.

1996 ♦ President Bill Clinton appointed the first Latino member of the Nuclear Regulatory Commission, scientist Nils J. Díaz (1938–). He served as chairman of the commission from 2003 to 2006. Díaz was a professor and the director of the Innovative Nuclear Space Power and Propulsion Institute of the University of Florida at Gainesville. He was also president and principal engineer of Florida Nuclear Associates.

Sources: "100 Influentials," *Hispanic Business*, October 1996, p. 58.

2000 ♦ Cuban-born psychiatrist Pedro Ruiz (1936–2023) became the first Latino to be elected president of the American College of Psychiatrists. He also served as president of other psychiatric associations, including the American Association of Social Psychiatry (2000–2002), the American Board of Psychiatry and Neurology (2002–2003), the American Psychiatric Association (2006–2007), and the World Psychiatric Association (2011–2014). After serving as a professor of psychiatry in New York City and Houston, he became professor, executive vice chair, and director of clinical programs in the Department of Psychiatry and Behavioral Sciences at the University of Miami Miller School of Medicine. His life's mission was to address disparities in health care to underserved communities. During his career, Ruiz sat on numerous boards and authored more than 1,000 articles.

Sources: "Former APA President Pedro Ruiz, M.D., Dies," *Psychiatric News*: https://psychnews.psychiatryonline.org/doi/10.1176/appi.pn.2023.05.5.14

2001 ♦ New York–born Puerto Rican pediatrician Helen Rodríguez Trías (1929–2001) was the first Latino to be presented with the Presidential Citizens Medal by Bill Clinton. It is the second highest civilian award in the United States. Rodríguez Trías was a pioneer in women's and children's health and was the first Latino to serve as president of the American Public Health Association. Among her vast and distinct achievements, she was the first to establish a center for the care of newborn babies in Puerto Rico. During her career, she also taught at Yeshiva University's Albert Einstein College of Medicine, Columbia, and Fordham.

Helen Rodríguez Trías

Sources: Wilcox, Joyce, "The Face of Women's Health: Helen Rodriguez-Trias." *American Journal of Public Health,* Vol. 92, no. 4 (April 2002): 566–569.

2001 ♦ Puerto Rican mechanical engineer Orlando Figueroa (1955–) was appointed director of NASA's Mars Exploration Program. At the time, it was the largest program at NASA. In 1993, Figueroa won NASA's Outstanding Leadership Medal.

Orlando Figueroa

Sources: Kanellos, *Latino Almanac*, p. 213.

2002 ♦ Cuban-born soil scientist Pedro A. Sánchez is the first Latino to be awarded the World Food Prize; its inscription states that he "pioneered scientific approaches to increase productivity of tropical soils, which had been long thought to be unsuitable for agriculture. His research helped open millions of hectares of land in Latin America to farming production, and his innovations in agroforestry dramatically improved productivity and ecological sustainability in Africa. By pioneering ways to restore fertility to some of the world's poorest and most degraded soils, Sánchez has made a major contribution to preserving our delicate ecosystem, while at the same time offering great hope to all those struggling to survive on marginal lands around the world." Sánchez became director of tropical agriculture at Columbia University's Earth Institute in 2003. He is an international authority and leader in the fight against hunger, having co-led the United Nations's Millennium Project Task Force on Hunger. After receiving all of his degrees at Cornell University, he served in or directed soil research programs in the Philippines, Africa, and Latin America.

Sources: "Pedro A. Sanchez: Director, Tropical Agriculture and the Rural Environment Program," Columbia Climate School: https://www.earth.columbia.edu/articles/view/2784.

2013 ♦ Mexican American astronaut Ellen Ochoa (1958–) became the first Latino to serve as director of the Johnson Space Center. She had previously served as deputy director and an astronaut before that. She had spent nearly 1,000 hours in space over four shuttle missions from 1993 to 2002. She was one of the first astronauts to dock with the newly orbiting International Space Station. Ochoa retired in 2018. Seven public schools, from California to Texas, are named in her honor.

Sources: "Ochoa Reflects on Historic Career, Lauds Current Diversity," *Houston Chronicle*, 8 April 2023, pp. 1, 5.

2013 ♦ Nobel Prize–winning chemical engineer Mario J. Molina (1943–2020) was presented with the Presidential Medal of Freedom by President Obama.

Sources: Kanellos, *Latino Almanac*, p. 214.

2014 ♦ Astrophysicist France Anne-Dominic Córdova (1947–) became the first Latino to be named director of the National Science Foundation. She had been serving as president of Purdue University.

Sources: Kanellos, *Latino Almanac*, p. 212.

Lydia Villa-Komaroff

2015 ♦ Cell biologist Lydia Villa-Komaroff (1947–) was named a distinguished woman scientist by the White House Office of Science and Technology Policy. The New Mexican native has also won the Leadership Award from the Women Entrepreneurs in Science and Technology (2011) and the Woman of Distinction Award from the American Association of University Women (2013), among others.

Sources: Kanellos, *Latino Almanac*, p. 216.

Albert Mark Galaburda

2017 ♦ Chilean-born Harvard University professor of neuroscience Albert Mark Galaburda (1948–) received the Dyslexia Foundation's Einstein Award, which honors an individual who is not dyslexic but has made significant contributions to increasing our understanding of dyslexia and improving the lives of individuals with dyslexia. Known for his development of the Geschwind-Galaburda hypothesis, which helps to explain differences in cognitive abilities on the basis of sex hormones and immunological characteristics, he is also a leading expert on the biological foundations of developmental dyslexia. Among his many other awards are the Pattison Prize in Neuroscience, Scientist of the Year from the Association for Children with Learning Disabilities, the Neuronal Plasticity Prize from the Fondation Ipsen of France, the Harold Amos Faculty Diversity Award from Harvard Medical School, and the Lifetime Achievement Award in Behavioral Neurology from the American Academy of Neurology.

Sources: Termini, Christina, "100 Inspiring Hispanic/Latinx Scientists in America": https://crosstalk.cell.com/blog/100-inspiring-hispanic-latinx-scientists-in-america.

2020 ♦ Molecular biologist Enrique M. de la Cruz (1969–) was named to Cell Press's "100 Inspiring Latinx Scientists in America." Since 2017, he has served as chair of Yale's Department of Molecular Biophysics and Biochemistry. In 2017, he received the Emily Gray Award in Education from the Biophysical Society.

Sources: Kanellos, *Latino Almanac*, p. 212.

2020 ♦ Mexican American botanist Ynés Mexía (1870–1938) was featured in a documentary, *Unladylike*, that aired on the Public Broadcasting Service (PBS). In a short career of just 13 years, Mexía collected as many as 500 new plant species in the Americas, as many as Darwin had on his voyage.

In all, she collected some 145,000 plant specimens during her travels, which are now housed at major museums and university collections in the United States. Fifty new species have been named after her.

Sources: Newton, David E., *Latinos in Science, Math, and Professions.* New York: Facts on File, 2007.

2023 ♦ Joseph Michael Acabá (1967–) was appointed chief of the Astronaut Office. In managing astronaut resources and operations, he is designated to have a central role in picking the astronaut for the Artemis Program to return to the Moon.

Sources: "NASA's New Astronaut Leader to Help Pick Next Moon Visitors," *Houston Chronicle,* 2 February 2023.

2023 ♦ Aeronautical engineer Robert Campos Treviño (1948–2023) received the Engineering Legacy Award from NASA after having worked at NASA for more than 50 years, during which time he innovated aspects of space suit design and extravehicular activity (EVA). His books on EVA won the Luigi G. Napolitano Award from the International Aeronautical Federation. In 2014, he was presented with the Lifetime Achievement Award by the Hispanic Engineers National Association. Born in Monterrey, Mexico, Campos Treviño was raised and educated in Texas.

Sources: "Captain Robert Campos Treviño, Ret.," *Houston Chronicle,* 15 October 2023.

ART AND DESIGN

1503 ♦ European-style architecture and design were introduced to the New World with the construction of the church of San Nicolas de Bari from 1503 to 1508 in the city of Santo Domingo. Other religious, civil, and military architecture, design, and decoration, including all types of pictorial and plastic arts, followed as the Spaniards colonized the Caribbean islands and North, Central, and South America.

Sources: Kanellos, *Chronology of Hispanic American History*, p. 14.

1751 ♦ On December 23, 1751, one of the first colonial artists to gain international fame, José Campeche (1751–1809), was born in San Juan, Puerto Rico. Campeche was the fifth of seven children of María Josefa Jordán Marqués, a Canary Islander, and Tomás de Rivafrecha Campeche, a freed slave who became a painter and musician employed by his local church. As a child, Campeche worked in his father's studio, learning both painting and music while receiving his education at the Dominican convent of Saint Thomas Aquinas. In 1772, Campeche began painting religious figures; his two earliest known paintings are portraits of Brother Sebastián Lorenzo Pizarro and Saint Joseph with the Christ Child. In 1776, Campeche became an associate of the exiled Spanish painter Luis Paret y Alcázar, who had recently arrived in Puerto Rico. Under Paret y Alcázar's influence and instruction, Campeche was transformed from a competent local painter into a colonial master. In the course of his career, Campeche would eventually outgrow the rigid academic training of Paret y Alcázar as he developed his own more fluid and humanistic style. In 1785, Campeche painted *La dama a caballo* (The Lady on a Horse), which marked his maturity as a draftsman and colorist. During this

José Campeche

period, Campeche became one of the leading portrait artists of the nobility and of the government. In San Juan in 1789, he painted portraits of the new king of Spain and the royal family when Charles IV inherited the throne, and from 1790 on, he became the principal portrait artist of the most prominent members of San Juan society. In 1797, Campeche began to receive commissions from other Spanish colonies. He painted *La Piedad* (Piety) for the Caracas Cathedral in Venezuela, among other works. In 1801, Campeche began to receive a number of distinguished commissions to paint religious scenes and portraits of saints; that same year, he painted *La visión de San Francisco* (Saint Frances's Vision) for the Church of Saint Frances. On November 7, 1809, José Campeche died of an infectious disease in the same house in which he had lived his whole life. He was buried at the Dominican convent.

Sources: Kanellos, *Chronology of Hispanic American History*, pp. 55, 62.

1783 ♦ The first academies of fine arts were founded in Mexico and Guatemala; these were the first in the Western Hemisphere, and Mexico's was the first in North America.

Sources: Kanellos, *Chronology of Hispanic American History*, p. 60.

1796 ♦ A unique style of religious painting and sculpture was started in New Mexico by an unknown wood carver, subsequently called the *Laguna Santero* by art historians. This sculptor and painter of religious works, including wooden saints, was active in New Mexico from 1796 to 1808, long enough for him to inspire a school of artists who copied his style. The design of his altar screens and paintings indicates that he may have been from the provinces of Mexico. The expression of religious piety in the works by the *Laguna Santero* are closer to images of medieval Europe than they are to the baroque style prevalent in Mexico during his life. *Santeros* (carvers of religious statuary) had been carving statues in New Mexico from about 1700, most of them anonymously and copying styles popular in Mexico.

Sources: Quirarte, *Mexican American Artists*, pp. 26–33.

Francisco Oller

1858 ♦ Puerto Rican painter Francisco Oller (1833–1917) traveled to Paris for a stay of seven years and became the only Latin American artist to participate in the development of Impressionism. After studying and interacting with the French founders of Impressionism, Oller returned to Puerto Rico and introduced much of what he had learned. During the rest of his life, he continued to visit France and Spain in the development of his career. Born Francisco Manuel Oller y

Cestero on July 17, 1833, in San Juan, Oller is also noted as being one of the first artists to really inspire his work in the landscape of Puerto Rico and the customs of its everyday people. In 1851, Oller traveled to Spain and studied at the Academy of San Fernando with Federico Madrazo y Kunts, director of the Prado Museum. In 1853, Oller returned to Puerto Rico, and in 1854, he received the silver medal in the first Puerto Rico Exposition.

In 1858, Oller moved to Paris, where he studied with Thomas Couture and became an official copyist at the Louvre. In 1859, he became a member of the Atelier de Gleyre with Pierre Renoir, Claude Monet, and Alfred Sisley, among others. In the following years, he became associated with many of the pioneers of Impressionism, including Camille Pissarro and Paul Cezanne, with whom he lived for a while. In 1865, Oller returned to Puerto Rico but continued to correspond with Cezanne, Pissarro, and other painters in Paris and to send his works there for exhibit and sale. In 1868, Oller exhibited 45 paintings at the San Juan Fair and was immediately proclaimed the best painter on the island. On September 1 of the same year, Oller opened and directed a Free Academy of Drawing and Painting, with an immediate enrollment of 200 students. On November 10, 1869, Oller was knighted by order of the king of Spain. On January 22, 1872, Oller was named painter of the royal court in Spain. From 1873 to 1884, Oller worked in Europe.

Upon his return to Puerto Rico in 1884, he learned that his school had been closed. In 1889, he founded the School of Painting and Drawing for Young Ladies. In 1892, Oller finished his monumental painting *El Velorio* (The Wake), based on Afro–Puerto Rican funerary customs. In 1893, Oller won the gold medal in the Puerto Rico Exposition for his 46 works exhibited. In 1895, he settled once again in Paris, where his *El Velorio* also became a sensation. Oller returned to Puerto Rico in 1896 with various paintings exhibiting the Impressionist style. In 1901, he opened another academy of drawing in San Juan. In 1902, Oller was named drawing professor in the Normal School, which would later become the University of Puerto Rico. Upon being fired from that post in 1904, he opened yet another school of art for young ladies. He later worked as a teacher in Bayamón and received a stipend while suffering a long illness that eventually resulted in his death on May 17, 1917.

Sources: Tardiff and Mabunda, *Dictionary of Hispanic Biography*, pp. 623–624.

1921 ♦ "Mexican Painters and Photographers of California," one of the first exhibitions of contemporary Mexican art in the United States, opened in Los Angeles.

Sources: Griswold et al., *Chicano Art*, p. 207.

1930 ♦ Painter Antonio García Encarnación (1901–1997) graduated from the Art Institute of Chicago and became the first, or one of the first, Mexican American painters of note. He was one of a generation of Mexican and Mexican American artists born between 1901 and 1912 who were raised and educated in the United States and developed an intercultural sensibility. Others were Octavio Medellín (1907–1999), Chelo González Amezcua (1903–1975), Pedro Salinas (1910–1973), and Margaret Herrera Chávez (1912–1992). García Encarnación was born in Monterrey, Mexico, in 1901 and moved to San Diego, Texas, with his family when he was 12 years old. In addition to exhibiting his paintings internationally, García Encarnación also painted murals, illustrated books, and taught art at Del Mar College in Corpus Christi.

Chelo González Amezcua was the first female painter to be considered a Mexican American artist. Born in Mexico in 1903, González Amezcua was a completely self-taught artist raised in Del Rio, Texas. She was offered a scholarship to attend the San Carlos Academy in Mexico City during the 1930s but had to refuse because of the need to support her family when her father died. In her early work and techniques, González Amezcua used ballpoint pen on paper, revealing no influence of other artists in her work. Only in the late 1960s was her work recognized, and she began to exhibit at museums and galleries outside of Del Rio. Pedro Salinas was born in Bastrop, Texas, to Mexican immigrant farmers. He painted Impressionist landscapes that became very popular. The daughter of New Mexico ranchers, Margaret Herrera Chávez worked with diverse media such as prints, watercolors, oils, ceramics, textiles, and sculpture and became one of the WPA artists during the Depression.

Sources: Quirarte, *Mexican American Artists*, pp. 41–42, 44–49.

1930s ♦ One of the first Latino folk artists to gain national attention was New Mexican *santero* (carver of religious statuary) Patrociño Barela (1900–1964), whose work was exhibited and studied throughout the 1930s. Since his time, *santeros* have continued to command attention in the art world.

Sources: Griswold et al., *Chicano Art*, p. 208.

1938 ♦ Mexican American sculptor Octavio Medellín (1907–1999) became the first U.S. Latino artist to join the faculty of a large university when he became a member of the art department of North Texas State University in Denton. In 1945, he took an appointment at Southern Methodist University, Dallas, where he taught until 1966. Medellín was born in Matehuala, Mexico, in 1907 and immigrated to the United

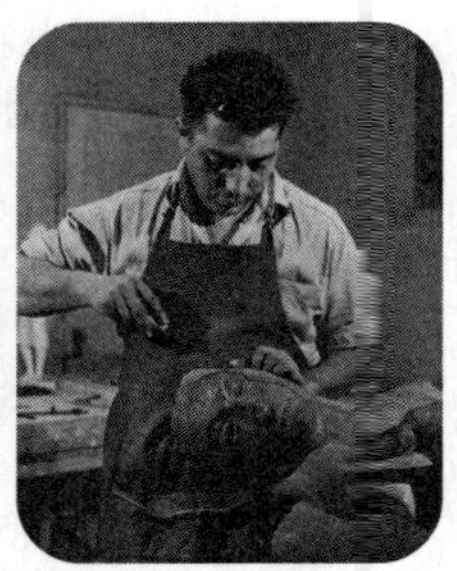

Octavio Medellín

States with his parents as refugees from the Mexican Revolution in 1920. He is considered a member of the first generation of artists with a Mexican American identity. Medellín's works are inspired by pre-Columbian sculpture; he works in stone and wood.

Sources: Quirarte, *Mexican American Artists*, pp. 49–52.

Patrociño Barela

1939 ♦ Patrociño Barela (c. 1900–1964) became the first Latino folk artist to have his works exhibited at a world's fair. The carver of saints, doors, and colonial-style furniture from wood was born in Bisbee, Arizona, and was selected to participate in the Federal Arts Project during the Depression. He came to national attention, and his sculptures were selected for exhibit at the 1939 New York World's Fair. Barela was self-taught but is considered by critics to have revealed the inner expression and psychological depth of the figures that he carved in a primitive style.

Sources: Meier and Rivera, *Dictionary of Mexican American History*, pp. 34–35.

1940 ♦ "Twenty Centuries of Mexican Art," the first large-scale and most influential exhibition of Mexican art ever, opened at the Museum of Modern Art in New York.

Sources: Griswold et al., *Chicano Art*, p. 208.

1949 ♦ Armando Baeza's (1924–) sculpture won an art prize in Los Angeles and became the first work by a Mexican American artist to be featured in a national news magazine: *Newsweek*.

Sources: Griswold et al., *Chicano Art*, p. 210.

1952 ♦ Puerto Rican painter Rufino Silva (1919–1993) was the first Latino to become a member of the faculty of the prestigious Art Institute of Chicago. Silva was born in Humacao, Puerto Rico, and studied at the Art Institute from 1938 to 1942.

Sources: Kanellos, *Latino Almanac*, pp. 291–292.

José Luis Sert

1953 ♦ Spanish-born architect José Luis Sert (1902–1983) became the first Hispanic to serve as dean of a major school of architecture: the Graduate School of Design at Harvard University. Sert was born and educated in Barcelona, Spain, and

The Institute of Puerto Rican Culture in San Juan was founded in 1955.

in 1939 moved to the United States, where he joined an architectural firm. During his career, he designed important structures not only in the United States but in Brazil, Colombia, and other countries. He is especially known for designing buildings at Harvard and Boston universities.

Sources: Hispanics in U.S. History, p. 31.

1954 ♦ The first annual Mexican American art exhibition was held in Los Angeles.

Sources: Griswold et al., *Chicano Art*, p. 210.

1955 ♦ The Institute of Puerto Rican Culture was founded in San Juan to preserve and nurture Puerto Rico's traditional arts and handicrafts. Through its school, workshops, exhibits, festivals, and publications, the institute has preserved and promoted traditional as well as avant-garde arts from folk dancing to theater and literature, operating annual and biennial festivals in many of the arts. Its founder and first director was the eminent folklorist and professor Dr. Ricardo Alegría (1921–2011). The work of the institute has been essential in the face of the onslaught of U.S. culture related to Puerto Rico's status as a colony of the United States.

Sources: "Historia," Instituto de Cultura Puertorriqueña: https://www.icp.pr.gov/historia/.

Amalia Peláez

1956 ♦ Amalia Peláez (1896–1968) became the first Latina artist to win a major award in the United States: first prize at the Gulf Caribbean Art Exhibition at the Museum of Fine Arts, Houston. Painter and ceramist Peláez was born in 1897 in Yaguajay, Cuba, one of nine children of a country doctor and his wife. She was familiar with the art world, however, because she was the sister of one of Cuba's most famous poets, Julián del Casal.

At the age of 15, Peláez began to study painting with Magdalena Peñarredonda. From 1916 to 1924, she studied at the San Alejandro Academy in Havana and also studied with the painter Leopoldo Romanach. She continued her studies in New York at the Art Students' League with George Bridgman, and from 1927 to 1934, she studied in Paris at the Grand Chaumier. Peláez eventually became a leader, with René Portocarrero and Wilfredo Lam, of the generation that was to bring Cuban painting into the 20th century. All three insisted on the artist's freedom to reinvent and represent reality.

Her solo exhibits included shows in Paris, New York, Havana, and Bogota. Peláez also won national awards in Havana. Among her most famous paintings is *Hibiscus* (1943), which demonstrates a fusion of Native, Creole, and imported elements. Peláez also had a distinguished career as a teacher, illustrator of books and magazines, and ceramist. Peláez died in Havana in 1968.

Sources: Kanellos, *Chronology of Hispanic American History*, p. 132.

Marisol Escobar

1963 ♦ Venezuelan American artist Marisol Escobar (1930–2016) became the first Latina to be given a room of her own at a show, "Americans, 1963," at the Museum of Modern Art in New York. Born in Paris on May 22, 1930, into a wealthy Venezuelan family, Escobar settled in Los Angeles with her father during World War II. After finishing high school in Los Angeles, Escobar studied art at the Académie des Beaux Arts in Paris, the Art Students' League in New York, and the New School for Social Research. She became a protege of Willem de Kooning in New York and began to exhibit in galleries in the late 1950s. By 1961, her work had begun appearing in the Museum of Modern Art and other important places, and *Life* magazine had published photos of her work. Throughout the next three decades, Escobar's fame as a sculptor grew, and in 1991, she was invited to exhibit her sculptures at the National Portrait Gallery in Washington, D.C.

Sources: Telgen and Kamp, *Latinas! Women of Achievement*, pp. 231–235.

1967 ♦ Dominican American fashion designer Oscar de la Renta (1932–2014) became the first U.S. Latino to win the Coty American Fashion Critics' Award. De la Renta went on to become one of the most important designers in the world.

Sources: Tardiff and Mabunda, *Dictionary of Hispanic Biography*, p. 277.

Antonio Martorell

1968 ♦ Puerto Rican painter and graphic artist Antonio Martorell (1939–) became the first Latino to win first prize in illustration from the American Art Institute for illustrating the children's book *ABC de Puerto Rico* by Isabel Freire de Matos and Rubén del Rosario.

Sources: Tardiff and Mabunda, *Dictionary of Hispanic Biography*, p. 531.

1968 ♦ The Chicano mural movement began with the works executed by artist Mario Castillo (1945–) in Chicago and with painter Antonio Bernal's (1937–) two-panel mural at San Diego's El Centro Cultural de la Raza. At about the same time, artists began executing murals in Austin, Houston, and San Antonio as well. Inspired by the murals of earlier Mexican master muralists, the movement would take hold throughout the Southwest, the Chicago area, and New York and would have its greatest activity and exponents in California during the 1970s.

Sources: Griswold et al., *Chicano Art*, p. 86.

1968 ♦ The first Chicano art galleries were Denver's El Grito de Aztlán Gallery and San Francisco's Galería de la Raza; they were followed in 1969 by the Plaza de la Raza in Los Angeles in 1969. Other Chicano art galleries followed, including La Raza Graphic Center, which opened in San Francisco in 1971. San Diego's El Centro Cultural de la Raza began serving as a gallery in 1970 as well.

Sources: Griswold et al., *Chicano Art*, pp. 225–226.

1968 ♦ The first major neighborhood or grassroots Chicano art show was the annual Arte del Barrio show, organized by René Yáñez (1942–2018) and Ralph Madariaga (1934–1985) of the Galería de la Raza in San Francisco.

Sources: Griswold et al., *Chicano Art*, p. 168.

1968: El Museo del Barrio

In 1968 El Museo del Barrio was founded in New York City by artist and educator Raphael Montañez Ortiz (1934–) and a coalition of Puerto Rican parents, educators, artists, and activists who noted that mainstream museums largely ignored Latino artists. The mission of El Museo del Barrio is to present and preserve the art and culture of Puerto Ricans and all Latin Americans in the United States. El Museo del Barrio fulfills its mission with its extensive collections (8,500 objects), varied exhibitions and publications, bilingual public programs, educational activities, festivals, and special events. *Sources:* "History," El Museo del Barrio: https://www.elmuseo.org/about/history-mission/.

1968 ♦ The first major Chicano art group was Oakland's Mexican American Liberation Art Front, founded in 1968. It held its first show of note, "New Symbols for la Nueva Raza," in 1969.

Sources: Griswold et al., *Chicano Art*, p. 223.

1970 ♦ The first annual Chicano art exposition, "The Tlacuilo Art Show," was initiated in San Antonio, Texas.

Sources: Griswold et al., *Chicano Art*, p. 215.

1971 ♦ The first Puerto Rican mural in the Midwest—perhaps in the continental United States—was *La Crucificción de Pedro Alvizu Campos*, created by the Puerto Rican Art Association in Chicago.

Sources: "Barrio Murals in Chicago," *Revista Chicano-Riqueña*, 4/4 (1976), pp. 58–59, 62.

1971 ♦ "Third World Women's Art" was the first exhibition of art by Latinas. It was organized by the Galería de la Raza in San Francisco.

Sources: Griswold et al., *Chicano Art*, p. 178.

1972 ♦ The first Hispanic performance art group to make living murals was Asco (Nausea), founded by Mexican American painters Gronk (1954–, born Glujio Nicandro), Patssi Valdez (1951–), Willie Herrón (1951–), and photographer Harry Gamboa (1951–). Their street performances, held mostly in East Los Angeles, included Day of the Dead celebrations, war protests, and

1972: Mujeres Muralistas

In 1972, at the height of the Chicano art movement, painter Patricia Rodríguez (1944–) led a group of Latino artists in founding Mujeres Muralistas, the first organization of Latina muralists, which was active until 1977 in the San Francisco Bay Area. The original members of the group were Patricia Rodríguez, Consuelo Méndez Castillo, Irene Pérez (1950–), and Graciela Carrillo de López. Over the next 10 years, more than 50 exhibitions of Chicana art were held around the country. Rodríguez was also the first to teach Chicano art history at the University of California. *Sources:* "Patricia Rodriguez Art," *Weebly*: https://patriciarodriguezart.weebly.com/biography-bibliography.html.

"instant murals": parodies of murals in the form of events staged against a wall. In 1972, Asco fused theater with murals and created "Walking Mural," which seemed to detach itself from the wall. Patssi Valdez played the Virgin of Guadalupe; Gronk was a walking Christmas tree and supported a large Masonite board that had figures with sculpted heads and arms projecting from it and flailing as he walked along.

Sources: Griswold et al., *Chicano Art*, pp. 148–149; Museum of Fine Arts, Houston, *Hispanic Art in the United States*, pp. 185–188.

1972 ♦ Los Angeles's Self-Help Graphics was founded as a workshop for artists in East Los Angeles through the efforts of Sister Karen Boccalero (1933–1997), a nun, who recognized the talent of youth in the barrio. Over the years, the workshop has grown into one of the most productive and influential training, production, and exhibition spaces for Chicano artists. Self-Help specializes in printmaking, and its workshop allows community members, whether novices or well-established printmakers, to make multiple-color silkscreen prints (serigraphs) of their works. By splitting the run with the artists, Self-Help sustains itself from sales of the prints to galleries and art collectors.

Sources: Hispanic, October 1995, pp. 68–72.

1973 ♦ The first truly national exhibition of Mexican American and Chicano art was held on November 10–11, 1973, at Trinity University in San Antonio, Texas. While representative, the short-lived show had little impact on the art scene in the United States.

Sources: Griswold et al., *Chicano Art*, p. 169.

1973 ♦ The Mexican Museum, the first museum in the United States to be completely dedicated to collecting and presenting Mexican art, received its charter in San Francisco. It opened its doors to the public with a group exhibition in 1975.

Sources: Griswold et al., *Chicano Art*, p 172.

1974 ♦ The first major exhibitions of Chicano art took place at the University of California at Irvine, the Los Angeles County Museum of Art, and several other institutions when the works of the mural-painting group Los Four came indoors. Los Four's was the first exhibition to be housed at a large museum such as the Los Angeles County Museum of Art, where it was organized by Jane Livingston. The group was comprised of painters Carlos Almaraz (1941–1989), Frank Romero (1941–), Gilbert Luján (1940–2011), and Beto de la Rocha (1937–).

Sources: Griswold et al., *Chicano Art*, p. 116; Museum of Fine Arts, Houston, *Hispanic Art in the United States*, p. 143.

1974 ♦ Artist Judith "Judy" Baca (1946–) founded the first City of Los Angeles mural program. She would go on to complete the largest mural in the world, the half-mile-long *The Great Wall of Los Angeles.*

Sources: Kanellos, *Latino Almanac*, p. 273.

1975 ♦ The Association of Hispanic Arts was founded in New York City to offer services to all nonprofit Latino arts organizations and individual artists in the United States. It assisted in community presentations, maintained a central information office on artists and arts organizations, and published the oldest and longest-lasting newsletter on Hispanic arts.

Sources: Furtaw, *Hispanic Americans Information Directory*, p. 4.

Judy Baca

1976 ♦ Chicana artist Judith "Judy" Baca (1946–) conceived of and executed the largest outdoor mural in the world, *The Great Wall of Los Angeles*, a half mile-long narrative mural on the Tujunga Wash drainage canal in the San Fernando Valley. Its subject is Los Angeles's multiethnic history from Neolithic times until the 1950s. *The Great Wall of Los Angeles* was painted over the course of nine years ending in 1976. Baca developed the concept, hired the people, and helped raise the money necessary for the project. Using the *Great Wall* project as a model, Baca went on to found the Social and Public Art Resource

Center (SPARC) in Venice, California, in 1976. SPARC involves multicultural youth in presenting and preserving murals and public art.

Sources: Telgen and Kamp, *Latinos! Women of Achievement*, pp. 28–29.

1976 ♦ "17 Artists, Hispano, Mexican American and Chicano" was the first exhibition of Latino art to travel widely and be shown in museums in Chicago; San Francisco; Boise, Idaho; and elsewhere. It was organized by Robert Glauber for the Illinois Bell Telephone Company.

Sources: Griswold et al., *Chicano Art*, p. 172.

1977 ♦ The first national Chicano arts festival, Canto al Pueblo, was held in Milwaukee, Wisconsin, from April 28 to May 9, 1977. Organized by Arnold Vento, Raymundo "Tigre" Pérez (1946–1995), and Ricardo Sánchez (1941–1995), the festival included art exhibitions, art happenings, musical performances, and literary readings.

Sources: Griswold et al., *Chicano Art*, p. 171.

1977 ♦ Sculptor Luis Jiménez (1940–2006) was the first U.S. Latino artist to receive the Hassan Fund Purchase Award from the American Academy and Institute of Arts and Letters. In 1979, he also received a fellowship from the American Academy in Rome.

Sources: Museum of Fine Arts, Houston, *Hispanic Art in the United States*, p. 193.

1977 ♦ The National Endowment for the Arts formed the first National Task Force on Hispanic Arts, chaired by art historian Jacinto Quirarte (1931–2012). The task force helped to create funding opportunities for artists and exhibitions.

Sources: Griswold et al., *Chicano Art*, p. 169.

1977 ♦ The first Latino art exhibition to travel widely and be shown in major museums was "Ancient Roots/New Vision," organized by Marc Zuver, executive director of Fondo del Sol in Washington, D.C. The exhibition opened at the Tucson Museum of Art and traveled to Chicago, Albuquerque, Colorado Springs, El Paso, Houston, Los Angeles, New York City, San Antonio, and Washington, D.C. It received extensive press coverage in those cities.

Sources: Griswold et al., *Chicano Art*, pp. 172–173.

Ana Mendieta

1978 ♦ Cuban American sculptor, painter, and video artist Ana Mendieta (1948–1985) became administrator of New York's Arts In Residence, Inc. (A.I.R. Gallery), the first gallery for women's art established in the United States. Mendieta, who came to the United States as a child refugee in 1961, devoted much of her artistic production to women's and Afro-Cuban themes.

Sources: "Ana Mendieta: Cuban-American Performance Artist, Sculptor, Painter, Photographer and Video Artist," *The Art Story*: https://www.theartstory.org/artist/mendieta-ana/.

Robert Graham

1978 ♦ Mexican-born sculptor Robert Graham (1938–2008) became the first Latino artist to receive a commission to work on a national monument in Washington, D.C. He and three others were commissioned to create the Franklin Delano Roosevelt Memorial, which has yet to be realized.

Sources: Museum of Fine Arts, Houston, *Hispanic Art in the United States*, p. 184.

1981 ♦ Haitian–Puerto Rican artist Jean-Michel Basquiat (1960–1988), born and raised in New York City, became the youngest artist ever to take part in the famed "Documenta" exhibition in Germany and then at 22 was the youngest artist ever to be included in the Whitney Museum of American Art's Biennial. He had his first American solo show in 1982.

Sources: Kanellos, *Latino Almanac*, p. 275.

1983 ♦ The National Hispanic Cultural Center was founded in Albuquerque, New Mexico, as a division of the New Mexico Department of Cultural Affairs. The center is dedicated to the preservation, promotion, and advancement of Hispanic culture, arts, and humanities. Its 20-acre campus houses the Roy E. Disney Center for Performing Arts, an art museum, a research library, a genealogy center, and a theater. The center's gallery is one of the principal places in the United States to show Latino art. The center's other activities include history and literary exhibitions, theater, music and dance productions, classic and contemporary films, and family and school events, along with readings and book signings by renowned authors and poets.

Sources: "About," National Hispanic Cultural Center: https://www.nhccnm.org/about/.

1984 ♦ The Hispanic Designers Association was founded in New York City by Hispanic fashion designers. Each year, it organizes a Hispanic Designers Gala Fashion Show and Benefit and recognizes leading designers with awards.

Sources: Hispanic Link Weekly Report, 28 August 1995, p. 4.

1985 ♦ The first comprehensive bibliography on Chicano art, *Arte Chicano*, was compiled by professors Shifra Goldman and Tomás Ybarra-Frausto.

Sources: Griswold et al., *Chicano Art*, p. 221.

1987 ♦ The first nationally touring exhibition of U.S. Hispanic art, "Hispanic Art in the United States: Thirty Contemporary Painters and Sculptors," was launched by the Museum of Fine Arts, Houston, and the Corcoran Gallery in Washington, D.C., under the leadership of Peter Marzio. Some controversy arose about the exhibition, curated by John Beardsley and Jane Livingston, because its curators were neither Latino nor specialists on the subject. The exhibition included not only the founding institutions on its itinerary but also major museums in Brooklyn, Los Angeles, Santa Fe, and elsewhere.

Sources: Griswold et al., *Chicano Art*, p. 174.

1987 ♦ Carolina Herrera (1939–) became the first Latina fashion designer to have her clothes worn by Jacqueline Kennedy Onassis, who, as First

1987: The Mexican Fine Arts Center Museum

The Mexican Fine Arts Center Museum opened its doors in 1987 with the goal of establishing an arts and cultural organization committed to accessibility, education, and social justice. The institution has grown, its audience has broadened, and its reach now extends across the United States and beyond, becoming the largest and most renowned of the Latino museums in the United States. In 2001, the museum expanded to a 48,000-square-foot, state-of-the-art facility in the heart of the Pilsen neighborhood of Chicago. In 2006, it changed its name to the National Museum of Mexican Art. Today, it is the only Latino museum accredited by the American Association of Museums. Founder and longtime director Carlos Tortolero (1954–) oversaw this growth and impact. He retired in December 2023. *Sources:* "History," National Museum of Mexican Art: https://nationalmuseumofmexicanart.org/history.

Carolina Herrera

Lady, set the standard for American fashion during the 1960s. Onassis also asked Herrera to create a wedding dress for her daughter, Caroline Kennedy. In 1987, the Venezuelan-born Herrera was named top Hispanic designer upon receiving the MODA Award. She began her rise to prominence with the founding of her House of Herrera fashion design business in New York City in 1981. She rose to become one of the most successful Hispanic fashion designers in the United States, eclipsed only by Dominican-born Oscar de la Renta (1932–2014). During the course of her career, she has been named to the Best Dressed Hall of Fame and named one of the Ten Most Elegant Women in the World.

Sources: Tardiff and Mabunda, *Dictionary of Hispanic Biography*, pp. 423–426; Telgen and Kamp, *Latinas! Women of Achievement*, pp. 181–186.

1990 ♦ The first national exhibition of Chicano art to travel to major museums throughout the United States was "Chicano Art: Resistance and Affirmation, 1965–1985," which included on its three-year itinerary the Wight Art Gallery of the University of California at Los Angeles, the Denver Art Museum, the Albuquerque Art Museum, the San Francisco Museum of Art, the Fresno Art Museum, the Tucson Museum of Art, the El Paso Museum of Art, the Bronx Museum of the Arts, and the San Antonio Museum of Art. In addition to showing representative Chicano works, the exhibit's catalog was an effort to write and illustrate the history of the Chicano art movement.

Sources: Griswold et al., *Chicano Art*, pp. 26-32.

1990 ♦ Mexican American sculptor Luis Jiménez (1940–2006) was the first Latino artist to have a place of honor for one of his works in front of the Smithsonian's American Art Museum, where it graced the entrance for many years before being moved to Moody Park in Houston, Texas. Made from epoxy and fiberglass, this and his other monumental sculptures withstand the extremes of weather.

Sources: "Vaquero," Smithsonian Institution: https://www.si.edu/object/vaquero% 3Asaam_1990.44.

César Pelli

1991 ♦ Argentine American architect César Pelli (1926–2019) became the first Latino to be named by the American Institute of Architects as one of the 10 most influential living architects. Pelli designed both public and private buildings throughout the United States and abroad. Pelli designed some of the world's tallest buildings, including the Petronas Towers in Kuala Lumpur and the World Financial Center in New York City. Other important structures are the San Bernardino City Hall, the Pacific Design Center in Los Angeles, and the U.S. Embassy in Tokyo. The World Financial Center is considered one of the 10 best works of American architecture designed since 1980.

Sources: Tardiff and Mabunda, *Dictionary of Hispanic Biography*, p. 661.

1991 ♦ Venezuelan American artist Marisol Escobar (1930–2016) became the first Latina sculptor to exhibit her works at the National Portrait Gallery in Washington, D.C. Escobar has been considered one of the most important figures in pop sculpture, according to H. Aronson's *History of Modern Art*.

Sources: Telgen and Kamp, *Latinas! Women of Achievement*, p. 235.

1992 ♦ The Whitney Museum of American Art organized its first retrospective for a Latino artist: its posthumous exhibition of the art, poetry, and commentary of Jean-Michel Basquiat (1960–1988), who had died of a heroin overdose in 1988. Over just 10 years of creative production, Basquiat had produced 1,500 drawings, 600 paintings, and numerous sculptures; his works were extensively exhibited and sold internationally.

Sources: Kanellos, *Latino Almanac*, p. 275.

1992 ♦ Amalia Mesa-Baines (1943–) became the first Latina visual artist to win a MacArthur Fellowship. Mesa-Baines has been one of the leading advocates of a Chicano artistic aesthetic. She specializes in creating interpretations of traditional Mexican American altars. She is also a critic and scholar of art, pioneering the documentation and interpretation of Mexican American art traditions. She has served as the director of the Visual and Public Art Department at California State University at Monterey Bay and is the author of *Ceremony of Spirit: Nature and Memory in Contemporary Latino Art* (1993). Her works have been exhibited nationally, including at the Los Angeles County Museum of Art, the San Francisco Museum of Art, the Whitney Museum of American Art, and the Studio Museum of Harlem. Born in Santa Clara, California, her education includes a B.A. (1966) from San Jose State University, an M.A. (1971) from San Francisco State University, and an M.A. (1980) and a Ph.D. (1983) from the Wright Institute in Berkeley, California.

Sources: Pérez, Laura E., and Esther Fernández, María, *Amalia Mesa-Bains: Archaeology of Memory,* University of California Press, 2023.

Oscar de la Renta

1993 ♦ Dominican American fashion designer Oscar de la Renta (1932–2014) became the first American to lead a French couture business when he was selected to direct the House of Balmain, Paris.

Sources: Tardiff and Mabunda, *Dictionary of Hispanic Biography*, p. 277.

1994 ♦ The first exhibition of photography from the oldest and largest Spanish-speaking cultures of the United States was held at Houston's FotoFest '94, a citywide international photographic biennial. The exhibition, entitled "American Voices: Latino/Chicano/Hispanic Photography in the US," featured the works of 39 Latino photographic artists. As part of the historic exhibition, FotoFest sponsored a symposium, "Across Cultures," which brought together artists, curators, and scholars from the United States, Mexico, and the Caribbean. FotoFest is the largest gathering of international photographers in the United States and is one of the largest in the world.

Sources: Hispanic, November 1994, p. 43.

1994 ♦ Sculptor of monumental works in fiberglass and epoxy Luis Jiménez (1940–2006) became the first Latino artist to be named to an endowed professorship at the University of Houston. Born in El Paso, Texas, in 1940, Jiménez studied art and then architecture at the University of Texas, where he received his B.A. in fine arts in 1964. Upon graduation, he received a grant to study at the National Autonomous University of Mexico. His was one of the most original and innovative approaches to sculpture in the United States; he produced full-color works able to withstand the weather. His pop art sensibility allowed him to satirize American and Chicano popular culture with surprising humor and pathos in a conventionally stoic medium. Jiménez received major commissions from cities around the country, and his works are held in some of the most important museums.

Sources: Museum of Fine Arts, Houston, *Hispanic Art in the United States*, pp. 191–193; Quirarte, *Mexican American Artists*, pp. 115–120.

1995 ♦ Argentine American architect César Pelli became the first Hispanic architect to receive the gold medal from the American Institute of Architects.

Sources: Tardiff and Mabunda, *Dictionary of Hispanic Biography*, p. 662.

1995 ♦ The first major exhibition featuring women artists of Latin America toured major museums in the United States. "Latin American Women Artists, 1915–1995" included works in diverse media by 35 artists from 11 different countries. Its itinerary, which lasted until April 29, 1996, included the Milwaukee Art Museum, the Phoenix Art Museum, the Denver Art Museum, and the National Museum of Women in the Arts in Washington, D.C.

Sources: Hispanic, July 1995, p. 15.

1995 ♦ Mexican American artist Leo Tanguma (1941–) received the first commissions to paint two murals at the Denver International Airport. His murals *Children of the World Dream of Peace* and *In Peace and Harmony with Nature* are located on Level 5 of the Jeppesen Terminal. Tanguma has an extensive portfolio of murals painted in schools, libraries, and prisons.

Sources: "Leo Tanguma: An Interview": https://zingmagazine.com/blog_posts/leo-tanguma-interview/.

1996 ♦ Born José Rafael Moneo Vallés, Spanish architect Rafael Moneo (1937–), who has designed many buildings in the United States, became the first Hispanic to win the major international Pritziker Architecture Prize, given by the Hyatt Foundation and the Pritziker family of Chicago. Among the buildings Moneo has designed are the Davis Museum and the Cultural Center in Wellesley, Massachusetts. Moneo also designed the Beck Building for the Museum of Fine Arts in Houston.

Rafael Moneo

Sources: "Museum Architect Wins Award," *Houston Chronicle*, 29 April 1996.

1996 ♦ Carlos Jiménez became the first Latino architect to be selected by the Architectural League of New York for inclusion in *40 Under 40*, a book identifying "design leaders of the next millennium." Jiménez graduated from the University of Houston in 1982 with an award for the best thesis design. Much of his work since graduation has been executed on marginal pieces of urban land and with stringent budgets. Among Jiménez's works is the Junior School and Administration Building of the Glassell School of the Museum of Fine Arts in Houston. He went on to win many other awards, including the Chicago Athenaeum Architecture Award (2004), AIA Indianapolis Honor Awards (2003), and awards from *Architecture* (2002) and *Architectural Record* (1990, 1994, 1996, 2004).

Sources: Fields, Darrel, and Brooke Hodge, eds.. *Carlos Jiménez: House and Studio*, Harvard Graduate School of Design, 2006.

1996 ♦ Artist Judith "Judy" Baca (1946–) was the first Latina to be commissioned to paint a mural in the Denver International Airport. Her mural *La Memoria de Nuestra Tierra* (Our Land Has Memory) is located where hundreds of thousands of travelers can see it.

Sources: Kanellos, *Latino Almanac*, p. 273.

2004 ♦ Washington D.C.'s Hirshhorn Museum and Sculpture Garden organized a major retrospective of Cuban American artist Ana Mendieta's (1948–1985) work: "Earth, Body, Sculpture and Performance," which traveled to major museums around the United States.

Sources: "Ana Mendieta: Cuban-American Performance Artist, Sculptor, Painter, Photographer and Video Artist," *The Art Story*: https://www.theartstory.org/artist/mendieta-ana/.

2006 ♦ Sculptor Manuel Neri (1930–2021) received the Lifetime Achievement Award in Contemporary Sculpture from the International Sculpture Center. Born in Sanger, California, Neri was in the forefront of the punk art movement of the 1960s. While experimenting with many media and forms, Neri's work is generally based on the human figure in plaster, bronze, and marble.

Sources: "Artist Manuel Neri," *SAAM*: https://americanart.si.edu/artist/manuel-neri-6624.

2008 ♦ Mexican American sculptor Jesús Bautista Moroles (1950–2015) became the first Latino sculptor to be awarded the National Medal of Arts. Moroles's monumental sculptures explore geometric creations in granite. The 1978 graduate of the University of North Texas received commissions from around the United States; his largest public commission was the Houston Police Officers Memorial in Houston, a massive granite earthwork completed in 1992. Moroles was celebrated with numerous other awards, including the Texas Medal of the Arts in 2007 and being named Texas State Artist in 2011.

Sources: "Artist Jesús Moroles," *SAAM*: https://americanart.si.edu/artist/jesus-moroles-5827.

2008 ♦ Mexican American sculptor Luis Jiménez (1940–2006) suffered a tragic accident in 2006, when the monumental sculpture he was finishing fell on him and put an end to his life. The 32-foot-tall, cast-fiberglass *Blue Mustang/Mesteño Azul* he was preparing was for the first commission ever for a monumental outdoor sculpture at a major airport in the United States. Jiménez's family finished the piece and installed it in 2008 at the Denver International Airport posthumously.

Sources: Cameron, Bailey, "Blucifer: The Story of Denver Airport's 'Blue Mustang' Sculpture from Luis Jimenez": https://www.uncovercolorado.com/blucifer-blue-mustang-statue-denver-airport/.

2008 ♦ The Council on Tall Buildings and Urban Habitat presented Argentine American architect César Pelli (1926–2019) with the Lynn S. Beedle Lifetime Achievement Award.

Sources: Bernstein, Fred A., and Paul Goldberger, "Cesar Pelli, Designer of Iconic Buildings Around the World, Dies at 92," *New York Times*, 20 July 2019: https://www.nytimes.com/2019/07/20/arts/cesar-pelli-dead.html.

2010 ♦ Mexican American muralist Judith "Judy" Baca (1946–) was conferred with the National Award for Public Art by Americans for the Arts. In 2011, a Los Angeles school was named in her honor: the Judy F. Baca Arts Academy.

Sources: Kanellos, *Latino Almanac*, p. 273.

2013 ♦ The Smithsonian American Art Museum organized the groundbreaking exhibition "Our America: The Latino Presence in American Art," which consisted of works in all media by 72 leading modern and contemporary Latino artists; 63 of the works were from the Smithsonian's own collection. The exhibition was organized by E. Carmen Ramos, curator of Latino art at the Smithsonian American Art Museum.

Sources: "Our America: The Latino Presence in American Art": https://americanart.si.edu/exhibitions/our-america.

Camilo José Vergara

2013 ♦ Documentary photographer Camilo José Vergara (1944–) was awarded the National Humanities Medal by President Barack Obama. Born in Chile but a graduate in sociology from Notre Dame (B.A. 1968) and Columbia University (M.A. 1977), he began photographic New York Cityscapes in the 1970s and developed a technique of showing the deg-

2015: The U.S. Latina/o Art Forum (USLAF)

The U.S. Latina/o Art Forum (USLAF) (today known as U.S. Latinx Art Forum) was founded in 2015 to support the creation of a more equitable art world. It was born of the conference "Imagining a U.S. Latina/o Art History" at the 2015 Annual Conference of the College Art Association (CAA) in New York. Among a variety of programs, USLAF provides advocacy and support to artists through fellowships, mentorship programs, and virtual public programs in partnership with museums. USLAF provides a forum for online conversations among artists, interviews artists, and curates online exhibitions. *Sources:* U.S. Latinx Art Forum History and Timeline: https://uslaf.org/history-timeline/.

radation of buildings and sites over time. He published his photos in three university press award-winning books and on his website; he has also had numerous exhibitions, including one at the National Building Museum in 1999.

Sources: "Camilo José Vergara Photographs: Tracking Time to Document America's Post-Industrial Cities," *Library of Congress*: https://guides.loc.gov/vergara-collection-guide.

2013 ♦ Artist and performer Chris E. Vargas founded the Museum of Transgender Hirstory and Art (abbreviated as MOTHA) in San Francisco, California. Its mission is to preserve and represent transgender and gender-nonconforming history and art. Without an exhibition space, the museum is floating, curating shows at other institutions and public spaces. Among the institutions that have housed its show are the Henry Art Gallery, Cooper Union, ONE National Gay & Lesbian Archives, the Yerba Buena Center for the Arts, and the Hammer Museum.

Sources: Morley, Jack Balderrama. "Transhistorical Aesthetics: The Museum of Trans History & Art (MOTHA) Queers Monument Design," *The Architect's Newspaper*: https://www.archpaper.com/2018/10/motha-stonewall-memorial-new-museum/.

2017 ♦ Brownsville native Miki García (1947–) was the first Latina to be appointed director of a major university art museum: the Arizona State University Art Museum. She was previously the executive director and chief curator of the Museum of Contemporary Art in Santa Barbara from 2005 to 2017. Prior to this, she worked at the Public Art Fund in New York from 2001 to 2004. From 1999 to 2001, García was a curatorial associate at the Museum of Contemporary Art in San Diego and has also worked at the

Blanton Museum of Art at the University of Texas at Austin and the San Antonio Museum of Art.

Sources: "Miki García," ASU Search: https://search.asu.edu/profile/3211210.

2020 ♦ Congress enacted legislation in 2020 to establish the National Museum of the American Latino as part of the Smithsonian Institution in Washington, D.C. As an intermediate step toward the building of a Latino museum on the National Mall, the Molina Family Latino Gallery was opened in 2022 at the National Museum of American History of the Smithsonian, exhibiting art, historical artifacts, and information from the 15th century to the present.

Sources: "Latino History Is US History": https://latino.si.edu/gallery.

2020 ♦ Cuban American painter Carmen Herrera (1915–2022), at the age of 105, received a major retrospective show, "Carmen Herrera: Structuring Surfaces," at the Museum of Fine Arts in Houston; it celebrated some nine decades of productivity and recognition. In 2016, the Whitney Museum of American Art organized a show of some 50 of her works in "Carmen Herrera: Lines of Sight."

Sources: "Carmen Herrera: Structuring Surfaces," Museum of Fine Arts, Houston: https://www.mfah.org/exhibitions/carmen-herrera-structuring-surfaces.

Emilio Ambasz

2020 ♦ Argentine American architect Emilio Ambasz (1943–), known as a "green architect" for his integration of buildings within the natural environment, was the first Latino to have the Museum of Modern Art create an institute named in his honor: the Emilio Ambasz Institute for the Joint Study of the Built and the Natural Environment. (Ambasz had served as curator for design at MOMA from 1969 to 1979.) Ambasz is known for creating buildings with integrated gardens. Among his noteworthy awards are the grand prize of the International Interior Design Award of the United Kingdom in 1987 and the IDEA Award from the Industrial Designers Society of America. A true giant in architecture, Ambasz has been the subject of a dozen books and numerous articles.

Sources: "A Green-Architecture Pioneer, Emilio Ambasz Creates Buildings That Belong to the Landscape," *New York Times*, 7 May 2023.

2021 ♦ The U.S. Postal Service issued four stamps featuring the paintings of artist Emilio Sánchez (1921–1999). In the 1940s, Sánchez moved to the

United States and studied at Yale, the University of Virginia, and New York City's Art Students' League. With an emphasis on images of Caribbean architecture, his work recovers the colors, lines, and ambience of buildings, many of which revive the lines of colonial Cuba. In 1974, he won first prize in the San Juan (Puerto Rico) Biennial.

Sources: "Emilio Sánchez Biography": https://emiliosanchezfoundation.org/sanchez.html.

2021 ♦ E. Carmen Ramos became the first woman and first person of color to be named chief curatorial and conservation officer at the National Gallery of Art in Washington, D.C. Ramos earned her Ph.D. in art from the University of Chicago in 2011 and had previously served as the acting chief curator and conservator of Latinx art at the Smithsonian American Art Museum.

Sources: "National Gallery of Art Announces Appointment of New Chief Curatorial and Conservation Officer E. Carmen Ramos," National Gallery of Art, 13 May 2021: https://www.nga.gov/press/2021/carmen-ramos.html.

2022 ♦ Jorge Zamanillo (1969–) was named the inaugural director of the National Museum of the American Latino, which was established by U.S. Congress in 2020. Zamanillo is an archaeologist, curator, and museum administrator who previously served as the CEO of HistoryMiami and president of the Florida Association of Museums.

Jorge Zamanillo

Sources: McGlone, Peggy. "Smithsonian Selects Miami Museum Leader as Founding Director of Latino Museum," Washington Post, 4 February 2022.

2022 ♦ Dr. María Rosario Jackson became the first Mexican American and the first African American to direct the National Endowment for the Arts, a government agency. To take the directorship, Jackson went on leave from her position as the tenured institute professor in the Herberger Institute for Design and the Arts at Arizona State University. For some 10 years, she also served as a senior advisor for arts and culture and strategic learning, research, and evaluation at the Kresge Foundation, and beginning in 2012, she served on the National Council for the Arts and Culture. Her board service includes the Performing Arts Center of Los Angeles County (The Music Center), the Association of Arts Administration Educators, and the Alliance for California Traditional Arts.

Sources: "Dr. María Rosario Jackson," National Endowment for the Arts: https://www.arts.gov/about/leadership-staff/dr-maria-rosario-jackson.

2023 ♦ Chilean-born fashion designer María Cornejo (1962–) received the Geoffrey Beene Lifetime Achievement Award from the Council of Fashion Designers of America (CFDA). The child of exiles from dictator Augusto Pinochet's era in Chile, Cornejo relocated from Paris to New York in 1996 and in 1998 remodeled a garage into her store to house the designs of her house, named Zero. She became the designer selected by many celebrities, including Michelle Obama. Among her other awards are the 2006 Fashion Prize of the Cooper Hewitt Smithsonian National Design Award and the 2018 Fashion Group International's Sustainability Award.

Sources: Friedman, Vanessa, "Independence Fortifies a Survivor," *New York Times*, 26 November 2023.

2023 ♦ Mexican American painter Gladys Roldán-de-Moras (1963–) was the first Mexican-born woman to be inducted in the National Cowgirl Hall of Fame. A painter of western scenes who has received numerous awards for her painting, Roldán-de-Moras immigrated to the United States shortly after her birth in Monterrey. Born into a ranching family, the principal subject of her art is cowgirls, especially of the Mexican *charro* tradition. Her most recent award is the 2023 Frederic Remington Award at the Prix De West at the National Cowboy & Western Heritage Museum.

Sources: Gladys Roldán-de-Moras, Artist: https://www.roldandemoras.com/about.

2024 ♦ The El Paso–Ciudad Juárez Border Biennial featured an open call for artists along the border, from Tijuana–San Diego to Brownsville–Matamoros, for works of art relating to theme of "Bad Hyphens Separate; Good Hyphens Attach," exploring the interrelationship of the cultures along both sides of the border. This year's biennial was particularly poignant, given the political conflict over migration and undocumented border crossing. Organized by the El Paso Museum of Art and the Museo de Arte de Ciudad Juárez, the show was curated by Las Cuces, New Mexico, native Claudia S. Preza (1993–).

Sources: Lescaze, Zoe, "Striking a Balance," *New York Times*, 28 April 2024.

LITERATURE

1598 ♦ In the mission to colonize New Mexico led by Don Juan de Oñate (c. 1550–1630), there were literary men who imported the first European-style drama and poetry to an area that would become part of the United States. Among his men was an amateur playwright, Captain Marcos Farfán de los Godos, who wrote a play based on their colonizing adventure that the soldiers performed. This was the first play in a European language written and performed in what became the present-day United States. The soldiers also had in their repertoire the folk play, often performed on horseback, entitled *Los moros y los cristianos* (The Moors and the Christians), which dramatized the reconquest of the Spanish peninsula from the Moors during the Crusades. Finally, the poet Gáspar Pérez de Villagrá (c. 1550–1620), also one of Oñate's soldiers, penned an epic poem memorializing the expedition, "La conquista de la Nueva Méjico" (The Conquest of New Mexico), which was later published in Spain. It is considered an important literary work in the Hispanic world and is still studied today. This was the first or one of the first epics written in a European language in the New World.

Sources: Kanellos, *Chronology of Hispanic American History*, p. 47.

1654 ♦ The first Spanish-speaking community in the northeast of what would become the United States was a colony of Sephardic Jews who established an oral and literary tradition that was unbroken until the present day.

Sources: Diner, Hasia, *The Jews of The United States, 1654 to 2000*, Internet Archive: https://archive.org/details/diner-hasia-j-auth-the-jews-of-the-united-states-1654-to-2000.

1732 ♦ Miguel de Quintana (1677–1748), a New Mexico peasant, became the first writer in the history of the Southwest to be tried by the Inquisition. The poet's verses came under suspicion, and on March 17, 1732, formal charges were made against Quintana to the Holy Office in Santa Fe, whereupon depositions and evidence were collected and sent to Mexico City. On May 22, 1734, the Inquisition office in Mexico City ruled that it did not have enough evidence to prosecute Quintana, although it advised that he be "examined for lesions of the head and questioned intensively regarding his claim to a divine inspiration behind his writing." The case was reopened in 1735, resulting in warnings being leveled at Quintana from the Mexico City offices, but the case was closed abruptly in 1737.

Sources: Gallegos, *Literacy, Education, and Society in New Mexico 1693–1821*, pp. 70–73.

1776 ♦ Probably the first documented library (other than private libraries) in New Mexico and much of the Southwest was in existence and use by this date at the Santo Domingo mission, according to a report by Fray Anastacio Domínguez, who was studying the schools and churches in New Mexico. The catalog listed some 256 titles, but this number did not include sets and duplicates, which were extensive.

Sources: Gallegos, *Literacy, Education, and Society in New Mexico 1693–1821*, pp. 53–54.

1803 ♦ The first literary work in the Spanish language published in the United States was that of the Cuban priest José Agustín Caballero (1731–1865): *Sermón fúnebre en elogio del excelenttsimo senor Don Christóbal Colón* (Funereal Sermon in Eulogy of That Excellent Gentleman Don Christopher Columbus), issued in Philadelphia by printers Eaken & Mecum.

Sources: Online Computer Library Center.

1808 ♦ The first book of exile literature, a popular Latino genre in the United States over the next two centuries, was *España ensangrentada* (Bloodied Spain), written anonymously by "Viejo castizo espanol" ("an old Spaniard of pure blood") and published in New Orleans. It was written in protest of the French invasion of Spain and of Napoleon's puppet Francisco Godoy.

Sources: Online Computer Library Center.

1811 ♦ The first Spanish-language novel published in the United States was by a Spanish philosopher born in Peru, Pablo de Olavide (1725–1803), using his pseudonym Atanasio Céspedes y Monroy: *La paisana virtuosa* (The Virtuous Countrywoman), issued by Mathew Carey in Philadelphia. That same year, Carey issued another novel by "Céspedes," *La presumida orgullosa* (The Presumptuously Proud Woman).

Pablo de Olavide

Sources: Online Computer Library Center.

Francisca Josefa de la Concepción de Castillo

1817 ♦ The first Spanish-language autobiography published in the United States was that of a nun in New Granada (the Spanish colony that became Colombia), Francisca Josefa de la Concepción de Castillo (1671–1742): *Vida de la V. M. Francisca Josefa de la Concepción* (Life of ...), published in Philadelphia by T. H. Palmer, who specialized in publishing Spanish-language books. She is considered the first recorded woman writer in what is now Colombia.

Sources: Online Computer Library Center.

1821 ♦ The first great eulogy by a Hispanic recorded in history was that of Captain Jacob de la Motta (1789–1845), a Sephardic Jewish doctor who resided in Charleston but gave the speech in New York on the death of the famed Reverend Gershom Mendes Seixas, also a Sephardic Jew. The eulogy was of particular relevance to Hispanic Jews in that it compared the freedom that Jews encountered in the United States with their persecution in Europe. Many of Charleston's Jews were immigrants or descended from immigrants who had to leave Spain and Portugal when they were persecuted by the Inquisition. Like de la Motta, a medical doctor and army surgeon who had served with distinction in the War of 1812, many of the Sephardic Jews became founding and leading citizens in South Carolina and Georgia (which had originally belonged to Spain). So effective and moving was de la Motta's eulogy that two former U.S. presidents, James Madison and Thomas Jefferson, congratulated him on it in writing.

Sources: Simonhoff, *Jewish Notables in America, 1776–1865*, pp. 189–192.

1822 ♦ The first anthology of Spanish literature, *Extractos de los más célebres escritores y poetas españoles* (Excerpts from the Most Celebrated Spanish Writers and Poets), was published in Baltimore for use as a textbook in St. Mary's School.

Sources: Online Computer Library Center.

Félix Varela

1824 ♦ In Philadelphia, the first philosophical work by the great Cuban patriot, novelist, journalist, and Catholic priest Félix Varela (1778–1853), *Lecciones de filosofía* (Lessons in Philosophy), was published. Varela was the first Catholic vicar of New York and one of the leaders of the Cuban independence movement.

Sources: Cortina and Leal, "Introduccion," in Felix Varela, *Jicoténcal*, p. xi.

José María Heredia

1825 ♦ The first collection of poems by a Hispanic writer, *Poesías de José María Heredia* by Cuban exile José María Heredia (1803–1839), was published in New York. Heredia, who produced many of his poems in the United States, is considered to be one of the greatest poets of Spanish America.

Sources: Online Computer Library Center.

1826 ♦ The first Latino novel written and published in the United States, *Jicoténcal*, attributed to Cuban philosopher Félix Varela (1778–1853), was issued in Philadelphia. The novel relates the wars of Spanish conquest over the Amerindians of Mexico and thus indirectly supported the Cuban independence movement by equating Spanish Americans with Indians. The novel, which was first published anonymously, was also the first historical novel ever written in the Spanish language. The historical genre entered Hispanic literature through the influence of Sir Walter Scott and James Fenimore Cooper.

Sources: Varela, *Jicoténcal*.

1828 ♦ The first collection of poetry by a Mexican author published in the United States, *Poesías de un mexicano* (The Poems of a Mexican) by Anastasio María de Ochoa y Acuña (1783–1833), was issued in New York.

Sources: Online Computer Library Center.

1828 ♦ The first collection of Spanish Golden Age plays to be read and studied as literature in U.S. colleges and universities was compiled and published in Boston by Francis Sales. *Selección de obras maestras dramáticas por Calderon de la Barca, Lope de Vega y Moreto* (A Selection of Dramatic Master Works by ...) included plays by three of the greatest playwrights of Spain's theatrical flowering in the 17th century. This anthology and others that followed helped to canonize these authors in the American college curriculum. During the

1820s, Sales published a number of anthologies and collections of Spanish literature.

Sources: Online Computer Library Center.

Lorenzo de Zavala

1834 ♦ Lorenzo de Zavala (1788–1836) wrote and published the first book of travel literature by a Hispanic author touring the United States, *Viage a los Estados Unidos de America* (Voyage to the United States of America). Zavala, a Mexican citizen, later became important in the Texas Revolution and became a vice president of Republic of Texas. That same year, another travel book written by a Mexican author, *Viage par los Estados Unidos del Norte* (Voyage to the United States of the North) by Rafael Reynal, was published in the United States in Cincinnati.

Sources: Online Computer Library Center.

1840 ♦ The first edition by a mainstream publisher of Spanish Golden Age playwrights, *Obras maestras de Lope de Vega y Calderon de la Barca* (Master Works by ...), published in New York by Henry Holt, was issued for use in the study of Spanish literature in U.S. colleges and universities.

Sources: Online Computer Library Center.

1858 ♦ The first autobiography written by a Mexican American in the English language was Juan Nepomuceno Seguín's *The Personal Memoirs of John N. Seguín* by the embattled and disenchanted political figure of the Republic of Texas and former mayor of San Antonio. Seguín was born on October 27, 1806, and became a politician and one of the founders of the Republic of Texas. Born into a prominent family of French extraction in San Antonio, Texas, by the age of 18 he had been elected mayor of San Antonio. One of the developers of a nationalist spirit in Texas, Seguín led Texans in opposition to the centrist government of Antonio López de Santa Anna in the 1830s. In the struggle for independence from Mexico, Seguín served as a captain in the Texas cavalry, eventually achieving the rank of lieutenant colonel. After the war of independence, Seguín once again served at the head of the San Antonio government but this time as commander. In 1838, he was elected to the Texas senate, and in 1840, he was elected again to the mayoralty of San Antonio. He was active in defending Tejanos against profiteering Anglos that were rushing into the state to make their fortune at all costs. Unjustly accusing him of favoring invading Mexican forces and betraying the Santa Fe Expedition to foment revolt in New Mexico against Mexico,

Anglos forced Seguín to resign as mayor in April 1842. He moved with his family across the Rio Grande into Mexico in fear of reprisals. In Mexico, he was jailed and forced to serve in the Mexican army, including in battle against the United States during the Mexican War. In 1848, he once again moved to Texas, only to return to live out his days in Nuevo Laredo, Mexico, from 1867 until his death in 1890.

Sources: Tardiff and Mabunda, *Dictionary of Hispanic Biography*, p. 836.

1858 ♦ The first anthology of Hispanic exile literature, *El laúd del desterrado* (The Lute of the Exiled), was published in New York by a group of Cuban exile poets and included the works of José María Heredia (1803–1839), Miguel Teurbe Tolón (1819–1858), Juan Clemente Zenea (1832–1871), and others. The anthology was an important indication that these writers were aware of the whole tradition of Hispanic literary exile and established political exile as one of the bases for literary creation by Latinos in the United States to the present.

Sources: Matías Montes Huidobro, ed., *El laúd del desterrado.*

1872 ♦ The first novel written and published in English by a Latino of the United States was by María Amparo Ruiz de Burton (1832–1895), a domestic novel entitled *Who Would Have Thought It?* Originally published anonymously, the novel reconstructs antebellum and Civil War society in the North and engages the dominant U.S. myths of American exceptionalism, egalitarianism, and consensus, offering an acerbic critique of opportunism and hypocrisy as it represents northern racism and U.S. imperialism. The novel was the first by a U.S. Latino to address the disenfranchised status of women.

María Amparo Ruiz de Burton

Sources: Ruiz de Burton, *Who Would Have Thought It?*

1881 ♦ The first fictional narrative written and published in English from the perspective of the conquered Mexican population of the Southwest was *The Squatter and the Don* by María Amparo Ruiz de Burton (1832–1895); it was self-published under the pseudonym C. Loyal in San Francisco. The novel documents the loss of lands to squatters and banking and railroad interests in southern California shortly after statehood. Ruiz de Burton was a member of the landed gentry in southern California, and she witnessed the disintegration of the old order, shifts in power relations, and the rapid capitalist development of the California Territory, all of which led to the disruption of everyday life for Californios. In *The Squatter and the Don*, a historical romance, Ruiz de Burton laments land loss and calls for justice and redress of grievances. The novel questions U.S. expansionism, the rise of corporate monopolies, and their power over government policy.

Sources: Ruiz de Burton, *The Squatter and the Don.*

1881 ♦ The first Spanish-language novel written and published in the Southwest was the romantic adventure novel *La historia de un caminante, o Gervacio y Aurora* (The History of a Traveler on Foot, or Gervasio and Aurora), written by Manuel M. Salazar (1854–1911). The novel created a colorful picture of pastoral life in New Mexico at the time.

Sources: Kanellos, *Latino Almanac*, p. 299.

George Santayana

1889 ♦ Spanish-born philosopher George Santayana (1863–1952) became the first Latino philosopher and writer to receive a Ph.D. from Harvard. He went on to become a noted poet, philosopher, and professor in the United States and Europe. He published his first book, *The Sense of Beauty*, on aesthetics, in 1896. In 1890, he was named assistant professor in the philosophy department at Harvard and published his first book of poems, *Lucifer: A Theological Tragedy*.

Sources: Tardiff and Mabunda, *Dictionary of Hispanic Biography*, p. 824.

1915 ♦ The first novel of the Mexican Revolution, *Los de abajo* (The Underdogs) by Mariano Azuela (1873–1952), was published in El Paso, Texas. It was the first and most important in a long line of novels of revolution published in exile and is also an important work in the history of Hispanic exile literature.

Mariano Azuela

Mariano Azuela, one of Mexico's greatest novelists and chroniclers of the Mexican Revolution, was born on January 1, 1873, in Lagos de Moreno, Jalisco, Mexico. Educated as a physician (University of Guadalajara, M.D., 1898), Azuela actually developed his career as a writer while practicing medicine until his death of a heart attack on March 1, 1952.

Azuela's early career as a writer, in fact, was developed while participating in the revolution firsthand as a physician in the army of Francisco "Pancho" Villa. Azuela wrote more than 40 novels, most of them based on Mexico's political life from the point of view of a skeptic and critic bent on reforming social and political life in his native land. In many of his works, he documents the loss or corruption of the ideals that were fought for during the revolution.

True to his immediate appreciation of social reality, Azuela's keen ear for dialogue and deft appropriation of characters from social reality contributed a recognition of grassroots Mexican culture that had not really appeared in Mexican letters before, especially within the context of political analysis through literature. True to a tradition of Hispanic literature in exile, Azuela's greatest and most renowned novel, *Los de abajo*, was written while he was a fugitive in El Paso, Texas. In *Los de abajo*, Azuela examines the revolution through the eyes of a common soldier and comes to condemn the uncontrollable whirlwind of violence that the revolution had become. But Azuela's condemnation was a pointed indictment of the forces of corruption and greed in converting the revolution into the murderer of those it was meant to protect and vindicate, such as the rural, grassroots protagonist who is ultimately killed on the very spot where his involvement in the struggle began.

Throughout his career, Azuela was a productive novelist. His other works include *María Luisa* (1907), *Los fracasados* (The Failures, 1908), *Mala yerba* (1909; translated as *Marcela: A Mexican Love Story* in 1932) *Andrés Pérez* (1911), *Sin amor* (Without Love, 1912), *Los caciques* (1917; translated as *The Bosses* in 1956), *Las moscas* (1918; translated as *The Flies* in 1956), *Las tribulaciones de una familia decente* (1918; translated as *The Trials of a Respectable Family* in 1963), and many others.

Sources: Kanellos, *Chronology of Hispanic American History*, p. 172.

1916 ♦ The first literary book to be published by a Dominican author in the United States was *El nacimiento de Dionisos* (The Birth of Dionysus) by Pedro Henríquez Ureña (1884–1946). At the time, Henríquez Ureña was the editor of the New York newspaper *Las novedades* (The News); he also was a brilliant teacher and literary critic.

Sources: Kanellos, *Latino Almanac*, p. 300.

1917 ♦ The first immigration novel published in the United States was written by Colombian immigrant Alirio Díaz Guerra (1862–?). *Lucas Guevara* is the story of a young South American student who immigrates to the grand metropolis of New York, becomes disillusioned, and commits suicide.

Sources: Díaz Guerra, *Lucas Guevara.*

1935 ♦ The first novel written by a U.S. Hispanic to be nominated for the Pulitzer Prize was George Santayana's *The Last Puritan: A Memoir in the Form of a Novel.*

Sources: Tardiff and Mabunda, *Dictionary of Hispanic Biography*, p. 824.

1939 ♦ Brother Angélico Chávez (1910–1996) published his first book of poetry, *Clothed with the Sun*, and eventually became the greatest religious poet among Latinos in the United States. Born on April 10, 1910, in Wagon Mound, New Mexico, he was raised in Mora and attended St. Francis Seminary in Cincinnati, Ohio, and colleges in the Midwest. Chávez was the author of some 20 books, and he was also a historian of his order and of the Catholic Church in New Mexico. What unifies Chávez's large output as a poet and historian is his interest in New Mexico's past and his own Catholicism. Beginning as a religious poet, he later took an interest in historical fiction and, finally, in the history of the region itself, as in his most famous historical essay, *My Penitente Land: Reflections on Spanish New Mexico* (1947). Chávez's reputation as a creative writer rests upon an important body of poetic works that includes *Clothed with the Sun* (1939), *Eleven Lady Lyrics and Other Poems* (1945), *The Single Rose; The Rose Unica and Commentary of Fray Manuel de Santa Clara* (1948), and *The Virgin of Port Lligat* (1959). Although Chávez's poetry and all of his works are grounded in New Mexican Catholicism, his poems are not local color pieces celebrating New Mexico's picturesque landscape; instead, they depict Chávez's inner life.

Sources: "Angélico Chávez," *Dictionary of Literary Biography, Volume 82: Chicano Writers*, pp. 86–90.

1945 ♦ Chilean Gabriela Mistral (1889–1957) became Latin America's first Nobel Prize winner for poetry. After becoming a Nobel laureate, she spent many years in the United States as an ambassador to the League of Nations and the United Nations for Chile. Mistral was born in Vicuña, Chile, and trained as a teacher. As she became well known in the world of letters, she left teaching to serve as a consul and later as an ambassador. As Latin America's first Nobel laureate, she traveled extensively throughout the Americas and became known as a great humanitarian, an active promoter of public education, and a wonderful speaker. Her poetry reveals Mistral as a great humanitarian of broad erudition in world literature and the classics, but her overriding theme was always love. Her work was also rooted in a deep religiosity and the condition and circumstances of women, spanning the gamut of preoccupations from maternity to sterility. Mistral's first book, *Desolación* (Desolation), was published in New York by the Hispanic Institute in 1922. Of her 20-some books of poetry, *Desolación* and *Tala* (1938) are considered her best works. She died in Hempstead, New York, on January 10, 1957.

Gabriela Mistral

Sources: Ryan, *Hispanic Writers*, pp. 222–223.

William Carlos Williams

1950 ♦ William Carlos Williams (1883–1963) was the first person and the first Latino to win the National Book Award for Poetry, recognizing both the third volume of *Paterson* and *Selected Poems.* Considered one of the greatest American modernist poets, Williams was born and raised in Rutherford, New Jersey, in a bilingual household, the son of a Puerto Rican mother and an English father who had been raised in the Dominican Republic. A medical doctor by profession, Williams nevertheless rose to be recognized as a distinguished writer, the author of numerous books and his five-volume epic poem *Paterson* (1946–1958). In addition to *Paterson,* his major works are *Spring and All* (1923), *The Desert Music and Other Poems* (1954), and *Pictures from Brueghel and Other Poems* (1962). In 1963, Williams was posthumously awarded the Pulitzer Prize for *Pictures from Brueghel and Other Poems* (1962) and the gold medal for poetry from the National Institute of Arts and Letters; he was the first Latino to receive these distinctions.

Sources: Leibowitz, Herbert, *"Something Urgent I Have to Say to You": The Life and Works of William Carlos Williams.* New York, Farrar, Straus and Giroux, 2011.

1958 ♦ Novelist Floyd Salas (1931–2021) became the first U.S. Hispanic writer to receive a Rockefeller grant to study creative writing at the prestigious Centro Mexicano de Escritores in Mexico City. Upon returning to California from Mexico, Salas worked on Bay Area campuses as a creative writing instructor and became active in the campus protest movement as well as immersed in the drug and hippie subcultures.

These experiences became grist for his novels *What Now My Love?* (1970) and *State of Emergency* (1996). His first published book, *Tattoo the Wicked Cross* (1967), was made possible by his winning the prestigious Joseph Henry Jackson Award and a Eugene F. Saxton Fellowship on the basis of early drafts of that novel. *Tattoo the Wicked Cross* is an exposé of the brutality of juvenile jail as seen by a street youth (*pachuco*) who is raped and abused; the brutalized protagonist ends up committing murder.

The raw power and passion of Salas's narration left reviewers believing that Salas had experienced this brutality firsthand, but he actually based the story on tales he had heard. The overwhelming acclaim the novel received from reviewers projected Salas into a resplendent career. *The Saturday Review of Literature* gave the most important canonizing response to *Tattoo*: "One of the best and certainly one of the most important first novels published in the last 10 years."

Sources: Kanellos, *The Hispanic Literary Companion*, p. 293.

1959 ♦ José Antonio Villarreal (1924–2010) published what is considered to be the first Chicano novel in contemporary times. *Pocho*, a developmental novel in which the protagonist has a classic identity crisis, was also the first Chicano novel to be published by a major commercial house, Doubleday.

Sources: "José Antonio Villarreal," *Dictionary of Literary Biography, Volume 82: Chicano Writers*, pp. 282–288.

1962 ♦ Nuyorican writer Piri Thomas (1928–2011) was the first Latino writer to receive a grant from the Louis M. Rabinowitz Foundation. The grant enabled him to finish writing his groundbreaking autobiography, *Down These Mean Streets* (1967). The work brought national attention to Nuyorican literature. It was the first agonizing tale of the search for identity among conflicting cultural, racial, ethnic, and linguistic alternatives presented to Latinos in general and to Afro-Latinos in the United States in particular. It was such a milestone that the Nuyorican and Latino literature that followed it either continued its themes or totally rejected its poetic melange of street language and psychodrama as a naive and unsophisticated cry out of the culture of poverty.

Piri Thomas

Thomas was born John Peter Thomas on September 30, 1928, in New York City's Harlem Hospital to a light-skinned Puerto Rican mother and an Afro-Cuban father of the working class. In his upbringing, he experienced racism in the most intimate of settings when his siblings' lighter skin was preferred over his obviously dark African inheritance. This prejudice, of course, presented one of the principal causes of anguish in his life and is reflected in his books. When his family attempted to escape the ills of the city by moving to Babylon, Long Island, he again faced rejection at school and in the neighborhood because of his skin color. In part, this is the subject of his second book, *Savior, Savior, Hold My Hand*, which also deals with the hypocrisy he faced while working with a Christian church.

Thomas grew up on the streets of Spanish Harlem, where he became involved in gang activity and criminality. In 1950, he participated in an armed robbery of a nightclub that left him and a policeman wounded; he was sentenced to and served seven years in jail, the subject of his *Seven Long Times* (1974). While in prison, Thomas became part of the black pride movement, converted to Islam, earned a G.E.D., and began writing. As a former convict, in 1962, he was befriended by an editor from Knopf and supported by a grant for five years from the Louis M. Rabinowitz Foundation, with which he was able to produce the modern classic autobiography that forever changed his life and the trajectory of Latino and ethnic literatures in the United States.

Sources: Kanellos, *The Hispanic Literary Companion*, pp. 327–328.

1963 ♦ Jose Yglesias (1919–1995) became the first Cuban American creative writer to be published by a mainstream press with the publication of *A Wake in Ybor City*, based on the Cuban-Spanish community in Tampa, Florida. Yglesias was one of the pioneers of Latino literature in English; it could also be said that he was the first writer with a Cuban American consciousness. For more than 30 years, he wrote novels and stories based on Latino life in the United States, and he saw them published by some of the largest and most respected publishing houses in the country. Yglesias was born in the cigar-making community of Ybor City on November 29, 1919.

He was the child of a Cuban mother and a Spanish father, who returned home to Galicia when Yglesias was only a child. Among the cigar rollers, a proud and intellectual lot, he learned about Hispanic literature, history, and politics, interests that would inform his fiction and nonfiction writing his entire life. Like the tobacco workers, Yglesias was largely self-educated. Two days after graduating from high school, he went to New York City. After serving in the U.S. Navy during World War II, he attended Black Mountain College for one year (1946–1947). He returned to New York City, married, and began a family while working for a pharmaceutical company, where he eventually became an executive.

During the 1950s, Yglesias began writing reviews and articles for magazines and in 1963 saw his first novel published. *A Wake in Ybor City*, like most first novels, is highly autobiographical. Yglesias soon became a full-time writer of stories for such magazines as *The New Yorker*, *Esquire*, the *Atlantic*, the *Nation*, and the *New York Times Magazine*; novels that deal mostly with Latinos in the United States; and journalistic books about such topics as Franco's Spain and Castro's Cuba. Two of his stories were included in *The Best American Short Stories* and form a part of his posthumous collection *The Guns in the Closet* (1996). In all, he wrote 10 books of fiction, three of which were published posthumously. He died of cancer in December 1995.

Sources: Kanellos, *The Hispanic Literary Companion*, pp. 389–390.

1964 ♦ The first literary magazine founded by Cuban exiles from the Cuban Revolution, *Cuadernos desterrados* (Exiled Notebooks), was established in Miami, Florida.

Sources: García, *Havana USA*, p. 262.

1965 ♦ Ediciones Universal, the first and largest publishing house to serve the Cuban refugee community, was founded in Miami, Florida, by Juan Manuel Salvat (1940–). It publishes the works of leading emigré scholars and literary figures. It was not until the 1970s and 1980s that other Cuban and Cuban American publishing houses began to appear, such as Editorial SIBI, Editorial Persona, Editorial Arcos, and Linden Lane Press.

Sources: García, *Havana USA*, p. 195.

1966 ♦ San Antonio, Texas, poet Angela de Hoyos (1940–2009) became the first Latino poet to win international recognition by winning the Bronze Medal of Honor (poetry) from Centro Studi e Scambi Internazionale (CSSI) in Rome, Italy, in 1966. She also won the Silver Medal of Honor (literature) from CSSI in 1967; the Diploma di Benemerenza (literature) from CSSI in 1968; the Diploma di Benemerenza (poetry) from CSSI in 1969 and 1970; and the Distinguished Service Citation from World Poetry Society Intercontinental in India in 1970. Angela de Hoyos is a pioneer of modern Chicano poetry; when there was little opportunity for her works to be published and recognized in the United States, she began disseminating her poetry internationally. Finally, in the early 1970s as the Chicano literary movement was peaking, her work became part of the basis for the Chicano literary flowering. She was the first of the women poets to gather a following in the movement and became an inspiration for other early writers, such as Evangelina Vigil-Piñón (1949–), who followed in her path.

Sources: Tardiff and Mabunda, *Dictionary of Hispanic Biography*, p. 274.

1967 ♦ The most influential Chicano magazine, *El grito* (The Shout), was founded in Berkeley, California, by two University of California professors, Octavio I. Romano-V. (1923–2005) and Herminio Ríos. *El grito* and the publishing house Editorial Quinto Sol (Fifth Sun), which they established in 1968, launched the careers of the most important writers of the Chicano Movement, such as Alurista (1947–), Tomás Rivera (1935–1984), Rudolfo Anaya

1967: First Chicano Epic Poem Published

In 1967 Rodolfo "Corky" Gonzales (1928–2005), founder of a militant Chicano civil rights organization, the Crusade for Justice, wrote and published the first Chicano epic poem, "I Am Joaquin/Yo Soy Joaquín," which influenced the development of Chicano literature and the nationalist ideology. The poem was widely read and emulated and was even the basis of a film created by El Teatro Campesino and narrated by Luis Valdez (1940–). *Sources:* Rosales, *Chicano! History of the Mexican American Civil Rights Movement*, pp. 180, 217.

(1937–2020), and Rolando Hinojosa (1929–2022), as well as defined Chicano literature and established the canons of that literature by publishing those works that best exemplified Chicano culture, language, themes, and styles.

The very name of the publishing house emphasized its Mexican/Aztec identity as well as the Spanish language; "quinto sol" referred to an Aztec belief in a period of cultural flowering that would take place sometime in the future, in a fifth age, which conveniently coincided with the rise of Chicano culture. In its publications, there was a definite insistence on working-class and rural culture, as exemplified in the works of Rivera, Anaya, and Hinojosa, and there was also a promotion of works written bilingually or in dialect.

Sources: Tatum, Charles, M. *Chicano and Chicana Literature.* University of Arizona Press, 2006.

1969 ♦ Nuyorican poet Victor Hernández Cruz (1949–) became the first Latino poet to be published by a mainstream publishing house when Random House issued his *Snaps*. Cruz is the Nuyorican poet who was discovered as a precocious street poet while still in high school in New York; he has become one of the most recognized and acclaimed Latino poets ever by the mainstream. Despite his early acceptance into creative writing circles, culminating with *Life* magazine's canonizing him in 1981 as one of the 25 best American poets, Cruz has resisted estheticism and academic writing to remain very much an oral poet, a jazz poet, a poet of the people and popular traditions, a bilingual poet, and a poet of intuition and tremendous insight.

Victor Hernández Cruz was born on February 6, 1949, in Aguas Buenas, Puerto Rico. He moved with his family to New York's Spanish Harlem at the age of 5. Cruz attended Benjamin Franklin High School, where he began writing poetry. In the years following graduation, his poetry began to appear in *Evergreen Review, The New York Review of Books*, and many other magazines. Beginning in 1970, he worked with poetry-in-the-schools programs in New York, such as the Teachers and Writers Collaborative. In 1973, Cruz left New York and took up residence in San Francisco, where he worked for the U.S. Postal Service and served as a visiting poet at area colleges. From 1973 to 1975, he took up the life of the traveling troubadour, covering the full expanse of the United States from Alaska and Hawaii to Puerto Rico, reading and performing his works while also continuing to write. Thereafter, he alternated living in San Francisco and Puerto Rico and finally settled down in Puerto Rico to dedicate himself mostly to writing and accepting engagements nationally to read from his works.

Cruz received fellowships from the National Endowment for the Arts and the Guggenheim Foundation in 1980 and 1991, respectively. His poetry books include *Papo Got His Gun* (1966), *Snaps* (1969), *Mainland* (1973), *Tropicalization* (1976), *By Lingual Wholes* (1982), *Rhythm, Content and Flavor* (1989),

1970: First National Award for Chicano Literature

Editorial Quinto Sol established the first national award for Chicano literature, Premio Quinto Sol, in 1970. The Premio included a $1,000 prize and publication of the winning book manuscript. For the first three years, the prize went to books that are still seen as exemplary Chicano novels: Tomás Rivera's *...y no se lo tragó la tierra/... And the Earth Did Not Part*, Rudolfo Anaya's *Bless Me, Ultima*, and Rolando Hinojosa's *Estampas del Valley y otras obras/Sketches of the Valley and Other Works. Sources:* Martín-Rodríguez, Manuel M. *Life in Search of Readers: Reading (In) Chicano/a Literature.* University of New Mexico Press, 2003, p. 18.

Red Beans (1991), *Maraca: New and Selected Poems, 1966–2000* (2001), *The Mountain in the Sea: Poems.* (2006), *In the Shadow of Al-Andalus* (2011), and *Beneath the Spanish* (2017).

Sources: Kanellos, *Latino Almanac*, p. 343.

1969 ♦ Editorial Quinto Sol published the first (or one of the first) anthologies of Chicano literature, *El Espejo/The Mirror*, edited by Octavio I. Romano-V. It included the works of such notable and still-studied authors as Alurista, Miguel Méndez, and Tomás Rivera.

Sources: Griswold et al., *Chicano Art*, p. 215.

1970 ♦ Texas novelist Tomás Rivera (1935–1984) won the first national award for Chicano literature, Premio Quinto Sol, for his novel of migrant worker life, *... y no se lo tragó la tierra /... And the Earth Did Not Part.*

Sources: Kanellos, *Latino Almanac*, pp. 309–310.

Rudolfo Anaya

1971 ♦ Rudolfo Anaya's (1937–2020) novel *Bless Me, Ultima*, the second winner of the Premio Quinto Sol, became a best-selling Chicano novel, selling more than one million copies over a 20-year period, according to the publishers. A straightforward narrative written in poetic and clear English, the novel is about a boy's coming of age in rural New Mexico and having to mediate the competing Indian and Spanish traditions of his maternal and paternal heritages. *Bless Me, Ultima* was the first U.S. Hispanic book to reach a broad segment of non-Hispanic readers.

Sources: Kanellos, *Latino Almanac*, pp. 310–311.

1971 ♦ *Floricanto en Aztlán* by Alurista (born Alberto Baltazar Urista, 1947–) became the first Chicano poetry book to be published by a university, the University of California at Los Angeles, through its Chicano Studies Publications. The book was highly influential in integrating pre-Columbian culture and symbolism into rising Chicano nationalism. It was also an exemplary model of bilingualism in poetry.

Sources: Griswold et al., *Chicano Art*, p. 217.

1972 ♦ The first journal for the study and promotion of Puerto Rican culture of the mainland United States, *The Rican Journal*, was founded and published by a Northeastern Illinois University sociology professor, Samuel Betances, in Chicago. In addition to publishing social science articles, the journal published original literature by Nuyoricans.

Sources: Chabrán, Rafael, and Richard Chabrán, "The Spanish-Language and Latino Press in the United States," in Kanellos and Fabregat, *Handbook of Hispanic Culture in the United States: Literature*, p. 378.

1972 ♦ Festival Floricanto, the first national Chicano literature festival, was held in Los Angeles.

Sources: Griswold et al., *Chicano Art*, p. 217.

1973 ♦ Nicholasa Mohr (1935–) became the first Latina in modern times to have her literary works published by major commercial publishing houses, and she has developed a longer career as a creative writer for these publishing houses than most other Latino writers. Mohr's books for such publishers as Dell/Dial, Harper & Row, and Bantam, in both the adult and children's literature categories, have won numerous awards and outstanding reviews. Part and parcel of her work is the experience of growing up female, Latina, and a minority in New York City.

Born on November 1, 1935, in New York City, Nicholasa Mohr was raised in Spanish Harlem. Educated in New York City schools, she finally escaped poverty after graduating from the Pratt Center for Contemporary Printmaking in 1969. From that date until the publication of her first book, *Nilda* (1973), Mohr developed a successful career as a graphic artist. *Nilda*, a novel that traces the life of a young Puerto Rican girl confronting prejudice and coming of age during World War II, won the Jane Addams Children's Book Award and was selected by *School Library Journal* as a Best Book of the Year. It was the first book by a U.S. Latino author to be so honored.

1973: *Revista Chicano-Riqueña* Founded

In 1973 the first national magazine of U.S. Latino literature, *Revista Chicano-Riqueña* (The Chicano-Rican Review), was founded at Indiana University Northwest in Gary, Indiana, by coeditors Nicolás Kanellos (1945–) and Luis Dávila (1938–2015). The magazine was published for 25 years, becoming the longest-lasting Latino literary magazine to date; it changed its title for the last decade of its life to *The Americas Review.* It moved to the University of Houston in 1980, from where it promoted pan-Latino culture in the United States and launched the careers of most of the important writers of Latino literature of its time, including Lorna Dee Cervantes, Sandra Cisneros, Ana Castillo, Tato Laviera, and many others. In 1979, the magazine founded its own literary press, Arte Público Press, which grew to be the largest noncommercial publisher of literature in the United States. *Sources:* Kanellos, *Latino Almanac*, p. 355.

The Society of Illustrators presented Mohr with a citation of merit for the book's jacket design. After *Nilda*'s success, Mohr was able to produce numerous stories, scripts, and the following titles: *El Bronx Remembered* (1975), *In Nueva York* (1977), *Felita* (1979), *Rituals of Survival: A Woman's Portfolio* (1985), *Going Home* (1986), and others.

Sources: Telgen and Kamp, *Latinas! Women of Achievement*, pp. 247–254.

1973 ♦ Ricardo Sánchez (1941–1995) became the first Chicano poet to have a book published by a mainstream commercial publishing house when Anchor/Doubleday issued his *Canto y grito mi liberación* (I Sing and Shout for My Liberation). It was also the first bilingual poetry book published by a major commercial publisher. Sánchez was one of the most prolific Chicano poets, one of the first creators of a bilingual literary style, and one of the first to be identified with the Chicano Movement. He was a tireless and popular oral performer and social activist whose creative power expressed itself in innovative uses of both Spanish and English in poetry, frequently through the creation of interlingual neologisms and abrupt linguistic contrasts. His verse is as overwhelming in sheer power as his aggressive personality, which was forged in hard prison labor.

Sánchez was born the youngest of 13 children in the notorious *Barrio del Diablo* (Devil's Neighborhood) in El Paso, Texas. He received his early education there and became a high school dropout, an army enlistee, and later a repeat offender sentenced to prison terms in Soledad Prison in California and Ramsey Prison Farm Number One in Texas. At these institutions, he began his literary career before his last parole in 1969.

Much of his early life experience of oppressive poverty and overwhelming racism, as well as his suffering in prisons and his self-education and rise to a high level of political and social consciousness, is chronicled in his poetry, which, although very lyrical, is the most autobiographical of all the Latino poets. Sánchez always envisioned himself participating, in fact leading, a sociopolitical consciousness-raising movement. His many travels and itinerant lifestyle—always in search of a permanent job in academia—resulted in his functioning as a troubadour model for the developing Chicano literary movement. His poetry announced and exemplified the authenticity of a bilingual writing style that had roots in oral tradition and community concerns.

Sources: "Ricardo Sánchez," *Dictionary of Literary Biography, Volume 82: Chicano Writers*, pp. 239–245.

1974 ♦ Estela Portillo Trambley (1926–1998) became the first woman to win the national award for Chicano literature, Premio Quinto Sol, for her collection of short stories, *Rain of Scorpions.* Her winning marked the ascendancy of Mexican American women into the Chicano literary movement, which had been so dominated by males.

Sources: Kanellos, *Latino Almanac*, p. 383.

1974 ♦ A group of young and radical Cuban emigrés founded the first pro–Cuban Revolution magazine in the United States: *Areíto.* Headed by Lourdes Casal (1938–1981), the magazine supported the Cuban government, which it stated had created a more egalitarian society. The magazine's stance prompted the defection of various sponsors and a hostile reaction from the Cuban refugee press and intellectuals. Despite the hostility, *Areíto* survived well into the 1980s.

Sources: García, *Havana USA*, pp. 201–203.

1975 ♦ The first anthology of Nuyorican literature, *Nuyorican Poetry: An Anthology of Puerto Rican Words and Feelings*, was compiled by Miguel Algarín (1941–2020) and Miguel Piñero (1946–1988). Algarín owned and administered the Nuyorican Poets Cafe, which promoted the distinct identity of Puerto Ricans born or raised on the mainland, and Piñero was the first Nuyorican writer to gain national acclaim with his play *Short Eyes.*

Sources: Kanellos, *The Hispanic Literary Companion*, pp. 244–246.

1975 ♦ New York Puerto Rican novelist Nicholasa Mohr's second book, *El Bronx Remembered*, was awarded *New York Times*'s Outstanding Book Award in teenage fiction and received the Best Book Award from the *School Library Journal. El Bronx Remembered* was also a National Book Award finalist in children's literature.

Sources: Telgen and Kamp, *Latinas! Women of Achievement*, p. 252.

1975 ♦ Chicano poet Gary Soto (1952–) became the first Latino writer to win the nationally prestigious Academy of American Poets Prize. That same year, he won the *Nation*'s Discovery Award. Soto is a prolific poet and writer of books for children and young adults.

Gary Soto

Sources: Kanellos, *Latino Almanac*, p. 314.

Rolando Hinojosa

1976 ♦ Rolando Hinojosa (1929–2022) became the first Latino writer and the first American to win the prestigious international award *Premio Casa de las Américas* (House of the Americas Prize) from Cuba for his novel *Klail City y sus alrededores* (Klail City and Surroundings). He was the first Chicano novelist to win an international award.

Sources: Kanellos, *Latino Almanac*, pp. 352–353.

1977 ♦ San Antonio poet Evangelina Vigil-Piñón (1949–) became the first Latino writer to win the National Literary Contest of the Coordinating Council of Literary Magazines for work published in a small magazine. Vigil-Piñón is the Chicana poet who has most sensitively portrayed and celebrated working-class culture. She is also one of the leading exponents of bilingual code-switching in poetry: Vigil-Piñón is a natural at transference from English to Spanish and back as conversation at the kitchen table. Working at the center of Latino literature as the poetry editor for the leading Latino literary magazine *Revista Chicano-Riqueña/The Americas Review*, Vigil-Piñón has also been a leader in the Latina women's movement as an anthologizer, speaker, and host of writers on tour.

Sources: Kanellos, *The Hispanic Literary Companion*, pp. 358–360.

1978 ♦ A group of young Cuban emigrés publishing the pro-Cuban Revolution magazine *Areíto* in New York published their first anthology, *Contra viento y marea* (Against Wind and Waves), in Cuba. The writings of these refugees, who had been forced to accompany their parents into exile from Cuba at an early age, recounted their experiences as refugees in a foreign culture and their allegiance to communist Cuba. In 1978, the anthology was awarded

Cuba's highest literary award, one regarded as one of the most distinguished in all of Spanish America: *Premio Casa de las Américas* (House of the Americas Prize).

Sources: García, *Havana USA*, p. 201.

1978 ♦ Puerto Rican novelist and short story writer José Luis González (1926–1996) became the first Latino writer to win Mexico's most prestigious literary award, the Xavier Viallurrutia Award for Fiction, for his novel *Balada de otro tiempo* (Ballad of Another Time), which is set to the background of the U.S. invasion of Puerto Rico during the Spanish-American War.

Sources: Kanellos, *Chronology of Hispanic American History*, p. 262.

1979 ♦ Arte Público Press organized the First National Latino Book Fair in Chicago, Illinois. In addition to exhibiting and selling books by the few Hispanic presses and magazines that existed in the United States at that time, the book fair featured readings by some of the most important writers of the period, such as Ana Castillo, Lorna Dee Cervantes, Sandra Cisneros, Abelardo Delgado, Sandra María Esteves, Tato Laviera, and Rolando Hinojosa.

Sources: Kanellos, *Latino Almanac*, p. 355.

1980 ♦ Prize-winning novelist Rudolfo Anaya (1937–2020) was the first Hispanic novelist to receive a gubernatorial award, the New Mexico Governor's Award for Excellence in the Arts. Anaya is the author of one of the most celebrated Latino novels, *Bless Me, Ultima* (1972). Anaya was born on October 30, 1937, in the village of Pastura, New Mexico, in surroundings similar

1979: Arte Público Press Founded

The oldest and largest publisher of Latino literature, Arte Público Press, was founded in 1979 at the University of Houston by Nicolás Kanellos, a professor and founding editor of *Revista Chicano-Riqueña*, one of the longest-lasting Latino literary magazines in the United States. Over the years, the press has won numerous awards and launched the careers of most of the prominent Latino writers. By the early 1990s, the press had become the largest non-commercial publisher of literature in the United States, issuing more than 30 titles per year. The first book published by Arte Público Press was Tato Laviera's groundbreaking collection of poems, *La Carreta Made a U-Turn*. *Sources:* Kanellos, *Latino Almanac*, p. 355.

to those celebrated in his famous novel about growing up in the rural culture of New Mexico. He attended public schools in Santa Rosa and Albuquerque and earned both his B.A. (1963) and his M.A. (1968) in English from the University of New Mexico. In 1972, he also earned an M.A. in guidance and counseling from the same university. From 1963 to 1970, he taught in public schools, but in 1974, he became a member of the English department of the University of New Mexico.

With the success of his writing career, Anaya rose to become the head of the creative writing program at the University of New Mexico. Included among his many awards are an honorary doctorate from the University of Albuquerque, the New Mexico Governor's Award for Excellence in the Arts, the President's National Salute to American Poets and Writers in 1980, and the Premio Quinto Sol in 1972 for *Bless Me, Ultima*. Anaya is also a fellow of the National Endowment for the Arts and the Kellogg Foundation, through whose auspices he was able to travel to China and other countries for study.

Sources: Kanellos, *The Hispanic Literary Companion*, pp. 41–42; "Rudolfo Anaya," *Dictionary of Literary Biography, Volume 82: Chicano Writers*, pp. 24–35.

1980 ♦ Mexican American poet Luis Omar Salinas (1937–2008) became the first Hispanic writer to win the Stanley Kunitz Memorial Prize and the Earl Lyon Award for his collection *Afternoon of the Unreal*. Salinas is one of the most beloved and enduring poets to emerge from the Chicano literary movement. His productivity has spanned the entire contemporary movement, with his first poems appearing in newspapers, magazines, and anthologies about the time when the first Chicano literary magazines and presses were being founded in the late 1960s. He always provided a broadly romantic and highly lyrical inspiration to Chicanos in search of roots rather than solely basing his works in the sociopolitical reality of an ethnic minority struggle. Highly influenced by Spain's Federico García Lorca and Chile's Pablo Neruda, Salinas has created a somewhat surreal, thoughtful, and very personal ongoing text in what otherwise has been the development of an epic and communal literature. Salinas has said that his poetic ideal is to "somehow come to terms with the tragic and through the tragic gain a vision which transcends this world in some way."

Sources: Tardiff and Mabunda, *Dictionary of Hispanic Biography*, pp. 795–796.

1981 ♦ Jesús Abraham "Tato" Laviera (1950–2013) became the first Latino to win the American Book Award of the Before Columbus Foundation, which recognizes and promotes multicultural literature. Laviera was the best-selling Latino poet of the United States. Born on September 5, 1950, in Santurce, Puerto Rico, he immigrated to New York City at the age of 10 with his family, who settled in a poor area of the Lower East Side. After finding himself in an alien society and with practically no English, Laviera was able to adjust and eventually graduate high school as an honor student. Despite having no other degrees, his intelligence, aggressiveness, and thorough knowledge of his community led to his developing a career in the administration of social service agencies.

After the publication of his first book, *La Carreta Made a U-Turn* (1979), Laviera gave up administrative work to dedicate his time to writing. Since 1980, Laviera's career included not only writing but touring nationally as a performer of his poetry, directing plays he had written and producing cultural events. In 1980, he was received by President Jimmy Carter at the White House Gathering of American Poets. In 1981, his second book, *Enclave*, was the recipient of another American Book Award.

Sources: Kanellos, *Latino Almanac*, pp. 320–321, 356–357.

1981 ♦ Cherríe Moraga (1952–) and Gloria Anzaldúa (1942–2004), two Chicana lesbian writers, became the first to compile an anthology of the literature and thought of women of color: *This Bridge Called My Back: Writings by Radical Women of Color.* The book has become the most famous and best-selling anthology of its kind, and it has inspired a movement of Latina feminist and lesbian writers.

Cherríe Moraga

Sources: Kanellos, *Latino Almanac*, pp. 330–331, 362.

1981 ♦ *Yerba buena* (Mint) by New York poet Sandra María Esteves (1948–) was the first Latino book to win the award for Best Small Press Publication. Esteves, the daughter of Puerto Rican and Dominican parents, is one of the leading exponents of bilingual feminist poetry; she is also one of the most noted oral performers of poetry. Her other works include *Tropical Rains: A Bilingual Downpour* (1984) and *Bluestown Mockingbird Mambo* (1990).

Sources: Telgen and Kamp, *Latinas! Women of Achievement*, pp. 121–123.

1981 ♦ Victor Hernández Cruz became the first Latino poet to be canonized as one of the few great American poets when the April 1981 issue of *Life* magazine proclaimed him a national treasure by including him among a handful of outstanding American poets without making reference to his race or ethnicity.

Sources: Kanellos, *Latino Almanac*, p. 343.

1981 ♦ The Mexican American Hernández brothers—Jaime, Gilbert, and Mario—self-published the first issue of their groundbreaking comic book series *Love and Rockets*; its popularity has endured into the 21st century, become the subject of academic studies, and spawned numerous followers. *Rolling Stone* ranked *Love and Rockets* as the greatest non-superhero graphic novel of all time, likening it to the *Clash*, *REM*, and *Run-DMC*. *Time* magazine included the Hernández brothers in its top 100 21st century innovators. It is one of the very few non-superhero graphic novels to have met the test of time.

Two of the Hernández brothers (Jaime in foreground and Gilbert in the middle) sign copies of *Love and Rockets* at San Diego Comic-Con 2007.

Sources: Rayner, Alex. "Love and Rockets Rides Again: 'We Influenced a Whole Lot of Cartoonists,'" *The Guardian,* 10 August 2016: https://www.theguardian.com/books/2016/aug/10/love-and-rockets-california-punks-jaime-gilbert-hernandez.

1982 ♦ Poet Evangelina Vigil-Piñón (1949–) became the first Latina to win the American Book Award from the Before Columbus Foundation for her *Thirty an' Seen a Lot.* Vigil-Piñón was born in San Antonio, Texas, on November 19, 1949, the second of 10 children of a very poor family that lived for years in public housing. In her later childhood years, Vigil-Piñón lived with her maternal grandmother and uncle, from whom she learned much of the oral lore that has become such an important basis for her poetry; Vigil-Piñón's mother was also an avid reader who gave her daughter a love of books. From her grandmother, she learned "to observe and listen for words of wisdom which come only with experience." And, indeed, the predominant narrator in her first full-length collection of poems, *Thirty an' Seen a Lot* (1982), is that of the acute but anonymous observer, the observer of the life of working-class people in her beloved West Side barrio of San Antonio, the recorder of their language and diction, their proverbs and music, their joys and sorrows. Despite the apparently natural vernacular of her writing, Vigil-Piñón's poetry is the product of great craftsmanship, obtained through extensive reading and self-education as well as through formal study. She obtained a B.A. in English from the University of Houston in 1974 and took post-graduate courses at various institutions afterward. She also served as an adjunct faculty member for the University of Houston.

Sources: "Evangelina Vigil," *Dictionary of Literary Biography, Volume 122: Chicano Writers*, pp. 306–312.

1983 ♦ *Revista Mariel*, the first magazine published by Cuban refugees from the Mariel Boatlift, was founded. Established in Miami initially by Reinaldo Arenas (1943–1990), Roberto Valero (1955–1994), and Juan Abreu (1952–), it was later moved to New York and specialized in publishing the works of authors who had been silenced by the Castro regime, as had its leading editor and literary figure, Reinaldo Arenas.

Sources: García, *Havana USA*, p. 195.

1983 ♦ Texas Mexican American writer Lionel G. García (1935–2013) was the first Latino to win the PEN Southwest Discovery Award for his novel *Leaving Home*. García went on to become the first and only Latino to win the two other major awards for fiction in the Southwest: the Texas Literary Award from the Southwestern Booksellers Association and the Texas Institute of Letters Jesse Jones Award for his 1989 novel, *Hardscrub*. García is a novelist who has created some of the most memorable characters in Chicano literature in a style that is well steeped in the traditions of the Texas tall tale and Mexican American folk narrative.

Born in San Diego, Texas, on August 20, 1935, García grew up in an environment in which Mexican Americans were the majority population in his small town and on the ranches where he worked and played. In order to make a living, García became a veterinarian, but he always practiced his first love: storytelling and writing. In 1983, he won the PEN Southwest Discovery Award for his novel in progress, *Leaving Home*, which was published in 1985. This and his second novel, *A Shroud in the Family* (1987), drew heavily on his family experiences and small-town background; both are set in a quaint village very much like San Diego, Texas, where he grew up, and follow the antics of children similar to those friends and family members that surrounded him as a child, who reappear in his collection of autobiographical stories, *I Can Hear the Cowbell Ring* (1994).

García's prize-winning novel *Hardscrub* (1989) is a departure from his former works; it is a realistically drawn chronicle of the life of an Anglo child in an abusive family relationship. It won the Best Novel Award from the Texas Institute of Letters and the Southwestern Booksellers Association Prize for Fiction.

Sources: "Lionel G. García," *Dictionary of Literary Biography, Volume 82: Chicano Authors*, pp. 123–124.

1983 ♦ Luis Omar Salinas (1937–2008) became the first Hispanic writer to win the General Electric Foundation Younger Writers Award in recognition for poems he published in the literary magazine *Revista Chicano-Riqueña.*

Sources: Tardiff and Mabunda, *Dictionary of Hispanic Biography*, pp. 785–786.

1984 ♦ El Paso poet Pat Mora's (1942–) first collection of poems, *Chants*, was the first Latino book to win the Southwest Book Award, given by the Border Regional Library Association. *Chants* is a celebration of women and the culture of the United States–Mexican border. Of all the Latino poets, Pat Mora has developed the broadest audiences for her poetry in the United States. Her clean, crisp narrative style and the healing, all-embracing messages in her verse have allowed her poetry to reach out to both adults and young people. In fact, Mora's poems have been reprinted in more elementary, middle, and high school textbooks than any other Latino poet in the United States. Pat Mora was born and raised in El Paso, Texas. She attended El Paso public schools and received all of her higher education in this border city, including a B.A. and an M.A. in English from the University of Texas at El Paso. After graduating from college in 1963, she worked as an English teacher in the El Paso public schools and the El Paso Community College; eventually, she made her way back to the University of Texas at El Paso as an instructor and, from 1981 to 1988, served as a university administrator and museum director.

Pat Mora

Mora began publishing poetry in little magazines, such as *Revista Chicano-Riqueña* in the late 1970s and early 1980s, as part of the first wave of Chicana writers to grab the reins of the Chicano literary movement and assume its leadership. It was her first books of poetry, however, that firmly established her reputation as a lyric shaman and celebrant of biculturalism. For *Chants* (1984) and *Borders* (1986), Mora received Southwest Book Awards, critical acclaim, and entry into the college and high school curricula. Her publication in 1991 of *Communion* consolidated her dominant themes and solidified her reputation in academia. Many more books of poetry and essays for adults and children's books followed.

Sources: Telgen and Kamp, *Latinas! Women of Achievement*, pp. 255–260.

1985 ♦ Oscar Hijuelos (1951–2013), who later won a Pulitzer Prize, became the first U.S. Hispanic writer to win the prestigious American Academy in

Rome Fellowship from the American Academy and Institute of Arts and Letters.

Sources: Kanellos, *The Hispanic Literary Companion*, p. 117.

1986 ♦ *The Americas Review* (formerly *Revista Chicano-Riqueña*) became the first Hispanic magazine ever to win the Citation of Achievement from the Coordinating Council of Literary Magazines. *The Americas Review* went on to win the citation again in 1987.

Sources: Kanellos, *The Hispanic Literary Companion*.

1986 ♦ Novelist and poet Julia Alvarez (1950–) became the first Latina and first Dominican to win the General Electric Foundation Award for Young Writers. The daughter of Dominican immigrants, Alvarez is the author of novels and poetry about growing up biculturally in the United States. Her most successful work is a novel, *How the García Girls Lost Their Accent*, published in 1991.

Julia Alvarez

Sources: Telgen and Kamp, *Latinas! Women of Achievement*, pp. 19–24.

1986 ♦ Michael Nava (1954–) published his first novel, *The Little Death*, becoming the creator of the first Latino gay detective series. As of 1996, six novels have been published in the series that features gay detective Henry Ríos.

Sources: "Who We Are: Michael Nava," *Publishers Weekly*, 30 September 1996, p. 49.

1988 ♦ Poet Pat Mora (1942–) was the first Hispanic writer to be named to the *El Paso Herald-Post* Writers Hall of Fame. An El Paso native who had won two Southwest Book Awards, Mora was also inducted into the Texas Institute of Letters the same year.

Sources: Telgen and Kamp, *Latinas! Women of Achievement*, p. 258.

1988 ♦ Nicolás Kanellos (1985–), the founder and publisher of Arte Público Press, became the first Latino publisher ever to be honored with the Hispanic Heritage Award for Literature, presented at the White House by President Ronald Reagan.

Sources: Unterburger, *Who's Who among Hispanic Americans*, p. 355.

1988 ♦ Mexican American lawyer Michael Angel Nava (1954–) was the first Latino writer to win the Lambda Literary Award for his novel *Goldenboy*, which features a criminal defense lawyer, Henry Ríos, who is to be the protagonist in the 10 mystery books in the series. Ríos is the first openly gay protagonist in Latino mystery/detective novels. Seven of the books in the series have won Lambda Literary Awards.

Sources: Olivas, Daniel, "Spotlight on Michael Nava," La Bloga: https://labloga.blogspot.com/2006/04/spotlight-on-michael-nava.html.

1989 ♦ Poet Carolina Hospital (1957–) compiled the first anthology of Cuban American literature, *Cuban American Writers: Los Atrevidos*, thus announcing the birth and acceptance of Cuban American literature rather than a literature of exile and immigration. Carolina Hospital has been in the forefront of developing a Cuban American aesthetic in literature. Not only does her poetry demonstrate the particular bilingual-bicultural nature of Cubans developing their literary sensibility in the United States, but her editorial work has helped to announce and define this aesthetic. Born in Havana just two years before the triumph of the revolution, she accompanied her family into exile in 1961 and was raised and educated in Florida. Like so many other children of exiles who had no say in their being transported into another culture and raised in an educational system that utilized a language different from that of the home, she became part of a generation of young people who knew only the United States as home but were constantly encouraged by parents and relatives to identify with an island of the past that they could only recreate in their imagination. The tensions between the U.S. reality and a mythical Cuba formed by the nostalgia of exiles, between the institutional English and Anglo-American culture of the outside world and the nurturing Spanish of the home and tradition, and between growing up as an immigrant rather than viewing life as an exile dominate the works of Carolina Hospital and the generation of writers that she identified in her groundbreaking anthology.

Sources: Kanellos, *The Hispanic Literary Companion*, pp. 138–139.

Helena María Viramontes

1989 ♦ Short story writer and novelist Helena María Viramontes became the first Latino writer to win the Storytelling Award of the Sundance Institute, the famed workshop for screenwriters. Viramontes is one of the most distinguished craftspeople of short fiction that Latino literature has produced. Her writing career began while she was still young and affiliated with one of the most avant-garde Chicano magazines, the streetwise *ChismeArte*, for which she served as literary editor.

The magazine was emblematic of her own writing style, still very much in touch with her upbringing on the streets of East Los Angeles, and very hip and polished, owing to her college education and her studies in creative writing and film. She is the author of *The Moths and Other Stories* (1985) and the novels *Under the Feet of Jesus* (1995) and *Their Dogs Came with Them* (2007).

Sources: "Helena María Viramontes," *Dictionary of Literary Biography, Volume 122: Chicano Writers*, pp. 322–328.

1989 ♦ The first television documentary on Latino literature of the United States, *Birthwrite: Growing Up Hispanic*, directed by Jesús Salvador Treviño, was aired by the Public Broadcasting Service. Treviño is also a renowned short story writer.

Sources: Kanellos, *Latino Almanac*, pp. 260–261, 442–445.

1989 ♦ Nicolás Kanellos (1945–), publisher of Arte Público Press, became the first publisher to be honored with the American Book Award in the publisher-editor category of the Before Columbus Foundation. Arte Público Press, founded by Kanellos in 1979, is the largest Latino publisher in the United States and has accrued more awards and launched more Latino authors into mainstream acceptance than any other press.

Sources: Unterburger, *Who's Who among Hispanic Americans*, p. 355.

Judith Ortiz Cofer

1990 ♦ Poet-novelist Judith Ortiz Cofer (1952–2016) became the first Hispanic writer to receive a PEN/Martha Albrand Special Citation in Nonfiction for *Silent Dancing: A Partial Remembrance of a Puerto Rican Childhood* (1990), a collection of autobiographical essays and poems. The book was also awarded the Pushcart Prize in the essay category, it was selected for the New York Public Library System list of Best Books for the Teen Age, and the title essay was chosen by Joyce Carol Oates for *The Best American Essays* (1991).

Sources: Kanellos, *The Hispanic Literary Companion*, pp. 231–232.

Oscar Hijuelos

1991 ♦ Oscar Hijuelos (1951–2013) became the first Latino to win the Pulitzer Prize for Fiction. Born to Cuban American working-class parents in New York City, Hijuelos was educated in public schools and obtained a B.A. in 1975 and an M.A. in 1976, both in English, from City College of New York of the City University of New York. Hijuelos is one of the few

Latino writers to have formally studied creative writing at that time and to have broken into Anglo-dominated creative writing circles, participating in prestigious workshops such as the Breadloaf Writers Conference and benefiting from highly competitive fellowships such as the American Academy in Rome Fellowship from the American Academy and Institute of Arts and Letters (1985), the National Endowment for the Arts Fellowship (1985), and the Guggenheim Fellowship (1990).

Hijuelos is the author of various short stories and the following novels: *Our House in the Last World* (1983), *The Mambo Kings Play Songs of Love* (1989), *The Fourteen Sisters of Emilio Montez O'Brien* (1993), *Mr. Ives' Christmas* (1995), *A Simple Habana Melody* (2002), *Dark Dude* (2008), *Beautiful Maria of My Soul* (2010), *Thoughts Without Cigarettes: A Memoir* (2011), and *Twain & Stanley Enter Paradise* (2015). *The Mambo Kings Play Songs of Love*, the winner of the Pulitzer Prize, is more than just a story of immigration. It examines a period in time when Latino culture was highly visible in the United States and was able to influence American popular culture: the 1950s during the height of the mambo craze and the overwhelming success of Desi Arnaz's television show *I Love Lucy*. Written in a poetic but almost documentary style, the novel follows two brothers who are musicians trying to ride the crest of the Latin music wave. While providing a picture of one segment of American life never seen before in English-language fiction, the novel also indicts womanizing and alcoholism.

Sources: "Pulitzer Prize Winner Oscar Hijuelos Dies at 62," *The Guardian*: https://www.theguardian.com/world/2013/oct/14/pulitzer-prize-winner-oscar-hijuelos-dies.

1991 ♦ Victor Villaseñor's (1940–) family autobiography, *Rain of Gold*, became the first book published by a Hispanic press, Arte Público Press, to make it onto the bestseller lists in the United States.

Victor Villaseñor

Sources: Kanellos, *Chronology of Hispanic American History*, pp. 214, 259.

Lorna Dee Cervantes

1991 ♦ Mexican American poet Lorna Dee Cervantes (1954–) became the first Latino to win the prestigious Paterson Poetry Prize for her second book, *From the Cables of Genocide: Poems of Love and Hunger.* It was also awarded the Latin American Writers Institute Award that same year. Cervantes is the most celebrated Latina poet of the United States. Cervantes's poems are so finely crafted and insightful of Mexican American and women's cultures that they are the among the most reprinted in anthologies and textbooks of any Latino poet.

Of Mexican and Amerindian ancestry, Cervantes was born into a very poor family in the Mission District of San Francisco, California. Despite this poverty, she was able to discover the world of books at a very early age. Cervantes began writing poetry when she was six years old; poems written when she was 14 were eventually published in a magazine after she had established her career as a writer. In 1990, she left her Ph.D. studies in philosophy and aesthetics at the University of California at Santa Cruz before finishing her dissertation. She then went on to teach creative writing at the University of Colorado in Boulder.

Cervantes's early career as a poet achieved recognition in 1974, when her work was published in *Revista Chicano-Riqueña.* She was one of the first Chicana poets to achieve publication and quickly assumed leadership in the literary movement by founding and editing a literary magazine, *Mango*, out of San Jose, California. Her work was quickly circulated throughout the Chicano literary movement and soon began to appear in anthologies and textbooks nationwide. Many of these early movement poems, poems dealing with identity and roots, became part of *Emplumada* (Plumed, 1981), Cervantes's first collection of poems, published in the prestigious University of Pittsburgh Press Poetry Series. The predominant themes include culture conflict, oppression of women and minorities, and alienation from one's roots. Cervantes's poetry is very well crafted and has the distinction of using highly lyrical language while at the same time being direct and powerful. Cervantes's second book, *From the Cables of Genocide: Poems of Love and Hunger*, which is very much the work of a mature poet, deals with the great themes of life, death, social conflict, and poverty. Her most recent books are *Ciento: 100-Word Love Poems* (2011) and *Sueño: New Poems* (2013).

Sources: Telgen and Kamp, *Latinas! Women of Achievement*, pp. 67–70.

1992 ♦ Mexican American novelist Lucha Corpi (1945–) became the first Hispanic writer to win the PEN Oakland/Josephine Miles Literary Award for her book *Eulogy for a Brown Angel*, in which Corpi created the astute Chicana detective Gloria Damasco, who unravels the mysterious assassination of a young boy during the protest activities of the 1970 Chicano Moratorium against the Vietnam War. Described as a feminist detective novel, *Eulogy* is fast-paced, suspenseful, and packed with an assortment of interesting characters. The feminist protagonist, Gloria Damasco, is somewhat of a clairvoyant who is able to use more than reason and logic in solving a very puzzling crime. In addition to the PEN Oakland Award, *Eulogy* also received the Multicultural Publishers Exchange Best Book of Fiction award. In 1995, Gloria Damasco returned in a mystery set against the background of the

United Farm Workers movement in California, *Cactus Blood.* The other books in the series are *Black Widow's Wardrobe* (1999) and *Crimson Moon* (2004).

Sources: "Lucha Corpi," *Dictionary of Literary Biography, Volume 82: Chicano Writers*, pp. 91–98.

1992 ♦ Mexican American Jungian psychologist Clarissa Pinkola Estés (1945–) became the first Latina to have her book *Women Who Run with the Wolves: Myths and Stories of the Wild Woman Archetype* make *New York Times* bestseller list. Making the list just five weeks after its publication, the book also remained on the list longer than any other book written by a Latina. *Women Who Run with the Wolves* contains original stories, folktales, myths, and legends by Estés, along with psychoanalytic commentary based on women's lives. *Hispanic* magazine hailed it as a "feminine manifesto for all women, regardless of age, race, creed, or religion, to return to their wild roots." Estés founded and now directs the C. P. Estés Guadalupe Foundation, which has as one of its missions the broadcasting of strengthening stories, via short-wave radio, to trouble spots around the world. In 1994, Estés was awarded the Associated Catholic Church Press Award for Writing, and in 1995, she won the National Association for the Advancement of Psychoanalysis Gradiva Award.

Sources: Tardiff and Mabunda, *Dictionary of Hispanic Biography*, p. 318; Telgen and Kamp, *Latinas! Women of Achievement*, pp. 115–120.

Cristina García

1992 ♦ Cristina García (1958–) was the first Cuban American woman to experience mainstream success as a novelist in the United States through the publication of her first novel. *Dreaming in Cuban*, issued by Knopf. Her journalistic background and interest in politics led her into the world of writing and the examination of her Cuban American circumstances, which have been so shaped by the political history of the United States and Cuba. Cristina García was born in Havana, Cuba, on July 4, 1958, and immigrated to the United States when her parents went into exile after the triumph of the Cuban Revolution. García was an excellent student and was able to attend elite American universities; she graduated from Barnard College with a degree in political science in 1979 and from the Johns Hopkins University with a master's in Latin American studies.

She was able to land a coveted job as a reporter and researcher with *Time* magazine, where she was able to hone her writing skills. She quickly ascended to bureau chief and correspondent at *Time* but left the magazine in 1990 to pursue her career as a creative writer. Her highly acclaimed novel was the first one authored by a woman to give insight into the psychology of the generation of Cubans born or raised in the United States who grew up under the looming myth of the splendors of the island in the past and the evils of Castro, a group, however, that never really had firsthand knowledge of their parents' homeland. In addition, the novel closely examines a woman's perspective on the dilemma of living between two cultures.

Sources: Kanellos, *The Hispanic Literary Companion*, pp. 93–95.

1993 ♦ Mexican American poet Luis Rodríguez's (1954–) memoir of life on the streets, *Always Running*, became the first Hispanic book to win the Carl Sandburg Literary Award for Non-Fiction. It also won the *Chicago Sun-Times* First Prose Book Award in 1994.

Sources: Tardiff and Mabunda, *Dictionary of Hispanic Biography*, p. 760.

1993 ♦ Chicana playwright, essayist, and lesbian theorist Cherríe Moraga (1952–) was the first Latina to win the Lambda Literary Award for Poetry for her book *The Last Generation.* In 1981, Moraga coedited the groundbreaking anthology *This Bridge Called My Back: Writings by Radical Women of Color* with Gloria Anzaldúa and then in 1983 went on to cofound, with Barbara Smith and Audre Lord, Kitchen Table: Women of Color Press, which was also groundbreaking for its time. In 2007, Moraga was named one of the United States Artists and received a grant of $50,000. In 1994, Moraga also won a Lamba Literary Award for her collection of plays, *Heroes and Saints & Other Plays.* To date, Moraga has written or coedited some dozen volumes and has seen a like number of her plays produced.

Sources: Kanellos, *Latino Almanac,* pp. 315, 331, 358.

1993 ♦ Cuban exile writer Reinaldo Arenas (1943–1990) was the first Latino writer to win the Lambda Literary Award for Autobiography for his book *Antes que anochezca*, published in English as *Before Night Falls* (1993). The book, which was also made into a highly reviewed film, documents his struggles in Cuba as a writer and gay man, his having to smuggle his writings out of his homeland to be published abroad, and his incarceration in one Cuba's most horrific prisons. Arenas escaped to the Unted States as part of the Mariel Boatlift and received acclaim for his novels and plays but died of AIDS in 1990.

Sources: McDowell, Edwin, "Reinaldo Arenas, 47, Writer Who Fled Cuba, Dies," *New York Times*, 9 December 1990.

1994 ♦ Puerto Rican novelist, short story writer, and poet Judith Ortiz Cofer (1952–2016) was the first Latino to win the O. Henry Prize for short stories.

That same year, she also won the Anisfield-Wolf Book Award in Race Relations for her novel *The Latin Deli.* Among her other important works are *Silent Dancing: A Partial Remembrance of a Puerto Rican Childhood* and *Line of the Sun.*

Sources: Tardiff and Mabunda, *Dictionary of Hispanic Biography*, p. 236.

1994 ♦ Rafael Campo (1964–) became the first Latino to win a Lambda Literary Award for Poetry for his collection *The Other Man Was Me: A Voyage to the New World.* As a gay poet and medical doctor, his writing has served as an inspiration for artists engaging with the AIDS crisis and discrimination against members of the LGBTQ+ community.

Sources: "Rafael Campo," Poets.org: https://poets.org/poet/rafael-campo.

1995 ♦ *The Desert Is My Mother/El desierto es mi madre*, a poetry and picture book for children by Pat Mora (1942–), became the first Latino book to win the Skipping Stones Honor Award in Nature and Ecology.

Sources: Kanellos, *The Hispanic Literary Companion*, p. 226.

Sandra Cisneros

1995 ♦ Mexican American poet and novelist Sandra Cisneros (1954–) became the first Latina to win the prestigious MacArthur Fellowship. Cisneros is the short story writer, essayist, and poet who has brought Chicana writing into the mainstream of literary feminism. She is also the first Chicana writer to be published and promoted by mainstream commercial publishing houses. Born on December 20, 1954, in Chicago into a Mexican American working-class family, Cisneros nevertheless benefited from a private education, graduating with a B.A. in English from Loyola University (1976) and later with an M.F.A. in creative writing from the Iowa Workshop (1978).

Cisneros's first novel, *The House on Mango Street* (1983), remains her most important contribution in that it captures the hopes, desires, and disillusionment of a young female writer growing up in the city. In *Mango Street*, Esperanza Cordero functions in a similar manner to the unidentified narrator in Tomás Rivera's classic *... y no se lo trago la tierra* (*... And the Earth Did Not Part*), observing the behavior and attitudes of the people who populate their environments. In Esperanza's urban Chicago world, children naively internalize the attitudes about gender and class of their adult Latino models; however, somehow the spirit of independence and creativity grows in Esperanza and leads her to escape the barrio in search of a house of her own: her own personality and identity, presumably through literature.

For *Mango Street*, Cisneros was awarded the American Book Award of the Before Columbus Foundation (1985), and she began touring college campuses for readings. Her other awards include a Dobie-Paisano Fellowship (1986) and NEA Creative Writing Fellowships in fiction and poetry (1982, 1990). In 1991, publishing giant Random House issued a collection of essays and short stories, *Woman Hollering Creek and Other Stories*, and two previous titles: *The House on Mango Street* and *My Wicked Wicked Ways*; Cisneros became one of the very few Latino writers of the United States to be supported by the commercial establishment at that point in history. Her other books include *Loose Woman: Poems* (1994); *Caramelo, or, Puro cuento* (2002); *Have You Seen Marie?* (2012); *A House of My Own* (2015); *Puro Amor* (2018); and *Martita, I Remember You/Martita, te recuerdo* (2018). Despite these sparse publications over the years, *The House on Mango Street* remains her best known and most cited work, having secured a place in college and high school curricula.

Sources: "Sandra Cisneros," *Dictionary of Literary Biography, Volume 122: Chicano Writers*, pp. 77–81.

1995 ♦ Mexican American author Helena María Viramontes was the first Latino to receive the John Dos Passos Prize for Literature for her novel *Under the Feet of Jesus.* The award criteria were "a substantial body of published work that displays an intense and original exploration of specifically American themes, an experimental approach to form, and an interest in a wide range of human experience."

Sources: "Helena María Viramontes," *Dictionary of Literary Biography, Volume 122: Chicano Writers*, pp. 322–328.

1995 ♦ Lionel G. García became the first Latino to win first place in the Texas Playwright Festival for his play *An Acorn on the Moon*, produced by Stages Repertory Theatre in 1995.

Sources: Kanellos, *The Hispanic Literary Companion*, p. 101.

1995 ♦ Tina Juárez's historical novel *Call No Man Master* was the first Hispanic book to win the Austin Writer's League Violet Crown Book Award and the Presidio La Bahia Award, the latter presented by the Sons of the Republic of Texas.

Sources: Juárez, *Call No Man Master.*

1996 ♦ Puerto Rican novelist Alba Ambert (1946–) became the first Latina to win the Carey McWilliams Award for Multicultural Literature, presented by the *Multicultural Education Review*, for her novel *A Perfect Silence*. Alba Ambert creates penetrating psychological narrative in fiction, much of which is based on her rise from abject poverty in Puerto Rico to literary acclaim. A poet and scholarly writer as well, Ambert combines lyrical and rhapsodic narrative style with minute attention to detail.

Born and raised in an infamous slum in San Juan, Puerto Rico, Alba Ambert was one of those "scholarship" children who, through force of will and extraordinary intelligence, are able to pull themselves up out of adversity and not only make something of themselves but also contribute greatly to humanity. Ambert followed a roundabout route to becoming a barrio teacher in Boston and later a successful creative writer. She studied philosophy at the University of Puerto Rico, graduating with a B.A. in 1974 with great distinction; thereafter, Ambert received M.A. and Ed.D. degrees in psycholinguistics from Harvard University in 1975 and 1980, respectively.

Not only was Ambert a bilingual teacher, but she also specialized in the teaching of bilingual special education students, curriculum writing, and theory, and some of this experience and study is reflected in the scholarly books that she has written. In 1986, Ambert began teaching and researching in Europe, which also gave her time to devote to her creative writing. Always interested in poetry and writing since her childhood, Ambert began publishing her poetry in Europe and then in the United States, but a milestone in her career was the writing of her highly autobiographical novel *A Perfect Silence*, which charts the protagonist's psychological struggles in resolving her previous poverty-stricken life with her highly successful intellectual career.

Sources: Kanellos, *The Hispanic Literary Companion*, pp. 22–23.

1996 ♦ Initiative, courage, and inventiveness are what win the day in Ofelia Dumas Lachtman's (1919–2018) novel *The Girl from Playa Blanca*, which received critical acclaim and was the first Hispanic book to win the Benjamin Franklin Award for Juvenile Young Adult Fiction. This exciting book follows a teenager and her little brother from her Mexican seaside village to Los Angeles in search of her father, who has disappeared while working to support his two children back in Mexico. The young protagonist unravels the mystery behind a major crime and not only succeeds in finding her father in the grand metropolis but also falls in love along the way.

Sources: Kanellos, *The Hispanic Literary Companion*, pp. 64–66.

Junot Díaz

1996 ♦ Junot Díaz (1968–) became the first Dominican American author to be "discovered" by a major publisher with his book of short stories, *Drown*, published by Putnam's Riverhead Books. Díaz received the greatest reception of any new Latino author ever, with articles appearing in *Newsweek* and other mass-market publications. Díaz, who was born in the Dominican Republic, received his B.A. from Rutgers University and his M.F.A. in creative writing from Cornell.

Sources: "New Faces of 1998," *Newsweek*, January 1996.

Richard Blanco

2013 ♦ Cuban American poet Richard Blanco (1968–) became the first Latino selected to read a poem at the inauguration of a U.S. president, Barack Obama. He was only the fifth poet to perform that poetic inauguration and the first immigrant and openly gay writer to do so. He was also the youngest writer to receive that distinction. Blanco is the author of a number of poetry collections, which have won some of the most prestigious awards for poetry in the United States, including *City of a Hundred Fires*, which won the Agnes Lynch Starrett Poetry Prize; *Directions to the Beach of the Dead*, which won the Beyond Margins Award from the PEN American Center; and *Looking for the Gulf Motel*, which won the Paterson Poetry Prize and the Thom Gunn Award. In 2023, President Joe Biden awarded Blanco the National Humanities Medal.

Sources: "Richard Blanco": https://richard-blanco.com/.

2014 ♦ Rolando Hinojosa (1929–2022) was awarded the Ivan Sandrof Lifetime Achievement Award by the National Book Critics Circle for his sustained, outstanding production of the Klail City Death Trip Series, a continuing novel written over some three decades chronicling the lives of a host of characters living along the Lower Rio Grande Valley of Texas. Hinojosa wrote many of his novels in one language, Spanish or English, and then rewrote them in the other language; his *Mi querido Rafa* (1981, Dear Rafe), however, was written bilingually, requiring an in-depth knowledge of not only both languages but also of Mexican American dialect. For his *Klail City y sus alrededores* (1976, Klail City and Surroundings), he was awarded one of Latin America's most prestigious prizes, the Premio Casa de las Américas.

Sources: Kanellos, *Latino Almanac*, pp. 309–311, 352–353.

Juan Felipe Herrera

2015 ♦ Juan Felipe Herrera (1948–) was the first Latino to be appointed poet laureate of the United States, from 2015 to 2017. Herrera is the author of 30 books of poetry, novels for young adults, and collections for children, including *Half the World in Light: New and Selected Poems* (2008), and winner of the National Book Critics Circle Award. Herrera was the poet laureate of California from 2012 to 2015. In 2016, he won the Robert Kirsch Award for Lifetime Achievement and the *Los Angeles Times* Book Prize.

Sources: "Juan Felipe Herrera," Library of Congress: https://www.loc.gov/programs/poetry-and-literature/poet-laureate/poets-laureate/item/n79033227/juan-felipe-herrera/.

2022 ♦ Californian Ada Limón (1976–) was the first Latina to be named poet laureate of the United States. The author of seven books of poetry had won the National Book Critics Circle Award for her *Bright Dead Things* (2015). In 2023, she received a MacArthur Fellowship and was named to an unprecedented second term as poet laureate until 2025.

Ada Limón

Sources: "U.S. Poet Laureate Ada Limón Appointed for a Historic Two-Year Second Term," Library of Congress: https://www.loc.gov/item/prn-23-040/u-s-poet-laureate-ada-limon-appointed-for-a-historic-two-year-second-term/2023-04-24/.

2023 ♦ Puerto Rican Ricardo Alberto Maldonado (1981–) was the first Latino to be named executive director and president of the Academy of American Poets. A renowned poet himself, he is the author of *The Life Assignment* (Four Way Books, 2020), which was a finalist for the Poetry Society of America's Norma Farber First Book Award and silver medalist for the Juan Felipe Herrera Best Poetry Book Award. Among its other activities, each year, the Academy of American Poets awards more than $1.3 million to more than 200 poets at various stages of their careers. Maldonado had served as the codirector of one of the most important poetry institutions, the 92NY's Unterberg Poetry Center in New York City.

Sources: "Ricardo Alberto Maldonado," poets.org: https://poets.org/poet/ricardo-alberto-maldonado.

Cristina Rivera Garza

2024 ♦ Mexican writer Cristina Rivera Garza (1964–), writing in English, became the first Latina to win the Pulitzer Prize for Memoir or Autobiography for her book exploring her sister's murder, *Liliana's Invincible Summer: A Sister's Search for Justice* (2023). Rivera Garza, who has a Ph.D. in history from the University of Houston, shifted her career and became a prize-winning novelist, nonfiction writer, and translator. She has won some of the most prestigious literary awards in Spanish America, including the José Rubén Romero National Book

Award, the IMPAC/CONARTE/ITESM National Award for Best Published Novel, and the Sor Juana Inés de la Cruz Prize for her novel *Nadie me verá llorar* (No One Will See Me Cry). She is also a MacArthur Fellow (2020) and is the M.D. Anderson Distinguished Professor in the Department of Hispanic Studies of the University of Houston, where she founded and now directs the United States' first Ph.D. program in creative writing in Spanish.

Sources: "Cristina Rivera Garza," Hispanic Studies, University of Houston: https://uh.edu/class/spanish/faculty/rivera-garza-c/.

PRINT MEDIA

1513 ♦ Explorer Juan Ponce de León's (1474–1521) search for the land of Bimini, described to him by the natives of Puerto Rico, took him to Florida, where he explored most of the coastal regions up to Apalachi Bay and some of the interior. At the time, there were an estimated 100,000 natives living there. This was the first introduction of a written language into what would become the mainland United States. Juan Ponce de León recorded his travels in his diaries. From this point on, the history of literacy, books, and writing in what was to become the United States was developed by Spanish, *mestizo*, and mulatto missionaries, soldiers, and settlers. From then on, there were civil, military, and ecclesiastical records in what eventually would become the southern and southwestern United States. Of course, this was followed by the importation of books, the penning of original historical and creative writing, the use of the printing press, and the publication of newspapers and other written products.

Sources: Kanellos, *Chronology of Hispanic American History*, p. 30.

1539 ♦ The printing press was brought to the Americas, namely to Mexico City. The printer was Juan Pablos (born Giovanni Paoli, c. 1500–c. 1560). By the mid-17th century, seven printers were operating in Mexico City, issuing everything from contracts and religious books to public notices and literary works. Among the first books printed were catechisms, religious books, grammars of the indigenous languages, dictionaries, and some technical and scientific books.

Sources: Kanellos, *Chronology of Hispanic American History*, pp. 35–36.

1699 ♦ The first book published in Spanish in what would become the United States was Cotton Mather's *La fe del Christiano* (The Christian Faith), a translation of his work in English, published in Boston by B. Green and J. Allen. It was published to be sent to the Spanish "so that they would open their eyes and be converted from darkness and the power of Satan to God," Mather said.

Sources: Online Computer Library Center.

1722 ♦ *La gaceta de México* (The Mexico Gazette), founded by Juan Ignacio Castorena (1668–1773), became the first newspaper in the Americas. Shortly thereafter, others appeared in Guatemala, Lima, Buenos Aires, and elsewhere. The history of journalism in North America began here.

Sources: Kanellos, *Chronology of Hispanic American History*, p. 54.

1779 ♦ The first history of colonial Texas was written by a Franciscan missionary, Juan Agustín Morfi (1735–1783). Morfi's *History of Texas, 1673–1779* documented the life of the missions, villages, and presidios using his service there.

Sources: Jenkins, *Basic Texas Books*, p. 387.

c. 1780 ♦ Revolutionary War hero and Sephardic Jew (originally from Spain) Benjamín Nones (1757–1826) became the first official interpreter of Spanish and French (Nones had lived in exile in Bordeaux, France) for the U.S. government.

Sources: Simonhoff, *Jewish Notables in America, 1776–1865*, p. 101.

1793 ♦ The first book published by a Hispanic printer/publisher in the United States was W. H. Dilworth's *The Complete Letter Writer, or Young Secretary's Instructor*, issued by Benjamin Gómez in New York. Gómez was the first Latino publisher and printer on record in the United States. He was the great-grandson of underground Sephardic Jews from Madrid, Spain, who fled to France, then to Canada, and finally to New York to escape persecution during the Inquisition. Although Gómez belonged to the wealthiest Jewish (and Spanish) family in the United States, he chose to go into the book trade and issued mostly works in English, some of them of great importance to the history of literature in the United States: John Bunyon's *Pilgrim's Progress*, William Blackstone's *Commentaries*, and Henry Fielding's *Tom Jones*.

Sources: Simonhoff, *Jewish Notables in America, 1776–1865*, pp. 112–116.

1791: First Latino Newspaper Editor

In 1791 Jacob Newton Cardozo (1786–1875), the son of a Sephardic Jewish immigrant and American Revolutionary War hero, was the first U.S.-born Latino to become an editor of a newspaper, Charleston's *The Southern Patriot*. In 1823, Cardozo was able to buy the newspaper and became its publisher. Cardozo also became a respected author and expert on commerce and finance with the publication of his book *Notes on Political Economy*, published in 1826. But it was as an editor that Cardozo made his greatest contribution, editing *The Southern Patriot* until 1845 and, later, newspapers in Mobile, Alabama, and Atlanta, Georgia. *Sources:* Simonhoff, *Jewish Notables in America, 1776–1865*, pp. 264–267.

1795 ♦ The first book written and published by a Latino in the United States was Hipólito San Joseph Giral del Pino's *A New Spanish Grammar*, published in Philadelphia by Colerick and Hunter. The book also included an English grammar for use by Spaniards.

Sources: Online Computer Library Center.

1798 ♦ The first printed book in the southern part of what would become the United States was Louisiana governor Manuel Gayoso de Lemos's (1747–1799) *Deseando mantener el buen orden y tranquilidad publica ...* (Wishing to Maintain Good Order and Public Tranquility), issued in New Orleans. It was also the first bilingual publication in what would become the United States, with Spanish and French parallel columns.

Sources: Online Computer Library Center.

1806 ♦ The first newspaper in Puerto Rico was *La gaceta de Puerto Rico* (The Puerto Rican Gazette), which was a government organization.

Sources: Kanellos and Martell, *Hispanic Newspapers in the United States: A Brief History and Bibliography*, p. 11.

1808 ♦ The first Spanish-language newspaper was founded in the United States: New Orleans's *El Misisipí.* Shortly thereafter, other newspapers were founded: Nacogdoches, Texas's *La Gaceta de Texas* (The Texas Gazette) in 1813 and New York's *El Mensajero Semanal* (The Weekly Messenger) in 1828. Hundreds of Spanish-language newspapers were subsequently founded in

Latino communities throughout the Southwest, Louisiana, Florida, and the Northeast in the years to come. During the 19th century, the newspapers were the principal medium for the publication of literature; they functioned not only to facilitate business and publish news but also to entertain and reinforce the Spanish language and Latino culture. They flourished especially in the first half of the 20th century and provided news and advertising of importance to Latinos as well as the cultural information and reinforcement that helped them to preserve their identity and protect their civil rights.

Sources: Kanellos and Martell, *Hispanic Newspapers in the United States: A Brief History and Bibliography*, pp. 4–5.

1823 ♦ The first Spanish–English bilingual newspaper, *El Correo de Texas/ The Texas Courier*, was published in San Antonio by the Texas Government Printing House.

Sources: Kliener, Diana J., "San Antonio Texas Courier" Texas State Historical Association: https://www.tshaonline.org/handbook/entries/san-antonio-texas-courier.

Narciso Gener Gonzales

1903 ♦ The first Latino journalist to pay with his life for exposing corruption through investigative reporting was Narciso Gener Gonzales (1858–1903), the son of a Cuban immigrant. Gonzales founded *The State* newspaper in Charleston, South Carolina, in 1881; in his editorials, he crusaded for a woman's right to vote and against child labor and the lynching of blacks. He also attacked corrupt politicians, one of the worst of which was the governor of South Carolina, Jim Tillman. In 1903, Tillman lost the gubernatorial election and blamed Gonzales for his defeat. In retaliation, Tillman confronted Gonzales on a busy street and shot him dead. Tillman was exonerated at his trial by jury, which found the shooting to be "justifiable" because of the injury to Tillman's reputation.

Sources: Hispanics in U.S. History, p. 12.

1904 ♦ Teacher and poet Sara Estela Ramírez (1881–1910) became the first Latina to publish and edit a newspaper, *Aurora*, in Laredo. She also edited *La corregidora* (The Corrector), named for an important heroine of Mexican independence from Spain. Ramírez, an important activist for workers' and women's rights, was followed by other women editor-publishers in Texas, such as Jovita Idar (1885–1946) and Andrea (1881–1963) and Teresa (1883–?) Villarreal.

Sources: Kanellos and Martell, *Hispanic Newspapers in the United States: A Brief History and Bibliography,* pp. 23-24.

1958 ♦ Harry Caicedo (1928–2004) became the first Hispanic chief of the news bureau for a major U.S. daily newspaper on assuming that role for the *Miami Herald.* Born in New York City on April 1, 1928, the son of Colombian parents, Caicedo received his bachelor's degree in journalism from the University of Missouri in 1954.

Sources: Kanellos, *Latino Almanac*, p. 252.

1965 ♦ Journalist Rubén Salazar (1928–1970) was promoted to foreign correspondent for the *Los Angeles Times*, thus becoming the first Mexican American to hold such a position at a major newspaper. He covered the U.S. invasion of the Dominican Republic that year and was one of two *Times* correspondents in Vietnam during the period of increased U.S. involvement in that war. Later, he was named *Times* bureau chief in Mexico City, covering Mexico, Cuba, and Central America.

Rubén Salazar

Sources: Hispanic Link Weekly Report, 14 August 1995, p. 2.

1976 ♦ The *Miami Herald* became the first major daily to publish a Spanish-language insert in its issues, entitled *El Herald.* By 1979, *El Herald* was delivered to more than 76,000 households.

Sources: García, *Havana USA*, p. 105.

1982 ♦ The National Association of Hispanic Publications was founded to represent some 100 Hispanic newspapers and magazines being published in the United States. The organization promotes Latino print media as a valuable means of communication and encourages the recruitment and training of Latinos as print journalists.

Sources: Furtaw, *Hispanic Americans Information Directory*, p. 25.

1984 ♦ Journalist Harry Caicedo (1928–2004) became the founding editor of the nation's first Latino mass-circulation magazine, *Vista*, which was distributed as a Sunday supplement in major daily newspapers.

Sources: Kanellos, *Latino Almanac*, p. 252.

1986 ♦ Mexican American lawyer Patricia Díaz Dennis (1946–) became the first Hispanic woman and only the second female to serve on the Federal Communications Commission. She was appointed by President Ronald Reagan. Prior to her appointment, she had served in management of ABC-TV in Hollywood, California, and on the National Labor Relations Board.

Sources: Tardiff and Mabunda, *Dictionary of Hispanic Biography*, p. 285.

1987 ♦ Newspaper publisher Knight-Ridder became the first U.S. media corporation to launch a Spanish-language daily newspaper, *El Nuevo Herald*, which grew out of the Spanish-language insert published by the *Miami Herald.*

Sources: García, *Havana USA*, p. 105.

1989 ♦ Mónica Lozano (1956–) became the first Hispanic woman to be named publisher of a Spanish-language daily newspaper in the United States when she assumed the position of associate publisher of *La Opinión*, which was founded in Los Angeles by her grandfather in 1926. *La Opinión* is one of very few major Spanish-language dailies being published in the United States today. Among the others are New York's *El Diario–La Prensa* and Miami's *El Nuevo Herald.*

Sources: Telgen and Kamp, *Latinas! Women of Achievement*, pp. 213–218.

1990 ♦ Elizabeth Martínez (1943–) became the first Latina to serve as the director of the Los Angeles County Public Library system. In that capacity, she revitalized the county's 63 branches and supervised the construction of 23 new branches, including the central library, built at a cost of $214 million. Born on April 14, 1943, in Pomona, California, where she grew up in the poorest part of town, Martínez fell in love with books and spent all the time she could reading in the local library. She graduated from the University of California at Los Angeles in 1965 with a degree in Latin American studies and in 1966 secured her master's degree in library science from the University of Southern California. She further studied management, earning certificates in 1978 and 1986. In 1966, the year Martínez obtained her library science degree, there were only five Mexican American librarians in the country. She joined the Los Angeles library system and worked her way up through the ranks, recruiting Hispanic librarians along the way. She has also mentored many librarians, taught at universities, and published articles on library management and on racism. In 1993, Martínez was honored with the PEN West Freedom to Write Award.

Sources: Telgen and Kamp, *Latinas! Women of Achievement*, pp. 237–240.

1992 ♦ Mónica Lozano (1956–), associate publisher of Los Angeles's *La Opinión* newspaper, was the first Latina to receive the National Organization

1990: First Hispanic to Head a Major Daily Newspaper

In 1990 Roberto Suárez (1928–2010) became the first Hispanic to head a major city daily newspaper as president of the *Miami Herald*. He also became publisher of the Spanish-language daily that is the *Herald*'s subsidiary, *El Nuevo Herald*. Born in Havana, Cuba, Suárez received his primary and secondary education there and went on to study economics and finance at Villanova University, where he graduated with a B.S. in 1949. He joined the *Herald* staff in 1962 as a mailer and worked his way up. *Sources:* Weber, Bruce, "Roberto Suarez, Founder of *El Nuevo Herald*, Dies at 82," *New York Times*, 10 June 2010: https://www.nytimes.com/2010/07/11/business/media/11suarez.html.

of Women's (NOW) Legal Defense and Education Fund Award for her contributions as a woman in the media.

Sources: Telgen and Kamp, *Latinas! Women of Achievement*, p. 218.

1995 ♦ The first magazine dedicated exclusively to reviewing books by and about Latinos in the United States, *The Latino Book Review*, was founded at the State University of New York at Albany by Professor Edna Acosta-Belen.

Sources: The Latino Book Review, 1/1 (1995).

Alma Guillermo Prieto

1995 ♦ Alma Guillermo Prieto (original surname, Guillermo Prieto; 1949–) became the first Latino journalist to win the prestigious MacArthur Foundation Fellowship. An immigrant from Mexico, Guillermo Prieto has written for the *The New Yorker* and *The New York Review of Books*, among many others. Her writings document modern Latin America. In 1983, as a *New York Times* writer, she was one of the first to report on the military massacres of civilians in El Salvador.

Sources: Hispanic Link Weekly Report, 19 June 1995, p. 2; *Hispanic Link Weekly Report*, 26 June 1995, p. 3.

1996 ♦ *Hispanic Business* was the first Latino magazine to win a Maggie Award for Best Business and Finance Magazine by the Western Publications Association.

Sources: Hispanic Link Weekly Report, 13 May 1996, p. 8.

1996 ♦ For the first time in U.S. publishing history, mainstream popular magazines began targeting Latino readers in the United States. (Previously, such magazines as *Selecciones de Readers' Digest* and *Cosmopolitan* in Spanish were targeted more to readers in the Spanish American countries and Spain.) Time-Warner Communications launched *People en Español* and Essence Communications launched *Latina*, specifically targeted for Latinas in the United States. Also, *Newsweek en Español* became the first mainstream news magazine to enter this market. These publications joined a host of other periodicals that targeted Latinos in both languages, some 230 magazines being distributed in the United States.

Sources: "Whose Media Is This Anyway?" *Hispanic*, December 1996, pp. 53–58.

1996 ♦ Miguel Laosa (1955–) became the first Latino to serve as publisher of a major city English-language daily newspaper, the *Austin American-Statesman*, in Austin, Texas. He is the former president of Cox Arizona Publications.

Sources: "100 Influentials," *Hispanic Business*, October 1996, p. 62.

Alberto Ibargüen

1998 ♦ Alberto Ibargüen (1944–) was named publisher of the *Miami Herald*. Under his leadership, the newspaper won three Pulitzer Prizes during his tenure until 2005. Born in Puerto Rico to Cuban parents, Ibargüen had served as publisher of *El Nuevo Herald* since 1995. He later served as president and CEO of the John S. and James L. Knight Foundation until 2023.

Sources: "Alberto Ibargüen Steps Down at Knight Foundation after 18 Years," Knight Foundation: https://knightfoundation.org/press/releases/alberto-ibarguen-steps-down-at-knight-foundation-after-18-years/.

1999 ♦ Alfonso Chardy, Manny García, John Lantigua, Patricia Maldonado, María Morales, and Sandra Márquez were part of a team that won a Pulitzer Prize for Investigative Reporting at the *Miami Herald*. The team "revealed pervasive voter fraud in a city mayoral election, that was subsequently overturned."

Sources: "The 1999 Pulitzer Prize Winner in Investigative Reporting," The Pulitzer Prize: https://www.pulitzer.org/winners/staff-44.

2008 ♦ David González (c. 1958–), a South Bronx–raised journalist, received the Distinguished Writing Award from the American Society of Newspaper

Editors for his three-part series, "House Afire," on the life of a struggling Pentecostal storefront church. González worked for more than 30 years at *New York Times*, during which time he reported on such diverse topics as terrorism in Latin America, the civil wars in Central America, problems with the U.S. census, and devastation in the South Bronx. González was also a photojournalist who shot many of the photographs accompanying his stories, especially when he served as the Central American/Caribbean bureau chief from 1999 to 2003.

Sources: González, David, "A Family Divided by 2 Words, Legal and Illegal," *New York Times*, 26 April 2009.

2019 ♦ Peruvian American journalist Carlos Lozada (1971–) was the first Latino to receive the Pulitzer Prize for Criticism. As the nonfiction book review editor and reviewer, Lozada was acknowledged by the Pulitzer committee for "trenchant and searching reviews and essays that joined warm emotion and careful analysis in examining a broad range of books addressing government and the American experience."

Carlos Lozada

Sources: "Carlos Lozada of *The Washington Post*," The Pulitzer Prize: https://www.pulitzer.org/winners/carlos-lozada-washington-post.

2024 ♦ Médar de la Cruz became the first Latino to win the Pulitzer Prize for Illustrated Reporting and Commentary. The Pulitzer committee cited his story "The Diary of a Rikers Island Library Worker," on the "Rikers Island jail using bold black-and-white images that humanize the prisoners and staff through their hunger for books," which was published in *The New Yorker*. The Miami-born Dominican American is a freelance cartoonist and illustrator. He is also the author of several graphic novels. De la Cruz works as a jail and prison services assistant for the Brooklyn Public Library.

Sources: "Medar de la Cruz, Contributor, *The New Yorker*," The Pulitzer Prizes: https://www.pulitzer.org/winners/medar-de-la-cruz-contributor-new-yorker.

[illegible] part [illegible] the first [illegible] in Latin America [illegible] the South Bronx [illegible] 1999 to 2010.

Source: González, David. "A Family Divided [illegible]" *The New York Times* [illegible].

Carlos Lozada

2019 • First [illegible] American [illegible] Carlos Lozada (1971–) was the first Latino [illegible] the Pulitzer Prize for Criticism. As the nonfiction book critic and reviewer, Lozada was acknowledged by the Pulitzer committee [illegible] reviews and essays that [illegible] and [illegible] about [illegible] and [illegible].

Source: "Carlos Lozada of *The Washington Post*." The Pulitzer Prize. https://www.pulitzer.org/winners/carlos-lozada-washington-post.

2019 • [illegible] Pulitzer [illegible] for Illustrated Reporting and Commentary [illegible] Pulitzer committee [illegible] story [illegible] published in *The New Yorker* [illegible] Dominican [illegible] He is also the author [illegible].

Source: "[illegible] *The New Yorker*." The Pulitzer Prize. https://www.pulitzer.org/winners/[illegible].

Dance and Theater

DANCE

1831 ♦ The first record of a professional dance troupe in performance in the United States is that of the theatrical company Compañía Española de Teatro, which performed in New Orleans at the Orleans Theater. Like many dramatic companies throughout the Spanish-speaking world, it presented dances, monologues, and more minor entertainments during acts as well as before and after the acts of the main play, which often numbered as many as five. *La abeja* (The Bee) trilingual newspaper stated that the company was performing national dances (of Spain), such as boleros and fandangos, as well as a fandango-style minuet, performed by "two well-known and celebrated dancers," Tiburcio López and Mrs. Martínez (dates unknown for both dancers). Throughout the 19th century and the early 20th century, Hispanic theatrical companies included dances in their offerings, most of which represented the regional dances of Spain; in the 20th century, the regional dances of Mexico, Cuba, and Puerto Rico gradually became more popular.

Sources: La abeja, 5 April 1831.

1932 ♦ Dancer José Limón (1908–1972) participated in the first appearance of modern dance on Broadway with the Humphrey-Weidman Company in the play *Americana.*

Sources: Tardiff and Mabunda, *Dictionary of Hispanic Biography*, p. 486.

José Limón

1945 ♦ José Limón (1908–1972), a Mexican immigrant raised in Los Angeles, began touring his own modern dance company and thus became the first Mexican American professional modern dancer to make a living and achieve renown with this art form. After serving in the U.S. Army during World War II, Limón reestablished his company and went on to outstanding international acclaim, but he was financially hard-pressed and therefore had to rely on teaching at various institutions. In 1950, he turned down an invitation from the Mexican government for a permanent post as a choreographer. Limón often toured the world under the auspices of the U.S. State Department. He viewed dance as the highest expression of humanity. His most famous master works include "Lament for Ignacio Sánchez Mejía," "La Malinche," "The Moor's Pavane," and "Danza de la Muerte" (Dance of Death).

Sources: Meier and Rivera, *Dictionary of Mexican American History*, pp. 194–195; Tardiff and Mabunda, *Dictionary of Hispanic Biography*, pp. 48, 57.

1953 ♦ Ballerina Lupe Serrano (1930–2023) became the first Latina to serve as principal dancer for the American Ballet Theatre. During the nearly two decades that Serrano performed with the American Ballet Theatre, she appeared in more than 50 different roles. Born in 1930 in Santiago, Chile, to a Spanish Argentine musician father and a Mexican mother while they were on a performance tour, Serrano grew up in a performing arts environment. Her formal ballet training began in Mexico City at the age of 13, and by the age of 18, she went on tour with the famed Cuban ballerina Alicia Alonso. She later performed with the famed Ballet Folklórico de México. At the age of 20, Serrano was accepted into the Ballet Russe de Monte Carlo in New York City, where she was featured in her first solo performance. After becoming a principal dancer for the American Ballet Theatre, Serrano became one of its main attractions both in New York and around the world. She retired in 1971 to devote herself to teaching dance.

Lupe Serrano

Sources: Tardiff and Mabunda, *Dictionary of Hispanic Biography*, p. 844.

1995 ♦ A song composed and recorded by a little-known Spanish flamenco duo, Los del Río, became the music for a line dance similar to the "Hokey Pokey," which took the United States by storm. "La Macarena" became so popular that it has become standard fare in all ballroom and school dances and even is performed in "human wave" fashion by spectators during football and baseball games. In the summer of 1996, a remix by the Bayside Boys made "La Macarena" the number-one song on the Billboard pop chart.

Fans of "La Macarena" dance in Quito, Equador. The dance was popular worldwide.

Sources: Moreno, Carolina. "The Real Meaning Behind the 'Macarena' Will Crush Your '90s Soul," *HuffPost*: https://www.huffpost.com/entry/the-macarena-meaning-crush-90-soul_n_55e738c9e4b0b7a9633b491d.

2023 ♦ Colombian American choreographer Miguel Gutiérrez (1972–) was the first Latino to have three of his dance compositions in performance on three different stages concurrently: *Cela Nous Concerne Tous* (This Concerns All of Us), *I As Another,* and *Variations on Themes from Lost and Found: Scenes from a Life and Other Works by John Bernd.* After struggling for many years to have his art recognized and his pieces performed, Gutiérrez was actually becoming celebrated in the heart of American dance theater: New York City.

Sources: Burke, Siobhan, "An Artist of Ordered Excess," *New York Times*, 16 April 2023.

THEATER

1598 ♦ Don Juan de Oñate's (c. 1550–1630) colonizing mission to New Mexico marked the introduction of European theater into lands north of the Rio Grande. The soldiers in the company, led by a certain Captain Marcos Farfán de los Godos, performed the folk play *Moros y Cristianos*, a pageant reenactment of the victory of Spanish Christian forces over Moors in medieval Spain, which accompanied Spanish soldiers all over the world as they saw themselves battling paganism. The troupe also improvised plays based on their historic journey. As missionaries began evangelizing the Native Americans in the Southwest, they also introduced religious plays, such as *Los Pastores* (The Shepherds), that eventually would become a staple part of the folk theater of the U.S. Southwest and survive well into the 20th century.

Sources: Kanellos, *Latino Almanac*, pp. 46, 297.

1789 ♦ In what became the Southwest of the United States, the first plays for subscription (i.e., professional or semiprofessional) were performed as early as 1789. The manuscript copy of a three-act cloak-and-dagger play, Fermin de Reygadas's *Astucias por heredar un sobrino a su tío* (The Clever Acts of a Nephew in Order to Inherit His Uncle's Wealth), bears that date and shows evidence of having been toured through California settlements. By the 1840s, there was a steady stream of itinerant theatrical companies performing Spanish melodramas at the ranches and settlements in Alta California.

Sources: Kanellos, *A History of Hispanic Theater in the United States*, pp. 1–3.

1825 ♦ The first Spanish-language play was published in the United States. Spaniard Félix Megía's (1776–1853) two-act play *Lafayette en Mount Vernon*, dramatizing the ideas of American democracy, was also published that same year in English translation, *Lafayette in Mount Vernon*, making it the first English-language translation of a Spanish-language play in the United States. Both were issued in Philadelphia.

Sources: Online Computer Library Center.

1831 ♦ The first Spanish-language professional theatrical company on record in the South was the Compañía Española de Teatro, which performed for a season in New Orleans at the Orleans Theater. Included in its repertory were five-act melodramas, such as *Bolero*, and three-act plays by the Spanish master Lope de Vega (1562–1635; full name Félix Lope de Vega y Carpio), which were performed along with music, dance, and shorter comic pieces, such as *Madre e hija* (Mother and Daughter). The leading actor of the company was Bernardo Arsilla, who had made his reputation on the stages of Spain. According to *La abeja* (The Bee) newspaper, all of the actors in the small company—which had to be reinforced with local amateurs—were Spanish and had performed in Europe and the Americas.

Lope de Vega

Sources: La abeja, 5 April 1831.

1846 ♦ The first Mexican circus theaters were documented as performing in the Monterey, California, area. Tent-covered performing companies offered a mixture of circus acts and melodrama, Spanish operetta (*zarzuela*), and song and dance. For the next 100 years, numerous Hispanic circuses and tent theaters would crisscross what would become the U.S. Southwest. By the 1870s, Mexican circuses were the most frequent professional performing companies in the Southwest, and by the 1870s, San Antonio had become a home base for circuses and theatrical tent shows.

Sources: Kanellos, *A History of Hispanic Theater in the United States*, pp. 96–103.

1848 ♦ The first Spanish-language theater house in the Southwest was Antonio F. Colonel's (1817–1894) Teatro del Merced in Los Angeles. It was built as an addition to his house and seated 300; it included a covered stage with a proscenium, a drop curtain, and a good supply of scenery. Before then, professional performances were housed in halls or billiard parlors or held in the open air. Various other theaters were opened in the decades to follow in Los Angeles, but the real flowering of the stage, especially in Los Angeles and San Antonio, took place in the 1920s when numerous houses, bearing such names as Teatro California, Teatro México, Teatro Hidalgo, Teatro Nacional, and Teatro Zendejas, were opened.

Sources: Kanellos, *A History of Hispanic Theater in the United States*, pp. 2–3.

1860 ♦ By the 1860s, resident Spanish-language theatrical companies were established in the Southwest as such formerly itinerant groups as the Compañía Española de la Familia Estrella settled down in San Francisco. The company was led by leading actor Gerardo López del Castillo (?–1902), who is known in the history of the Mexican stage as the first impresario to take theater on tour to the provinces.

Sources: Kanellos, *A History of Hispanic Theater in the United States*, pp. 3–6.

1890 ♦ Following the construction of railroads along the U.S.–Mexican border, Mexican theatrical companies began performing along a circuit that started at Laredo and extended west to California. During the early 20th century, the Southwest would see a flowering of the Spanish-language professional stage in the major cities of the Southwest and West, such as Laredo, San Antonio, El Paso, Tucson, Los Angeles, and San Francisco.

Sources: Kanellos, *A History of Hispanic Theater in the United States*, pp. 17–20.

1891 ♦ A portion of the Cuban cigar industry was transferred to Florida when Ybor City was founded in the swamps just outside of Tampa in 1886. The factory owners and workers soon constructed mutual aid societies to serve the transplanted cigar-making community. The societies were the first Latino mutual aid societies to house theaters in their buildings and to run full-range theatrical programs by and for the workers as well as to house professional companies on tour from Cuba, Spain, and later New York and other parts of the United States. The first of these societies to open was the Centro Español in 1891.

The Centro Español's original building included a theater hall, which was used for dramatic and musical comedy productions as well as for dances and other community events. A new building, proudly erected in 1912, included a first-rate theater with a stage 28 by 35 feet with a proscenium arch 24 feet high, an orchestra pit, box seats, 231 seats in the balcony, and 465 seats in the orchestra. Over the years, Ybor City became a Latino theatrical center that launched the careers of many professional theater people as well as entire companies. During the Depression, it was the only community to support a Hispanic Federal Theater Project company as part of the Works Progress Administration.

Sources: Kanellos, *A History of Hispanic Theater in the United States*, pp. 146–175.

1911 ♦ The first Spanish-language play supporting women's rights and exhorting women to liberate themselves, *Julia y Carlota*, was written; excerpts from the play were published anonymously in Tampa's *Centro Obrero* (Workers' Center) newspaper *La Federación* on November 2, 1911. The excerpt that appeared in the newspaper exhorted Carlota to break the bonds of family and religion that are meant to keep women in their place, oppressed, and divorced from politics so that they do not reform civil laws.

Sources: Kanellos, *A History of Hispanic Theater in the United States*, p. 169.

1914 ♦ The Centro Asturiano mutual aid society in Ybor City included in its newly constructed center a first-rate, 1,200-seat theater with a stage 27

Teatro Carmen in Tucson, Arizona, was the foremost Spanish-language theater in the area from 1915 through the 1920s. The building is currently being restored by Stratford Art Works, which bought it in 2021.

by 80 feet for productions by its own company and by professional theater companies on tour to the Tampa area. It is the only theater constructed before World War II by Latinos still in use today as a theater. In addition, it was the only theater to house a Hispanic Federal Theater Project during the Depression.

Sources: Kanellos, *A History of Hispanic Theater in the United States*, p. 152.

1915 ♦ The first Hispanic woman to become a theater impresario was Carmen Soto Vásquez (1861–1934), who constructed and operated the most important theater house for Tucson, Arizona's Mexican community. Teatro Carmen was Tucson's largest theater to that date, seating 1,400 spectators. During its heyday, from 1915 to 1922, the theater hosted both professional Spanish-language touring companies and local amateurs performing melodramas, comedies, *zarzuelas*, operettas, and musical concerts. According to Thomas E. Sheridan, "To the Mexican elite of Tucson, Teatro Carmen was a powerful symbol of self-identity, living proof of the depth, power, and beauty of their culture.... The dramas of Spain's Golden Age or contemporary works of Mexico's finest playwrights and composers gave lie to the derogatory stereotypes of Mexicans so prevalent in the Southwest."

Sources: Kanellos, *A History of Hispanic Theater in the United States*, pp. 185–186; Sheridan, *Los Tucsonenses*, pp. 200–201.

1919: First Spanish-Language Theater in New York

The first Spanish-language theater house was founded in 1919 in New York. El Teatro Español, which was the former Park Theatre, was leased by Spanish director and leading man Manuel Noriega (1880–1961) in partnership with other businessmen. Prior to this date, Spanish-language theatrical companies leased theaters only for the run of plays or to house companies on tour. Noriega formed a stock company, Gran Compañía de Opera y Zarzuela, to occupy the house when touring companies were not performing there. *Sources:* Kanellos, *A History of Hispanic Theater in the United States*, pp. 109–111.

1921 ♦ The Teatro Principal in Los Angeles became the first Latino theatrical entity in the United States to establish a playwriting contest. Following this lead, playwriting contests sponsored by the many Spanish-language theaters in Los Angeles gave rise to a boom in original works written for the stages of the Southwest. Many of the plays were based on local themes, and some even elaborated plots based on Hispanic culture of the Southwest dating back to missionary and colonial times. Locally written plays became so popular in Los Angeles that the largest crowds were registered at the theaters every time that new plays by local writers were featured. The Teatro Principal invited local playwrights to submit works in any theatrical genre in prose or verse. The winning works were chosen for production by director Romualdo Tirado (1880–1963), and their authors were paid royalties based on the box office sales. At the end of the run, the newly produced plays competed in an additional contest in which the plays were judged by a panel and audience acclamation. The first- and second-place winners were awarded prizes of $100 and $50, respectively.

Sources: Kanellos, *A History of Hispanic Theater in the United States*, pp. 44–45.

1922 ♦ The first Puerto Rican play to be published in New York was Gonzalo O'Neill's *La india borinqueña* (The Puerto Rican Indian). O'Neill was a prosperous businessman who was also a poet and playwright and an investor in the most important theater house of the 1930s, the Teatro Hispano. He wrote nationalistic plays that supported Puerto Rican independence and identity, such as his *Bajo una sola bandera* (Under One Flag), which was produced onstage and published in 1928.

Sources: Kanellos, *A History of Hispanic Theater in the United States*, pp. 140–143.

1924 ♦ The first playwright contracted to write works to be produced on a Hispanic stage in the United States was Guz Aguila (born Antonio Guzmán Aguilera, 1894–1958). Impresario and theater-owner Meyer Trallis hired the renowned Mexican author of musical-comedy revues for $1,000 per month to write original *revistas* (revues) for production at the Teatro Hidalgo in Los Angeles. The Teatro Hidalgo also committed a company of 30 performers to be directed by Guz Aguila as well as new scenery and costumes. The production of original material based on the lives and culture of Mexicans in Los Angeles had become so important in the intensely competitive theatrical environment of Los Angeles that such publicity and production strategies had become common. The contracting of playwrights led to the greatest boom in Spanish-language playwriting ever experienced in the United States. Over the next several decades, numerous other theaters were leased or purchased and rebaptized as Hispanic houses, such as the Teatro Campoamor, the Teatro Cervantes, the Teatro Hispano, the Teatro San José, and the Teatro Variedades.

Sources: Kanellos, *A History of Hispanic Theater in the United States*, pp. 64–65.

1930 ♦ Beatriz Escalona (1903–1980), known onstage as La Chata Noloesca, split from the Hermanos Areu (Areu Brothers) vaudeville company to form her own touring company, made up mainly of Mexican American young women from San Antonio, Texas. She was the first U.S.-born Hispanic to not only become an outstanding theatrical performer but also rise to the status of the greatest vaudeville actress ever.

Born on August 20, 1903, in San Antonio, Texas, Escalona was discovered while working as an usherette and box office cashier at the Teatro Nacional. She became associated with the Spanish-Cuban troupe of Hermanos Areu—she married José Areu—and played everything from melodrama to vaudeville with them beginning in 1920, when she made her stage debut in El Paso.

Over the course of the 1920s, Escalona developed and perfected her comic persona of the streetwise maid, a *peladita* or underdog character, who maintained a spicy and satirical banter. By 1930, La Chata Noloesca had split from the Areu Brothers and formed her own company, Atracciones Noloesca, and continued to tour the Southwest and northern Mexico.

In 1936, she reformed her company in her native San Antonio and set out to weather the Depression by performing in Tampa, Chicago, and New York—as well as Puerto Rico and Cuba—as the Compañía Mexicana. La Chata Noloesca's novel idea was to bring to the Cubans, Puerto Ricans, and other Mexicans vaudeville, music, folklore, and her own brand of humor.

In 1941, the company set down roots in New York for a stretch of nine years, during which time it was a mainstay on the Hispanic vaudeville circuit made up of the Teatro Hispano, the Teatro Puerto Rico, the Teatro Triboro, and the 53rd Street Theater. Back in San Antonio, she periodically performed for special community events until her death in 1980.

Sources: Kanellos, *Chronology of Hispanic American History*, pp. 108, 149.

1936 ♦ The Tampa Hispanic unit of the Federal Theater Project (FTP) was the only Latino company involved in the effort by the historically important Works Progress Administration's (WPA) effort to save the American stage by employing theatrical artists. The company was directed by professional leading actor and director Manuel Aparicio, who had risen from the Ybor City stages to perform in New York, Cuba, and Spain. Manuel Aparicio became the only Hispanic director in all of the FTP. The company, headquartered at the Centro Asturiano, performed mostly standard *zarzuelas*, along with some other works required by the FTP. Ultimately, because of language differences and misunderstandings about citizenship, the Hispanic unit lost 25 of its members in 1937 when Congress passed the ERA Act of 1937, which effectively removed foreigners from the WPA. This led to the demise of the unit.

Sources: Kanellos, *A History of Hispanic Theater in the United States*, pp. 156–160.

1937 ♦ The first play published by a Puerto Rican woman playwright of New York was *Los Hipócritas* (The Hypocrites) by Franca de Armiño (b. 1900). It was also the first play of record by a U.S. Latina produced on the stages of New York. *Los Hipócritas*, which debuted in three performances at the Palace Theatre in New York on April 15 and 16, 1933, produced by the Compañía Manuel Santigosa, is an anarchist drama in four acts and eight scenes. The author dedicated the play to the oppressed of the world and to those who work for social renovation. Franca de Armiño was a labor organizer and a columnist for *Gráfico* (Graphic) newspaper. She had been a tobacco worker and labor organizer in Puerto Rico.

Sources: Kanellos, *A History of Hispanic Theater in the United States*, pp. 139–140.

1937 ♦ The first Latino theater to conscientiously support the solidarity of a pan-Hispanic identity was New York's Teatro Hispano, which opened in August 1937. Under the leadership of Mexican impresario Senor del Pozo, the Teatro Hispano developed a formula for featuring the national culture of the diverse Hispanic ethnic groups of the New York community. The theater would offer a week of Puerto Rican theater and variety acts, then one Cuban, followed by Spanish or Mexican or Argentine, in an effort to bring all of the diverse ethnic groups together and, of course, benefit financially from this cooperation and solidarity.

Sources: Kanellos, *A History of Hispanic Theater in the United States*, pp. 131–134.

Chita Rivera

1952 ♦ Puerto Rican dancer Chita Rivera (1933–2024) became the first Latina star dancer on Broadway in 1952 when she accepted a role as a principal dancer in *Guys and Dolls*. She went on to star in numerous Broadway hit musicals during the golden age of musicals, including *Can-Can*, *Mr. Wonderful*, and *West Side Story*. She also became the first Latina show dancer to be featured on all of the top television variety shows, including *The Garry Moore Show*, *The Ed Sullivan Show*, *The Arthur Godfrey Show*, *The Sid Caesar Show*, and others. Rivera performed on Broadway in shows until 2015 and won three Tony Awards.

Sources: Telgen and Kamp, *Latinas! Women of Achievement*, pp. 313–319.

1957 ♦ Panamanian American director José Quintero (1924–1999) became the first Latino director to be nominated for a Tony Award for a Broadway production: *Long Day's Journey into Night*. Quintero is one of the few Latino directors to have made a career on Broadway and in major American theaters, directing the works of such international masters as Federico García Lorca, Jean Genet, Thornton Wilder, and Tennessee Williams. The José Quintero Theatre on West 42nd Street in Manhattan was named in his honor. In 1979, he was inducted into the American Theater Hall of Fame.

José Quintero

Sources: Tardiff and Mabunda, *Dictionary of Hispanic Biography*, p. 718.

1957 ♦ Broadway musical *West Side Story* was the first mainstream production to have a Latino theme and to showcase the talents of Latino actors and dancers, some of whom, such as Chita Rivera (1933–2024) and Rita Moreno (1931–), went on to make important contributions to stage and film. The musical ran for 732 performances on Broadway and garnered a Tony nomination for Chita Rivera, the first such nomination for a Latina performer.

Sources: Telgen and Kamp, *Latinas! Women of Achievement*, p. 316.

1963 ♦ The first play that can be called "Chicano" was Luis Valdez's *The Shrunken Head of Pancho Villa*, which he wrote while he was a student at San Jose State University. The drama department produced the play in 1963, making it the first produced Chicano play. Luis Valdez (1940–) went on to be called by many critics "the father of Chicano theater" for his founding of El

Teatro Campesino in 1965 and defining, introducing, and promoting a form and style of people's theater called *teatro chicano.*

Sources: González Broyles, *El Teatro Campesino.*

Luis Valdez

1965 ♦ Luis Valdez (1940–) founded El Teatro Campesino, the first farm worker theater, in Delano, California. His efforts inspired young Chicano activists across the country to use theater as a means of organizing students, communities, and labor unions. Valdez was born into a family of migrant farm workers in Delano, California. Although his education was constantly interrupted, he finished high school and went on to San Jose State University, where he majored in English and pursued his interest in theater.

In 1965, Valdez enlisted in César Chávez's mission to organize farm workers in Delano into a union. It was there that Valdez brought together farm workers and students in El Teatro Campesino to dramatize the plight of the farm workers. The publicity and success gained by the troupe led to the spontaneous appearance of a national Chicano theater movement. In 1967, Valdez and El Teatro Campesino left the unionizing effort to expand their theater beyond agitprop and farm worker concerns. Since then, Valdez and the theater have explored most of the theatrical genres that have been important to Mexicans in the United States.

During the late 1960s and the 1970s, El Teatro Campesino produced many of Valdez's plays, including *Los vendidos* (The Sell-Outs, 1967); *The Shrunken Head of Pancho Villa* (1968); *Bernabé* (1970); *Dark Root of a Scream* (1971); *La Carpa de los Rascuachis* (1974); and *El Fin del Mundo* (The End of the World, 1976). In 1978, Valdez later broke into mainstream theater and film with his play *Zoot Suit.* In 2015, he was awarded the Presidential Medal of the Arts.

Sources: González Broyles, *El Teatro Campesino.*

María Irene Fornés

1965 ♦ Cuban American playwright María Irene Fornés (1930–2018) became the first Latina playwright to win an Obie for Distinguished Plays for *The Successful Life of Three.* She went on to win eight other Obies, the most of any Latino playwright, for her plays *The Danube*, *Mud*, *Sarita*, *The Conduct of Life*, and *Abingdon Square.* During her career, she had some 40 of her plays produced. In 2002, she was awarded the PEN/Laura Pels International Foundation for Theater Award for a Master American Dramatist.

Sources: Tardiff and Mabunda, *Dictionary of Hispanic Biography*, pp. 345–347; Telgen and Kamp, *Latinas! Women of Achievement*, pp. 141–148.

1967 ♦ Broadway and Hollywood actress Miriam Colón (1936–2017) founded the first mobile Puerto Rican theater in the United States, the Puerto Rican Traveling Theater (PRTT), to take full-scale productions, often including salsa bands, into the neighborhoods and parks of New York City. Unlike the community-based Chicano theater, which performed short improvisational *actos*, the PRTT produced full-length conventional plays by Latin American and Latino playwrights in Spanish and English.

Miriam Colón

Sources: Kanellos, *Latino Almanac*, p. 412.

1968 ♦ Luis Valdez's El Teatro Campesino became the first Mexican American company (and the first Mexican American playwright) to win an Obie. Valdez (1940–) would win two more Obies, in 1972 and 1978.

Sources: Tardiff and Mabunda, *Dictionary of Hispanic Biography*, p. 911.

1968 ♦ Luis Valdez (1940–) and El Teatro Campesino left the struggle to establish a farm worker union in order to dedicate themselves to establishing a national theater for Chicanos. They founded Teatro Nacional de Aztlán (TENAZ), at first with the idea that the best members of companies from around the country would join TENAZ to form a national performing company, but, in fact, it was El Teatro Campesino that became the national company for Chicanos. In the mid-1970s, Valdez and El Teatro Campesino left TENAZ, which had become an association of Chicano theaters, organizing festivals, seminars, and conferences. Valdez had been severely criticized for not abandoning religious mysticism and for not becoming as radical as many of the other groups had become.

Sources: Kanellos, *Latino Almanac*, pp. 423–424.

1969 ♦ The only Hispanic repertory company specializing in production of the classics of the Spanish Golden Age as well as contemporary drama, the Teatro Repertorio Español was founded in New York City and continues to be the most active Latino company in the United States. It is also one of the few companies in the United States to stage 19th-century *zarzuelas*. Operating today out of the Gramercy Arts Theater, which has a tradition of Spanish-language theater that goes back to the 1920s, the Teatro Repertorio Español caters to both educational and community-based audiences with productions in both Spanish and English.

Sources: Kanellos, *Latino Almanac*, p. 408.

1971 ♦ Cuban American playwright Iván Acosta's (1943–) play *Abdala-José Martí* was the first Spanish-language play produced at the Lincoln Center Theater Festival.

Sources: Sánchez-Grey, Alba, "El Tema del Desarraigo en el Teatro de Iván Acosta," *Círculo: Revista d e Cultura* 24 (1995): p. 119.

1973 ♦ José Quintero (1924–1999) became the first Latino to win a Tony Award for Best Direction in a Play for his work on the Broadway production of *A Moon for the Misbegotten* by Eugene O'Neill.

Sources: Tardiff and Mabunda, *Dictionary of Hispanic Biography*, p. 718.

Carmen Zapata

1973 ♦ Actress Carmen Zapata (1927–2014) launched the Bilingual Foundation of the Arts, the first Latino theater to serve as a showcase of Latino acting and playwriting for Hollywood.

Sources: Tardiff and Mabunda, *Dictionary of Hispanic Biography*, p. 966.

1973 ♦ Luis Valdez (1940–) and El Teatro Campesino were the first Latino theatrical director and troupe to win a special Emmy for the PBS broadcast of the television version of their play *Los vendidos* (The Sellouts).

Sources: Tardiff and Mabunda, *Dictionary of Hispanic Biography*, p. 518.

1974 ♦ The first Broadway hit play by a Latino was *Short Eyes* by Miguel Piñero (1946–1988). It was also the first Latino-authored play to win major drama awards on Broadway, including the New York Drama Critics Circle Award for Best American Play, an Obie, and the Drama Desk Award. After the success of *Short Eyes*, Piñero went on to write other successful plays and scripts for such television dramas as *Barreta*, *Kojak*, and *Miami Vice*. In all, Piñero wrote 11 plays that were produced, most of which are included in his two collections, *The Sun Always Shines for the Cool; A Midnight Moon at the Greasy Spoon; Eulogy for a Small-Time Thief* (1983) and *Outrageous One-Act Plays* (1986). Piñero also authored of a book of poems, *La Bodega Sold Dreams* (1986). In 2010, Arte Público Press published his complete works under the title of *Outlaw: The Complete Works of Miguel Piñero.*

Sources: Kanellos, *Chronology of Hispanic American History*, pp. 224, 260.

1974 ♦ The Puerto Rican Traveling Theater became the first Latino theater to open a theater house in the off-Broadway section of New York City and to be accepted and reviewed as an off-Broadway house. Founded by Miriam Colón (1936–2017) in 1967, the theater had previously performed in the open air in various Latino neighborhoods of New York City.

Sources: Kanellos, *Latino Almanac*, p. 412.

1975 ♦ Rita Moreno (1931–) became the first Latina actress to win a Tony Award for Best Featured Actress in a Play in the Broadway production of *The Ritz*, which ran for more than 400 performances.

Sources: Telgen and Kamp, *Latinas! Women of Achievement*, p. 266.

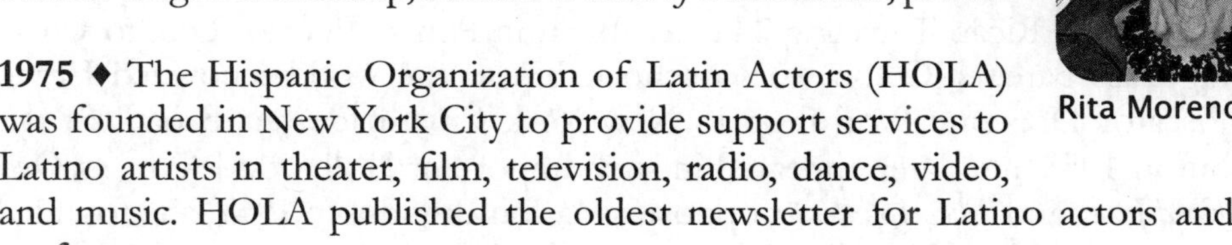

Rita Moreno

1975 ♦ The Hispanic Organization of Latin Actors (HOLA) was founded in New York City to provide support services to Latino artists in theater, film, television, radio, dance, video, and music. HOLA published the oldest newsletter for Latino actors and performers.

Sources: Furtaw, *Hispanic Americans Information Directory*, p. 15.

1978 ♦ Luis Valdez (1940–) became the first Mexican American playwright to break into mainstream theater with Los Angeles's Mark Taper Forum's production of his *Zoot Suit* and the 1979 Broadway production of the same play. In 1986, his play *I Don't Have to Show You No Stinking Badges* had a successful run at the Los Angeles Theater Center.

Sources: Tardiff and Mabunda, *Dictionary of Hispanic Biography*, p. 518.

1981 ♦ Puerto Rican actor-director-producer José Ferrer (1912–1992) became the first Latino actor inducted for acting into the Theater Hall of Fame.

Sources: Kanellos, *Chronology of Hispanic American History*, p. 167.

Dolores Prida

1981 ♦ Cuban American playwright Dolores Prida (1943–2013) became the first Latina to receive a special award from the Third World Theatre Competition in Caracas, Venezuela, for her play *La era latina* (The Latin Era). Written and first produced in 1980, this bilingual musical comedy toured to more than 30 Latino neighborhoods in New York City for open-air staging by the Puerto Rican Traveling Theater. This foray into bilingual theater next led her to write her most important and far-reaching work, *Coser y cantar* (Sewing and Singing, 1981), an experimental, psychological play about bilingualism-biculturalism and the conflicting roles that Latinos, especially women, must play in U.S. society. By dividing the Americanized part of a woman's psyche from her "old country" consciousness, creating a character around each, and engaging the characters in bilingual dialog, Prida was able to illustrate the tensions and contradictions that need to be resolved by Latinos everywhere in the United States.

Sources: Kanellos, *Latino Almanac*, pp. 419–420.

1982 ♦ Actress, director, and producer Miriam Colón (1936–2017) became the first Hispanic artist to be awarded the New York City Mayor's Award of Honor for the Arts and Culture for her work as founder and director of the Puerto Rican Traveling Theater. Born in Ponce, Puerto Rico, to working-class parents, Colón won a scholarship to the world-renowned Erwin Piscator Dramatic Workshop in New York City, made her Broadway debut in 1953, and later appeared in such important Hollywood films as *One-Eyed Jacks* and *The Appaloosa*, opposite Marlon Brando. In 1967, she founded the Puerto Rican Traveling Theater to take Spanish-language and Hispanic theater into the neighborhoods of New York City in open-air productions. Later, she created a theater house from an old firehouse in the off-Broadway section to house more conventional productions of Latino and Latin American plays.

Sources: Telgen and Kamp, *Latinas! Women of Achievement*, pp. 93–96.

1982 ♦ Cuban American playwright María Irene Fornés (1930–2018) became the first Latina to win an Obie for sustained achievement in theater. This was in addition to numerous other Obies that she had won during her career for individual plays.

Sources: Telgen and Kamp, *Latinas! Women of Achievement*, p. 147.

1983 ♦ Playwright, director, and screenwriter Luis Valdez (1940–) became the first Latino playwright to be awarded the National Medal of Arts.

Sources: Tardiff and Mabunda, *Dictionary of Hispanic Biography*, p. 518.

1985 ♦ Cuban American writer María Irene Fornés (1930–2018) became the first Latino playwright to win the prestigious American Academy and Institute of Arts and Letters Award in Literature, bestowed in recognition of sustained achievement.

Sources: Telgen and Kamp, *Latinas! Women of Achievement*, p. 147.

1987 ♦ Luis Valdez (1940–) became the first Mexican American screenwriter-director to break into Hollywood commercial films with his writing and directing of *La Bamba* (the name of a dance from Veracruz), the screen biography of Chicano rock and roll star Ritchie Valens (1941–1959). Valdez's screenwriting career began with early film and television versions of Corky Gonzales's poem "I Am Joaquin" (1969) and the play *Los vendidos* (The Sellouts) and gathered momentum with a film version of *Zoot Suit* (1982). Valdez's plays, essays, and poems have been widely anthologized. He has published three collections of plays: *Luis Valdez—The Early Works* (1990), *Zoot Suit and Other Plays* (1992), and *Mummified Deer and Other Plays* (2005). Valdez's awards include an Obie (1968), Los Angeles Drama Critics Circle Awards (1969, 1972, and 1978), a special Emmy Award (1973), and a Best Musical award from the San Francisco Bay Critics Circle (1983).

Sources: Kanellos, *Chronology of Hispanic American History*, p. 274.

1987 ♦ Director José Quintero (1924–1999) became the first Latino to win the Unique Contributions to the Theatre Award from the Drama League. The Panamanian-born Quintero made a career of directing works by the great American playwrights Tennessee Williams and Eugene O'Neill.

Sources: Tardiff and Mabunda, *Dictionary of Hispanic Biography*, p. 718.

1985: The Hispanic Playrights Project

The Hispanic Playwrights Project was founded in 1985 in Costa Mesa, California, to take plays by Latinos through readings and workshops and produce the best of them in an annual national festival, which showcases them for theaters around the United States. Since its founding, more than half of the plays produced by the festival have gone on to be produced by larger companies. Inaugurated in 1986, HPP prompted the submission of over 1,000 manuscripts, of which more than 50 received workshops and more than half went on to full productions at SCR and other resident theaters. The program lasted until 2004. *Sources:* "Hispanic Playwrights Project," Southcoast Repertory Theater: https://www.scr.org/about/about-scr-landing/the-scr-story/scr-production-history/history-landing-page/play-reading-history/reading-landing-page/hispanic-playwrights-project-history/.

1989 ♦ Arte Público Press received a grant from the Ford Foundation to publish collections of Latino plays, the first ever concerted effort to issue the works of Latino playwrights of the United States. In the following three years, the press published anthologies of Chicano, Cuban American, and Puerto Rican plays, respectively, as well as individual collections of plays by such playwrights as Iván Acosta, Carlos Morton, Miguel Piñero, Dolores Prida, and Luis Valdez. The press also issued anthologies of plays by Latinas and plays for children.

Sources: "Drama," Arte Público Press Catalog, pp. 64–65: https://artepublicopress.com/wp-content/uploads/2023/10/2023-Complete-Catalog_final-with-cover_9-7-2023.pdf.

Josefina López

1989 ♦ Josefina López (1969–), as a 17-year-old Mexican immigrant, became the youngest Latina playwright to have a play, *Simplemente María, or The American Dream*, air nationally on the Public Broadcasting Service. López has since then continued to write plays for production and gone on to become a scriptwriter for television and film.

Sources: Hispanic, August 1995, p. 28.

1990 ♦ Carmen Zapata (1927–2014) of the Bilingual Foundation of the Arts was the first Latino director to receive the prestigious Civil Order of Merit from His Majesty Juan Carlos I, King of Spain, in recognition of her commitment to Latinos in theater and film and for her community service. In 1991, she, along with eight other artists and organizations, was conferred the California Governor's Award for the Arts.

Sources: Tardiff and Mabunda, *Dictionary of Hispanic Biography*, p. 966.

1996 ♦ New York's Teatro Repertorio Español became the first Latino theatrical company to win an honorary Drama Desk Award for its excellence in presenting plays in Spanish and English.

Sources: Hispanic Link Weekly Report, 13 May 1996, p. 8.

2002 ♦ Chita Rivera (born Dolores Conchita Figueroa del Rivero, 1933–2024) became the first Latino dancer to receive a Kennedy Center Honor. The Puerto Rican Broadway musical dancer often appeared on television variety shows and over her career won three Tony Awards and the Presidential Medal of Freedom.

Sources: Tardiff and Mabunda, *Dictionary of Hispanic Biography*, p. 739; Telgen and Kamp, *Latinas! Women of Achievement*, pp. 313–319.

2011 ♦ Dominican-born, Bronx-raised Broadway costume designer Emilio Sosa (1967–) received the Henry Hewes Design Award and the Lucille Lortel Award for his work on *By the Way, Meet Vera Stark*. He had previously received the LA Ovation Award for the musical *Twist* and was actually the first designer of color to work on the Christmas Show at Radio City Music Hall in 2018. The *New York Times* noted that in 2023, he was the designer for five shows, dressing 94 actors and designing 450 costumes.

Sources: "Broadway's Hardest Working Man," *New York Times*, 4 June 2023.

2015 ♦ *Hamilton: An American Musical* by Nuyorican Lin-Manuel Miranda (1980–) premiered off-Broadway at the Public Theater. It officially opened on Broadway on August 6, 2015. It opened to rave reviews and is the highest-grossing musical ever. As of the time of publication of *Latino Firsts*, *Hamilton* is still on Broadway and touring the country with various companies. In 2020, the Disney Channel aired the video production of *Hamilton* nationally, which made it accessible to the millions of people who could not afford Broadway's most expensive ticket.

Lin-Manuel Miranda

Hamilton won the Tony Award for Best Musical, and Miranda won the Tony Awards for Best Original Score and Best Book of a Musical; the *Hamilton* cast album won the Grammy Award for Best Musical Theater Album. If that were not enough, *Hamilton* was awarded the Pulitzer Prize.

Hamilton is a truly revolutionary work of art for the stage in many regards: 1) its cast of actors playing the Founding Fathers was predominantly made up of people of color, 2) the entire play is sung and spoken in rap, and 3) it presents a subtle message about immigration—Hamilton was an immigrant—to a Broadway audience, which is traditionally adverse to political messages. Just the sheer phenomenon is overwhelming of an artist who is studied and intelligent enough to write such an intricate play based on history as well as compose the music, perform in the lead role, sing, and dance; it is especially overwhelming considering that the predominantly old, white, and well-to-do patrons of Broadway musicals rarely ever see a Puerto Rican in any of these roles.

After leaving the stage production of *Hamilton*, Miranda worked on various television and film productions and costarred in *Mary Poppins Returns* in 2019. A Hollywood production of his first Tony Award–winning musical, *In the Heights* (2008), reached theaters and the Disney Channel in 2021.

In 2019, the Smithsonian National Portrait Gallery awarded Miranda the Portrait of a Nation prize; he also received a star on the Hollywood Walk of Fame. Miranda should be considered the greatest Latino Broadway star ever as a Nuyorican playwright, composer, actor, and singer.

Sources: "Lin-Manuel Miranda," Biography: https://www.biography.com/actors/lin-manuel-miranda.

2017 ♦ Cuban-born, Argentine-raised Riccardo Hernández was the first Latino scenic designer to win an Obie Award for Sustained Excellence of Set Design for Thornton Wilder's play *The Skin of Our Teeth.* In 2020, he was awarded the Princess Grace Statue. Hernández has designed the scenery for more than 250 Broadway and off-Broadway plays. He is the cochair of design at the David Geffen School of Drama at Yale University.

Sources: Riccardo Hernández—Scenic Design: https://www.riccardohernandez.com/bio.

Lyndsay Méndez

2018 ♦ California-born actress Lyndsay Méndez (1981–) won a Tony Award for Best Featured Actress in a Musical for her work in the revival of the musical *Carousel.* In 2023, she was again nominated for the same Tony for her work in the revival of *Merrily We Roll Along.*

Sources: Henderson, Kathy. "Lindsay Mendez," Broadway Buzz: https://www.broadway.com/buzz/6633/lindsay-mendez/.

2022 ♦ New Mexico native Montana Levi Blanco (1984–) was the first Latino to win a Tony Award for Best Costume Design in a Play for his work on the Thornton Wilder play *The Skin of Our Teeth.* His grandmother, who was a lampshade artisan, inspired his early love of fabric, color, and beauty. An M.F.A. graduate in Design from the David Geffen School of Drama at Yale University, Blanco is booked up for new shows for all of 2024 and 2025.

Montana Levi Blanco

Sources: "Montana Levi Blanco Costume Design": https://www.montanaleviblanco.com/about.

Film, Radio, and TV

FILM

1912 ♦ The first actor to establish the stereotype in film of the "Latin lover" was the Spanish-born Antonio Moreno (born Antonio Garrido Monteagudo, 1887–1967), who in 1912 began appearing in films by D. W. Griffith. Moreno played a dapper Latin lover in numerous Hollywood silent films and was especially popular during the 1920s, when he played leads opposite such actresses as Gloria Swanson, Greta Garbo, Pola Negri, and Bebe Daniels. His foreign accent limited his career in talkies, where he was seen mainly in character roles. He appeared in hundreds of films, including *The Voice of the Millions* (1912), *The Musketeers of Pig Alley* (1912), *The Song of the Ghetto* (1914), *The Loan Shark King* (1914), *Sunshine and Shadows* (1914), *In the Latin Quarter* (1915), *The Quality of Mercy* (1915), *My American Wife* (1922), *The Spanish Dancer* (1923), *Romance of the Rio Grande* (1929), *Rose of the Rio Grande* (1938), *Captain from Castille* (1947), *Creature from the Black Lagoon* (1954), and *The Searchers* (1956).

Sources: Kanellos, *Latino Almanac*, p. 460.

1916 ♦ The Puerto Rican film industry was established with the founding of the Sociedad Industrial Cine Puerto Rico in 1916 by Rafael Colorado D'Assoy (1869–1959) and Antonio Capella Martínez (1880–1968). The Sociedad produced three films that year; its first film was *Por la Hembra y el Gallo* (For Women and Fighting Cocks).

Sources: Kanellos, *Latino Almanac*, p. 446.

1920 ♦ Juan Emilio Viguie Cajas Sr. (1891–1966) became the first commercially successful producer of films in Puerto Rico, primarily producing newsreels for continental enterprises such as Pathe, Fox Movietone, and MGM. He also produced many documentaries for private enterprises and for the government.

Sources: Kanellos, *Latino Almanac*, pp. 446–447.

Ramón Novarro

1922 ♦ In 1922, Ramón Novarro (1899–1968) was cast in the leading role in the silent film *The Prisoner of Zenda* and became the first Latino matinee idol in the United States. In 1913, Novarro moved to Los Angeles, California, with his family as refugees from the Mexican Revolution. The family experienced abject poverty, which led Novarro to work as a child, including taking small acting and dancing parts on-screen and stage. Largely because of his ability as a dancer, Novarro was cast in the film that would launch his career as a romantic actor: *The Prisoner of Zenda.* Novarro quickly became a success as a romantic matinee idol, rivaled only by Rudolph Valentino in sexy Latin- and Arab-lover roles. Among his notable films were *Ben-Hur: A Tale of the Christ* (1925), *The Student Prince in Old Heidelberg* (1927), *Son of India* (1931), *Mata Hari* (1931), and *The Cat and the Fiddle* (1934). His last film was *Heller in Pink Tights* (1960). Novarro was found beaten to death at his home on October 31, 1968.

Sources: Kanellos, *Latino Almanac*, p. 460.

1925 ♦ The first Latina leading lady in Hollywood films, Dolores del Río (1904–1983), made her debut in *Joanne*, which was the first of 15 silent films she made between 1925 and 1929. Her three most important films were *What Price Glory?*, *Resurrection*, and *Ramona.* Del Río became one of Hollywood's top 10 moneymakers during the 1920s. In 1942, after starring in 23 U.S. films, she left the country for Mexico, where she became important in the film industry of her native country. Born Dolores Asúnsolo y López Negrete to a wealthy family in Durango, Mexico, del Río came to the United States in 1925 at the invitation of Hollywood director Edwin Carewe, who directed her in *Joanne.*

Dolores del Río

Sources: Telgen and Kamp, *Latinas! Women of Achievement*, pp. 103–108.

1926 ♦ Lúpe Vélez (born María Guadalupe Vélez de Villalobos, 1908–1944), the second of two Latina leading ladies (Dolores del Río actually had her de-

Lúpe Vélez

but a few months earlier, in 1925) in Hollywood films, made her debut in a film directed by Hal Roach. She became a star the following year as the leading lady in *The Gaucho*, opposite Douglas Fairbanks. Known as a fiery leading lady both in silent and sound films, she later made positive use of her Spanish-accented English to reposition herself as a comedienne in the *Mexican Spitfire* series. Her volatile personal life, including a romance with Gary Cooper and marriage to Johnny Weissmuller, ended in suicide. Her films included *The Gaucho* (1927), *Stand and Deliver* (1928), *Lady of the Pavements* (1929), *The Squaw Man* (1931), *The Cuban Love Song* (1931), *Hot Pepper* (1933), *The Girl from Mexico* (1939), *Mexican Spitfire* (1940), and *Redhead from Manhattan* (1943).

Sources: Kanellos, *Latino Almanac*, pp. 429–430.

1934 ♦ Juan Emilio Viguie Cajas Sr.'s (1891-1966) film *Romance Tropical* (Tropical Romance) was the first Puerto Rican feature film of the sound period. Written by the poet Luis Palés Matos (1898–1959), the film depicts a lovesick young musician who attempts to seek his fortune at sea in a tiny boat.

Sources: Kanellos, *Latino Almanac*, pp. 446–447.

Rita Hayworth

1935 ♦ Rita Hayworth (1918–1987) made her screen debut and was on her way to becoming the first Latina sex goddess in Hollywood films. Born as Margarita Carmen Cansino in Brooklyn, New York, she was the daughter of Spanish dancer Eduardo Cansino and his Ziegfeld Follies partner Volga Hayworth. By the age of 13, Hayworth had danced professionally in Mexican night spots in Tijuana and Agua Caliente, where she was eventually noticed by Hollywood scouts. She made her screen debut in 1935, playing bit parts under her real name. In 1937, she married Edward Judson, under whose guidance she changed her name and was transformed into an auburn-haired sophisticate. For the remainder of the 1930s, Hayworth was confined to leads in B pictures, but throughout much of the 1940s, she became the undisputed sex goddess of Hollywood films and the hottest star at Columbia Studios. Her tempestuous personal life included marriages to Orson Welles, Aly Khan, and singer Dick Haymes. As Rita Cansino, her films included *Under the Pampas Moon* (1935), *Charlie Chan in Egypt* (1935), *Dante's Inferno* (1935), *Meet Nero Wolfe* (1936), *Trouble in Texas* (1937), *Old Louisiana* (1937), and *Hit the Saddle* (1937). As Rita Hayworth, she acted in *The Shadow* (1937), *Angels Over Broadway* (1940), *The Strawberry Blonde* (1941), *Blood and Sand* (1941), *Cover Girl* (1944), *Gilda* (1946), *The Lady from Shanghai* (1947), *The Loves of Carmen*

(1948), *Salome* (1953), *Miss Sadie Thompson* (1953), *Pal Joey* (1957), *Separate Tables* (1958), *They Came to Cordura* (1959), *The Happy Thieves* (1961), *The Money Trap* (1965), *The Wrath of God* (1972), and *Circle* (1976).

Sources: Meares, Hadley Hall, "The Love Goddess: Rita Hayworth's Tragic Quest," *Vanity Fair*, 23 September 2020.

1941 ♦ The first Latina actress to be considered a model of American beauty and sensuality was Rita Hayworth, who in 1941 was dubbed "The Great American Love Goddess" by Winthrop Sargent in *Life*. The actress and cabaret dancer Rita Cansino had so successfully molded her identity to the needs of Hollywood that in the early 1940s, she was making $6,000 a week as Columbia Pictures's leading actress. This was in contrast to other Latina actresses, who were repeatedly cast in the stereotype of the Latin spitfire.

Sources: Telgen and Kamp, *Latinas! Women of Achievement*, pp. 169–173.

1949 ♦ The Puerto Rican government founded a production facility in San Juan to spur the film industry on the island. Administered by the *División de Educación de la Comunidad* (Division of Community Education), this unit produced more films than any other entity in Puerto Rico. By 1975, it was able to produce 65 shorts and two features.

Sources: Kanellos, *Latino Almanac*, pp. 446–447.

1950 ♦ Puerto Rican actor José Ferrer (1912–1992) became the first Puerto Rican and first U.S. Latino to win the Academy Award for Best Actor. Ferrer was one of the most distinguished Latino actors to have made a career in mainstream films and onstage in the United States. The star of numerous Hollywood films and of many stage productions was born in Santurce, Puerto Rico, on January 8, 1912. Raised and educated in Puerto Rico, he graduated from Princeton University in 1933.

José Ferrer

As an actor or director, his stage credits include *Let's Face It* (1943), *Strange Fruit* (1945), *Cyrano de Bergerac* (1946), *Design for Living* (1947), *Twentieth Century* (1950), *Stalag 17* (1951), and *Man of La Mancha* (1965), among many others. As an actor, director, or producer, he has been associated with some of the most famous Hollywood films, including *Joan of Arc* (1948), *Moulin Rouge* (1952), *The Caine Mutiny* (1954), *Return to Peyton Place* (1961), *Lawrence of Arabia* (1962), *Ship of Fools* (1965), and others. His awards include the Gold Medal from the American Academy of Arts and Sciences (1949), the Academy Award for Best Actor in *Cyrano de Bergerac* (1950), and induction into the Theater Hall of Fame (1981), among many others. The U.S. Postal Service honored Ferrer with a stamp in 2012.

Sources: Kanellos, *Chronology of Hispanic American History*, p. 167.

1951 ♦ Viguie Film Productions became the first large Puerto Rican film producer. Founded by Juan Emilio Viguie Cajas Jr. (1923-2004) and journalist Manuel R. Navas, the company produced documentaries for both commercial and government use. In 1974, the company changed names and financial backing and became Guastella Film Producers, currently the largest producer in Puerto Rico.

Sources: Kanellos, *Latino Almanac*, pp. 446–447.

Anthony Quinn

1952 ♦ Actor Anthony Quinn (1915–2001) became the first Mexican American to win the Academy Award for Best Supporting Actor for his role as Emiliano Zapata's brother in *Viva Zapata!* Born in Chihuahua, Mexico, of Irish-Mexican parentage, Quinn lived in the United States since childhood. He began his career as a film actor in 1936. Quinn went on to win a second Academy Award for *Lust for Life* (1956), and he began playing leads that emphasized his earthy and exotic qualities.

He appeared in more than 100 films and wrote his autobiography, *The Original Sin*, in 1972. Among his many films are *Parole!* (1936), *The Buccaneer* (1938), *King of Alcatraz* (1938), *Texas Rangers Ride Again* (1940), *Blood and Sand* (1941), *The Ox-Bow Incident* (1943), *Guadalcanal Diary* (1943), *Back to Bataan* (1945), *California* (1947), *Sinbad the Sailor* (1947), *Black Gold* (1947), *The Brave Bulls* (1951), *Viva Zapata!* (1952), *Against All Flags* (1952), *Ride, Vaquero!* (1953), *Lust for Life* (1956), *Man from Del Rio* (1956), *The Black Orchid* (1959), *The Guns of Navarrone* (1961), *Barabbas* (1961), *Requiem for a Heavyweight* (1962), *Lawrence of Arabia* (1962), *Zorba the Greek* (1964), *A High Wind in Jamaica* (1965), *The Shoes of the Fisherman* (1968), *The Magus* (1968), *The Secret of Santa Vittoria* (1969), *The Greek Tycoon* (1978), *The Children of Sanchez* (1978), *The Salamander* (1981), *Ghosts Can't Do It* (1990), and *Revenge* (1990).

Sources: Kanellos, *Chronology of Hispanic American History*, p. 172.

1952 ♦ Puerto Rican actor José Ferrer became the Latino with the most Academy Award nominations (three) when he was nominated for best actor for his role in *Moulin Rouge.*

Sources: Kanellos, *Chronology of Hispanic American History*, p. 339.

1956 ♦ Francisco "Chico" Day (1907–1995) became the first Latino assistant director in Hollywood and the first Latino to be inducted into the Directors Guild of America. Born Francisco Alonso in Juarez, Mexico, on October 16, 1907, Chico, as he was affectionately called, was raised in El Paso, Texas, and Los Angeles, California. He began working in motion pictures as a bit player and extra alongside his older brother, the famed actor Gilbert Roland. In 1956, he became the first assistant director to Cecile B. DeMille on the production of *The Ten Commandments.* Chico Day went on to be the unit production manager on such films as *The Magnificent Seven*, *Patton*, *Hello Dolly*, and *Islands in the Stream.* In 1981, Day was awarded the Frank Capra Achievement Award from the Directors Guild of America. Today, an annual award in his name is given to outstanding Hispanic directors by the Latino Committee of the Directors Guild.

Sources: Reyes, Luis, "Hollywood's Hispanic Heritage," *DGA News*, August/September 1994, pp. 18–19.

1956 ♦ Anthony Quinn (1915–2001), the Irish-Mexican actor born in Chihuahua, Mexico, became the first Latino to win two Academy Awards. His first Oscar was for the role of Emiliano Zapata's brother in *Viva Zapata!* (1952) and the second for his depiction of Vincent Van Gogh in *Lust for Life* (1956). Anthony Quinn appeared in more than 100 films, acting in English, Spanish, and Italian.

Sources: Gates, Anita. "Anthony Quinn Dies at 86; Played Earthy Tough Guys," *New York Times*, 4 June 2001.

1961 ♦ Puerto Rican actress Rita Moreno (1931–) became the first Latina to win an Academy Award for Best Supporting Actress. Actress, dancer, and singer Moreno was born Rosita Dolores Alverio in Humacao, Puerto Rico. A dancer from childhood, she reached Broadway at 13 and Hollywood at 14. She won a 1961 Academy Award as Best Supporting Actress for *West Side Story* and has been in several films important for understanding the Hollywood depiction of Latinos, including *A Medal for Benny* (1945), *The Ring* (1952), and *Popi* (1969). Her other films include *Pagan Love Song* (1950), *Singin' in the Rain* (1952), *Latin Lovers* (1953), *Fort Vengeance* (1953), *Jivaro* (1954), *Garden of Evil* (1954), *The King and I* (1956), *The Vagabond King* (1956), *The Deerslayer* (1957), *West Side Story* (1961), *Summer and Smoke* (1961), *Marlowe* (1969), *Carnal Knowledge* (1971), *The Ritz* (1976), *The Boss' Son* (1978), *Happy Birthday, Gemini* (1980), *The Four Seasons* (1981), and *Life in the Food Chain* (1991). At first typecast as a hot-blooded exotic, she was able to break away and earn more well-rounded roles that led her to become one the most recognizable and awarded actresses in the United States. She received the Screen Actors Guild Lifetime Achievement Award in 2014.

Sources: Moreno, Rita. *Rita Moreno: A Memoir*. New York: Penguin, 2013.

1969 ♦ Actor Ricardo Montalbán (1920–2009) founded the first organization to promote equal opportunities for Latino actors and actresses in Hollywood. The Nosotros organization sought to improve the image of Latinos in the movies and on television. It sponsored the Golden Eagle Awards to recognize outstanding performances by Latinos.

Ricardo Montalbán

Sources: Tardiff and Mabunda, *Dictionary of Hispanic Biography*, p. 563.

1971 ♦ The first two Chicano documentary films were made, David García's *Requiem-29*, which described the Chicano moratorium on the Vietnam War, and Jesús Salvador Treviño's *América Tropical*, about the whitewashing of a David Alfaro Siqueiros mural in Los Angeles.

Sources: Kanellos, *Latino Almanac*, pp. 260–261.

Jesús Salvador Treviño'

1972 ♦ Jesús Salvador Treviño's (1946–) documentary film *Yo Soy Chicano* (I Am Chicano) was the first film by a Chicano to be nationally televised. The film dealt with the Chicano Movement from its pre-Columbian roots to modern activism.

Sources: Kanellos, *Latino Almanac*, pp. 260–261.

1972 ♦ The feature film based on Luis Valdez (1940–) and El Teatro Campesino's play *Los Vendidos* was the first nationally televised Chicano feature film. It was a satire of the stereotypes traditionally used to depict Mexicanas and Mexican Americans. *Los Vendidos* may also be considered the first Chicano feature film.

Sources: Kanellos, *Latino Almanac*, pp. 444–445; Valdez, Luis, and El Teatro Campesino, *The Early Works*, Arte Público Press, 1990.

1978 ♦ Spanish Cuban cinematographer Nestor Almendros (1930–1992) became the first Latino to win an Oscar for Best Cinematography. A graduate of the University of Havana in philosophy and literature, Almendros began his career in film with an amateur eight-millimeter film with the great Cuban director Tomás Gutiérrez Alea in 1950. He later studied film with Hans Richter at the City University of New York and studied cinematography at the Centro Sperimentale di Cinematografia in Rome. In the mid-1960s, he began collaborating regularly with director Eric Rohmer and later with director Francois Truffaut.

He won the Academy Award for Best Cinematography for the 1978 film *Days of Heaven*. Included among his many outstanding films are *The Wild Racers* (U.S., 1968); *The Gun Runner* (U.S., 1969); *Ma nuit chez Maud/My Night at Maud's* (France, 1969); *L'enfant sauvage/The Wild Child* (France, 1970); *Le genou de Claire/Claire's Knee* (France, 1970); *L'amour l'apres-midi/Love in the Afternoon* (France, 1972); *L'histoire d'Adele H./The Story of Adele H.* (France, 1975); *Days of Heaven* (U.S., 1978); *Kramer vs. Kramer* (U.S., 1979); *The Blue Lagoon* (U.S., 1980); *The Last Metro* (France, 1980); *Sophie's Choice* (U.S., 1982); *Places in the Heart* (U.S., 1984); *Heartburn* (U.S., 1986); and *New York Stories* (U.S., 1989). Almendros also directed several noteworthy documentaries, including *Improper Conduct* (1984) and the anti-Castro film *Nobody Listened* (1988). Almendros was the author of an important autobiographical book on cinematography, *Un homme à la caméra/A Man with a Camera*, published first in French in 1980 and then in English translation in 1984.

Sources: Almendros, Nestor, *Man with a Camera*, New York: Farrar, Straus & Giroux, 1986.

1978 ♦ The first Chicano film nominated for an Academy Award was the short documentary *Agueda Martinez: Our People, Our Country* by Esperanza Vázquez and Moctezuma Esparza (1949–), which depicts the lifestyle of an elderly woman in northern New Mexico.

Sources: Kanellos, *Latino Almanac*, p. 442.

1979 ♦ The first Cuban American comedy film, the award-winning *El Super*, based on the play by Iván Acosta (1943–) and directed by León Ichaso (1948–2023), was produced. The film, using the working-class dialect of New York City Cubans, deals with Cuban American culture shock and the adjustment of Cuban exiles to permanent residency in the United States. In addition to launching the career of Ichaso as a producer-director, it launched the career of Elizabeth Pena (1959–2014), the first Cuban American Hollywood actress in contemporary times, who went on to star in numerous Hollywood films and television productions.

Sources: Canby, Vincent, "The Screen: 'El Super,' a Cuban American Tale: The Cast," *New York Times*, 29 April 1979.

1979 ♦ The nation's longest-running Latino film festival, Cine Festival, was founded by the Guadalupe Cultural Arts Center in San Antonio. At first focusing on local and regional Mexican American films in various categories, over the years, the festival has expanded to focus on all Latino filmmaking in the United States while also airing movies from the rest of the Hispanic world. Like most film festivals, Cine Festival awards juried prizes for the best films in various categories.

Sources: Cine Festival: https://guadalupeculturalarts.org/cine-festival/.

1981 ♦ *Seguín* by Jesús Salvador Treviño—the first Chicano western—was filmed, followed by Moctezuma Esparza's *The Ballad of Gregorio Cortez* in 1982. Both films broke the mold of the genre by focusing on the recuperation of lost or suppressed aspects of Chicano history. *Seguín* was the first Latino version of the fall of the Alamo since it was first depicted on the screen in 1911, whereas *The Ballad of Gregorio Cortez* dealt with the adventures of a folk hero who was cast as a bandit by Anglo-Texan law.

Sources: Kanellos, *Latino Almanac*, pp. 260–261.

1984 ♦ Actor César Romero (1907–1994) became the Latino actor with the longest, or one of the longest, acting careers in Hollywood films. In 1984, he received an award from the Hollywood International Celebrity Banquet for achieving 50 years in the film industry. That same year, he received the Nosotros Golden Eagle Award for success as a Latino in show business. In 1991, Romero, who played the suave Latin lover in so many films, also won the IMAGEN Hispanic Media Image Award for Lifetime Achievement.

César Romero

Sources: Tardiff and Mabunda, *Dictionary of Hispanic Biography*, p. 768.

Gregory Nava

1985 ♦ Gregory Nava (1949–) became the first Latino screenwriter to have a film nominated for an Academy Award. His highly acclaimed *El Norte* is the story of a peasant couple's journey of immigration to the United States.

Sources: Tardiff and Mabunda, *Dictionary of Hispanic Biography*, p. 599.

1985 ♦ José Ferrer (1912–1992) was the first Latino actor to be awarded the National Medal of Arts by President Ronald Reagan.

Sources: Kanellos, *Chronology of Hispanic American History,* p. 167.

1985 ♦ Edward James Olmos (1947–) was the first Latino to win the Primetime Emmy for Outstanding Supporting Actor in a Drama Series for his role as Lieutenant Castillo in the television series *Miami Vice.*

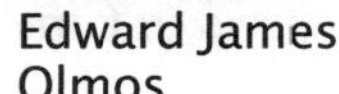
Edward James Olmos

Sources: Kanellos, *Latino Almanac*, p. 461.

1987 ♦ *La Bamba*, the screen biography of rock star Ritchie Valens (1941–1959), written and directed by Luis Valdez (1943–), was the first Hollywood film marketed successfully in both English and Spanish versions to audiences in the United States. A record 77 Spanish-language prints were released, and the Latino market provided a two-to-one return over mainstream audiences on costs, representing 10 percent of the receipts. The movie was nominated for Best Motion Picture: Drama at the Golden Globes. It also introduced broad audiences to actors Lou Diamond Philips (1962–) and Esai Morales (1962–) as well the music of Los Lobos.

Sources: Machado, Yolanda, "'La Bamba' and the Lives It Changed," *New York Times*, 3 May 2021.

1988 ♦ The award-winning film *Stand and Deliver* was the first Hollywood feature film in which virtually the entire production, including scripting, producing, financing, directing, and acting, was conducted by Latinos. The film presented the inspirational true story of a Bolivian math teacher, Jaime Escalante (1930–2010), in East Los Angeles, who prepared numerous poor, inner-city students for college against all odds. Actor Edward James Olmos (1947–) was able to provide a second life for the film through massive distribution to educational institutions in the United States in conjunction with such sponsors as PepsiCo.

Sources: Kanellos, *Latino Almanac*, p. 461.

1988 ♦ Mexican American filmmaker Jesús Salvador Treviño (1946–) became the first U.S. Latino director to win a Directors Guild of America award for Best Daytime Drama for his film *Gangs.*

Sources: Tardiff and Mabunda, *Dictionary of Hispanic Biography*, p. 900.

1990 ♦ Jimmy Smits (1955–) won the Primetime Emmy Award for Outstanding Supporting Actor in a Drama Series for his work in the television

Jimmy Smits

series *L.A. Law.* Known mostly for acting in police and legal television dramas, Smits was born in Brooklyn, New York, to a Surinam Dutch father and a Puerto Rican mother. He has acted in some two dozen feature films, plus the entire series of *L.A. Law* from 1986 to 1992; *NYPD Blue* from 1994 to 1998 and 2004; and *The West Wing* from 2004 to 2006.

Sources: Brady, James, "Jimmy Smits (TV and Film Actor)," *Parade Magazine*, 2 January 2005: http://www.parade.com/articles/editions/2005/edition_01-02-2005/in_step_with_1.

1991 ♦ A coming-of-age comedy-drama, *Hangin' with the Homeboys*, directed by Joseph Vásquez (1962–1995), was the first Latino film to win the prestigious Waldo Salt Screenwriting Award at the Sundance Film Festival. It was also nominated for various Independent Spirit Awards that year.

Sources: Holden, Stephen. "Review/Film; Homeboys Hangin' Downtown," *New York Times*, 24 May 1991.

1991 ♦ Filmmaker Jesús Salvador Treviño's (1946–) feature film *Raíces de Sangre* (1977) was the first film by a U.S. Hispanic to be named one of the top 25 Latin American films of all time by the Valladolid (Spain) Film Festival.

Sources: Tardiff and Mabunda, *Dictionary of Hispanic Biography*, p. 900.

Robert Rodríguez

1993 ♦ Film student Robert Rodríguez (1968–) broke all records by making a critically acclaimed film, *El Mariachi*, on a budget of only $7,000 in an era when films cost millions of dollars to make. Columbia Pictures picked it up, and the movie brought in more than $2 million. *El Mariachi* effectively launched Rodríguez's Hollywood career, and his next film was a fully funded Hollywood production, *Desperado*, starring Antonio Banderas (1960–), which opened in 1995 to mixed reviews. For *Desperado*, Rodríguez insisted on an 80 percent Latino crew, and the film provided Spanish actor Antonio Banderas with his first American lead. The female lead went to Salma Hayek (1966–), the first Mexican actress since Dolores del Río to take the lead in an American film.

Sources: Hispanic, July 1995, p. 26; Tardiff and Mabunda, *Dictionary of Hispanic Biography*, p. 763.

1995 ♦ The Gregory Nava (1949–) film *My Family* had the highest per-screen average revenue ($5,375) for all movies released on the weekend of May 5–7, 1995. The importance of this figure is that it brought Hollywood a step closer to recognizing the value of producing Latino-content films with real Latino actors. The year 1995 saw a record number of releases with Latino themes, including *The Perez Family*, *Desperado*, *A Walk in the Clouds*, and *Roosters*, which was based on a play by Milcha Sanchez-Scott (1953–). For *My Family*, Nava assembled the most prestigious Latino cast in film history, which included Jimmy Smits (1955–), Esai Morales, and Edward James Olmos. Hollywood was not only beginning to react to the demographic strength of Latinos in the United States but also to their representing the highest level of video renters among all segments of society.

Sources: Hispanic, July 1995, pp. 22–26.

1996 ♦ Jimmy Smits (1955–) won the Golden Globe for Best Actor in a Television Series: Drama.

Sources: Brady, James, "Jimmy Smits (Tv and Film Actor)," *Parade Magazine* 2 January 2005: http://www.parade.com/articles/editions/2005/edition_01-02-2005/in_step_with_1.

2000 ♦ The first hit children's series to feature a Latina protagonist, *Dora the Explorer*, debuted on Nickelodeon. Created by three non-Latinos—Chris Gofford, Valerie Walsh Valdés, and Eric Weiner—the animated series enchanted children around the world and spawned various spin-offs and copies; it lasted until 2019. In 2024, a sequel series debuted entitled *Dora*. Whereas the first Dora was presented as a pan-Latina character, the new Dora's mom is Peruvian and her father Mexican and Cuban. Kathleen

The media franchise Dora the Explorer, created by Chris Gofford, Valerie Walsh Valdés, and Eric Weiner, includes books, movies, and a TV series featuring a Latina protagonist.

Herles (1990–) voiced the first Dora and Diana Zermeño (2013–) the new, somewhat older Dora.

Sources: Guerra, Joey, "The Return of Just 'Dora,'" *Houston Chronicle,* 16 April 2024.

Benicio del Toro

2001 ♦ Benicio del Toro (1967–) was the first Latino actor to win a National Film Critics Award for Best Supporting Actor for his role as Javier Rodríguez in *Traffic.* Puerto Rican–born Benicio Monserrate Rafael del Toro Sánchez has acted in more than 40 feature films and garnered some of the most prestigious awards, including a 2001 Academy Award for Best Actor and a Golden Globe Award for Best Supporting Actor: Motion Picture in *Traffic*; a 2001 British Academy Award for Best Supporting Actor in *Traffic*; a 2008 Cannes Film Festival Award for Best Actor in *Che Guevara*; and numerous other national and international awards. Del Toro's breakthrough had come in 1995 with his performance in *The Usual Suspects*, for which he won an Independent Spirit Award for Best Supporting Male. He won the award again the following year for *Basquiat* (1996).

Sources: Ugwu, Reggie, "Benicio Del Toro, Hollywood's Instant Antihero, Goes the Distance," *New York Times*, 27 June 2018.

Martin Sheen

2001 ♦ Martin Sheen (1940–) won a Golden Globe Award for Best Actor in a Television Series: Drama for his portrayal of a U.S. president in *The West Wing* television series. Sheen (born Ramón Antonio Gerardo Estévez) was born in Dayton, Ohio, to an Irish-immigrant mother and a Spanish-immigrant father. One of the most well-known television and film actors ever, Sheen has a filmography that includes more than 60 feature films and more than 30 television movies; he also was the narrator of dozens of documentaries. His most successful and long-lasting series was *The West Wing* (1999–2006), for which he had numerous award nominations and finally won the Golden Globe in 2001 as well as other more minor awards over those years.

Sources: "Martin Sheen Biography," *Monsters & Critics*: https://web.archive.org/web/20131105095713/http://www.monstersandcritics.com/people/Martin-Sheen/biography/.

2001 ♦ Cuban-born director León Ichaso (1948–2023) was awarded the Spotlight Award by the National Board of Review for *Piñero*, the biopic of playwright/poet Miguel Piñero. Throughout his movie-directing and -producing career, Ichaso focused on bringing Latino stories to the silver screen, such as in *El Super* (1979), *Crossover Dreams* (1985), *Azúcar Amarga* (1996), and *El Cantante* (2006). He also directed episodes of such TV crime dramas as *Miami Vice* and *The Equalizer.*

Sources: "Leon Ichaso, 74, Latino Filmmaker Who Explored Assimilation and Exile," *New York Times*, 28 May 2023.

Lourdes Portillo

2001 ♦ Mexican American documentary filmmaker Lourdes Portillo (1943–2024) received the following awards for her *Senorita Extraviada: Missing Young Women*: the Special Jury Prize at the Sundance Film Festival, Best Documentary at the Havana International Film Festival, and the Nestor Almendros Award at the Human Rights Watch Film Festival. The most distinguished Chicana filmmaker to arise from the Chicano civil rights movement, Portillo has some 19 documentaries to her name, many of them award winners.

Sources: Mayorquín, Orlando, "Lourdes Portillo, 80, Documentary Filmmaker Who Was Nominated for an Oscar," *New York Times*, 28 April 2024.

Justina Machado

2004 ♦ Justina Machado (1972–) received the Actors Guild Award for Outstanding Performance by an Ensemble in a Drama Series for her starring role in HBO's *Six Feet Under.* She was a repeat winner for the 2005–2006 season. The Chicago native of Puerto Rican ancestry has acted in numerous television shows, including *Grey's Anatomy*, *Ugly Betty*, *Bones*, *Body of Proof*, and *Desperate Housewives.* Her starring role in the 2023 Amazon black comedy *The Horror of Dolores Roach* was particularly noteworthy. She has also acted in almost two dozen films.

Sources: "The Empanadas Are Just to Die for," *New York Times*, 9 July 2023.

2005 ♦ Producer/director Robert Rodríguez's (1968–) film *Sin City* won the Technical Grand Prize at the Cannes Film Festival. It also won the Online Film Critics Society Award (2006) for Best Cinematography. Rodríguez is the most successful Latino filmmaker, with numerous mainstream hits and box office successes.

The San Antonio–born Mexican American broke into national movie history when his film *El Mariachi* (1992) broke the record for lowest-budget film to earn more than $1 million (according to the Guinness World

Records) by grossing $2.6 million from his $7,000 of expenditures. This led to commercial backing for two sequels; his eventually opening his own studio in Austin, Texas; and a string of highly successful commercial movies, including the *Spy Kids* (beginning in 2001) franchise, *Sin City* (2005) and its sequel, and *From Dusk to Dawn* (1996) and its two sequels. In 2013, Rodríguez founded his own cable television channel, El Rey. Rodríguez remains in demand as a director for major film and television projects for Disney, Fox, and others.

Sources: Martínez, José, and Christin Devine, "Hispanic Blood: An Interview with Robert Rodriguez," *Creative Screenwriting,* 21 December 2015: https://www.creativescreenwriting.com/hispanic-blood-an-interview-with-robert-rodriguez/.

2005 ♦ Movie producer Moctezuma Esparza opened his first multiplex in what would become a Maya Cinemas chain in Salinas, California. The 14-screen movie house introduced the Maya design that would be followed by the other 16 multiplexes Esparaza opened, many of which featured films in Spanish and/or were subtitled in Spanish.

Sources: Bernstein, David, "A New Multiplex Is Aiming to Capture a Bilingual Audience," *New York Times*, 1 August 2005.

Eva Longoria

2007 ♦ Producer Eva Longoria's (1975–) hit series *Ugly Betty* won the Golden Globe for Best Television Series: Musical or Comedy. While still enjoying a flourishing acting career, Longoria founded her own production studio, Unbelievable Entertainment, in 2005, which is dedicated to creating projects centered on the Latino experience. Beginning in 2013, Longoria was one of the executive producers for the television series *Devious Maids*; she began directing the series as well in 2014.

Sources: "Latino Power List: 45 Trailblazers Making Waves in Hollywood," *The Wrap*: https://www.thewrap.com/latino-power-list-eva-longoria-jenna-ortega/#helmers.

America Ferrera

2007 ♦ America Ferrera won the Golden Globe for Best Actress in a Television Series: Musical or Comedy in the hit television series *Ugly Betty.* For acting in this role, she also won a Primetime Emmy Award, a Screen Actors Guild Award, and a Satellite Award.

Sources: Maxwell, Erin, "Satellite Award Winners Announced," *Variety,* 17 December 2007.

2008 ♦ Benicio del Toro won the Cannes Film Festival Award for Best Actor for the movie *Che*, which he also produced.

Sources: Ugwu, Reggie. "Benicio Del Toro, Hollywood's Instant Antihero, Goes the Distance," *New York Times*, 27 June 2018.

2009 ♦ Spanish-born, U.S.-educated screenwriter–director Eva Vives's (1976–) *Five Feet High and Rising* won the Best Short Prize at the Sundance Festival and the Cannes Film Festival. She then cowrote the feature adaptation of that short as *Raising Victor Vargas* (2002), which was nominated for Best First Screenplay at the Independent Spirit Awards.

Sources: Schwartz, Dana, "Mary Elizabeth Winstead Is a Comedian Who Blurs the Line between Life and Art in *All About Nina*: EW Review," *Entertainment Weekly*: https://ew.com/movies/2018/09/28/mary-elizabeth-winstead-all-about-nina-review/.

2009 ♦ Rita Moreno was the first Latina actress to be awarded the National Medal of Arts, presented by President Barack Obama.

Sources: Moreno, Rita, *Rita Moreno: A Memoir*, New York: Penguin, 2013.

2013 ♦ Oscar Isaac (1979–) was the first Latino to win the National Film Critics Award for Best Actor for his leading role in *Inside Llewyn Davis.* Guatemalan-born Óscar Isaac Hernández Estrada is known for breaking stereotypes about Latinos in Hollywood films. In 2017, *Vanity Fair* named him the best actor of his generation, and in 2020, the *New York Times* considered him among the 25 greatest actors of the 21st century.

Oscar Isaac

Sources: Mengiste, Maaza, "The Dream of Oscar Isaac," *Esquire,* 30 March 2022.

2015 ♦ Rita Moreno became the first Latina actress to receive the Kennedy Center Honors Lifetime Artistic Achievement Award.

Sources: Moreno, Rita, *Rita Moreno: A Memoir,* New York: Penguin, 2013.

2016 ♦ Oscar Isaac (1979–) was the first Latino to win a Golden Globe for Best Miniseries or Motion Picture: Television for *Show Me a Hero.*

Sources: Mengiste, Maaza, "The Dream of Oscar Isaac," *Esquire,* 30 March 2022.

2017 ♦ Anthony González (2004–) won the Outstanding Individual Achievement in Voice Acting by a Male Performer in an Animated Feature Production for his role as Miguel Rivera in the hit animated movie *Coco.* He also won the Teen Choice Award for this role. The Los Angeles native has acted in television dramas and also as a voice actor for video games.

Anthony González

Sources: Rossi, Madison, "From Street Performer to Disney Star," *Time*: https://time.com/collection/american-voices-2017/5042022/american-voices-anthony-gonzalez/.

Rosario Dawson

2018 ♦ Rosario Dawson (1979–) won the Behind the Voice Actors Award for Best Female Lead Vocal Performance in a Feature Film for the voice of Batgirl/Barbara Gordon in *The Lego Batman Movie.* In 2006, she won a Satellite Award for Outstanding Actress in a Supporting Role: Comedy or Musical in the movie *Rent* and a Gamer's Choice: Breakthrough Performance Award for her work in *Marc Eckō's Getting Up: Contents Under Pressure.*

Sources: "Rosario Dawson," Biography.com, 2 July 2018.

2022 ♦ Lin-Manuel Miranda (1980–) won the Audie Award for Best Male Narrator for the audiobook version of Benjamin Alire Saenz's *Aristotle and Dante Dive into the Waters of the World* (2021). The award is made annually by the Audio Publishers Association.

Sources: "Lin-Manuel Biography (1980–)," Biography.com, 14 September 2020.

2023 ♦ Producer/director Eva Longoria won the Breakthrough Director: Film Award from the Critics Choice Association's Celebration of Cinema & Television for her directing of the movie *Flamin' Hot.*

Sources: "Eva Longoria Awards," IMDb: https://www.imdb.com/name/nm0519456/awards/.

2024 ♦ Film director/producer Eva Longoria was named *USA Today*'s Woman of the Year in recognition of women who have made a significant impact in their communities and across the country. She has been recognized with a Critics Choice Award and SXSW and Palm Springs International Film Festival honors. Her directorial debut with the Amazon film *Flamin' Hot* (2023) won her an Imagen Foundation Award.

Sources: Avila, Pamela, "Eva Longoria, Director, Producer, Champion for Latino Community, Is Woman of the Year Honoree," *USA Today* 29 February 2024: https://www.usatoday.com/story/entertainment/celebrities/2024/02/29/eva-longoria-woman-of-the-year/72308679007/.

2024 ♦ America Ferrera won the People's Choice Award for Supporting Actress for *Barbie.*

Sources: Hammond, Pete, "The Critics Choice Is 'Barbie' with 18 CCA Nominations; 'Oppenheimer', 'Poor Things' Follow with 13 Each," *Deadline*: https://deadline.com/2023/12/critics-choice-film-nominations-2023-1235665954/.

RADIO

1924 ♦ Pedro J. González (1895–1996) started the first Spanish-language radio program in the United States. Between 1924 and 1934, González aired his show *Los Madrugadores* (The Early Risers), which brokered airtime from Los Angeles station KMPC each day from 4:00 to 6:00 A.M. The program, broadcast with 100,000-watt power, could be heard throughout the Southwest.

Sources: Gutiérrez and Schement, *Spanish-Language Radio in the Southwestern United States*, pp. 56–58; Schement and Flores, "The Origins of Spanish-Language Radio."

1939: The International Broadcasting Company Is Founded

In 1939 the first Spanish-language radio network, International Broadcasting Company (IBC), was established to supply Spanish-language programming across the country. IBC was founded in El Paso, Texas. It is estimated that by 1941, IBC and other radio networks were supplying 264 hours of programming per week. *Sources:* Gutiérrez and Schement, *Spanish-Language Radio in the Southwestern United States*, pp. 56–58; Schement and Flores, "The Origins of Spanish-Language Radio."

1946 ♦ Raúl Cortez (1905–1971) established the first full-time Spanish-language radio station in a major market: 100,000-watt KCOR in San Antonio, Texas. Nine years later, Cortez expanded into Spanish-language television.

Sources: Gutiérrez and Schement, *Spanish-Language Radio in the Southwestern United States*, pp. 56–58; Schement and Flores, "The Origins of Spanish-Language Radio."

1973 ♦ Caballero Spanish Media was founded in New York City and eventually became the largest Latino radio advertising agency, with sales reaching as high as $26 million in 1994. Founded by Cuban immigrant Eduardo Caballero (1930–2023), the media company began selling syndicated Spanish movies and television advertising in 1973 and switched exclusively to airtime sales for Spanish-language radio in 1975. The first major advertiser Caballero landed was Colgate Palmolive. Caballero opened six other offices in cities with large Latino populations. Caballero worked with about 130 Spanish-language stations, whose listeners accounted for 90 percent of the Latino radio audience in the United States. Caballero was elected to both the Broadcasting & Cable Hall of Fame and the American Advertising Federation's Advertising Hall of Fame.

Sources: Hispanic, September 1995, pp. 30–31.

1976 ♦ The first Spanish-language news service, Spanish Information Systems, was founded in Dallas, Texas. The service provided news in Spanish via satellite to radio and television stations nationwide.

Sources: Kanellos, *Latino Almanac*, pp. 244–245.

1983 ♦ Cuban immigrant Pablo Raúl Alarcón and his son, Raúl Alarcón Jr., bought radio station WSKQ-AM in New York and founded the Spanish Broadcasting System, which grew into the largest Latino-owned media entity in the United States, with revenues of approximately $94 million by 1994. By 1990, the Alarcón family had acquired and was operating six stations in Florida, Los Angeles, and New York. Their KLAZ-FM became the first Spanish-language station in Los Angeles to hit number one in 1993. Their WSKQ-AM became the first Spanish-language station to break into the top three in New York City in 1995.

Sources: Hispanic, September 1995, p. 30.

1985 ♦ After extensive lobbying by the Cuban American National Foundation (CANF), directed by Jorge Mas Canosa (1939–1997), U.S. Congress founded Radio Marti, a radio station designed to broadcast news, features,

1993: First Number-One Station in Los Angeles

In 1993 Spanish Broadcasting System station KLAZ-FM became the first Spanish-language station in Los Angeles to hit number one in 1993. Spanish Broadcasting System is the largest Hispanic-owned media entity. *Sources: Hispanic,* September 1995, p. 30.

and entertainment to Cuba in order to counter the censored or ideologically biased broadcast media run by the Castro regime. Funded initially at an estimated $10 million to $12 million per year, it was established on Marathon Key, Florida. The radio station had an immediate impact; it is believed that because of its series on AIDS, the Cuban government was forced to acknowledge and address this important health issue.

Sources: García, *Havana USA*, pp. 147–148; Tardiff and Mabunda, *Dictionary of Hispanic Biography*, p. 533.

María Hinojosa

1986 ♦ María Hinojosa (1961–) became the first Latina in broadcast journalism to win a Silver Cindy Award for her work on the National Public Radio program *Immigration and Detention.* Born on July 2, 1961, in Mexico City, Hinojosa was raised in the Chicago area. While a student at Barnard, Hinojosa entered the field of radio by founding a Latino radio show at Columbia University; she went on to become the program director for the radio station. When she graduated magna cum laude in 1985, she became an intern at National Public Radio and nine months later was hired as a production assistant. She has gone on to become a leading socially responsible Latino radio journalist and a published author. In 2012, Hinojosa was awarded the John Chancellor Award for Excellence in Journalism.

Sources: Telgen and Kamp, *Latinas! Women of Achievement*, pp. 187–192.

1988 ♦ Orange County Broadcasting purchased station KPLS-AM in Los Angeles and dedicated it to "all talk." It is the first all-talk Spanish-language station in southern California (there are four "talk" stations in the Miami market).

Sources: Kanellos, *Latino Almanac*, p. 240.

1989 ♦ María Hinojosa became the first Hispanic journalist to win the Corporation for Public Broadcasting Silver Award; she won the award for her piece "Day of the Dead."

Sources: Telgen and Kamp, *Latinas! Women of Achievement*, p. 190.

1992 ♦ Amador Bustos bought 92.1 KSZA-FM in Sacramento, which grew into the Z-Spanish Network, at that time becoming the nation's largest Hispanic-owned satellite radio network with revenues of $4.5 million by 1994. Born in Michoacan, Mexico, Bustos came to the United States as a child and worked as a farm laborer. After earning a college degree, he worked as a teacher and then decided to try radio. After succeeding with his first station, he acquired others in California and Arizona and decided to link them into a satellite-based network. In addition to reaching listeners all over California and Arizona, the Z-Spanish Network reached another 500,000 listeners in Mexico. In 2000, Bustos sold the chain to Entravision Communications. In 2006, Bustos Media once again was on the radio as well as television, administering 25 radio stations across the United States and several television stations by 2009.

Sources: "Bustos Makes a Comeback," *Media Moves*, 27 January 2011: https://www.mediamoves.com/2011/01/bustos-makes-a-comeback.html.

1995 ♦ Public radio journalist María Hinojosa (1961–) became the first Hispanic journalist to win the prestigious Robert F. Kennedy Award for Excellence in Journalism for her piece "Manhood behind Bars," a story for NPR about jail time becoming a rite of passage for men. She has also won the John Chancellor Award for Excellence in Journalism, the National Association of Hispanic Journalists' Radio Award, and a Pulitzer Prize, among many other honors.

Sources: Telgen and Kamp, *Latinas! Women of Achievement*, p. 191.

1996 ♦ *Universo*, the daily Spanish-language astronomy radio program, became the most widely syndicated Spanish-language radio program in the United States, airing on 150 stations in 28 of the top 30 U.S. Latino markets. The second most syndicated Spanish-language program was *CNN Noticias*, the news program. The Spanish-language astronomy program is produced by the University of Texas McDonald Observatory as part of its program to keep students in school and interested in the sciences. Production and distribution are made possible by grants from the National Science Foundation and the National Aeronautics and Space Administration (NASA). The program shut down in 2011 due to insufficient funding.

Sources: "Universo Radio Program to Cease Regular Production," UT News 6, July 2011: https://news.utexas.edu/2011/07/06/universo-radio-program-to-cease-regular-production/.

1997 ♦ The Hispanic Radio Network (HRN) became the first Latino media entity to win the 1996 Population Institute Global Media Award in Excellence. HRN won the award for its program *Buscando la Belleza* (Searching for Beauty), which informed listeners on a wide range of educational subjects. HRN was the only Latino-owned national Spanish radio network at the time, producing and syndicating programs that aired on more than 165 stations.

Sources: Hispanic Link Weekly Report, 13 January 1997, p. 8.

2007 ♦ The Latino Public Radio Consortium (LPRC) was founded to develop strategies that would significantly increase Latino participation in public broadcasting. In 2008, the group drafted a "brown paper" outlining how the public media could better serve Latinos. The document was then disseminated throughout the public broadcasting system. It highlighted the diversity of the Latino public in language, age, income, and ethnicity and supported the distribution of multiple program streams. It called for assistance to the Latino public programs that were already in existence to facilitate their growth and build their capacity. And, of course, it called for hiring and training more Latinos for public broadcasting.

Sources: Kanellos, *Latino Almanac*, p. 241.

Lourdes García-Navarro

2017 ♦ Lourdes "Lu Lu" García-Navarro (1972–) was the first Latino to host a major series on National Public Radio when she became the host of *Weekend Edition Sunday*. The London-born daughter of Cuban and Panamanian parents grew up in Miami; she spent 17 years of her career at NPR, then in 2021, she accepted a position on the *New York Times*'s *Open Audio* program. She is the winner of two Peabody Awards (2005 and 2012) and an Edward R. Murrow Award (2012), among others.

Sources: "The Corporation for Public Broadcasting Honors NPR's Lourdes García-Navarro with the Edward R. Murrow Award": https://cpb.org/awards/corporation-public-broadcasting-honors-nprs-lourdes-garcia-navarro-edward-r-murrow-award.

TELEVISION

1951 ♦ *Buscando Estrellas* (Looking for Stars), thought to be the first Spanish-language television program in the United States, began broadcasting from San Antonio, Texas. Produced and hosted by José Pérez del Río (1909–1994), the show was a weekly entertainment variety and talent-search pro-

The cast of *I Love Lucy* included (left to right) Desi Arnaz, Lucille Ball, Vivian Vance, and William Frawley.

gram. Its production and broadcasting rotated every 13 weeks to three other Texas cities: Corpus Christi, Harlingen, and Laredo. Between 1956 and 1961, Pérez del Río also produced *Cine en Espanol*, which featured old films from Spain, Mexico, and Argentina.

Sources: Subervi-Vélez, Federico A., "Mass Communications and Hispanics," *Handbook of Hispanic Cultures in the United States: Sociology*, Ed. Félix Padilla, p. 334.

1952 ♦ The record-breaking sitcom *I Love Lucy* was the first television comedy to feature a Latino as a star, Desi Arnaz (1917–1986). Eventually lasting nine years, Arnaz and Lucille Ball modified the Latin lover and dumb blonde stereotypes to capture the attention of television audiences, who were also engaged by the slightly titillating undercurrent of a mixed marriage between an Anglo and a Latino who played and sang Afro-Cuban music. The formula pairing a White Anglo-Saxon Protestant (WASP) and a minority or outcast has been duplicated on television to this date through such programs as *Chico and the Man*, *Who's the Boss?*, *The Nanny*, and others. Under the direction of famed bandleader and minor movie star Desi Arnaz, Desilu Productions was formed and grew into a major television studio. *I Love Lucy* can still be seen streaming in black-and-white reruns in many parts of the United States.

Sources: Pérez-Firmat, *Life on the Hyphen*, pp. 48–52.

1955 ♦ KCOR-TV, the first Spanish-language television station in the United States, opened for business in San Antonio, Texas.

Sources: Kanellos, *Latino Almanac*, p. 243.

1961 ♦ Emilio Azcárraga Vidaurreta (1895–1972), the most prominent media magnate in Mexico, and René Anselmo (1926–1995), along with a group of minority investors, founded the first national Spanish-language television network, Spanish International Network (SIN). At that time, most of the programming was purchased from Televisa, Azcárraga Vidaurreta's company in Mexico. When the network started using satellites in 1976, SIN programs were being disseminated to Spanish-language communities around the world. By 1979, SIN was feeding more than 64 hours of programming to eight affiliates in the United States by Westar satellite, 50 hours of which came from Televisa. The remainder originated in the United States or was imported from Venezuela, Spain, Argentina, or Brazil. The network feed consisted primarily of *novelas* (soap operas), variety shows, and news from Mexico City.

Sources: Kanellos, *Latino Almanac*, pp. 243–246.

Geraldo Rivera

1971 ♦ Journalist and lawyer Geraldo Miguel Rivera (1943–) became the first Latino to win the New York State Associated Press Broadcasters Association Award for his investigative series "Drug Crisis in East Harlem." He also became the first Latino to be named Broadcaster of the Year; he was named to this honor again in 1972 and 1974.

Sources: Tardiff and Mabunda, *Dictionary of Hispanic Biography*, p. 746.

1976 ♦ Spanish International Network (SIN) became the first major broadcasting company, preceding CBS, ABC, and NBC, to distribute programming directly to its affiliates via domestic satellites. SIN signals reached the San Antonio station from Mexico City by terrestrial microwave and from there were distributed by the Westar satellite.

Sources: Kanellos, *Latino Almanac*, pp. 244–245.

1978 ♦ Cuban-born Luis Santeiro (1947–) became the first Latino screenwriter and producer to work for the most important children's television show in history, *Sesame Street.* Over the course of his career, he has won 14 Daytime Emmy Awards.

Sources: Kanellos, *Latino Almanac*, p. 259.

1979 ♦ Spanish International Network (SIN) became the first Spanish-language network to pay cable franchise operators to carry its satellite signals. Today, SIN's successor, Univision, is by far the largest Spanish-language media company in the United States, its television broadcasts reaching 98 percent of Latino households. Its empire includes some 62 television stations; radio and television networks; and Galavisión, which is the largest Spanish-language cable network in the world.

Sources: Kanellos, *Latino Almanac*, pp. 244–246.

1982 ♦ Teresa Rodríguez (1966–) became Spanish-language network television's first Latina female newscaster for Univision's predecessor, SIN. Over the course of her career, she has won 11 Emmys for broadcast journalism.

Sources: Hispanic, July 1994, p. 54.

1984 ♦ Mexican American actor A. Martinez (born Adolfo Larrue Martínez III, 1948–) was the first Latino actor to break into daytime drama (soap operas) with a leading role; he played police officer Cruz Castillo in *Santa Barbara.* Martinez performed in the soap opera throughout its run, until 1992. Martinez went on to star or be featured in numerous film and television productions. He is the winner of a Daytime Emmy.

Sources: Tardiff and Mabunda, *Dictionary of Hispanic Biography*, pp. 525–526.

1984 ♦ NBC became the first major network to offer a news anchor position to a Latino. Teresa Rodríguez (1966–) of Univision was offered the position once held by Connie Chung in hosting *Sunrise.* Rodríguez reportedly turned down the job because she did not want to be separated from her family in Miami. It was not until 1994 that a major news network hired a Latina as a full-time anchor: NBC's Jackie Nespral (1966–). Nespral, also a Cuban American residing in Miami, commuted to New York at least three times a week to work at the network.

Sources: Hispanic, July 1994, p. 54.

1985 ♦ Puerto Rican dancer and Broadway star Chita Rivera (born Dolores Conchita Figueroa del Rivero, 1933–2024) became the first Latina to be named to the Television Academy Hall of Fame. Rivera was one of the most popular dancers ever featured on such classic television variety shows as *The Garry Moore Show*, *The Ed Sullivan Show*, *The Arthur Godfrey Show*, and *The Sid Caesar Show*. Over her career, Rivera won two Tony Awards, two Drama Desk Awards, and a Drama League Award. She was the first Latino to receive a Kennedy Center Honor in 2002. In 2009, she was awarded the Presidential Medal of Freedom.

Sources: Tardiff and Mabunda, *Dictionary of Hispanic Biography*, p. 739; Telgen and Kamp, *Latinas! Women of Achievement*, pp. 313–319.

1987 ♦ Geraldo Miguel Rivera (1943–) became the first Latino to host a nationally syndicated talk show, *Geraldo*. Rivera, a journalist and television personality, was born in New York City. He studied at the University of Arizona and Brooklyn Law School and received a law degree from the University of Pennsylvania and a degree in journalism from Columbia University. Rivera went on to become one of the nation's most celebrated and respected investigative television journalists, writing and producing various award-winning documentaries. He has won a Peabody Award and 10 Emmys for distinguished broadcast journalism. After beginning his career as a reporter for WABC-TV in New York in 1970, he went on to become a reporter, producer, and host for various television news and entertainment shows. Today, Rivera is still one of the most visible and successful Latinos in media and entertainment.

Sources: Kanellos, *Chronology of Hispanic American History*, pp. 221, 274.

1989: Spanish Audio Debuts on HBO

With the debut of *Selections in Spanish* in 1989, Home Box Office (HBO) became the first U.S. cable network to provide its subscribers the option of Spanish-language audio for the telecast of motion pictures and some sporting events. By the end of 1989, HBO was offering an average of 20 dubbed movies per month, and by 1991, *Selecciones en Español* was carried by 182 cable operators in the United States. Following up on its U.S. success with *Selecciones*, in 1991, HBO launched the HBO-Olé pay TV service in Latin America and the Caribbean Basin, which allowed cable subscribers in more than 20 Latin American countries prompt access in Spanish to HBO programs. *Sources:* Kanellos, *Latino Almanac*, pp. 249–250.

1990 ♦ Jesús Garza Rapport founded *International TeleMúsica*, the first show featuring international music videos primarily in the Spanish language, entertainment news, promotions, and lifestyle segments. The programs were produced in Hollywood, using various California settings. The program reached its targeted youth audience throughout the Western Hemisphere on the Spanish International Network (SIN) via satellites and affiliates.

Sources: Kanellos, *Latino Almanac*, p. 249.

1991 ♦ Giselle Fernández (1961–) became the first Latina to anchor a national morning news and features television show, *CBS This Morning*. Born on May 15, 1961, in Mexico City, at the age of 4, Fernández and her family moved to East Los Angeles, where her father was a flamenco dancer and her mother a university professor. She graduated with a degree in journalism from the University of Southern California in 1983. Her first job in television news was as a reporter in Colorado Springs, Colorado. She was working as a weeknight anchor in a Miami station in 1989 when the CBS network offered her the anchor position.

Sources: Telgen and Kamp, *Latinas! Women of Achievement*, pp. 133–135.

1991 ♦ Univision network's *El Show de Cristina* became the first Spanish-language talk show to win an Emmy. Rated number one in daytime television and among the top 10 Spanish-language programs in the United States, the show was produced and hosted by Cristina Saralegui (1948–), a former *Cosmopolitan en Español* editor.

Sources: Telgen and Kamp, *Latinas! Women of Achievement*, pp. 345–346.

Nelly Galán

1992 ♦ Nelly Galán (1963–), president of Galán Entertainment (a production company fully funded by Fox Television and devoted to the production of Latino-themed projects), cofounded HBO's Latino division, Tropix. One of her first projects to air was *Loco Slam*, a highly popular series of stand-up comedy specials in English featuring Latino comedians. Over her career, she produced more than 700 episodes of television in Spanish and English for a variety of companies from HBO to Telemundo.

Sources: Nelly Galán: https://nelygalan.com/about-nely/bio/.

1994 ♦ The first Spanish-language national sports network, La Cadena Deportiva Nacional, was launched as a subsidiary of the Prime Ticket Network.

It began in 1993 as a southwestern network; it was carried successfully in 750,000 homes in the Southwest.

Sources: Hispanic, July 1994, p. 9.

1994 ♦ NBC became the first major network to hire a Latina as a full-time anchor: Cuban American Jackie Nespral (1966–). In 1991, she had become the first Latino news cohost for NBC's *Today.*

Sources: "Jackie Nespral," *Miami Herald,* 5 February 2014: https://www.miamiherald.com/latest-news/article1959536.html.

1995 ♦ After considerable pressure (ABC was the focus of an ongoing boycott by the National Hispanic Media Coalition) was applied to the television networks to hire Latino talent and improve the portrayal of Latinos on the screen, ABC became the first network in history to create a program to recruit Latino writers to work on prime-time shows. As part of the ABC Latino Freelance Writers Project, ABC issued a call for any Latino who had previously written for or sold written material to any production company to submit scripts. The project was cosponsored by the Writers Guild of America.

Sources: Hispanic Link Weekly Report, 19 June 1995, p. 8; *Hispanic Link Weekly Report,* 26 June 1995, p. 4.

José Díaz-Balart

1996 ♦ José Díaz-Balart (1960–) became the first Latino anchor of a morning network news program, *CBS This Morning.* Díaz-Balart had previously served as anchor for an NBC-owned station in Miami. Before that, he was bureau chief in Washington, D.C., for the Spanish-language network Telemundo.

Sources: Hispanic Link Weekly Report, 13 May 1996, p. 8.

1996 ♦ HTV, the 24-hour, all Spanish-language music network launched in August 1995, became the first music channel to be carried by SCOLA, a nonprofit educational service that reaches five million subscribers in the United States and Canada at educational institutions and through cable systems. In addition, HTV was distributed to more than four million homes in Venezuela, Ecuador, Nicaragua, Spain, and Portugal. The new music network was created by Robert Behar (1949–) and Daniel Sawicki, partners in Hero Communications of Florida, Inc.

Sources: Hispanic Business, April 1996, p. 66.

1996 ♦ Telemundo became the first Spanish-language network to enter into a coproduction agreement with a foreign company. Telemundo Group established a first-of-its-kind agreement with the Mexican network Televisión Azteca to coproduce programming, with an emphasis on Spanish-language soap operas, for an international audience. The organizations share facilities, talent, and each other's markets as they compete with Mexico-based giant Televisa.

Sources: Hispanic Business, June 1996, p. 150.

1996 ♦ The Cisneros Group and Playboy Enterprises launched the first Spanish-language channels for adult entertainment: PlayboyTV/Latin America and AdulTV/Latin America; both channels were offered on Galaxy Latin America's DirecTV satellite service.

Sources: "About Cisneros": www.cisneros.com.

1996 ♦ Soledad O'Brien (1966–) became the first Latina to host an interactive cable online news program, *The Site*, which was a joint venture of *NBC News* and Microsoft Corporation. O'Brien discussed technology issues in the daily program. A national total of 22.5 million cable subscribers could view the program nightly. O'Brien is the daughter of a Cuban mother and an Australian father. Born and raised in St. James, Long Island, O'Brien is a graduate of Harvard University and is the winner of an Emmy Award for her work as cohost of The Discovery Channel's *The Know Zone.* From July 2003 to April 2007, she was co-anchor of the program *American Morning*, CNN's flagship morning program that aired live. In June 2013, O'Brien founded Starfish Media Group, a production and distribution company for which she has produced documentaries. In 2022, she won a Peabody Award for *The Rebellious Life of Mrs. Rosa Parks.*

Soledad O'Brien

Sources: "Soledad O'Brien, Host of MSNBC's *The Site*," *Hispanic*, October 1996, pp. 9–10.

1997 ♦ Cable News Network (CNN) launched the first 24-hour Spanish-language news channel for Latin America. The initiative came under the directorship of Carlos I. Díaz, president of Turner International Latin America in Atlanta, Georgia.

Sources: "100 Influentials," *Hispanic Business*, October 1996, p. 58.

2022 ♦ Radio and TV journalist María Hinojosa (1961–) and her company, Futuro Media, won a Pulitzer Prize for Audio Reporting for its seven-part podcast series *Suave.* She had previously been honored with the Robert F. Kennedy Journalism Award for Reporting on the Disadvantaged and four Emmy Awards.

Sources: Futuro Media: https://www.futuromediagroup.org/.

MUSIC

1598 ♦ With the colonizing expedition into New Mexico led by Don Juan de Oñate (c. 1550–1630), both European and *mestizo* ecclesiastic and secular music were introduced to the Southwest, and they have continued as part of religious and folk tradition to this day. In particular, the folk music, as represented by ballads and other songs, is the oldest folk music in the United States except for that of the American Indians. Because the missionaries discovered that music was especially effective in evangelizing the Indians, it was taught more extensively to the natives than any other subject at the missions.

Sources: Campa, *Hispanic Culture in the Southwest*, pp. 234–242; Rosaldo et al., *Chicano*, p. 143.

1700 ♦ By the turn of the century, operas were not only being performed but also composed in Mexico City and Peru. Thus, the first opera and European classical music was introduced to North America by the Spaniards, and it has had an unbroken tradition to date.

Sources: Kanellos, *Chronology of Hispanic American History*, p. 53.

1824 ♦ The first conservatory of music in the Americas was founded by José Mariano Elízaga (1786–1842) in Mexico City. He is considered the first great Mexican composer.

Sources: Kanellos, *Chronology of Hispanic American History*, p. 81.

1912 ♦ The first Hispanic operatic diva in the United States was Lucrezia Bori (1887–1960), who made her debut at the Metropolitan Opera in New

Lucrezia Bori

York City in 1912. Born in Valencia, Spain, on December 24, 1888, Bori studied opera in Milan, Italy, and began her career there. However, she spent the better part of her career with the Met in New York from 1921 to 1936. During this time, she also appeared frequently in Latino theatrical productions in New York. When the Met's existence was threatened because of economic problems during the Depression, she became chairperson of the "Save the Metropolitan Opera" initiative, and thanks to her leadership, the opera survives to this day. After Bori went into retirement in 1936, she became the first woman opera singer to be elected a member of the board of directors of the Metropolitan Opera. She served on the board until her death in 1960.

Sources: Hispanics in U.S. History, p. 26.

1927 ♦ With Luisa Espinel's (1892–1963) debut recital at New York's famed Edith Totten Theater, the singing and dramatic career of the first U.S.-born and -bred Latina musical star in both Latino and Anglo mainstream venues was launched. During the 1930s, Espinel—the Tucson, Arizona, native changed her name from Ronstadt—toured Southwest theaters, opera houses, and college campuses singing the folk music of Spain in a bel canto voice. Espinel had received formal training in San Francisco, Paris, and Madrid and had personally researched the folk songs and dances of Spain by traveling the Spanish countryside and living among the folk.

Luisa Espinel

Sources: Sheridan, *Los Tucsonenses,* pp. 190–191.

1930 ♦ By the early 1930s, modern Mexican American *conjunto* music had been born. When Narciso Martínez (1911–1992) began his commercial recording career, the first steps had been taken toward cementing the core of the modern *conjunto*—the accordion and bajo sexto combination. These two instruments would later become inseparable. Meanwhile, Martínez, who is considered the father of modern *conjunto*, devised a new technique for the accordion, one that differed radically from the old Germanic style. He stopped using the left-hand base-chord buttons, leaving the accompaniment to the bajo sexto. The resulting sound was dramatically novel: a clean spare treble and a staccato effect that contrasted sharply with the Germanic sound of earlier northern Mexican accordionists. The Martínez style quickly took hold and became the standard that younger accordionists emulated, particularly those who established themselves after World War II.

Sources: Peña, Manuel. *The Texas-Mexican Conjunto: History of a Working-Class Music.* Austin: University of Texas Press, 1985.

Arsenio Rodríguez

1930 ♦ Cuban popular musician Arsenio Rodríguez (1911–1970) became the father of modern salsa music. In the early 1930s, the basic *son* of Afro-Cuban music was upgraded when Rodríguez added a second trumpet, conga drums, and, most importantly, a piano, giving the ensemble a more urban and sophisticated sound. Rodríguez also anticipated some of the greatest modern *salseros* (salsa musicians) by moving away from romantic themes of earlier *sones* and incorporating texts that addressed nationalist and social issues.

Sources: García, David, *Arsenio Rodríguez and the Transnational Flows of Latin Music*, Temple University Press, 2006.

1933 ♦ Xavier Cugat (1900–1990) and his band became the first Latino music group to have its own radio program, *Dinner at the Waldorf.* This was followed by *Let's Dance* in 1934 and 1935, *RCA Magic Key* in 1936, and *Xavier Cugat's Rumba Review* in 1941 and 1942.

Xavier Cugat

Sources: Tardiff and Mabunda, *Dictionary of Hispanic Biography*, p. 263.

1936 ♦ Spanish-born opera star Lucrezia Bori (1887–1960) became the first female opera singer to be elected to the board of directors of the Metropolitan Opera of New York. She served until her death in 1960.

Sources: Hispanics in U.S. History, p. 26.

Ernesto Lecuona

1940 ♦ The first Latino music to cross over into American popular music were the songs and compositions composed by Ernesto Lecuona (1896–1963). They became standards beginning in the 1940s. Lecuona, the beloved Cuban composer of popular and semiclassical music, was born in Guanabacoa, near Havana, into a family of musical performers. Having been afforded piano lessons from early childhood, Lecuona was composing by the age of 11 and teaching music in the city schools by the age of 16. At 17, he graduated from the Conservatorio Nacional de Cuba and later studied with Joaquín Nin.

His musical training and virtuosity as a pianist took him to the founding of what became a very successful and historically important band, the Lecuona Cuban Boys, which cut numerous records. Much of the Latin music recording business emanated from New York during the 1940s, and Lecuona spent quite a bit of time there. Some of his popular compositions became standards of not only Latin music but also American popular music; most noteworthy of these are "Siboney" (the name of a pre-Columbian Indian tribe of Cuba) and "Malagueña" (a girl from Malaga, Spain). Lecuona also composed serious music, such as his "Rapsodia Negra" (Black Rhapsody) for piano and orchestra, as well as numerous *zarzuelas* (Hispanic operettas) and radio scores. After the triumph of the Cuban Revolution, Lecuona went into exile in Santa Cruz de Tenerife, Canary Islands, where he died on November 19, 1963.

Sources: Kanellos, *Chronology of Hispanic American History*, p. 130.

1956 ♦ "Pancho Lopez," a satiric version of the hit song "Davy Crockett," became one of the first crossover hit recordings nationally for composer and performer Eduardo "Lalo" Guerrero (1916–2005), a native of Tucson, Arizona. Guerrero performed and recorded his songs for more than four decades, expressing the humor and popular sentiments of the working classes in his compositions. Another burlesque of a mainstream standard is his "Tacos for Two."

Sources: Sheridan, *Los Tucsonenses*, pp. 246–247.

1956 ♦ The Casals Music Festival was founded in San Juan, Puerto Rico, in honor of the greatest cellist that ever lived, Pablo Casals (1876–1973). The yearly classical music festival, which takes place every June for 16 days, was the first classical music festival to honor a Hispanic virtuoso. Casals had moved to Puerto Rico from his native Spain as a refugee from the Spanish Civil War.

Sources: "Sobre Nosotros; Festival Casals," Internet Archive Wayback Machine: https://web.archive.org/web/20120411212319/http://www.festcasalspr.gobierno.pr/abouteng.html.

1957 ♦ At the age of 22, Jorge Mester (1935–) became the youngest teacher-conductor at the Juilliard School of Music and for years was conductor at the Juilliard Opera Theatre. Born in Mexico City to Hungarian immigrant parents, he immigrated to the United States and received his higher education in southern California. In 1967, he became the conductor of the Louisville Orchestra and in 1970 became the director of the annual Aspen Festival.

Sources: Meier and Rivera, *Dictionary of Mexican American History*, p. 219.

Ritchie Valens

1958 ♦ Ritchie Valens (born Ricardo Valenzuela, 1941–1959) became the first Mexican American rock star with his hit recording of "Come On, Let's Go." In October of the same year, he became the first Mexican American rocker to be featured on the national television show *American Bandstand* in Philadelphia. His second recording in 1958 was his most important, with both sides, "La Bamba" and "Donna," becoming hits. Both climbed to the top 10 by December. Just as his career was taking off, Valens died in a plane crash with other rock stars. In 1987, Luis Valdez wrote and directed a hit movie biography of Valens entitled *La Bamba.*

Sources: Tardiff and Mabunda, *Dictionary of Hispanic Biography*, p. 914.

Celedonio Romero

1960 ♦ Spanish classical guitarist Celedonio Romero (1908–1996) formed the first classical guitar quartet to tour and perform with major symphony orchestras in the United States. The quartet went on to become the most important classical guitar dynasty in American music. Romero formed the quartet with his three sons, Angel, Pepe, and Celin, and in addition to performing at symphonies also performed at the White House and at the Vatican. Romero composed and recorded hundreds of works for guitar, including 10 concerts for guitar and orchestra. After dictator Francisco Franco's death, Spain embraced Romero, and King Juan Carlos presented him with the Order of Isabel the Catholic Queen, the monarch's highest civilian honor. The Vatican made Romero a knight of the Holy Sepulchre in 1991. Romero died in San Diego, California, in 1996.

Sources: Kozinn, Allan, "Celedonio Romero, 83, Guitarist Who Formed a Family Quartet," *New York Times,* 11 May 1996.

1962 ♦ Mexican American singer Joan Baez (1941–) became the first Latino entertainer to appear on the cover of *Time* magazine after she sang to a crowd of 350,000 gathered at the Lincoln Memorial for Martin Luther King Jr.'s "I Have a Dream" speech. Along with Bob Dylan, Baez was one of the moving forces behind the pop and folk music support for the 1960s generation's youth activism and protest against the Vietnam War. During this time, Baez's recording albums were very successful; her first such album, entitled *Joan Baez,* reached number three on the charts.

Joan Baez

Sources: Tardiff and Mabunda, *Dictionary of Hispanic Biography*, pp. 81–82.

1964 ♦ Lead guitarist Jerry García (1942–1995) founded the Grateful Dead, one of the greatest rock bands of all time. The son of a musician who emigrated from La Coruña, Spain, García was ranked among the top 10 moneymaking Latino performers at the time of his death in 1995. So popular was García's band that it became the subject of a cult followed by thousands of "Deadheads."

Jerry García

Sources: Hispanic Link Weekly Report, 14 August 1995, p. 1.

Vikki Carr

1967 ♦ Vikki Carr (1940–) became the first Latina singer or entertainer to be invited to a command performance for Queen Elizabeth II in London. The following year, she set a precedent for sold-out concerts in Germany, Spain, France, England, Australia, Japan, and Holland. In the United States, she became a favorite of the White House, performing repeatedly for each of the last four presidents. Carr recorded 49 bestselling records, including 15 gold albums. In 1985, she won a Grammy for her Spanish-language album *Simplemente Mujer* (Simply a Woman). For her Spanish-language records, she won gold, platinum, and diamond records. Her 1989 album *Esos Hombres* won gold records in Mexico, Chile, Puerto Rico, and the United States. Among her other awards are the *Los Angeles Times* Woman of the Year in 1970, the American Guild of Variety Artists' Entertainer of the Year in 1972, the Hispanic Woman of the Year in 1984, and the Girl Scouts of America Award in 1991.

Sources: Kanellos, *Chronology of Hispanic American History*, pp. 215, 257, 272.

1968 ♦ Cuban-born Tania J. León (1943–) became the first musical director of the Dance Theater of Harlem. She is one of a very small handful of women conductors in the United States. Since 1968, she has maintained a busy schedule as a composer, recording artist, and guest conductor at most of the important symphonies throughout the United States and Puerto Rico, as well as in Paris, London, Spoleto, Berlin, and Munich. From 1977 to 1988, she was the director of the Family Concert Series for the Brooklyn Philharmonic Community. In 1985, León joined the faculty of Brooklyn College as an associate professor teaching both composition and conducting. She has also served as music director for Broadway musicals, such as *The Wiz*. Her honors include the Dean Dixon Achievement Award in 1985, the ASCAP Composer's Award from 1987 to 1989, the National Council of Women

Tania J. León

Achievement Award in 1980, the 1991 Academy-Institute Award in Music from the American Academy and Institute of Arts and Letters, and many others.

Sources: Kanellos, *Chronology of Hispanic American History*, pp. 219, 252.

José Feliciano

1968 ♦ Pop singer José Feliciano (1945–) became the first Puerto Rican artist to win a Grammy Award. Actually, he won two: one for Best New Artist and the other for Best Contemporary Pop Vocal Performance: Male. The Grammys were awarded for his rendition of "Light My Fire."

Sources: Hispanics in American History: 1865 to the Present, p. 49.

1969 ♦ Mexican American rock musician Carlos Santana (1947–) and his group were the first pop group to experiment with the fusion of rock and salsa styles and to perform at Woodstock, which led to the group's being the first Latino salsa-rock group to appear on television's *The Ed Sullivan Show*. In his career, Santana has recorded more than 30 albums, with nine of them achieving platinum status and 16 achieving gold status.

Carlos Santana

Sources: Tardiff and Mabunda, *Dictionary of Hispanic Biography*, p. 818.

1970 ♦ Pop singer José Feliciano (1945–) composed and recorded "Feliz Navidad," which became one of the most played Christmas songs in the world and has been covered by hundreds of artists. It won a place in the Grammy Hall of Fame; Feliciano himself is a seven-time Grammy winner. In 1987, in recognition of his pioneering composing, guitar-playing, and performing, Feliciano was accorded a place on the Hollywood Walk of Fame. Feliciano has also been honored with the renaming of Public School 155 as the Jose Feliciano Performing Arts School.

Sources: Deming, Mark, "José Feliciano Biography," All Music: https://www.allmusic.com/artist/jos%C3%A9-feliciano-mn0000271113#biography.

1971 ♦ Princeton University professor and composer Mario Davidovsky (1937–2019) won the Pulitzer Prize for his "Synchronism No. 6." Davidovsky was born in Buenos Aires, Argentina, but immigrated to the United States in 1960 and developed his musical career here.

Sources: "Mario Davidovsky, Composer Who Made Electronics Sing," *New York Times*, 30 August 2019.

1974 ♦ Mexican Eduardo Mata (1942–1995) became the first Latino conductor of a major American symphony, the Phoenix Symphony. From 1977 until the 1993–1994 season, Mata led the Dallas Symphony as music director while also touring extensively and even continued to serve as the principal conductor and musical advisor of the Phoenix Symphony until 1978. He also served as the principal guest conductor of the Pittsburgh Symphony beginning in 1989. Mata was named conductor emeritus of the Dallas Symphony beginning with the 1994 season.

Eduardo Mata was born in Mexico City and became one of Mexico's most outstanding symphonic directors. Educated at the National Conservatory of Music from 1954 to 1963 and through private instruction, he began his conducting career in 1964 with the Guadalajara Symphony Orchestra. From 1966 to 1975, he was music director and conductor of the Orquesta Filarmónica of the National University in Mexico City. In 1975, he became director of the National Symphony in Mexico City and also directed a number of international music festivals, including the 1976 Casals Festival in Mexico.

Sources: "Eduardo Mata Is Dead at 52," *New York Times*, 5 January 1995.

Freddy Fender

1975 ♦ Singer Freddy Fender (1937–2006), born Baldemar Garza Huerta) became the first Mexican American country and western star to have a national hit song, "Before the Next Teardrop Falls," cross over to pop and become a gold record. He also released his first album that year, which also became gold. In 1976, he became the first Latino to receive a Country Music Association Award for Single of the Year and a Grammy for Best Country Vocal Performance: Male.

Sources: Tardiff and Mabunda, *Dictionary of Hispanic Biography*, p. 327.

1978 ♦ Cuban American composer-conductor Tania J. León (1943–) became the first Latina to serve as the music director and conductor for a Broadway hit musical, *The Wiz*, as well as for the *Dance in America* series for public television. León has served as guest conductor for symphonies throughout the United States and has had her compositions recorded.

Sources: Tardiff and Mabunda, *Dictionary of Hispanic Biography*, p. 479.

1982 ♦ The Guadalupe Cultural Arts Center in San Antonio, Texas, founded the annual Tejano Conjunto Festival to celebrate Tejano music, the Texas brand of northern Mexican music, which has become one of the most popular varieties of Latino dance music. Today, the festival draws bands from throughout the United States, Mexico, and as far away as Japan. Prizes and honorable mentions are awarded annually in four related categories. In addition, each year, the Conjunto Hall of Fame honors the giants in the field of Tejano music at the festival. Today, the festival transpires over five days of live performances and dancing in various locations in San Antonio.

Sources: "Tejano Conunto Festival 2024," Guadalupe Cultural Arts Center: https://guadalupeculturalarts.org/tejano-conjunto-festival/.

1984 ♦ The recording "Conga" by Cuban American singer Gloria Estefan (1957–) and her band, Miami Sound Machine, was the first record in history to make it onto Billboard's pop, dance, black, and Latin charts simultaneously. The single was part of Miami Sound Machine's first English-language album, *Eyes of Innocence.*

Gloria Estefan

Sources: Tardiff and Mabunda, *Dictionary of Hispanic Biography*, p. 316.

Irene Cara

1984 ♦ Singer/actress Irene Cara (born Irene Escalera, 1959–2022), raised in the Bronx by Puerto Rican and Cuban parents, shared the Oscar for Best Original Song for "Flashdance ...What a Feeling," which she cowrote for the hit film *Flashdance.* She also won a Grammy Award for Best Pop Vocal Performance: Female that year. She had previously played a character in the hit movie *Fame* (1980), for which she sang the title song. Cara has an extensive discography as well as Broadway, off-Broadway, film, and television credits.

Sources: "'Fame' and 'Flashdance' Singer-Actor Was Genius," *New York Times*, 27 November 2022.

1986 ♦ Salsa singer Celia Cruz (1925–2003) became the first Latino musical performing artist to be given the Ellis Island Medal of Honor, also known as the Mayor's Liberty Award, by the National Ethnic Coalition of Organizations.

Sources: Tardiff and Mabunda, *Dictionary of Hispanic Biography*, p. 257.

Celia Cruz

1987 ♦ Mexican American singer Linda Ronstadt (1946–) produced her first completely Spanish-language album, *Canciones de mi Padre*, which went double platinum. Ronstadt is considered to have broken ground for female rock stars, becoming the most popular female vocalist in the 1970s and 1980s.

Sources: Kanellos, *Latino Almanac*, p. 493.

1991 ♦ Mariah Carey (1970–) became the first Latina pop singer to win Grammys for Best Pop Vocalist Performance: Female and Best New Artist with her very first album, *Mariah Carey*. Carey was only the third artist in history to be nominated in the same year for Album of the Year, Song of the Year, and Best New Artist. The 11 songs on the album were cowritten by Carey, and she produced "Vanishing," a piano and vocal track. The track "Vision of Love" was number one on Billboard's pop, black, and adult contemporary charts. In the first year of the album's release, *Mariah Carey* remained number one for 22 weeks and sold some six million copies.

Mariah Carey

Sources: Tardiff and Mabunda, *Dictionary of Hispanic Biography*, p. 175; Telgen and Kamp, *Latinas! Women of Achievement*, pp. 51–55.

Tito Puente

1992 ♦ Salsa musician and composer Tito Puente (1923–2000) became the first Latino to record 100 albums. He was also the holder of four Grammy Awards and published more than 400 compositions. He was honored with a star on the Hollywood Walk of Fame.

Sources: Tardiff and Mabunda, *Dictionary of Hispanic Biography*, pp. 706–707.

1994 ♦ *Lydia Mendoza: A Family Autobiography*, edited by Chris Strachwitz and James Nicopolus, became the first Latino book to receive the Association for Sound Collections Award for Excellence in the field of ethnic music. The book was an edited transcription of the dictated memoirs of Lydia Mendoza (1916–2007) and her family of singers and vaudevillians. Mendoza was the first great Mexican American recording star, the first to sing in the vernacular rather than the cultivated operatic style, and the first to appeal to a broad section of working-class Mexican Americans. Beginning in the early 1930s, her career as a recording star and performer lasted well into the 1960s, and her fame extended throughout the Southwest, Mexico, Central America, and northern South America. In 1982, Mendoza was awarded a National Heritage Fellowship by the National Endowment for the Arts.

Sources: Strachwitz and Nicopolus, *Lydia Mendoza*.

1994 ♦ The "Queen of Salsa," Celia Cruz (1925–2003), the renowned singer of Afro-Cuban music, was the first Latina to receive the National Medal of Arts. Cruz began her career in Cuba performing with the famous Sonora Matancera band until she left for Mexico in 1960 as a refugee from the Cuban Revolution and, in 1962, settled in the United States. In the United States, she performed and recorded with practically all of the most popular salsa bands. Over her career, she recorded 37 albums and sold over 10 million recordings worldwide. In 1987, she was accorded a star on the Hollywood Walk of Fame and in 1999 was inducted into the International Latin Music Hall of Fame. In 2011, Cruz was featured on a U.S. postal stamp. In 2024, she became the first Afro-Latina to have her portrait on a U.S. quarter.

Sources: Kanellos, *Latino Almanac*, pp. 422, 478, 481, 487.

Plácido Domingo

1994 ♦ Plácido Domingo (1941–) and José Carreras (1946–), together with Luciano Pavarotti—the three most prominent living operatic tenors—began a series of concerts entitled "The Three Tenors" for the largest opera audiences in history, staging their events in stadiums and broadcasting them live internationally as well as marketing videos and CDs of the concerts. The first of these mega-opera events was held in San Francisco Giants Stadium on the eve of the World Cup finals before an audience of 58,000 people. Both Spanish tenors have performed often in the United States, with Domingo regarded by American aficionados as one of the greatest operatic tenors ever. So beloved is his voice that Domingo has recorded popular Latin American songs for the U.S. Hispanic audience as well as songs in English for American mainstream listeners. Born in Madrid in 1941, Domingo grew up in Mexico and made his debut there in 1961. He made his debut with the New York City Opera in 1965 and with the Metropolitan Opera in 1968. In 1996, Domingo became the director of the Washington (D.C.) Opera, becoming the first Hispanic to direct a major company in the United States.

José Carreras

Sources: Salazar, Francisco. "José Carreras & Placido Domingo to Reunite for Concert," OperaWire: https://operawire.com/jose-carreras-placido-domingo-to-reunite-for-concert/#google_vignette.

1995 ♦ Salsa singer Celia Cruz (1925–2003) became the first Latino pop singer to be awarded the National Medal of Arts, presented by President Bill Clinton. Cruz is the acknowledged "Queen of Salsa" and the female artist who has recorded the most salsa records in history. She immigrated to the United States as a refugee from communist Cuba and has sung with many of the leading salsa bands, including the Willie Colón band.

Sources: Tardiff and Mabunda, *Dictionary of Hispanic Biography*, pp. 255–258.

Israel "Cachao" López

1995 ♦ Cuban composer–bandleader Israel "Cachao" López (1918–2008) was the first male Latino recipient of the National Heritage Fellowship in a White House ceremony. The fellowships celebrate the lifelong achievements of masters of folk and traditional arts in the United States. Cachao is credited with starting or influencing many of the traditions that have made up salsa music, including contributing to the development of the mambo and the *descargas* (freestyle improvisational jam sessions). Cachao was born in 1918 into an extended family with some 50 musicians as members. As a string bassist, he made his debut at the age of 12 with the Havana Philharmonic and later, along with his brothers, played with the historically important *charanga* orchestra of Antonio Arcano. Cachao, who immigrated to the United States as a refugee, has won several Grammys.

Sources: "Cachao," *Hispanic Arts News*, October 1995, p. 12.

1995 ♦ Mexican American pop singer Selena (1971–1995) set the record for attendance at the largest venue for country and western concerts, the Houston Livestock Show and Rodeo. She drew a crowd of 60,000 at her performance in the same year that her life ended tragically.

Sources: Tardiff and Mabunda, *Dictionary of Hispanic Biography*, p. 837.

1995 ♦ Pop singer Selena's album *Dreaming of You*, issued posthumously, entered the Billboard 200 at number one—the second highest chart debut after Michael Jackson's *HIStory*.

Sources: Tardiff and Mabunda, *Dictionary of Hispanic Biography*, p. 838.

1996 ♦ Salsa bandleader-composer Tito Puente (1923–2000) was the first Latino popular musician to be honored by the Smithsonian Institution's National Museum of American History for his 60 years in the music industry. He donated a pair of timbales to the museum on the occasion. In 1997, he was presented the National Medal of Arts.

Sources: *Hispanic Link Weekly Report*, 14 October 1996, p. 1.

Daniel Catán

1996 ♦ The Houston Grand Opera staged the world premiere of the opera it commissioned by Mexican composer Daniel Catán (1949–2011), *Florencia en Amazonas*, based on a short story by Nobel Prize–winning writer Gabriel García Márquez. The libretto was written by Marcela Fuentes-Berain, a Mexican scriptwriter who has coauthored films with García Márquez. *Florencia en Amazonas* is the story of a famous opera singer traveling down the Amazon River searching for a lost love. It is the first Spanish-language opera commissioned by an American opera company. Up to that point, no operas in the standard opera repertoire had Spanish-language texts. After various productions around the United States and Mexico, *Florenica en Amazonas* debuted at the Metropolitan Opera of New York in 2023; it was its first Spanish-language opera in more than 100 years. Latina soprano Ailyn Pérez sang the lead role.

Sources: "Myth, Magic, and Spirit," *Houston Chronicle Zest Magazine*, 20 October 1996, pp. 8–9, 15.

1997 ♦ Eduardo "Lalo" Guerrero (1916–2005) became the first Chicano musician to receive the government's highest honor for an artist, the 1996 National Medal of Arts, presented by President Bill Clinton in a White House ceremony. He had also been declared a national folk treasure by the Smithsonian Institution in 1980. The main street in Cathedral City, California, in front of the Civic Center is named for him. Born in Tucson, Arizona, in 1917, Guerrero led a life devoted to composing and performing popular music. He scored his first hit, "La Canción Mexicana," when he was still in his teens and wrote and recorded hits throughout the 1940s and 1950s.

Sources: "National Heritage Fellowships: Eduardo 'Lalo' Guerrero," National Endowment for the Arts: https://web.archive.org/web/20200521082518/https://www.arts.gov/honors/heritage/fellows/eduardo-lalo-guerrero.

Ricky Martin

1999 ♦ "Livin' la Vida Loca," Puerto Rican singer Ricky Martin's (1971–) single on his hit album *Ricky Martin*, which sold 12 million copies, reached number one in many countries around the world and is considered the hit that ignited the Latin pop explosion and led to the breakthrough in English for many other Latino singers.

Sources: Kanellos, *Latino Almanac*, p. 491.

1999 ♦ Lydia Mendoza (1916–2007) was awarded the National Medal of Arts by President Bill Clinton. In 2003, her portrait was unveiled as a U.S. postal stamp.

Sources: Strachwitz and Nicopolus, *Lydia Mendoza.*

2003 ♦ *Rolling Stone* magazine placed Mexican American musician Carlos Santana (1947–) at number 15 among the 100 greatest guitarists of all time. Santana has been one of the most durable performers ever, with hits spanning four decades. At the age of 72, Santana was still touring.

Sources: Kanellos, *Latino Almanac,* p. 493.

Marcos Witt

2007 ♦ Marcos Witt (born Jonathan Mark Witt Holder, 1962–), one of the very few renowned Latino "Christian" stars, scored a Billboard Latin Music Award for Latin Christian/Gospel Album of the Year with his album *Alegría.* Witt is also one of the few religious singers to successfully cross over to secular music.

Sources: Kanellos, *Latino Almanac,* pp. 493–494.

2010 ♦ The Houston Grand Opera (HGO) inaugurated its trilogy of mariachi operas with *Cruzar la Cara de la Luna* (Crossing the Face of the Moon), written by José "Pepe" Martínez (1941–2016, music and lyrics) and Leonard Foglia (lyrics and book), with the assistance of and performance of the famed Mariachi Vargas de Tecatitlán. For the second and third operas, *El Pasado Nunca Se Termina* (The Past Never Ends, debuted by the Lyric Opera of Chicago in 2015) and *Milagro del Recuerdo* (The Miracle of Memory, 2019), Martínez's son Javier replaced him as composer. The HGO claims that these are the world's first mariachi operas. The HGO's sponsorship represented the first great recognition of and investment in the Mexican vernacular music form, and all three operas have subsequently been produced in opera houses around the United States.

Pauline Oliveros

Sources: "Mariachi at HGO," *Houston Grand Opera,* Vol. 63, No. 2 (2022): pp. 20–23.

2012 ♦ Pauline Oliveros (1932–2016), arguably the most distinguished Latino composer and performer of experimental music ever, received the John Cage Award from the Foundation for Contemporary Arts. Born in Houston, it is reported that she began performing music at the age of five and that she learned to play the accordion by the age of nine. She pursued her music education in different states, following some of the most distinguished masters of experimental music ever. She herself was widely acclaimed and taught at the University of California at San Diego, where she served as the director of the Center for Music Experiment (1967–1969). She is best known for developing the concepts of "deep listening" and "sonic awareness."

Sources: Smith, Steve. "Pauline Oliveros, Composer Who Championed 'Deep Listening,' Dies at 84," *New York Times*, 28 November 2016.

Emilio and Gloria Estefan

2015 ♦ The Cuban American husband and wife composer/singer/orchestra leaders Emilio (1953–) and Gloria Estefan (1957–) were jointly awarded the nation's highest civilian honor, the Presidential Medal of Freedom, by President Barack Obama. The producers of many top-10 hits, gold and platinum albums, and Grammys had been working together, and then married, since 1975.

Sources: Kanellos, *Latino Almanac*, p. 488.

2016 ♦ Mexican American singer Linda Ronstadt (1946–) received the Recording Academy's Lifetime Achievement Award. The winner of 11 Grammy Awards, she is also in the Rock and Roll Hall of Fame (2014) and has received a Kennedy Center Honor (2019). In the late 1970s, Ronstadt had been the most popular female rock singer and the highest earner. Over her career, Ronstadt had six platinum albums and numerous singles hits. In the late 1970s and 1980s, Ronstadt also won awards as a country music performer and blazed the path for many other female singers to follow.

Linda Ronstadt

Sources: "Linda Ronstadt," *Parade*, 11 September 2022, pp. 8–9.

Ailyn Pérez

2016 ♦ Mexican American opera singer Ailyn Pérez (1979–) was the first Latina to win the Beverly Sills Artist Award. Born in Chicago to Mexican immigrants, in 2012 Pérez was the first Latina to receive the equally prestigious Richard Tucker Award in its 35-year history; she also won the Plácido Domingo Award in 2012.

Sources: "Love Is in the Aria," *Vanity Fair*, June 2012: https://www.vanityfair.com/culture/2012/06/stephen-costello-ailyn-perez-opera-duets.

Jennifer López

2017 ♦ Jennifer López (1969–) became the executive producer and host of *World of Dance*, a televised dance competition that debuted with 9.7 million viewers. She had previously served as a judge (2011–2012 and 2014–2016) for the weekly television show *American Idol.* She interrupted her judging in 2012 to embark on her first world tour. In 2013, she was ranked as the fifth-highest-paid woman in music.

Sources: Kanellos, *Latino Almanac*, p. 490.

Martina Arroyo

2020 ♦ Opera soprano Martina Arroyo (1937–) was inducted into the American Classical Music Hall of Fame. Since winning the Metropolitan Opera Auditions of the Air in 1957, she became part of the first generation of Afro–Puerto Rican opera stars of the 1960s and 1970s. From 1965 to 1978, she served as the leading soprano for New York's Metropolitan Opera. In 2013, she received a Kennedy Center Honor.

Sources: Kanellos, *Latino Almanac*, pp. 494–495.

2021 ♦ The most popular *norteño* (Mexican northern region) band of all time, Los Tigres del Norte released their album *La Reunión*, topping the Billboard chart for Regional Mexican Airplay, thus achieving a number-one hit album over *six* decades. The group has received multiple Grammy Awards and Latin Grammy Awards, the Latin Recording Academy's Lifetime Achievement Award, and sold more than 40 million albums; 24 of the albums reached number one, and 50 singles reached number one.

Sources: "Los Tigres del Norte," California Museum: https://californiamuseum.org/inductee/los-tigres-del-norte/.

Bad Bunny

2022 ♦ Puerto Rican superstar Bad Bunny's (born Benito Antonio Martínez Ocasio, 1994–) *Un Verano Sin Ti* maintained number-one status for most of the year on Billboard's album chart; it was streamed billions of times. His tours and other live performances grossed $435 million. Each of the six albums Bad Bunny has released since 2018 has been a billion-streamer. What is noteworthy is that although he speaks perfect English, Bad Bunny has continued to record only in Spanish as compared to so many other Latino pop stars who cross over to English hoping to increase their audiences.

Sources: Pareles, Jon. "Another Year of Innovation for Latin Pop," *New York Times*, 25 December 2022.

2023 ♦ Puerto Rican superstar Bad Bunny's (born Benito Antonio Martínez Ocasio, 1994–) *Un Verano Sin Ti* became the first Spanish-language album to lead in sales in 2022; it was the world's best-performing album that year. It was also the first album by a Latino to top 10 billion streams and the first Spanish-language album to earn a Grammy nomination for Album of the Year.

Sources: "Beyoncé, Adele and Bad Bonny in Position to Make History," *Houston Chronicle*, 5 February 2023.

SPORTS

ARCHERY

2020 ♦ The first Latina to represent the United States in the Olympics in archery was Jennifer Muciño-Fernández (2002–), born in Boston and raised in Mexico City. She also won a place on the 2024 U.S. Olympic archery team. Muciño-Fernández is a self-taught archer, coached by her mother who also had no experience in the sport.

Sources: "Living the American Dream: Team USA Archery's Jennifer Muciño-Fernández," USA Archery News: https://www.usarchery.org/article/titles-to-fight-for-as-the-usat-qualifier-series-continues-with-the-socal-showdown.

BASEBALL

1871 ♦ Esteban Bellán (1849–1932) became the first Latin American ballplayer to play professional baseball in the United States. Bellán was an Afro-Cuban recruited from Fordham College to play for the Troy Haymakers the same year as the founding of the National Baseball Association. He played for three years in the majors. By the turn of the century, no blacks were allowed in the majors. Up until Jackie Robinson broke the color barrier, Latin American and Latino blacks became regular players in the Negro Leagues of the United States. White-looking Latinos, however, were allowed to play throughout the history of professional baseball in the United States.

Esteban Bellán

At times, teams went to extremes to prove the racial purity of their Latin American players, as did the Cincinnati Reds in 1911 in preparing affidavits to prove that their new Cuban players, Armando Marsans (1887–1960) and Rafael Almeida (1887–1969), had the purest Castilian blood running through their veins.

Sources: Kanellos, *Latino Almanac*, p. 499.

1878 ♦ La Liga de Béisbol Profesional Cubana, the Cuban professional baseball league, was founded just seven years after the National League was founded in the United States. Professional baseball in Latin America is almost as old as it is in the United States. The Cuban leagues became important contributors of players to the Negro and white professional leagues in the United States and also offered major league players a place to play during the offseason.

Sources: Kanellos, *Chronology of Hispanic American History*, p. 114.

José Méndez

1909 ♦ Cuban José Méndez (1886–1928) was the first Latin American pitcher to achieve the outstanding record of 44 wins with only two losses for his first two seasons of play. He accomplished this incredible feat while playing for the Cuban Stars of the Negro Leagues. Because of his African ancestry and dark skin, Méndez was never allowed to play in the majors. Instead, he played in the Negro National League and in Cuba, and thus, many of his statistics are missing. Such witnesses as Hall of Famer John Henry Lloyd said that he never saw a pitcher superior to Méndez, and Giants manager John McGraw said that Méndez would have been worth $50,000 in the majors, an unusually high figure in those days. During the winters, he played in Cuba, where he compiled a record of 62–17 by 1914. From 1912 to 1916, Méndez played for the Kansas City All Nations, a racially mixed barnstorming club. From 1920 to 1926, he served as a player-manager for the Kansas City Monarchs and led them to three straight Negro National League pennants from 1923 to 1925. During his long career, he also played for the Los Angeles White Sox, the Chicago American Giants, and the Detroit Stars.

Sources: Kanellos, *Chronology of Hispanic American History*, p. 121.

1921 ♦ The best batter in Cuban baseball, and probably one of the best to ever play the game, was Alejandro Oms (1895–1946), who played with the Cuban Stars and the New York Cubans in the Negro Leagues from 1921 to 1935. In the winter season, Oms managed to put in outstanding seasons in

Alejandro Oms

Cuba. Oms was born into a poor family in Santa Clara, Cuba, in 1895. As a child, he had to work in an iron foundry. He started playing organized baseball in 1910 as a center fielder. On the most famous Cuban team of all time, Leopardos de Santa Clara, Oms batted .436 in the 1922–1923 season. In Cuba, Oms achieved a lifetime batting average of .352; his average in the United States is unknown. He was batting champion on the island three times: in 1924–1925 with .393; in 1928–1929 with .432; and in 1929–1930 with .380. In 1928, he established a Cuban record for most consecutive games with hits: 30. In his last years, he was penniless and his vision had failed; he died at the age of 51 in 1946.

Sources: Kanellos, *Latino Almanac*, pp. 501, 512.

Dolf Luque

1923 ♦ Dolf Luque (Adolfo Domingo De Guzmán Luque, 1890–1957) became the first Latin American to play in the World Series as a member of the Cincinnati Reds. Luque, who was a Cuban, broke into the majors in 1914 with the Boston Braves, where he was incessantly jeered at and subjected to racial epithets. Despite his emotionally rocky career because of the racism he faced, he had one of the longest careers of any Latino baseball player, serving until 1935 for Boston, Cincinnati, Brooklyn, and New York teams. Luque pitched in two World Series, being credited with the decisive win in one of them. In 1923, Luque became the first Latino to win the pitching championship in professional baseball in the United States, with 27 wins, an earned-run average of 1.93, and six shutouts.

Sources: Kanellos, *Latino Almanac*, p. 499.

1930 ♦ One of the greatest baseball pitchers of all time, Vernon "Lefty" Gómez (1907–1989), began his major league career. Born in Rodeo, California, Gómez ranks third in regular-season wins in the history of baseball, with 189 for the New York Yankees. He also holds the record for World Series wins without a loss (6–0) and three wins against one loss in All-Star play. Gómez was active from 1930 to 1943, pitching 2,503 innings and winning 189 games to 102 losses, with an earned-run average of 3.34. He scored 20 wins or more in 1931, 1932, 1934, and 1937. Gómez is number 13 on the all-time winning percentage list. Gómez made All-Star teams every year from 1933 to 1939, and he is a member of the National Baseball Hall of Fame.

Vernon "Lefty" Gómez

During winter seasons, he played in Cuba, where he also served as manager of the Cienfuegos team, and once, he taught a class on pitching at the University of Havana. Gómez died on February 2, 1989, in San Rafael, California.

Sources: Kanellos, *Latino Almanac*, p. 508.

1938 ♦ Puerto Rico began winter-league baseball under the name of La Liga de Béisbol Profesional de Puerto Rico by hosting off-season Major League Baseball players and preparing many future star athletes in Class AAA play. Today, the Puerto Rican Winter League is the oldest such league in operation in the world.

Sources: Van Hyning, *Puerto Rico's Winter League*, p. 4.

Hiram Bithorn

1942 ♦ Hiram Bithorn (1916–1951) joined the Chicago Cubs, becoming the first Puerto Rican baseball player in the major leagues. Known as the "Tropical Hurricane," Bithorn pitched three seasons for the Cubs and one for the White Sox. Previous Puerto Rican players were not drafted because their skin color was too dark; the light-skinned Bithorn was able to break the color barrier, and after him, more Puerto Rican players were recruited.

Sources: Quevedo, Jane Allen, "Hi Bithorn," Society for American Baseball Research: https://sabr.org/bioproj/person/hi-bithorn/.

1951 ♦ Cuban Orestes "Minnie" Miñoso (Saturnino Orestes "Minnie" Armas Arrieta Miñoso, 1924–2015) became the first Latino ballplayer in professional baseball in the United States to steal the most bases (31) in a season. Miñoso had made his debut with the New York Cubans of the Negro Leagues in 1948 but made it to the Cleveland Indians in 1946 when the color barrier was broken. Miñoso had a long career playing for various teams. In 1976, when he served as a designated hitter for the Chicago White Sox, he became one of only six players to have been active over four decades. In 1996, he was inducted into the National Baseball Hall of Fame.

"Minnie" Miñoso

Sources: Kanellos, *Latino Almanac*, pp. 501, 511.

"Chico" Carrasquel

1951 ♦ The first Latino ballplayer to be selected for the All-Star Game was Venezuelan shortstop Alfonso "Chico" Carrasquel (1926–2005). Carrasquel served as the opening player in that position in 1951.

Sources: Kanellos, *Chronology of Hispanic American History*, p. 231.

1954 ♦ Mexican second baseman Roberto "Beto" Avila (1924–2004) became the first Latino to win the batting championship in professional baseball in the United States. Playing for Cleveland in 1954, he batted .341, drove in 67 runs, and scored 112 runs, 15 of them home runs.

Sources: Kanellos, *Chronology of Hispanic American History*, pp. 235–236.

1956 ♦ Venezuelan shortstop Luis Aparicio (1934–) became the first Hispanic American in U.S. professional baseball to be named Rookie of the Year. Playing for Baltimore in 1956, Aparicio drove in 56 runs, scored 69 runs, and led the leagues in stolen bases. He was inducted into the National Baseball Hall of Fame in 1984.

Luis Aparicio

Sources: Kanellos, *Latino Almanac*, pp. 403–404, 411–412.

1960 ♦ Cuban Orestes "Minnie" Miñoso (1925–2015) became the first Latino ballplayer in U.S. professional baseball to lead both leagues in hits, with 184 for the Chicago White Sox.

Sources: Kanellos, *Chronology of Hispanic American History*, p. 242.

1962 ♦ Pedro "Tony" Oliva (1938–), a native Cuban, became the only baseball player in history to win batting championships during his first two major league seasons. While playing for the Minnesota Twins, he won Rookie of the Year in 1964 and the league batting title in 1964, 1965, and 1971. Oliva also won the Gold Glove in 1966 as the league's best defensive right fielder. In 2021, he was inducted into the National Baseball Hall of Fame.

Pedro "Tony" Oliva

Sources: Kanellos, *Latino Almanac*, p. 512.

Juan Marichal

1963 ♦ Dominican pitcher Juan Marichal (1937–) became the first Latino to throw a no-hitter in professional baseball in the United States. Pitching for the San Francisco Giants, he beat Houston 1–0 on July 15, 1963.

Sources: Kanellos, *Latino Almanac*, p. 510.

1964 ♦ Minnesota Twins baseball player Pedro "Tony" Oliva (1938–) set the American League record for most hits by a rookie, 217.

Sources: Reichler, *The Great All-Time Baseball Record Book*, p. 305.

1967 ♦ Kansas City's Bert Campaneris (1942–) became the first Latino baseball player to hit three triples in a game, thus joining an elite club of the most triple hitters in one game in the major leagues.

Sources: Reichler, *The Great All-Time Baseball Record Book*, p. 98.

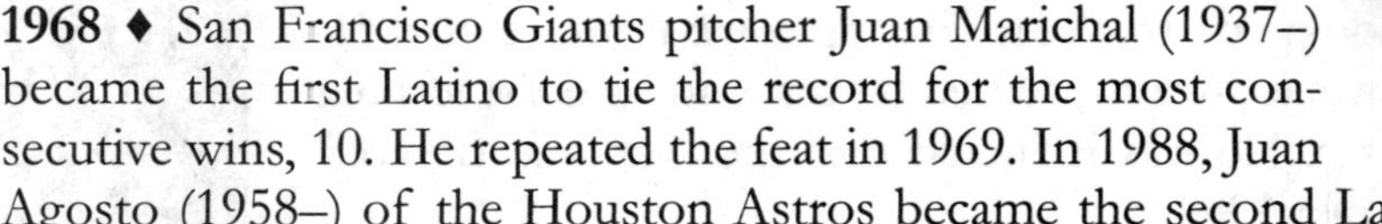

1968 ♦ San Francisco Giants pitcher Juan Marichal (1937–) became the first Latino to tie the record for the most consecutive wins, 10. He repeated the feat in 1969. In 1988, Juan Agosto (1958–) of the Houston Astros became the second Latino to join the exclusive club.

Bert Campaneris

Sources: Reichler, *The Great All-Time Baseball Record Book*, p. 241.

Preston Gómez

1969 ♦ Cuban-born Preston Gómez (born Pedro Gómez Martínez, 1923–2009) became Major League Baseball's first Latino manager, managing for the San Diego Padres. He only lasted two years because of consecutive losing seasons. He had more chances as a manager, for the Houston Astros from 1973 to 1974 and again in 1980 for the Chicago Cubs, but again did not prevail. He spent the rest of his baseball career as a coach for various teams until his retirement in 1984.

Sources: "Cardcorner: 1972 Topps Preston Gómez," National Baseball Hall of Fame: https://baseballhall.org/discover/card-corner/1972-topps-preston-gomez.

1970 ♦ Venezuelan shortstop Luis Aparicio (1934–) won the most Gold Gloves as the best American League shortstop in the history of baseball. He won every year from 1958 to 1962 and then again in 1964, 1966, 1968, and 1970. He led the American League shortstops in fielding for eight consecutive seasons and broke a major league record by leading the American League in assists for six straight years.

Sources: Tardiff and Mabunda, *Dictionary of Hispanic Biography*, p. 45.

1971 ♦ While playing for the Minnesota Twins, baseball player Pedro "Tony" Oliva (1938–) led the league in hits five times in his career and made All-Star teams from 1964 to 1971, tying Joe Dimaggio's record of having been named an All-Star in each of his first six seasons.

Sources: Kanellos, *Latino Almanac*, p. 512.

Roberto Clemente

1973 ♦ Roberto Clemente (1934–1972) became the first Puerto Rican baseball player to be named to the National Baseball Hall of Fame and was the first player in history for whom the Hall of Fame waived its five-year waiting period. Born in Carolina, Puerto Rico, Clemente rose from an impoverished background to become a star outfielder for the Pittsburgh Pirates from 1955 to 1972. He assisted the Pirates in winning two World Series in 1960 and 1971. Among Clemente's achievements as a player, he was four times the National League batting champion—in 1961, 1964, 1965, and 1967—and he was voted the league's Most Valuable Player in 1966. He was awarded 12 Gold Gloves and set a major league record in leading the National League in assists five times. He served on 14 All-Star teams, and he was one of only 16 players to have 3,000 or more hits during their career. Clemente was promising a great deal more before his untimely death in a plane crash while bringing relief to victims of an earthquake in Nicaragua. Clemente had accumulated 240 home runs and a lifetime batting average of .317.

Sources: Tardiff and Mabunda, *Dictionary of Hispanic Biography*, pp. 233–235.

1973 ♦ Orlando Cepeda (1937–) became the first Latino baseball player to tie the record for most doubles in a game, four, while playing for the Boston Red Sox. In 1986, two more Latino players, Dámaso García (1955–2020) and Rafael Ramírez (1958–), joined that elite group. In 1999, Cepeda was inducted into the National Baseball Hall of Fame.

Orlando Cepeda

Sources: Reichler, *The Great All-Time Baseball Record Book*, pp. 96–97.

Rod Carew

1977 ♦ Panama-born baseball player Rod Carew (1945–) received more than four million All-Star votes, more than any other player in history. Spending most of his career as an outfielder for the Minnesota Twins, Carew played in 18 consecutive All-Star Games and batted over .300 for 15 consecutive seasons. His career batting average is the highest of any Latino player ever: .328.

Sources: Kanellos, *Latino Almanac*, p. 504.

Al López

1977 ♦ When baseball player Al López (1908–2005) was elected to the National Baseball Hall of Fame, he was considered the seventh best catcher and the seventh best manager of all time. For many years, he held the record for the highest number of games caught in the major leagues (1918) and for the most years (12) spent in the National League, catching in 100 games or more. He tied the record for the most games caught in the National League without a passed ball (114) in 1941. As a manager for the Indians and the White Sox, he compiled a record of .581, the ninth all-time highest.

Sources: Kanellos, *Latino Almanac*, p. 509.

Fernando Valenzuela

1981 ♦ Baseball pitcher Fernando Valenzuela (1960–) became the first rookie ever to win the Cy Young Award. The Los Angeles Dodger led the league in strikeouts, and in the shortened season that year, he tied the rookie record for the most shutouts: eight. He also won the Rookie of the Year and *The Sporting News* Player of the Year awards.

Sources: Kanellos, *Latino Almanac*, p. 518.

1983 ♦ Juan Marichal (1937–) became the first Dominican baseball player to be inducted into the National Baseball Hall of Fame. Marichal started his career as a pitcher with the San Francisco Giants in 1962, and from 1962 to 1971, he averaged 20 wins per year. He led the National League in wins in 1963 with a record of 25–8 and in 1968 with 26–9 and in shutouts in 1965 with 10. He also had the highest earned-run average (ERA)—2.10—in 1969. He pitched in eight All-Star Games with a record of 2–0 and a 0.50 ERA for 18 innings. Marichal's total innings pitched were 3,509, for a record of 243–142 and an ERA of 2.89. He was an All-Star from 1962 to 1969 and again in 1972.

Sources: Kanellos, *Chronology of Hispanic American History*, pp. 209, 247, 269.

1984 ♦ Venezuelan Luis Aparicio (1934–) was inducted into the National Baseball Hall of Fame as one of the greatest shortstops of all time in professional baseball in the United States. He still holds the records for games played, assists, and double plays and the American League record for putouts. His record of 506 stolen bases still ranks among the highest. Playing most of his career for the Chicago White Sox, Aparicio began his career in

1956 as Rookie of the Year and continued to play inspired baseball until his retirement in 1973. Aparicio played on All-Star teams from 1958 to 1964 and again from 1970 to 1972. He won the Gold Glove 11 times.

Sources: Kanellos, *Latino Almanac*, pp. 403–404, 411–412.

1984 ♦ Roberto Clemente became the first Latino baseball player to be featured on a U.S. postage stamp; he was only the second baseball player to be so honored.

Sources: Tardiff and Mabunda, *Dictionary of Hispanic Biography*, pp. 233–235.

1986 ♦ Baseball pitcher Fernando Valenzuela (1960–) tied Carl Hubbell's record of five straight strikeouts in an All-Star Game. Valenzuela was selected for the All-Star team five times.

Sources: Kanellos, *Latino Almanac*, p. 518.

José Canseco

1988 ♦ José Canseco (1964–) became the only baseball player in history to hit 40 home runs (actually 42) and steal 40 bases in the same season. He accomplished this feat while playing for the Oakland A's; he also batted .307 and scored 120 runs that season.

Sources: Reichler, *The Great All-Time Baseball Record Book*, p. 85.

1989 ♦ Cuban American baseball player José Canseco (1964–) signed the highest-paying contract up to that point in baseball history—$23.5 million over five years—with the Oakland A's.

Sources: Tardiff and Mabunda, *Dictionary of Hispanic Biography*, p. 162.

1992 ♦ Bobby Bonilla (1963–) became the highest-paid baseball player in the major leagues, signing a contract with the New York Mets for $29 million over five years. He proved his worth in 1993: he was the sole Mets representative in the All-Star Game.

Bobby Bonilla

Sources: Tardiff and Mabunda, *Dictionary of Hispanic Biography*, p. 129.

1993 ♦ Linda Alvarado (1951–), the president of Alvarado Construction, became the first Latina to own a Major League

Baseball team in the United States. Alvarado became a partner in the Colorado Rockies franchise from its inception. This was also the first time a woman was in a bid for ownership of a major league franchise.

Sources: Telgen and Kamp, *Latinas! Women of Achievement*, pp. 15–17.

1994 ♦ Dominican Felipe Alou (1935–) became the first Latino in baseball to be named manager of the year. He was the first Dominican manager in MLB history. He managed the Montreal Expos (1992–2001) and the San Francisco Giants (2003–2006). As a player, Alou led the National League twice in hits and once in runs; he played all three outfield positions.

Felipe Alou

Sources: Alou, Felipe. *Alou: My Baseball Journey.* Lincoln: University of Nevada Press, 2018.

Héctor López

1994 ♦ Panama-born Héctor López (1929–2022) was one of three African-descendant baseball players to break the color line as managers of Class AAA baseball when he became manager of the Gulf Coast League Yankees, the rookie-league team. He had played Major League Baseball for the Kansas City Athletics and the New York Yankees from 1955 to 1966, including playing on the Yankee teams that won the World Series in 1961 and 1962. During his career, he played every position except for pitcher and catcher.

Sources: "Héctor López, 93, Dies; Manager Who Broke Baseball Color Barrier," *New York Times*, 2 October 2022.

1995 ♦ Montreal Expos manager Felipe Alou (1935–) became the first Latino to win baseball's Manager of the Year Award. He managed the Expos from 1992 to 2001. In 2015, Alou was elected to the Canadian Baseball Hall of Fame and in 2016 to the Caribbean Baseball Hall of Fame.

Sources: Hispanic Link Weekly Report, 29 August 1995, p. 1.

1996 ♦ Alex "A-Rod" Rodríguez (1975–) of the Seattle Mariners became the first shortstop to hit more than 30 home runs in a season. The 21-year-old also maintained a batting average of .360. It was with the New York Yankees, from 2004 to 2016, that he became Major League Baseball's highest-paid player. Over the years, Rodríguez's output was out-

Alex "A-Rod" Rodríguez

standing, leading to his being named to 14 American League All-Star Teams, three times as Most Valuable Player (2002, 2003, 2007). He also was named twice the *Baseball America* Player of the Year (2000, 2002) and three times *The Sporting News* Player of the Year (1996, 2002, 2007). He holds the record for the most career grand slams (25), the most runs in a season (141), the most extra base hits in a season (91), the highest slugging percentage (.631 in 1996), and the most total bases in a season (393). In his career, Rodríguez scored more runs than any other Latino player: 2021.

Sources: Kanellos, *Latino Almanac*, p. 514.

Edwin Rodríguez

2011 ♦ Edwin Rodríguez (1960–) became the first Puerto Rican full-time manager of a Major League Baseball team. He became interim manager of the Florida Marlins in 2010 and went on to be hired for the 2011 season. However, after only achieving a 32–29 record, he resigned before the season's end.

Sources: Links, Zachary, "Marlins Manager Edwin Rodriguez Steps Down," MLB Trade Rumors: https://www.mlbtraderumors.com/2011/06/marlins-manager-edwin-rodriguez-steps-down.html.

José Altuve

2017 ♦ Venezuelan second baseman for the Houston Astros, José Altuve (1990–), achieved 200 hits, only the fourth right-hander in Major League Baseball history and the first player in history to lead his league in hits in four consecutive seasons. He won the Hank Aaron Award and became *Baseball America*'s Major League Player of the Year in 2017. Signed by the Astros as a free agent after so many MLB teams passed him up because he was too short (5'6"), Altuve has numerous records and is a repeat All-Star. In 2017 as well, he became only the ninth player in MLB history to homer three times in a playoff game. In 2021, he became the first player in history to hit a lead-off home run the day after hitting a game-ending grand slam. Altuve has won the Silver Slugger Award six times and has three American League batting titles and two championship series MVP awards (2017 and 2019). He was named to the All-Star team eight times and helped the Astros win two World Series.

Sources: Kawahara, Matt, "Road to History," *Houston Chronicle*, 21 August 2023.

2018 ♦ Albert Pujols (born José Alberto Pujols Alcántara, 1980–) became the second player in Major League Baseball history to accrue 3,000 hits. A

Albert Pujols

Dominican-born immigrant to the United States (at the age of 16), Pujols was one of the most feared batters and also considered one the greatest all-time players, sure to be inducted into the National Baseball Hall of Fame when he becomes eligible in 2028. He was selected as Most Valuable Player of the National League in 2005, 2008, and 2009 and selected 11 times for the All-Stars (2001, 2003–2010, 2015, 2022). He won the Silver Slugger Award six times and twice led the National League in home runs. He also led the league once each in batting average, doubles, and runs batted in. He was only the fourth player in MLB history to have 700 home runs. He is second in major league history in runs batted in and in total bases, behind only Hank Aaron.

Sources: Hoffman, Benjamin. "Albert Pujols Passes Willie Mays in Home Runs, If Not Dominance," *New York Times*, 18 September 2020.

2019 ♦ The Panamanian pitcher who started playing ball with cardboard gloves and stick bats because his family could not afford better, Mariano Rivera (1969–) was inducted into the National Baseball Hall of Fame as one of the greatest relief pitchers ever. During his career, Rivera developed a cutter pitch that most batters found unhittable. In 19 seasons with the New York Yankees, Rivera posted a record 652 saves with a win–loss mark of 82–60. His career ERA of 2.21 ranks number one, and his 952 games finished also ranks number one for all time. He helped the Yankees win five World Series.

Mariano Rivera

Sources: "Marina Rivero, Pitcher," National Baseball Hall of Fame: https://baseballhall.org/hall-of-famers/rivera-mariano.

Jorge Soler

2021 ♦ Atlanta Braves outfielder Jorge Soler (1992–) made history when playing the Houston Astros in the World Series by homering at the top of the first inning. No one had ever achieved such a feat before. During that same series, Soler also made history by being the only player to hit a homer out of the park when the roof was open; the ball left the stadium and carried over railroad tracks close to the park.

Sources: "Feeling Grand: Some Milestone Highlights," *Houston Chronicle*, 3 November 2022.

2024 ♦ Dominican third baseman Adrián Beltré Pérez (1979–) was elected to the National Baseball Hall of Fame. Considered one of the greatest

Adrián Beltré Pérez

third basemen of all time, his leadership at bat and in fielding were recognized with numerous awards: four Fielding Bible Awards (2006, 2008, 2011, 2012), the Lou Gehrig Memorial Award (2014), two Rawlings American League Platinum Glove Awards (2011, 2012), five Rawlings Gold Glove Awards (2007, 2008, 2011, 2012, 2016), four Silver Slugger Awards (2004, 2010, 2011, 2014), four Texas Rangers Player of the Year Awards (2012, 2013, 2014, 2016), and a Wilson Defensive Player of the Year Award for the Texas Rangers (2012). He retired in 2018 as the only third baseman in history with both 3,000 career hits and 400 homers. Beltré Pérez had his number 29 retired by the Texas Rangers in 2019.

Sources: "Adrian Beltré," National Baseball Hall of Fame: https://baseballhall.org/hall-of-famers/beltre-adrian.

2024 ♦ Houston Astros eight-time All-Star player José Altuve (1990–) became Major League Baseball's highest-paid second baseman in history when he signed a contract extension—he would have become a free agent in 2025—for $125 million guaranteed through the 2029 season, when he will be aged 39. This sum means that Altuve will have more than $300 million in guaranteed career earnings. Altuve had already spent 13 years with the Astros, had maintained the highest batting average for the franchise at .307, and has three American League batting titles. Only one man in major league history has more postseason home runs than Altuve's 27: Manny Ramírez with 29.

Sources: "Altuve Agrees to Deal Running until Age 39," *Houston Chronicle*, 7 February 2024.

BASKETBALL

1991 ♦ Houston Rockets basketball forward Carl Herrera (1966–) became the first Venezuelan to be signed by the National Basketball Association. That year, he became only the fifth rookie in the team's history to shoot .500 or better. Herrera had previously played for the University of Houston Cougars, becoming their top offensive rebounder and winning the Southwest Conference Newcomer of the Year Award and the All-Southwest Conference first team choice in 1989–1990. Herrera was a member of the Houston Rockets's championship teams of the 1990s.

Carl Herrera

Sources: "100 Influentials," *Hispanic Business*, October 1993.

1995 ♦ Rebecca Lobo (1973–) became the first Latina basketball player to be named All-American center. Lobo led her team, the University of Connecticut, to a national championship with a record of 35–0. The 6'4" Southwick, Massachusetts, native scored record points (35) and record rebounds (17). She was the only Big East basketball player in history to win both Big East Player of the Year and Scholar-Athlete of the Year, and she accomplished this feat twice. Lobo went on to have a successful career in the Women's NBA from 1997 to 2003. After that, she became a television sportscaster.

Sources: Hispanic, August 1995, p. 28.

1996 ♦ The first Hispanic woman to win an Olympic gold medal in basketball was Rebecca Lobo, who competed on the undefeated championship team of the United States. Lobo had helped her college team, the University of Connecticut, win the 1995 National Collegiate Athletic Association championship, where she was named in the final four Most Valuable Players.

Sources: Hispanic Business, May 1996, p. 28.

Diana Taurasi

2004 ♦ Diana Taurasi (1982–) won the gold medal for basketball as a member of Team USA at the Athens Olympics. Born to Argentine parents in Glendale, California, Taurasi became one of women basketball's greatest players of all times. She helped her University of Connecticut team win three national championships. Considered the WNBA's GOAT, this legend has done it all as a professional: Rookie of the Year (2004), three-time WNBA champion with the Phoenix Mercury (2007, 2009, 2014), MVP (2009), and 11-time All-Star (2005, 2006, 2007, 2009, 2011, 2013, 2014, 2017, 2018, 2021, 2024). She also helped her teams in the EuroLeague and the Russian National League win multiple championships, and as part of Team USA she won six consecutive gold medals at the Olympics between 2004 and 2024. Only two other athletes, one from Germany and another from Hungary, have won as many Olympic gold medals over six appearances. Taurasi will surely be named to the Women's Basketball Hall of Fame after she retires.

Sources: "Diana Taurasi Voted by Fans as WNBA's Greatest Player of All Time," WNBA: https://www.wnba.com/news/diana-taurasi-voted-by-fans-as-wnbas-greatest-player-of-all-time.

2010 ♦ Rebecca Lobo (1973–) became the first Latina basketball player to be inducted into the Women's Basketball Hall of Fame and in 2017 into the Naismith Memorial Basketball Hall of Fame.

Sources: Kanellos, *Latino Almanac*, p. 509.

Devin Booker

2020 ♦ Devin Booker (1996–), the son of a Mexican-Puerto Rican mother and an NBA professional basketball player, Melvin Brooks, became the first Latino men's basketball player to make Team USA basketball for the 2020 and 2024 Olympics, winning a gold medal each year. Due to his mother's Mexican heritage, the Mexican national team had courted Booker for the Olympics, but he chose to play for Team USA. Born and raised in Grand Rapids, Michigan, predominantly by his mother while his father played ball around the United States and Europe, Booker nevertheless learned much from his father and followed in his footsteps. Recruited from the University of Kentucky by the Phoenix Suns, Booker earned Rookie of the Year in 2016 and in 2019 became the youngest player in history with consecutive 50-point games. Booker went on to become an All-Star four times and helped the Phoenix Suns reach the NBA finals in 2021.

Sources: "'I'm Definitely Going to Rep That Side of My Heritage, Always': Devin Booker Is Determined to Get More in Touch with His Mexican Heritage," *The Athletic*: https://www.nytimes.com/athletic/1458332/2019/12/13/im-definitely-going-to-rep-that-side-of-my-heritage-always-devin-booker-is-determined-to-get-more-in-touch-with-his-mexican-heritage/.

José Juan Barea

2021 ♦ Puerto Rican José Juan "J. J." Barea (1984–) became the first Latino basketball player to be hired as a player development coach for the Dallas Mavericks. Barea, at 5'10", was one of the shortest players in the NBA. He joined the Mavericks as a guard in 2006 and helped the team win the NBA championship in 2011. He played for the Minnesota Timberwolves for a few seasons and then returned to play for the Mavericks from 2014 to 2020. He had previously helped the Puerto Rican team win a silver medal in the Olympics.

Sources: Sefko, Eddie, "J. J. Barea: 'I Like Coaching, Every Time I Do It, I Like It Even More'," NBA: https://www.mavs.com/barea-coach/.

Manu Ginóbili

2022 ♦ One of the best shooting guards in basketball history, Argentine Emanuel David "Manu" Ginóbili (1977–) of the San Antonio Spurs was indicted into the Naismith Memorial Basketball Hall of Fame. He was an NBA All-Star in 2005 and

2011 and in 2008 won the NBA Sixth Man of the Year Award. He helped the Spurs win the NBA Championship in 2003, 2005, 2007, and 2014. His number 20 was retired by the Spurs. He is considered the greatest Latin American player of all time. Ginóbili also played in the EuroLeague and is one of only two players (along with Bill Bradley) to have won a EuroLeague title, an NBA championship, and an Olympic gold medal.

Sources: "The Best South American NBA Players of All Time," Ranker: https://www.ranker.com/list/south-american-nba-players/ranker-nba.

Pau Gasol

2023 ♦ NBA All-Star Pau Gasol (1980–) was inducted into the Naismith Memorial Basketball Hall of Fame. The Spaniard had an outstanding career, playing for the Los Angeles Lakers (2008–2014), the Chicago Bulls (2014–2016), the San Antonio Spurs (2016–2019), and the Milwaukee Bucks (2019). During his career, he scored more than 20,000 points and had more than 10,000 rebounds, 3,500 assists, and 1,500 blocks. He was an NBA All-Star in 2006, 2009, 2010, 2011, 2015, and 2016. He helped the Lakers win the national championship in 2009 and 2010, and in 2023, the Lakers retired his number 16.

Sources: "Pau Gasol Biography: Life, Career, Stats & Facts," Lakers Nation: https://lakersnation.com/pau-gasol-biography/#google_vignette.

2024 ♦ Diana Taurasi (1982–) became the first American athlete to compete in six consecutive Olympics, one of three to ever reach that mark in the world. The three-time WNBA champion won her sixth gold medal as part of Team USA at the Paris Olympics.

Sources: "Diana Taurasi Wins Basketball Record 6th Olympic Gold Medal," ESPN: https://www.espn.com/olympics/story/_/id/40823078/diana-taurasi-wins-basketball-record-6th-olympic-gold-medal.

BODYBUILDING

1980 ♦ Mexican American bodybuilder Rachel Elizondo McLish (1955–) became the first winner of the U.S. Women's Bodybuilding Championship. She went on to become Ms. Olympia in 1980 and 1983 and world champion in 1982. She became the most famous female bodybuilder of all time. Born in 1958 in Harlingen, Texas, to Rafael and Rachel Elizondo, Rachel Elizondo McLish found her way to athletics through the study of ballet and her father's interest in weightlifting. McLish intensified her weight training while in college at Pan American University in Edinburgh, Texas, and during that time began working as a trainer at a spa. In 1978, McLish graduated with a degree in health and physical education from Pan American and became a partner in the Sport Palace Spa, the first and largest health club in south Texas. She began competing in bodybuilding tournaments and soon became known as the world's first female bodybuilding champion. In January 1999, she was inducted into the IFBB Hall of Fame. During the 1990s, McLish began a successful film acting career. She also wrote books and designed sportswear.

Sources: Hispanic, September 1993, pp. 50–54.

BOWLING

1989 ♦ Venezuelan Amleto Andrés Monacelli (1961–) became the first Latino to win the U.S. Professional Bowlers Association Player of the Year Award. Monacelli began the Professional Bowlers Association tour in 1982 and by 1991 was winning $81,000 in prizes annually; in 1989, he even achieved a record $213,815. The list of tournaments he won includes the Japan Cup (1987), the Showboat Invitational (1988), the Miller Challenge (1989), the Wichita Open (1989, 1990), the Budweiser Touring Players Championship (1989), the Cambridge Mixed Doubles (1989, 1990), the Columbus Professional Bowling Classic (1990), the Quaker State Open (1991), and the True Value Open (1991).

Among his many awards are the Professional Bowlers Association Player of the Year (1989, 1990) and the Harry Smith Point Leader Award (1989). In 1990, he won the Budweiser Kingpin Competition for the highest average of the year, and in 1990, sportswriters named him Bowler of the Year; this was the first time that a foreigner had ever been named Bowler of the Year in the United States. In his professional career, Monacelli rolled 16 perfect games, seven of them during the 1989 season, which established a new record for perfect games in a year. Three of these were accomplished in the span of one week, tying the record. At the age of 54, Monacelli became the third oldest player to win a PBA tour title, and in 2019, he won a PBA tour title again just before turning 55. He was ranked number 21 on the PBA's 2008 list of "50 Greatest Players of the Last 50 Years."

Sources: Amleto Monacelli PBA Library, Bowlers Mart: https://www.bowlersmart.com/category/pba-tour/pba-bowling-player-video-library/amleto-monacelli-pba-library/.

BOXING

Kid Chocolate

1931 ♦ Cuba's Kid Chocolate became the first Latino boxer to win a world title in the junior lightweight class. He was born Eligio Sardiñas (1910–1988) in Havana and became an example of boxers who battle their way out of poverty into fame and temporary riches. After winning 86 amateur fights and 21 professional fights in Cuba, he made his New York debut in 1928 and over his career had 36 wins, with only 10 losses and 6 draws. He became a true champion, supported his community, and was memorialized onstage and on-screen. However, he was severely exploited by his managers and owners and ultimately was done in by poverty and alcoholism.

Sources: "Kid Chocolate," The Cyber Boxing Zone Encyclopedia: http://www.cyberboxingzone.com/boxing/kidchoc.htm

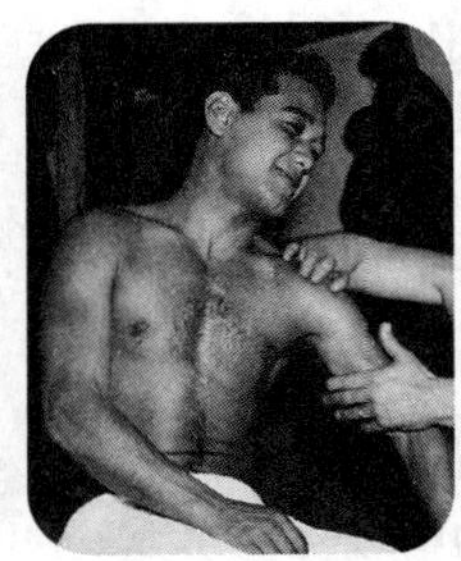
Sixto Escobar

1936 ♦ Sixto Escobar (1913–1979) became the first Puerto Rican boxer to win a world championship when he knocked out Tony Marino. Fighting as a bantamweight boxer, Escobar is one of only a very few boxers to have regained his crown—twice. In 2002, he was elected to the International Boxing Hall of Fame.

Sources: Kanellos, *Chronology of Hispanic American History*, p. 209.

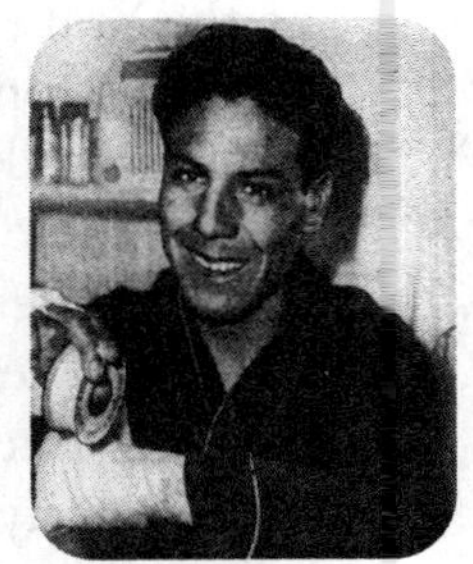
Manuel Ortiz

1942 ♦ Manuel Ortiz (1916–1970) of El Centro, California, became the first Mexican American to win the bantamweight boxing championship on August 7, 1942, when he beat Lou Salica. Over his career, Ortiz won 100 bouts: 54 by knockout and 46 by decision; he lost only 28 and had three draws. He never suffered a knockout himself. Ortiz tied Henry Armstrong in defending his title 20 times (only two fighters had defended more often). He was named one of the "80 Best Fighters of the Last 80 Years" by *The Ring* magazine.

Sources: "Manuel Ortiz," The Cyber Boxing Zone Encyclopedia: http://www.cyberboxingzone.com/boxing/ortiz-m.htm.

1956 ♦ José Luis "Chegui" Torres (1936–2009) became the first U.S. Latino to win a silver medal in the light middleweight boxing division of the Olympics. He was also the first Puerto Rican athlete on the American team and the first to win a medal. Torres went on to become a professional boxer, winning the middleweight championship in 1965 with a technical knockout of Willie Pastrano in Madison Square Garden. After finding no more rivals in the middleweight division, Torres rose to middle heavyweight and won the crown, which he defended successfully until 1966. In 1997, Torres was elected to the International Boxing Hall of Fame. Torres was born and raised in Ponce, Puerto Rico. He dropped out of high school and joined the U.S. Army, where he became a champion boxer. After the Army, Torres moved to New York and pursued his amateur and then professional boxing careers, but he also pursued a career as a singer and musician. The multitalented Torres later became a respected columnist for the *New York Daily News*.

Sources: Kanellos, *Chronology of Hispanic American History*, p. 239.

1969 ♦ Boxer Mando Ramos (born Armando Ramos, 1948–) became the first Mexican American to win the world lightweight championship with his victory over Carlos Cruz in Los Angeles. In 1972, he went on to win the World Boxing Congress lightweight championship over Pedro Carrasco.

Sources: Kanellos, *Latino Almanac*, p. 514.

Carlos Palomino

1974 ♦ Mexican American boxer Carlos Palomino (1949–) became the first Latino to win the world welterweight championship. Born in Sonora, Mexico, Palomino immigrated to the United States with his family when he was a child. While serving in the U.S. Army, he became the world military champion, and after compiling a record of 30 wins and one loss as a professional, he captured the world welterweight championship.

Sources: Meier and Rivera, *Dictionary of Mexican American History*, p. 270.

Paul Gonzales

1984 ♦ The Los Angeles Olympics registered the most U.S. Latinos to ever have competed on the U.S. Olympic team. Local hero Paul Gonzales (1964–) of East Los Angeles won a gold medal in boxing. He became the first Mexican American to win an individual gold medal for the United States.

Sources: Kanellos, *Chronology of Hispanic American History*, p. 271.

1985 ♦ Boxer Héctor "Macho" Camacho (Héctor Luis Camacho Matías, 1962–2012) became the first Puerto Rican to win

Héctor "Macho" Camacho

the World Boxing Council and World Boxing Organization championships in the lightweight division. He went on to win championships in three weight classes: WBC super featherweight, WBC lightweight, and WBO junior welterweight.

Sources: Tardiff and Mabunda, *Dictionary of Hispanic Biography*, p. 156.

1989 ♦ Panamanian boxer Roberto Durán (1951–) became the first Latino boxer in history to have held championship titles in four different weight divisions: lightweight, welterweight, junior middleweight, and middleweight. In 1989 at the age of 37, Durán won his last title in the World Boxing Council middleweight division.

Roberto Durán

Sources: Tardiff and Mabunda, *Dictionary of Hispanic Biography*, pp. 299–300.

1992 ♦ Oscar de la Hoya (1973–) became the only boxer to win a gold medal for the United States in the Summer Olympics, held in Barcelona. In 1995, de la Hoya became the first Mexican American boxer to win the International Boxing Federation Lightweight Championship. Born in Los Angeles in 1973, de la Hoya went on to win 11 professional world titles in six weight classes, including the lineal championship in three weight classes. De la Hoya was *The Ring* magazine's top-rated fighter in the world in 1997 and 1998. In 2002, de la Hoya became the first Mexican American to own a firm promoting combat sports: Golden Boy Promotions. He was one of the few boxers in history to take on promotional responsibilities while still active. In 2018, he also began promoting MMA matches.

Sources: Hispanic, October 1995, pp. 28–32.

1995 ♦ Rose Quiñones Trentman became the first woman to serve as a New York State Boxing Commissioner. Of Puerto Rican origin, Trentman was also a bilingual teacher in the New York City schools.

Sources: Hispanic, April 1995, pp. 8–9.

2012 ♦ Marlen Esparza (1989–) became the first American woman to win an Olympic medal for boxing; she won a bronze medal the year women's boxing was admitted to the Olympics in London. A native of Pasadena, Texas, Esparza went on to

Marlen Esparza

a professional boxing career and became the WBC, WBO, WBA, and *The Ring* female world flyweight champion. Esparza's professional record stands at 14 wins, two losses.

Sources: "Gabriela Alaniz Defeats Marlen Esparza by Split Decision, Wins Ring Lightweight Championship," *The Ring*: https://www.ringtv.com/current-issue/.

2014 ♦ Bonnie Canino (1962–), nicknamed "The Cobra," was the first Latina inducted into the International Women's Boxing Hall of Fame. She was one of seven initial inductees. She was originally a kickboxer, in large part because there were so few opportunities for women in the regular boxing ring. As a kickboxer, she fought some of the leading contenders, including Lisa Howarth, Bridgett Riley, Kathy Long, and Lucia Rijker, achieving a record of 27–4 and winning two world championships. She was inducted into the Martial Arts Hall of Fame in 2004 and the Broward County, Florida, Sports Hall of Fame in 2008.

As a professional boxer, her record was 11–4. Following her boxing career, Canino established a karate and boxing gym in Dania Beach, Florida, where she has trained two world title holders. She is a two-time Team USA coach for the World Games, and six times since 2006, she has been the promoter for the Women's National Golden Gloves championships.

Sources: "Bonnie Canino 2019 IWBHF Inductee," International Women's Boxing Hall of Fame: https://www.iwbhf.com/photosinductees/canino.htm.

2023 ♦ Mexican boxer Santos Saúl Álvarez "Canelo" Barragán (1990–) made the *Forbes* list of the highest-paid athletes in the world for 2019, 2022, and 2023. Canelo holds multiple world championships in four weight classes from light middleweight to light heavyweight. In May 2024, he defended his WBA (Super), WBC, IBF, WBO, and *The Ring* super middleweight titles against Jaime Munguía in Las Vegas for one of the largest pay-per-view audiences of all time. As of 2024, his record stood at 69 wins and two losses, with 39 knockouts.

Canelo Barragán

Sources: "Saul Alvarez," BoxRec: https://boxrec.com/en/proboxer/348759.

BREAKING

2014 ♦ Victor Montalvo (1995–) became the first of two male athletes to make the Olympic Breaking (also known as breakdancing) Team the first year it became an Olympic sport. Montalvo, also known as B-Boy Victor, is the holder of two world titles in breaking.

Sources: Shinn, Peggy, "The History of Breaking," Team USA: https://www.teamusa.com/news/2023/november/04/the-history-of-breaking.

CLIMBING

2024 ♦ At the Paris Olympics, Natalia Grossman (2001–) became the first Latina climber for Team USA. Born in Santa Cruz, California, of Mexican heritage, she moved with her family at the age of 15 to Boulder to pursue her climbing. She is a graduate of the University of Colorado in Boulder. Her prior credits include winning the gold medal at the 2023 Pan American Games and won gold and silver at the 2021 IFSC Climbing World Championships. In 2019, she also was undefeated in the bouldering National Cup Series and in 2020 won the USA Climbing: Bouldering Open National Championship.

Natalia Grossman

Sources: Hudges, Susie, "Natalia Grossman Is Making History as Team USA's First Latina Climber," *PS*: https://www.popsugar.com/fitness/natalia-grossman-rock-climbing-latina-representation-49352729.

CYCLING

1995 ♦ Mariano Friedrick became the first Latino cyclist to win a bronze medal in the world championships. His grandfather was a three-time national cycling champion in Argentina.

Sources: Hispanic Business, May 1996, p. 28.

1995 ♦ David "Tinker" Juárez (1961–), also known as the "Hollifield Flash" after a BMX track, became the first U.S. Latino to win a gold medal in cycling at the Pan American Games. In 1989, the Californian turned pro in mountain bike racing.

Sources: Hispanic Business, May 1996, p. 28.

2000 ♦ Cyclist Freddie Rodríguez (1973–), known as "Fast Freddie," won the National Road Championship. He went on to win it again in 2001, 2004, and 2013. In 2004, he also won the Giro d'Italia.

Sources: "Full Circle: 'Fast' Freddie Ends Career Where It Began,"" Velo: https://velo.outsideonline.com/road/full-circle-fast-freddie-ends-career-where-it-began/.

FENCING

1932 ♦ The first Latino athletes to make the U.S. Olympic team were fencer Miguel A. de Capriles (1906–1981) and triple jumper Roland Lee Romero (1914–1975). Capriles also became the first U.S. Latino to win a medal (bronze) in those games. He won another bronze in the 1948 Olympics.

Sources: Kanellos, *Chronology of Hispanic American History*, p. 201.

1951 ♦ Fencer Miguel A. de Capriles (1906–1981) became the first U.S. Hispanic to represent the United States in the Pan American Games. Capriles was born in Mexico and came to the United States at the age of 13. He made the U.S. Olympic team three times: in 1932, 1948, and 1951.

Sources: Kanellos, *Chronology of Hispanic American History*, p. 201.

1962 ♦ Argentina-born fencer Hugo M. Castello (1914–1994) became the coach of the first U.S. Olympic fencing training camp. In 1935 and 1936, he had been National Intercollegiate Foil Champion. In 1936, he competed with the U.S. Olympic team. From 1946 to 1975, he served as fencing coach at New York University, where he became one of a select number of coaches to have won at least 10 national collegiate team fencing championships. Only five other NCAA coaches in all sports have won 10 national team titles. Castello is a member of the Helms Sports Hall of Fame.

Sources: "Hugo Castello, Coach at N.Y.U., Dies at 79," *New York Times*, 29 March 1994.

1972 ♦ Fencer Alfonso Morales (1937–) became the first Latino athlete to compete four times in the Olympics: in 1960, 1964, 1968, and 1972.

Sources: Kanellos, *Chronology of Hispanic American History*, p. 258.

1989 ♦ Natalia Del Loretto Clovis (born Natalia Lederer, 1943–) became the first Latina fencer to win the U.S. national championship in epee. The Cuban-born Clovis had studied fencing and had belonged to the Cuban Professional Club before she immigrated to the United States. Over the years, she participated on numerous U.S. national teams in international championships and Olympic Games. In 1972, she won the Pacific Coast Women's Foil Championship, the Grand International Women's Foil Championship, and the Espada de Honor Trophy. In 1989, she won the gold medal in women's epee at the U.S. national championship.

Sources: "Natalia Clovis," Olympedia: https://www.olympedia.org/athletes/20993.

FLYING

1956 ♦ Korean War ace Manuel J. Fernández (1925–1980) set a new world record for air speed, flying at 666.661 miles per hour in his F-IOOC Super Sabre at the Bendix Trophy Race in September 1956.

Sources: Secretary of Defense, *Hispanics in America's Defense*, p. 35.

FOOTBALL

1967 ♦ Mexican American Thomas Jesse Fears (1922–2000) became the first Latino to serve as a head coach in the National Football League (1967–1970). Born in Guadalajara, Mexico, to a Mexican mother and an Anglo-American father, Fears was a star Los Angeles Rams wide receiver from 1948 to 1956, when he was a three-time reception leader and an All-Pro; he played on three NFL championship teams: 1951, 1962, and 1965. In 2011, Fears was inducted into the Pro Football Hall of Fame.

Thomas Jesse Fears

Sources: "Tom Fears," Pro Football Hall of Fame: https://web.archive.org/web/20111029014225/http://www.profootballhof.com/hof/member.aspx?PlayerId=66.

Steve Van Buren

1968 ♦ Honduras-born Steve Van Buren (1920–2012), a powerful running back for the Philadelphia Eagles (1944–1951), was the first Latino elected to the Pro Football Hall of Fame.

In eight NFL seasons, he won four NFL rushing titles. During the short seasons back then, he was the first NFL player to score more than 10 touchdowns and the first to have multiple 1,000-yard rushing seasons.

Sources: "Steve Van Buren, Philadelphia Eagles Player, Pro Football Hall of Fame Inductee," *Washington Post*, 24 August 2012.

Jim Plunkett

1970 ♦ Stanford University football quarterback Jim Plunkett (1947–) became the first Latino Heisman Trophy winner. Of German, Irish, and Mexican ancestry, Plunkett was born and raised in San Jose, California, and after college went on to become a record-breaking quarterback for the Boston (now New England) Patriots and the San Francisco 49ers.

Sources: Meier and Rivera, *Dictionary of Mexican American History*, p. 279.

1971 ♦ Jim Plunkett (1947–) became the first Latino to start as quarterback in the National Football League, and in his debut year, he became Rookie of the Year while playing for the Boston (now New England) Patriots, passing for 2,158 yards and 19 touchdowns.

Sources: Kanellos, *Latino Almanac*, pp. 503, 513.

Manny Fernández

1973 ♦ Manuel José "Manny" Fernández (1946–) received the highest distinction of any Hispanic in football: he was named to the All-Time Greatest Super Bowl All-Star Team. Fernández played on one of professional football's winningest teams, the Miami Dolphins, from 1968 to 1977. Fernández was voted the Dolphins's most valuable defensive lineman for six consecutive years from 1968 to 1973. He helped the Dolphins win two Super Bowls, in 1972 and 1973, and become the only undefeated team in National Football League history in 1973. Fernández may also be the only Latino football player to have started in three Super Bowls.

Sources: Tardiff and Mabunda, *Dictionary of Hispanic Biography*, p. 332.

Tom Flores

1978 ♦ Thomas Flores (1937–) was the second Latino to be named coach of a professional football team in the United States. He succeeded John Madden to the post for the Oakland Raiders in 1978 and was officially named in 1979. Flores, born on March 21, 1937, in Fresno, California, into a family of Mexican American farm workers, went on to become one of the most successful coaches in the history of the National Football League. He led the Raiders to two Super Bowl championships.

Sources: Kanellos, *Latino Almanac*, pp. 497, 503, 508.

1989 ♦ Outstanding coach of professional football Thomas Flores (1937–) became the first Latino president and general manager of an NFL team: the Seattle Seahawks. His was the highest rank ever attained by a Latino in professional sports in the United States.

Sources: Kanellos, *Latino Almanac*, pp. 497, 503, 508.

Anthony Muñoz

1991 ♦ Professional football player Anthony Muñoz (1958–) became the first Latino player to be named Offensive Lineman of the Year by the American Football Conference. Also, for several years, he held the unofficial title of the NFL's strongest man.

Sources: Tardiff and Mabunda, *Dictionary of Hispanic Biography*, p. 591.

Anthony David González

2019 ♦ Mexican American Anthony David González (1976–), considered one of the greatest tight ends of all time, was inducted into the Pro Football Hall of Fame. Starting in 1997, González played 12 seasons for the Kansas City Chiefs and another five for the Atlanta Falcons. González holds the record for receiving yards (15,127) and receptions by a tight end (916).

Sources: Lewis, Edward, "Tony Gonzalez to be inducted into Chiefs Hall of Fame," *Around the NFL*: https://web.archive.org/web/20180127015145/http://www.nfl.com/news/story/0ap3000000911162/article/tony-gonzalez-to-be-inducted-into-chiefs-hall-of-fame.

Chi Chi Rodríguez

GOLF

1963 ♦ Juan "Chi Chi" Rodríguez (1935–2024) became the first Puerto Rican and first Latino golfer to win the Denver Open. He went on to become one of golfing's all-time greats, also being the first Latino to win in more than a decade of open golfing competitions. Born in Rio Piedras, Puerto Rico, in 1935, Rodríguez came from an extremely impoverished family and found his way into golf as a caddy on the links that served Puerto Rico's booming tourism. His is one of the most famous Latino "rags to riches through sports" tales: his career earnings surpassed the $3 million mark. He contributed financially to numerous charities and to the Chi Chi Rodríguez Youth Foundation in Clearwater, Florida. Included among the important tournaments he won were the Denver Open (1963), the Lucky Strike International Open (1964), the Western Open (1964), the Dorado Pro-Am (1965), the Texas Open (1967), and the Tallahassee Open (1979). As a member of the Senior Professional Golf Association (PGA) Tour, he won numerous tournaments, including the Silver Pages Classic (1987), the GTE Northwest Classic (1987), the Sunwest Senior Classic (1990), and the Murata Reunion Pro-Am (1991).

Sources: Kanellos, *Chronology of Hispanic American History*, p. 207.

1968 ♦ Lee Treviño (1939–) became the first Mexican American to win a major professional golf championship at the U.S. Open, and he became the first player in history to shoot all four rounds of the event under par.

Lee Treviño

Born in Dallas, Texas, to a cleaning lady and raised by her and her father, a gravedigger, Treviño got involved in golf because their four-room farmhouse was located at the back of the Glen Lakes Country Club fairways. As a boy, Treviño studied the form of golfers on the course from his own backyard. He dropped out of school in the seventh grade and made his way into what was then an exclusively Anglo rich man's sport by working as a caddy and greenskeeper.

In 1966, Treviño became a professional golfer and achieved his first major victory in 1968 at the U.S. Open. In 1970, he was the leading money-winner on the Professional Golf Association (PGA) Tour. In 1971, Treviño won the U.S. Open for a second time, won five tournaments between April and July, and also won the British Open in that year and again in 1972. In 1971, Treviño became the first Hispanic ever named PGA Player of the Year, Associated Press Athlete of the Year, and *Sports Illustrated* Sportsman of the Year. After that, he won the 1974 PGA again, among many other tournaments. He was also awarded the Vardon Trophy for the fewest strokes per round (69.73 for 82 rounds), the lowest since Sam Snead in 1958. Treviño retired from the PGA Tour in 1985 with 30 victories and a total career earnings of more than $3 million (third highest). Treviño was elected to the Texas Sports, American Golf, and World Golf Halls of Fame.

Sources: Kanellos, *Chronology of Hispanic American History*, pp. 211, 257.

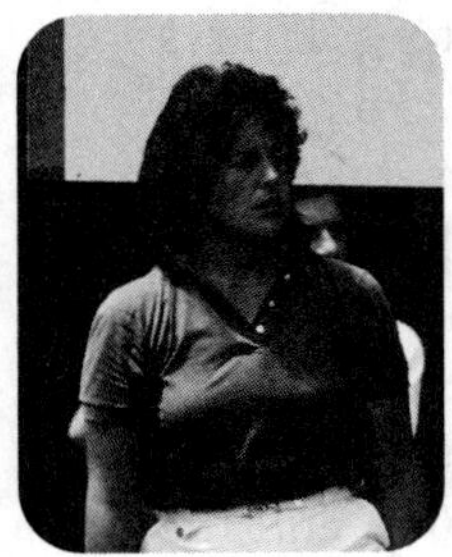

Nancy López

1978 ♦ Nancy López (1957–) became the first Hispanic to win the Ladies' Professional Golf Association Tournament. One of the greatest women's golf champions of all time, López was born in 1957 to Mexican American parents in Torrance, California. She was raised in Roswell, New Mexico, and rose to become one of the youngest women golfers to experience professional success. She learned golf from her father, and by the age of 11, she was already beating him. López won the New Mexico Women's Open when she was only 12. In high school, she was the only female member of the golf team, and as an 18-year-old senior, she placed second in the U.S. Women's Open. In 1978, during López's first full season as a pro, she won nine tournaments, including the Ladies' Professional Golf Association (LPGA). She was named Rookie of the Year, Player of the Year, and Female Athlete of the Year; she also won the Vare Trophy. Also in 1978, she set a new record for earnings by a rookie, $189,813. In 1983, López took a break from her career when she became the mother of Ashley Marie, the child of her marriage to baseball star Ray Knight. Two months after having Ashley, López began touring again, and by 1987, she had won 35 tournaments and qualified to become the 11th member of the Ladies' Professional Golf Association Hall of Fame; in all, López had 48 LPGA tournament victories. López's most outstanding year was 1985, when she won five tournaments and finished in the top 10 at 25 others; that year, she also won the LPGA title again. Through 1987, she had earned more than $2 million.

Sources: Telgen and Kamp, *Latinas! Women of Achievement*, pp. 209–212.

Lorena Ochoa Reyes

2017 ♦ Known as the best Latin American golfer of all time, Lorena Ochoa Reyes (1981–) was inducted into the World Golf Hall of Fame. Previously, Ochoa Reyes had received the 2003 Nancy Lopez Golf Achievement Award for the world's most outstanding female amateur golfer. Having started her amateur career in her birthplace, Guadalajara, Mexico, Ochoa Reyes was an outstanding member of the championship University of Arizona team, where during her second year, she set an NCAA record with seven consecutive victories in her first seven events. She graduated and became a professional, competing in the LPGA from 2003 to 2010, the year of her retirement. She was a Golf Writers Association of America Female Player of the Year in 2006, 2007, and 2008.

Sources: Shapiro, Leonard. "Say Hello to the Ochoa Era," *Washington Post*, 27 April 2007.

Abraham Ancer

2018 ♦ Mexican American golfer Abraham Ancer (1991–) was the first U.S. Latino to win the Emirates Australian Open. In 2021, he went on to win the 2021 WGC-FedEx St. Jude Invitational on the PGA Tour. Born in McAllen, Texas, Ancer is currently ranked 20th in the world, the highest ranked and the one earning the most cash prizes of all U.S.-born Latinos.

Sources: Lavner, Ryan. "Abraham Ancer Officially Announces Move to LIV Golf," NBC Sports: Golf: https://www.nbcsports.com/golf/news/abraham-ancer-announces-move-liv-golf.

GYMNASTICS

2022 ♦ Ruben Padilla (2001–) was the first Latino to win the gold medal in the double mini trampoline at the Trampoline Gymnastics World Championship. He also won a silver medal in the all-around team and a bronze medal in the double mini team event. The Californian started doing gymnastics when he was seven years old. In spite of having broken bones and disc problems in this demanding sport over the last two decades, he achieved these remarkable wins. He also went on to win gold medals in the double mini and team trampoline World Championships in Birmingham in 2023.

Sources: "Ruben Padilla," Trampoline & Tumbling National Team: https://members.usagym.org/pages/athletes/nationalTeamTT.html?id=266189.

Hezly Rivera

2024 ♦ Hezly Rivera (2008–) became the youngest member of Team USA at the Paris Olympics, joining the greatest all-time gymnast Simone Biles and other senior gymnasts. Born in Hackensack, New Jersey, to Dominican parents, the family moved to Texas for her training, and she attends high school online in order to devote herself to her sport. In 2022, she was second in the Junior World Artistic Gymnastics Championships, and in 2024, she was third in all-around at Winter Cup and tied for first on beam. Again in 2023, she was sixth in all-around at the U.S. National Gymnastics Championships and fifth in all-around at Olympic trials but tied for first on beam.

Sources: Galván, Astrid. "Gymnast Hezly Rivera Is the Youngest U.S. Athlete to Qualify for Paris Olympics," *Axios*, 1 July 2024: https://www.axios.com/2024/07/01/hezly-rivera-olympics-gymnastics.

HANDBALL

1985 ♦ Los Angeles native Sandra Lynn de la Riva-Baza (1961–), the daughter of Mexican immigrant parents, became the first Latina U.S. national champion in team handball. Beginning in the late 1970s, de la Riva-Baza played team handball, making the U.S. national team for nine years, including participating in the 1984 and 1988 Olympics. De la Riva-Baza was U.S. national champion in 1985 and 1986 and served as team captain in the 1986 world championships. She won gold medals at the 1987 U.S. Cup and the Pan American Games. At the 1988 U.S. national championships, she was selected Most Valuable Player. Beginning in 1994, de la Riva-Baza served as vice president of the U.S. Team Handball Foundation. She is the first Latina to accomplish all of these firsts in handball.

Sources: "Sandra de la Riva," Olympedia: https://www.olympedia.org/athletes/32929.

HORSE RACING

1974 ♦ Puerto Rican jockey Angel Cordero (1942–) won the Kentucky Derby to become the first Latino to win one of the races of the Triple Crown. Cordero went on to win the Derby again in 1976 and 1985. He also won the Belmont Stakes in 1976 and the Preakness Stakes in 1980 and 1984. In 1982, he was named Jockey of the Year.

Sources: Kanellos, *The Hispanic American Almanac*, p. 705.

1988 ♦ Puerto Rican jockey Angel Cordero (1942–) became the first Puerto Rican to be inducted into the Thoroughbred Racing Hall of Fame. In his 31-year career, Cordero won more than 7,000 races, including three Kentucky Derbies.

Sources: Tardiff and Mabunda, *Dictionary of Hispanic Biography*, p. 240.

2012 ♦ Puerto Rican jockey John Velásquez (1971–) was inducted into the Horse Racing Hall of Fame as one of the winningest jockeys of all time. A three-time Classic winner and two-time Eclipse Award winner, Velázquez had won a total of 26 riding titles at New York tracks. He holds the record for most wins of all time and most wins in one afternoon (6) at Saratoga. His Belmont victory with Rags to Riches marked the first time in 102 years that a filly was victorious in the final leg of the Triple Crown. He has accomplished 5,308 wins and accrued $324,066,825 in career earnings.

John Velásquez

Sources: "John Velásquez," ESPN: https://www.espn.com/blog/onenacion/post/_/id/541/latino-jockeys-in-the-hall-of-fame.

Víctor Espinoza

2015 ♦ Mexican Víctor Espinoza became the first Latino jockey to win horse racing's vaunted Triple Crown: riding American Pharoah, he won the Kentucky Derby, the Preakness Stakes, and the Belmont Stakes. He was also the oldest jockey to ever win the Triple Crown. In October, Espinoza rode American Pharoah to victory in the Breeder's Cup Classic, making him the first jockey ever to win the Grand Slam of four major thoroughbred races in one year.

Sources: Layden, Tim, "Victor and Jose Espinoza Share a Career but Lead Two Different Lives," *Sports Illustrated*, 15 May 2014.

JUDO

1988 ♦ René Capo (1961–2009) became the first Latino to compete on the Olympic men's judo team; he made the team for the 1988 and 1996 Summer Olympics. Capo was born in Pinal del Río, Cuba, in 1961 and had studied judo since the age of 6. Capo was ranked number one in the United States in his weight class of 95 kilos (210 pounds). He was a business management graduate of the University of Minnesota.

Sources: Hispanic Business, May 1996, p. 27.

1996 ♦ Celita Schultz (1968–) became the first Latina to make the U.S. Women's Olympic Judo Team and the first to be elected captain of the team. Born in Houston, Texas, in 1968, Schultz had been competing in judo since the age of 7. Schultz competed in the Summer Olympics of 1996, 2000, and 2004. She is a graduate in art from Yale University.

Sources: Hispanic Business, May 1996, p. 28.

2023 ♦ María Celia Laborde (1990–) became the first Latina and only the third Team USA judo athlete in history to win a medal at the Judo World Masters competition. A world-class judoka originally competing and winning competitions for Cuba since her senior World Judo Championship medal in 2014, Laborde moved to the United States in 2022 and qualified for Team USA for the Paris Olympics in 2024.

Sources: Jomantas, Nicole, "Maria Laborde Makes History with Silver at World Judo Masters," USA Judo: https://www.usajudo.com/news/2023/august/04/World-Masters-Day-1-Results.

OLYMPICS (GENERAL)

2024 ♦ Team USA at the Paris Olympics had the highest representation of Latino athletes in history. They were drawn from throughout the United States; notably, some athletes residing or training in the United States chose to represent their home countries, as was the case of Puerto Ricans from the archipelago and Mexicans. For the most part, Latinos winning medals for individual performances were scarce. However, many Latina women won gold and silver medals as part of team sports, such as basketball, artistic swimming, and soccer. The roster of Latinos on Team USA included Anita Alvarez (artistic swimming), Devin Booker (basketball, gold medal), Shaine Casas (swimming), Jordan Delacruz (weightlifting), Angelica Delgado (judo), Mariah Durán (skateboarding), Marcos Girón (tennis), Catalina Gnoriega (archery), Natalia Grossman (sport climbing), María Laborde (judo), Alyssa Mendoza (boxing), Victor Montalvo (breaking), Jennifer Muciño-Fernández (archery), Kevin Paredes (soccer), Daniella Ramírez (artistic swimming, silver medal), Hezly Rivera (gymnastics team, gold medal), and Diana Taurasi (basketball, gold medal).

Sources: Kanellos, Nicolás, my personal analysis of the 2024 Olympic Games.

RODEO

1883 ♦ One of the first champion riders, Mexican *vaquero* Antonio Esquivel (1862–1938), performed in Buffalo Bill Cody's "Wild West Show" intermittently from 1883 to 1905.

Sources: Slatta, *Cowboys of the Americas*, p. 146.

Vicente Oropeza

1900 ♦ The first cowboy to win the World Championship of Trick and Fancy Roping was Vicente Oropeza (1858–1923), a famous Mexican roper who had made his debut in competition in the United States in 1891 and became a star of Buffalo Bill Cody's touring "Wild West Show" for 16 years. He is credited with having introduced trick and fancy roping into the United States and was the most influential Latino rodeo performer of all time. Oropeza was inducted into the National Rodeo Hall of Fame in 1975.

Sources: LeCompte, Mary Lou, "The Hispanic Influence on the History of Rodeo," *Journal of Sports History*, 12 (Spring 1985), pp. 21–38.

1965 ♦ Ramón Ahumado, known as "*El Charro Plateado*" (The Silver-Plated Cowboy), was the first known Mexican rodeo champion in the United States. He was elected posthumously to the National Cowboy Hall of Fame. A real cowboy who punched cattle on the Mexican ranches of Arizona in the 1880s and participated in rodeo-type events, Ahumado was a dazzling horseman.

Sources: Sheridan, *Los Tucsonenses*, p. 98.

1991 ♦ Championship calf roper Juan Salinas (1901–1995) was inducted into the National Rodeo Hall of Fame. The Texas rancher won numerous awards on the national rodeo circuit and was a national finalist at Madison Square Garden every year from 1936 through 1946.

Sources: "Juan Salinas," National Rodeo Hall of Fame: https://nationalcowboymuseum.org/collections/awards/rodeo-hall-of-fame/inductees/5199/.

1979: National Rodeo Hall of Famer Leandro Jáuregui

Lifelong rancher and horse trainer Leandro "Andy" Jáuregui (1903–1990) was inducted into the National Rodeo Hall of Fame in 1979. During his career, he won numerous rodeo prizes, including the Steer Roper Championship in 1931 and the Team Roper Championship in 1934. So renowned was his prowess as a horseman, including breaking broncs, that he worked as a double in Hollywood films for such actors as Tom Mix and Joel McCrea. *Sources:* "Andy Jauregui," National Rodeo Hall of Fame: https://nationalcowboymuseum.org/collections/awards/rodeo-hall-of-fame/inductees/5102/.

2013 ♦ World championship bull rider John Quintana (1947–2013) of Idaho was inducted into the National Rodeo Hall of Fame. He made the National Finals Rodeo for six consecutive years from 1969 through 1974 and won the 1972 world bull-riding championship. He twice set world records for the highest-marked bull ride, scoring 94 points on Minick Rodeo Company's V-61 and 96 points at the 1974 Helldorado Days Rodeo in Las Vegas.

Sources: "John Quintana," National Rodeo Hall of Fame: https://nationalcowboymuseum.org/collections/awards/rodeo-hall-of-fame/inductees/5383/.

2023 ♦ Bareback, bull riding, and team roping champion J. C. Trujillo (1948–) was inducted into the National Rodeo Hall of Fame. After winning junior rodeo accolades, Trujillo won the 1968 Intercollegiate Bareback Championship as a member of the Arizona State University rodeo team. He went on to win numerous prizes, including the World Championship Bareback in 1981. Among the rodeos where he took first-place prizes were Prescott five times, Salinas four times, Ogden three times, the Pendleton Round-Up twice, and Calgary once. Trujillo was inducted into the Pro Rodeo Hall of Fame in 1994.

Sources: "J.C. Trujillo," National Rodeo Hall of Fame: https://nationalcowboymuseum.org/collections/awards/rodeo-hall-of-fame/inductees/j-c-trujillo/.

SKATING

1956 ♦ Catherine Machado (1936–) became the first U.S. Latino athlete ever to compete on the U.S. Winter Olympics team. She was the senior women's figure skating champion. She finished eighth in overall competition in women's singles.

Sources: Kanellos, *Chronology of Hispanic American History*, pp. 238–239.

1958 ♦ Catherine Machado (1936–) became the first Latino to win the World Professional Figure Skating Championship, held in England. After competing in the Olympics, Machado developed a career with the Ice Capades but also continued to compete professionally.

Sources: Kanellos, *Chronology of Hispanic American History*, pp. 238–239.

Rudy Galindo

1987 ♦ Rudy Galindo (1969–) became the first Latino to win the World Junior Championship in men's figure skating. He went on to win, as a single skater, the 1996 U.S. National Championship, the 1987 World Junior Championship, and the 1996 World Bronze medal; as a pairs skater, he competed with Kristi Yamaguchi and won the 1988 World Junior Championship and the 1989 and 1990 U.S. National Championship. Born to Mexican American parents in San Jose and educated in San Jose public schools, Galindo began skating at the age of 8. When he and his sister became outstanding skaters, their truck-driving father, Jess Galindo, worked overtime for many years to finance the lessons and the travel that his children needed to compete regionally and nationally. Beginning in 1987, when Rudy Galindo won the World Junior Championship and the Central Pacific Senior Championship, he became a leading figure in national and world competitions. Galindo was singles champion in the Pacific Coast Senior competition in 1992, 1993, 1994, and 1995. In March 1996, Galindo won first place in singles figure skating at the National Senior Figure Skating championship. Galindo's international titles include first place in the Vienna Cup in 1994 as well as second place in the Prague Skate in 1993. In 1996, he placed third in the World Figure Skating Championships.

Sources: "Edge of a Dream," *Time*, 18 March 1996.

SOCCER

Marcelo Balboa

1998 ♦ The son of immigrants from Argentina, Marcelo Balboa (1967–) became one of only three American players—Tab Ramos and Eric Wynalda were the other two—to play in three World Cups. Balboa was the first U.S-born Latino to play on the U.S. Men's National Team. In 2000, Balboa ended his career on the U.S. national team with 128 caps and 13 goals. Just before becoming a professional, Balboa was named the 1988 WSA MVP. He was U.S. Soccer Athlete of the Year in 1992 and 1994. From there, he went on to have an outstanding career with various pro teams. In 2005, he was made the MLS All-Time Best XI and was elected to the National Soccer Hall of Fame. After his career as a player, he became a sportscaster.

Sources: "Marcelo Balboa 2005 Inductee," National Soccer Hall of Fame: https://www.nationalsoccerhof.com/players/marcelo-balboa.html.

2008 ♦ Amy Rodríguez (1987–) won a gold medal at the Summer Olympics. The granddaughter of Cuban refugees, Rodríguez was the first pick in the 2009 Women's Professional Soccer Draft. In 2011, she played on the U.S. national team for the FIFA Women's World Cup and in 2012 competed in the Olympics in London, where she received her second gold medal. After retiring as a player in 2022, Rodríguez became the head coach of the professional Utah Royals FC.

Amy Rodríguez

Sources: Holt, Chandler, "Amy Rodriguez to Coach Utah Royals FC in 2024 NWSL Season," KSL Sports: https://kslsports.com/500588/amy-rodriguez-to-coach-utah-royals-fc-in-2024-nwsl-season/.

SOFTBALL

1996 ♦ The star pitcher for the first gold medal-winning women's softball team in the Summer Olympics was Lisa Fernández (1971–). Like her teammates, Fernández won her gold medal the same year that softball was admitted as an official Olympic sport. Born in Lakewood, California, in 1971, Fernández is the daughter of Cuban immigrant parents who played baseball and softball. She is considered among the greatest women softball players ever. In high school, she threw 69 shutouts and in college was a four-time All-American for the University of California at Los Angeles. As a pitcher, she helped UCLA win two National Collegiate Athletic Association Women's College World Series. Fernández was also an outstanding batter, leading the nation with a .510 average in 1993 and batting .382 during her college career. She holds the records for singles (225), runs scored (142), walks (65), hits (287), pitching wins (93), career percentage (.93), and no-hitters (11). Fernández pitched winning games in three consecutive Olympics and won gold medals in each as a member of Team USA: 1996, 2000, and 2004. In 2023, she was inducted into the ASA/USA Softball National Hall of Fame.

Lisa Fernández

Sources: Hispanic Business, May 1996, p. 8.

Jessica Mendoza

2011 ♦ Jessica Mendoza (1980–), professional fastpitch softball outfielder, was named Player of the Year. She also ranked in the top 10 for career batting average and slugging percentage. Born and raised as a second-generation Mexican American in Camarillo, California, Mendoza was a two-time Olympic softball team medal winner: gold in 2004 and silver in 2008. She also won gold at the Pan American Games in 2003 and 2007. After her athletic career, she became a color analyst for ESPN's *Sunday Night Baseball.* In 2015, she became the first female commentator for a Major League Baseball game in ESPN history, and by 2015, she became a full-time broadcaster for ESPN. In 2019, she had a career change, becoming a senior advisor to the general manager of the New York Mets. In 2020, Mendoza became the first female World Series analyst on any national broadcast platform while working at ESPN.

Sources: "Jessica Mendoza Signs Extension with ESPN, Resigns from Mets Adviser Role," ESPN, 7 February 2020: https://www.espn.com/mlb/story/_/id/28653997/jessica-mendoza-signs-extension-espn-resigns-mets-adviser-role.

STOCK CAR RACING

2021 ♦ Cuban American driver Aric Almirola (1984–) is the winningest Latino stock car racer in history. Among his accomplishments are winning the 2014 Coke Zero 400, the 2018 1000Bulbs.com 500, and the 2021 and 2023 Bluegreen Vacations Duel. In 2021, he won the NASCAR All-Star Race. In 2022, he retired from full-time racing but continued to race part-time. As recently as 2024, he earned a bonus of $100,000 for winning the first Dash 4 Cash race of the season.

Aric Almirola

Sources: "Aric Almirola Wins Inaugural Xfinity Series Race at Sonoma," NASCAR News: https://www.nascar.com/news-media/2023/06/10/aric-almirola-wins-inaugural-xfinity-series-race-at-sonoma/.

Daniel Suárez

2022 ♦ Mexican-born Daniel Suárez (1992–) became the first Latino driver to win a Cup Series race by winning at Sonoma Raceway in 2022. He repeated this in 2024 with a win at the Atlanta Motor Speedway. In 2015, he won the Sunoco Rookie of the Year Award and the next year won the series championship.

Sources: "Daniel Suárez," NASCAR: https://www.nascar.com/drivers/daniel-suarez.

SWIMMING AND DIVING

1964 ♦ At the Tokyo Olympics, Donna de Varona (1947–) became the first U.S. Latino to win a gold medal in swimming; she actually won two gold

Donna de Varona

medals, one in the 400-meter individual medley and one in the 4x100 freestyle. That same year, de Varona was named Most Outstanding Female Athlete in the World by both the Associated Press and United Press International. Donna de Varona was inducted into the International Swimming Hall of Fame and the San Francisco Bay Area Hall of Fame. She was a U.S. Olympic Hall of Famer and received the Olympic Order, the highest honor presented by the International Olympic Committee. In 1999, *Sports Illustrated for Women* named her as one of the "100 Greatest Athletes." In subsequent years, de Varona was an activist for youth sports and fitness and served five terms on the President's Council on Physical Fitness and Sports; she was appointed to presidential commissions by five presidents.

Sources: "Donna de Varona," National Women's Hall of Fame: https://www.womenofthehall.org/inductee/donna-de-varona/.

1965 ♦ Olympic gold medal swimmer Donna de Varona (1947–) became the youngest person (at 18 years old) and the first woman to be a sportscaster on network television. She continued in that career, often appearing as host and cohost for Olympic coverage. In addition, de Varona was one of the founders of the Women's Sports Foundation.

Sources: "Donna de Varona," National Women's Hall of Fame: https://www.womenofthehall.org/inductee/donna-de-varona/.

Tracy Ruiz-Conforto

1983 ♦ Swimmer Tracy Ruiz-Conforto (1963–) was the first U.S. Latina to win the gold in the Pan American Games in 1983, and she won again in 1987. In addition, she was the second U.S. Latina to win a gold medal in swimming at the Summer Olympics in 1984. In 1988, she won a silver medal in the Olympics. Ruiz-Conforto was inducted into the International Swimming Hall of Fame in 1993.

Sources: Faber, Nancy, "Candy Costie and Tracie Ruiz Are at Their Most Buoyant When They Get That Synching Feeling," *People*, 16 April 1984.

1985 ♦ Wendy Lucero-Schayes (1963–) became the first Latina diver to win the National Collegiate Athletic Association 1-meter diving championship; she also won the national title in the Phillips 66 National Championships in 1984 and 1985. For these years, she was also named Academic All-American for her performance in the classroom. Lucero-Schayes was born on June

26, 1963, the daughter of Don Lucero, the son of a Spanish immigrant, and Shirley Lucero, of Irish descent. In 1987, she also became the first Latina to win the America Cup II championship in 3-meter diving; that year, she also came in first in the U.S. Olympic Festival. She went on to compete in the 1988 Olympics in Seoul, South Korea. Lucero-Schayes was also voted the U.S. Female Diving Athlete of the Year in 1990 and 1991.

Sources: Telgen and Kamp, *Latinas! Women of Achievement*, pp. 219–226.

Dara Torres

2008 ♦ Dara Torres (1967–) became the first swimmer to compete in five Olympic Games (1984, 1988, 1992, 2000, and 2008); in the 2008 Games at the age of 41, she became the oldest swimmer in U.S. Olympic history. At her first Olympic competition in 1984, she won the gold medal in the 400-meter freestyle relay. Over the years, she went on to win 11 more Olympic medals (four gold, four silver, and four bronze). Torres is one of four women to win the most Olympic medals. Five of hers were won at the 2000 Olympics; she was the oldest member of the swim team at the age of 33 and was also a world-record holder in the three events. The daughter of a Cuban immigrant father and American mother who was a model, Torres was born in Los Angeles, California. In 2024, Torres became the head swimming and diving coach at Boston College.

Sources: Weil, Elizabeth, "A Swimmer of a Certain Age," *New York Times Magazine*, 29 June 2008.

Anita Alvarez

2016 ♦ Anita Alvarez (1996–) made Team USA in artistic swimming at the Rio de Janeiro Olympics and again in 2020 at the Tokyo Olympic games. At the age of 14, she had already competed in the 2012 Olympic trials. With the 2024 games, she earned a silver medal on the team in Paris. Born and raised in Amherst, New York, Alvarez was named Artistic USA Synchro Athlete of the Year in 2016 and again in 2019.

Sources: "Alvarez, Anita," USA Artistic Swimming: https://www.usaartisticswim.org/profiles/anita-alvarez-828944.

2024 ♦ Daniella Ramírez (2001–) won a silver medal at the Olympics in synchronized swimming. Ramírez had previously won a silver and a bronze medal at the Pan American Games (2019, 2023) and one silver and three bronze at four World Aquatics Championships (2019, 2022, 2023, 2024).

Born and raised in Miami, Ramírez is a third-generation swimmer of Venezuelan parents. She is a student at the University of California at Los Angeles.

Sources: "Daniella Ramírez," USA Artistic Swimming: https://www.usaartisticswim.org/profiles/daniella-ramirez.

TENNIS

Pancho González

1948 ♦ Richard Alonso "Pancho" González (1928–1995), one of the greatest tennis professionals ever, became the first Latino to win the U.S. singles championship at Forest Hills. He repeated this feat in 1949. After having won the U.S. grass, clay, and indoor championships, González turned pro. From 1954 to 1962, he was world professional singles champion. In 1968, he was named to the International Tennis Hall of Fame.

Sources: Kanellos, *Latino Almanac*, pp. 508–509.

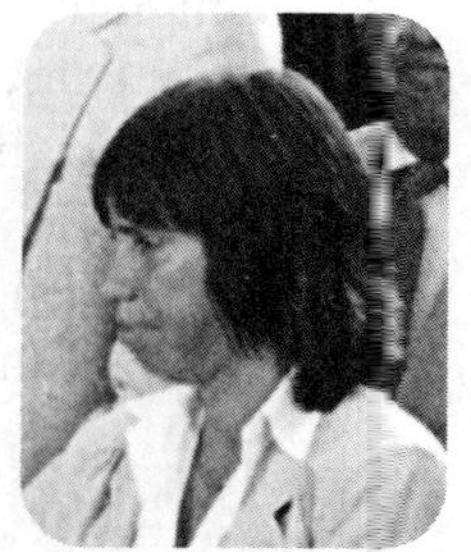

Rosemary Casals

1966 ♦ Rosemary Casals (1948–) teamed with Ian Crookenden to win the U.S. hard-court mixed doubles tennis championship. The daughter of Salvadoran immigrants thus became the first Latina to win the mixed doubles championship. In 1967, Casals joined Billie Jean King to win the doubles tennis championship at Wimbledon. They went on to win it again another four times. King and Casals also won the U.S. Ladies Association doubles championship twice at Forest Hills. In the years that followed, Casals and King won 56 titles in total to become one of the most successful doubles teams in history. Nine times, Casals was rated as number one in doubles by the U.S. Lawn Tennis Association. She was the first U.S.-born Latina to become a top-rated tennis professional.

Sources: Telgen and Kamp, *Latinas! Women of Achievement*, pp. 57–62.

1968 ♦ Richard Alonso "Pancho" González (1928–1995) became the first Latino tennis player to coach the U.S. Davis Cup team. That year, 1968, he also became the first Latino to be named to the International Tennis Hall of Fame.

Sources: Kanellos, *Latino Almanac*, pp. 508–509.

1970 ♦ In response to unfair and unequal prize money for women's professional tennis, Rosemary Casals (1948–) and other women players established the annual Virginia Slims Invitational Women's Tennis Tournament in Houston, Texas, despite the disapproval of the U.S. Ladies Tennis Association. Casals became the first winner of the tournament, taking home the top prize of $1,600. The success of the Virginia Slims Invitational led to Casals becoming a member of the Virginia Slims eight-tournament women's professional circuit, ending any financial problems she had experienced. She went on to become one of the top money winners.

Sources: Telgen and Kamp, *Latinas! Women of Achievement*, p. 61.

1973 ♦ Tennis player Rosemary Casals (1948–) collected the largest prize ever awarded in women's tennis up to that time, defeating Nancy Richey Gunter in the finals of the Family Circle Tournament and winning $30,000.

Sources: Telgen and Kamp, *Latinas! Women of Achievement*, p. 61.

1990 ♦ Dominican American tennis player Mary Joe Fernández (1971–) became the highest-ranked Latina singles tennis player in history. She also ranked fourth in the world from late 1990 to early 1991. In 1991, she became the first Latina and the 33rd woman to earn more than $1 million in prize money.

Mary Joe Fernández

Sources: Tardiff and Mabunda, *Dictionary of Hispanic Biography*, p. 334.

1990 ♦ Tennis player Rosemary Casals (1948–) became the first Latina to win the U.S. Open senior women's championship in doubles, teaming up with Billie Jean King.

Sources: Telgen and Kamp, *Latinas! Women of Achievement*, p. 62.

Gigi Fernández

1991 ♦ Gigi Fernández (1964–) became the first Puerto Rican professional women's tennis player to rank in the top 20 of the world's best players; she is also the first Puerto Rican tennis player to be ranked number one in doubles in the world. Just six years after her professional debut, Fernández ranked 17th in the world. Gigi Fernández was born in San Juan, Puerto Rico, and has been playing tennis since she was eight years old, when her parents enrolled her in tennis lessons. She has played consistently since then and went to Clemson University on a tennis scholarship. During her freshman year, she made the National Collegiate Athletic Association finals. She turned pro in 1985 and by 1991, she was ranked 17th in the world, her highest ranking to date. Fernández is the winner of six Grand Slam women's doubles titles, including the U.S. Open in 1988, 1990, and 1992; the French Open in 1991 and 1992; and Wimbledon in 1992. In 1991, she and her partner, Mary Joe Fernández (no relation), were ranked number one in doubles tennis. In the 1992 Barcelona Olympics, the two Fernándezes won the gold medal, making Gigi the first Puerto Rican to win an Olympic gold.

Sources: Telgen and Kamp, *Latinas! Women of Achievement*, pp. 129–131.

TRACK AND FIELD

1932 ♦ The first Latino athletes to make the U.S. Olympic team were triple jumper Roland Lee Romero (1914–1975) and fencer Miguel A. de Capriles (1906–1981). Capriles became the first Latino of the United States to win a medal, the bronze.

Sources: Kanellos, *Chronology of Hispanic American History*, p. 201.

1979 ♦ Cuban-born marathoner Alberto Bauduy Salazar (1958–) set the U.S. road record of 22:13 for five miles. In 1980, he made the U.S. Olympic team, but that was the year that the United States boycotted the games in Moscow. However, that same year, he went on to win the New York Marathon, becoming the first Latino to do so. In winning the marathon, he set the record for the fastest first marathon in history as well as the second fastest time ever run by an American.

Alberto Salazar

Sources: Kanellos, *Latino Almanac*, pp. 515–516.

1980 ♦ Alberto Bauduy Salazar (1958–) set a new world record in the New York Marathon of 2:08:13. That year, he was also selected as the top U.S. road racer. In 1982, Salazar won the Boston and New York marathons. In addition to his world record, Salazar has set six U.S. records, the most since Steve Prefontaine.

Sources: Kanellos, *Latino Almanac*, pp. 515–516.

1987 ♦ U.S. Latinos competing at the Pan American Games on the U.S. team won the most medals ever, 13. Mike Gonzales (1964–) won one in the decathlon. Gonzales tried for three years to make the U.S. Olympic team but was plagued with injuries and did not qualify.

Sources: "First Step, for Three Years, Michael Gonzales…," *Los Angeles Times*, 16 June 1992.

1994 ♦ Long-distance runner Alberto Bauduy Salazar (1958–) came back in 1994 after a long slump and a series of illnesses and stunned the sports world by winning the 53-mile super marathon in South Africa. He was the first Hispanic runner to do so.

Sources: Kanellos, *Latino Almanac*, pp. 515–516.

Jasmine Camacho-Quinn

2020 ♦ Jasmine Camacho-Quinn (1996–) became the only Puerto Rican track and field athlete of Afro-Latina descent and only the second Puerto Rican to represent Puerto Rico at the Olympic Games and win a gold medal when, at the 2020 Tokyo Olympics, she won the gold medal in the 100-meter hurdles. At the 2024 Paris Olympics, she won a bronze medal, becoming the only Puerto Rican to have won two Olympic medals. She also won gold in the 2023 Central American and Caribbean Games. Although born and raised in Charleston, South Carolina, to a Puerto Rican mother and an African American father, both track and field athletes, Camacho-Quinn qualified to represent Puerto Rico at the Olympic Games because her mother was born in Trujillo Alto, Puerto Rico. Nevertheless, Camacho-Quinn also identifies as Puerto Rican.

Sources: Miranda, Gabriela, "Black Puerto Rican Jasmine Camacho-Quinn's Gold Medal Represents More Than a Record Win," *USA Today:* 2 August 2021.

VOLLEYBALL

1992 ♦ Carlos Briceño (1967–) became the first Latino to win an Olympic medal in volleyball. In international play, Briceño consistently ranked among the top three and in 1995 shared the number one men's team ranking. At the 1992 Barcelona Olympics, Briceño won a bronze medal for the United States, and in 1993, he won a silver medal at the NORCECA championships.

Sources: Hispanic Business, May 1996, p. 28.

WATER POLO

2020 ♦ Margaret Ann Steffens (1993–), born in San Ramon, California, the daughter of a champion Puerto Rican water polo athlete and an Anglo-American mother, was the first Latina to win medals at the Olympics as soon as the sport was included. In fact, she helped Team USA win three consecutive gold medals in the 2012, 2016, and 2020 Olympics. Steffens established a new Olympic record at the 2020 Summer Olympics for the most goals scored (49) by an individual player. She also scored the most goals in the 2012 and 2016 Olympiads.

Sources: "Team USA's Maggie Steffens Breaks Water Polo Olympic Scoring Record," *Sports Illustrated,* 30 July 2021: https://www.si.com/olympics/2021/07/30/maggie-steffens-breaks-water-polo-scoring-record-tokyo-olympics.

WEIGHTLIFTING

1987 ♦ U.S. Latinos competing at the Pan American Games on the U.S. team won the most medals ever, 13. Weightlifter Mario Martínez (1957–2018) won three gold medals. Martínez competed in three Olympic games for the United States: 1984, 1988, and 1992. In 1984, he won a silver medal.

Sources: "Mario A. Martinez," *Californian*: https://www.legacy.com/us/obituaries/thecalifornian/name/mario-martinez-obituary?id=10039824&fhid=2348.

2012 ♦ Californian Sarah Elizabeth Robles (1988–) became the first Latina to represent the United States in weightlifting at the Olympics. Competing for the United States at the London games in 2012 without placing for a medal, she returned in 2016 and 2020 to win the bronze medal both years. In doing so, she became the first American woman to win two Olympic medals in weightlifting. Robles was also a three-time U.S. national champion. In 2022, she won a gold medal in the Pan American Weightlifting Championships.

Sources: "Sarah Robles Becomes First U.S. Woman to Win Two Olympic Weightlifting Medals," USA Weightlifting: https://www.teamusa.org/USA-Weightlifting/Features/2021/August/02/Sarah-Robles-Becomes-First-US-Woman-to-Win-Two-Olympic-Weightlifting-Medals.

WRESTLING

1958 ♦ The first Latino to compete on the U.S. Olympic wrestling team was Richard "Dick" Delgado (1931–1991) at the Melbourne Olympics. Born in National City, California, in 1931, Delgado rose to wrestling prominence as an All-American at the University of Oklahoma. He had begun to wrestle in high school and junior college in San Diego, California, where he won the AAU Junior National Championship, weighing in at 121 pounds. After that, while serving in the U.S. Navy (1950–1954) he won another three AAU National Championships. He was subsequently recruited to the University of Oklahoma, where he became an All-American and won two NCAA championships (1957, 1958), in addition to various conference titles. At the same time, he also won national AAU titles in 1956, 1957, 1958, 1959, and 1960. In 2011, Delgado was inducted into the National Wrestling Hall of Fame.

Sources: "Richard 'Dick' Delgado," National Wrestling Hall of Fame & Museum: https://read.uberflip.com/i/279748-latino-american-wrestling-experience/13.

Pedro Morales

1971 ♦ Puerto Rican professional wrestler Pedro Morales (1942–2019) won the WWWF World Heavyweight Championship, becoming the first Latino to win a national professional wrestling title. Born on the island of Culebra, Puerto Rico, Morales began his career as an amateur wrestler at age 13 in New York and became a professional in 1959 at age 17. Morales joined Worldwide Wrestling Associates (WWA) in 1965, and his career took off. He won numerous WWA and WWF titles in the 1960s. In 1971, he won the WWWF championship, which he would hold for one of the longest times in the history of the sport; he also held the Intercontinental Championship for 619 days. Morales was inducted into three halls of fame: the WWF Hall of Fame (1995), the Professional Wrestling Hall of Fame and Museum (2015), and the Wrestling Observer Newsletter Hall of Fame (2017).

Sources: "Pedro Morales": https://www.onlineworldofwrestling.com/profile/pedro-morales/#google_vignette.

Henry Cejudo

2008 ♦ The first Latino to win a medal for wrestling in the Olympics was Henry Cejudo (1987–) at the Beijing Olympiad. Born in Los Angeles to Mexican American immigrants in 1987, Cejudo was, for the most part, a bantamweight Mixed Martial Arts competitor who also had an outstanding career in freestyle wrestling. At the Beijing Olympics, he became the youngest freestyle wrestler (at age 21) to ever win a gold medal. Throughout his wrestling career, Cejudo won championships at local, state, and national levels as well as at the Pan American Games (2006, 2007, and 2008). He had an equally illustrious post-freestyle wrestling career as a Mixed Martial Arts fighter. In fact, in 2019, upon winning the UFC Bantamweight Championship, he became only the fourth fighter to hold championships in two weight divisions at the same time—the other being the UFC Flyweight Championship. In 2018, Cejudo was inducted into the National Wrestling Hall of Fame.

Sources: Gregory, Sean, "A US Shocker on the Wrestling Mat," *Time*: https://time.com/archive/6944189/a-us-shocker-on-the-wrestling-mat/.

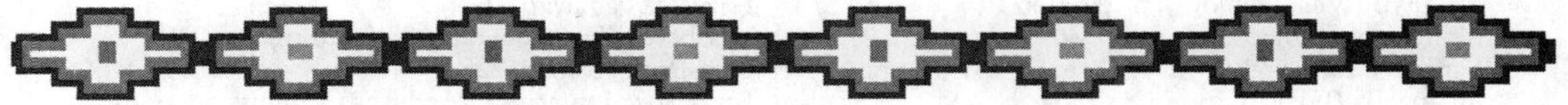

PHOTO SOURCES

aaa.si.edu: p. 201 (top).
ABC Network: pp. 282, 295 (top).
Jim Accordino: p. 356 (middle).
adelinalanepantla.blogspot.it: p. 49.
Bryan Allison: p. 375 (top).
Keith Allison: pp. 349 (top), 351 (middle), 363, 364 (bottom).
American Civil Liberties Union: p. 65.
americangallery19th.wordpress.com: p. 113 (bottom).
Sam Andre: p. 354 (middle).
Caroline Andrieu: p. 209 (top).
Artnexus.com: p. 197.
Associated Press: p. 355 (top).
Ballet Theatre Foundation/American Ballet Theatre/ photographer: Maurice Seymour: p. 270.
Barberry (Wikicommons): p. 104.
Baseball Digest: p. 346 (middle).
BD2412 (Wikicommons): p. 99 (top).
Jeffrey Beall: p. 249 (top).
Rob Bogaerts/Anefo: p. 333 (middle).
Bpowers88 (Wikicommons): p. 194 (bottom).
CC-BY-SA (Wikicommons): p. 326.
C. R. Bruce: p. 118 (top).
Bulldogbrown60 (Wikicommons): p. 251.
Bywaters Special Collections, Southern Methodist University: p. 200.
cabovolo.com: p. 184.
California State Senate: p. 83 (top).
Jarrett Campbell: p. 371 (bottom).
Tito Caraballo: p. 204.
Garrett Carey: p. 138.
Carl Van Vechten Photographs, Library of Congress: p. 279 (bottom).
CasaMagazine.com: p. 7 (bottom).
CasaRosada.gov.ar: pp. 143 (top), 211 (bottom).
CBS Television: p. 311.
cervantesvirtual.com: p. 110 (bottom).
COD Newsroom: p. 145.
Comiquero.com: p. 243.
Andrew Cordes: p. 134.
County of Los Angeles Board of Supervisors: p. 29 (middle).
Allan J. Cronin: p. 332 (bottom).
CSvBibra (Wikicommons): p. 151 (bottom).
Cubanball.com: p. 339 (top).
Dabryna (Wikicommons): p. 352.
Daily Morning Oasis: p. 116 (top).
Danvera (Wikicommons): p. 256 (bottom).
Digital-collections.csun.edu: p. 19 (bottom).
Dlodlodlo (Flickr): p. 16 (middle).
Donostia Kultura: p. 302 (top).
Erik Drost: pp. 351 (top), 362 (middle).
Dutch National Archives, The Hague: p. 374 (top).
Ealmagro (Wikicommons): p. 183.
Ebay.com: p. 344 (top).
Ebyabe (Wikicommons): p. 131.
Eric Enfermero: p. 347 (bottom).
Escogido Baseball Club: p. 348 (top).
ETH Library: p. 133 (top).
Gigi Fernandez: p. 377 (bottom).
Flickr: p. 3.
FloweringDagwood (Wikicommons): p. 365 (bottom).
Fort Worth Record-Telegram: p. 320 (bottom).
Glenn Francis: p. 345 (top).
Georgetown University Art Collection: p. 1.
GES 2016 (Flickr): p. 143 (bottom).
Aurora Gonzalez: p. 358.
GSAPPstudent (Wikicommons): p. 218.
Irwin Gooen: p. 179.
Goudey Gum: p. 339 (bottom).
Henry Cisneros Library: p. 20.
Matti Hillig: p. 213.
Valerie Hinojosa: p. 246.
HispanicHeritage.org: p. 248 (bottom).
Hispanic Lifestyle (Flickr): pp. 286, 295 (bottom).
Cal Hopkins: p. 378.
Jeffrey Hyde: p. 372 (bottom).
ima.umn.edu: p. 188 (bottom).
Norma Arbelo Irizarry: p. 202.
Janwikifoto (Wikicommons): p. 188 (top).
Jared (Wikicommons): p. 149.
James Jeffrey: p. 280 (top).
John D. and Catherine T. MacArthur Foundation: p. 106 (top).
John F. Kennedy Presidential Library and Museum: pp. 13 (top), 14.
Jose Gomez-Sicre Photographic Archives: p. 203 (top).
jpg1.lapl.org: p. 89.
Michelle Kells: p. 55.
Keyany (Wikicommons): p. 123.
Kheel Center: p. 73.
Kingkongphoto & www.celebrity-photos.com: pp. 325 (top), 328 (bottom).
Knight Foundation: p. 266.
Anthony L. Komaroff: p. 194 (top).
Jennifer Lapinel-Spincken: p. 280 (bottom).
Lázaro Galdiano Museum: p. 273.
Library of Congress: pp. 7 (top), 9 (bottom), 10 (top), 12 (top), 13 (bottom), 15, 23 (bottom), 79, 115 (top), 152, 203, 224 (top), 239 (top), 257 (top), 267, 269, 320 (top), 321 (middle), 338, 339 (middle).
Look magazine: p. 340 (middle).
Los Angeles County Metropolitan Transportation Authority: pp. 355 (bottom), 372 (middle).
Los Angeles Daily News: pp. 340 (top), 354 (bottom), 376 (top).
Los Angeles Times: pp. 100, 354 (top).
Los Angeles Times Photography Collection, UCLA: pp. 207, 209 (bottom).
John Mac: p. 350.
Manny's Baseball Land: p. 346 (top).
Mapache-Clandestino (Wikicommons): p. 242.
Maryland GovPics (Wikicommons): p. 367 (top).
MBDChicago (Wikicommons): p. 348 (bottom).
McGhiever (Wikicommons): p. 40.
John Mena: p. 372 (top).
Robbie Mendelson: p. 377 (top).
Metro-Goldwyn-Mayer: p. 290 (top).
MiamiDade.gov: p 22 (bottom).
Mike (Flickr): p. 351 (bottom).
Ministry of the Presidency of the Government of Catalonia: p. 201 (bottom).

MJNRJB (Wikicommons): p. 256 (top).
Montanabw (Wikicommons): p. 367 (bottom).
Larry D. Moore: pp. 94, 239 (bottom), 257 (bottom).
Mtamz305 (Wikicommons): p. 144.
David Munoz: p. 332 (top).
Museo del Prado: p. 175.
Museo Nacional de Historia, Mexico City: pp. 110 (middle), 127.
Narcy Studios: p. 327 (bottom).
NASA: pp. 171 (top and bottom), 172 (top and middle), 182 (top), 192 (bottom).
National Cancer Institute: p. 178.
National Center for Biotechnology Information: p. 192 (top).
National Endowment for the Arts: p. 248 (top).
National Museum of the U.S. Navy: p. 118 (bottom).
National Science Foundation: p. 189 (top).
Naval Museum of Madrid: p. 170.
NBC Television: pp. 281, 323 (middle), 324 (middle).
Azalia Negron: p. 356 (top).
New York Public Library Archives: p. 227 (top).
NobelPrize.org: p. 229.
Oakland Tribune: p. 361 (bottom).
PaulWie1 (Wikicommons): p. 331 (top).
Peabody Awards: p. 310.
Peter Norby: p. 235.
NPG.si.edu: p. 230.
oac.cdlib.org: p. 44 (top).Arturo Pardavila III: p. 346 (bottom).
Perezfan (Wikicommons): p. 333 (bottom).
Christopher Peterson: pp. 211 (top), 255.
Jay Phagan: p. 54.
proyectosalonhogar.com: p. 44 (bottom).
Alfredo Quiñones-Hinojosa: p. 182 (bottom).
Jerry Reuss: p. 344 (bottom).
Ritcheed (Wikicommons): p. 349 (bottom).
Poleth Rivas: p. 249 (bottom).
RKO: pp. 290 (bottom), 291 (top).
Rockero (Wikicommons): pp. 95, 247.
Rocoptics (Wikicommons): p. 190.
RR Auction: p. 323 (top).
Germán Saiz: p. 214.
Richard Sandoval: pp 142, 315, 356 (bottom).
Sba.gov: p. 133 (bottom).
Sdkb (Wikicommons): p. 136 (bottom)
Senadopr.us: p. 11.
Shutterstock: pp. 136 (top), 151 (top), 176, 271, 275, 279 (top), 283 (top), 287, 297 (bottom), 298, 299 (top), 300, 301 (top and bottom), 302 (bottom), 303 (top and bottom), 304, 305 (top and bottom), 312, 323 (bottom), 324 (top), 325 (bottom), 327 (top), 328 (top), 329 (top and bottom), 331 (bottom), 333 (top), 334 (top and bottom), 365 (top), 375 (bottom), 379.
sirismm.si.edu: p. 128 (top).
Gage Skidmore: pp. 27 (top), 80, 253, 299 (bottom), 381 (bottom).
Slgckgc (Flickr): p. 345 (bottom).
John Mathew Smith & www.celebrity-photos.com: p. 371 (top).
srlp.org: p. 81.
State Archives of Florida: p. 167.
Michael Steenbergen: p. 83 (bottom).
Supreme Court of the United States: p. 29 (top).
TaurusEmerald (Wikicommons): p. 373 (bottom).
TeachAids (Flickr): p. 361 (top).
John Telleria: p. 342 (top).
Telome4 (Wikicommons): p. 283 (bottom).
Tenayuca Family: p. 76.
texasbeyondhistory.net: p. 128 (bottom).
TexasProud.com: p. 225.
Texas State Library and Archives Commission: p. 245.
The Rudz (Wikicommons): p. 317.
Times-Picayune (New Orleans, LA): p. 12 (bottom).
Tomjc.55 (Wikicommons): p. 227 (bottom).
Tonklis (Wikicommons): p. 330.
Tradingcarddb.com: pp. 341 (all three photos), 342 (bottom), 343 (all three photos).
Trinka and Bill (Wikicommons): p. 28 (top).
uaemex.mx: p. 224 (bottom).
UCLA Library, *Los Angeles Times* collection: p. 263.
United Church of Christ: p. 308.
United Methodist News Service: p. 161.
University of New Mexico: p. 169.
University of Texas Libraries, The University of Texas at Austin: p. 165.
U.S. Air Force: pp. 116 (bottom), 119 (top).
U.S. Army: pp. 114, 115 (bottom), 116 (second from top), 172 (bottom), 362 (top and bottom).
U.S. Congress: pp. 18, 23 (top), 26 (bottom), 27 (bottom), 30 (bottom), 31 (top), 32 (bottom), 34 (bottom), 35 (bottom), p. 36 (top), 67.
U.S. Department of Commerce: p. 139.
U.S. Department of Defense: pp. 17, 120.
U.S. Department of Education: pp. 99 (bottom), 106 (bottom).
U.S. Department of Health and Human Services: p. 25.
U.S. Department of Homeland Security: p. 33.
U.S. Department of Justice: p. 28 (bottom).
U.S. Department of State: pp. 16 (top), 29 (bottom), 30 (top), 60, 316, 324 (bottom), 334 (middle).
U.S. Farm Security Administration: p. 68.
U.S. Government: pp. 10 (bottom), 31 (middle), 32 (top), 63, 142 (top).
U.S. House of Representatives: pp. 31 (bottom), 34 (top), 35 (top).
U.S. House Office of Photography: p. 2 (top).
U.S. Marines: p. 116 (second from bottom).
U.S. National Archives and Records Administration: p. 187.
U.S. Navy: pp. 117, 119 (bottom).
U.S. Postal Service: p. 27 (middle).
U.S. Senate Committee on Appropriations: p. 98.
U.S. Senate Judiciary Committee: p. 36 (bottom).
Utah Daily Chronicle: p. 361 (middle).
UTSA Libraries Special Collections: p. 47.
Ted Van Pelt: p. 364 (top).
Camilo José Vergara: p. 216.
Vimeo: p. 327 (middle).
Vintagecardprices.com: p. 360 (top and bottom).
Allan Warren: p. 297 (top).
White House Photographic Office: p. 376 (bottom).
whtime.cloudapp.net: p. 163.
Wikiart.org: p. 198.
Wrestling magazine: p. 381 (top).
Xiao Dai: p. 189 (bottom).
Y2kcrazyjoker4 (Wikicommons): p. 348 (middle).
YouTube.com: pp. 219, 265, 288 (top and bottom), 357.
Zach Catanzareti Photo: p. 373 (top).
Public domain: pp. 4, 5 (top and bottom), 6, 8, 9 (top), 16 (bottom), 19 (top), 22 (top), (top), 45, 48, 70, 86, 110 (top), 112, 113 (top), 125, 130, 166, 177, 180, 223 (top and bottom), 226, 231, 262, 291 (bottom), 292, 293, 321 (top and bottom), 337, 340 (bottom), 347 (top), 369, 374 (bottom).

BIBLIOGRAPHY

A

"About," National Hispanic Cultural Center: https://www.nhccnm.org/about/

"About Cisneros,": www.cisneros.com.

"About People," *Hispanic Business*, April 1996, p. 68.

"About Robert R. Dávila," Gallaudet University: https://web.archive.org/web/20070512204324/http://www.gallaudet.edu/x3566.xml

Acuña, Rodolfo F. *Occupied America: A History of Chicanos*, ninth edition, Pearson, 2019.

"Adelina 'Nina' Otero-Warren," National Women's History Museum: https://www.womenshistory.org/education-resources/biographies/adelina-nina-otero-warren

"Adrian Beltré," National Baseball Hall of Fame: https://baseballhall.org/hall-of-famers/beltre-adrian

"Adriana Ocampo," NASA: https://science.nasa.gov/people/adriana-ocampo/

Aikins-Núñez, Talia. *Men of the 65th: The Borinqueneers of the Korean War*. Wisconsin Rapids: Zest, 2023.

"Alberto Ibargüen Steps Down at Knight Foundation after 18 Years," Knight Foundation: https://knightfoundation.org/press/releases/alberto-ibarguen-steps-down-at-knight-foundation-after-18-years/

"Alfredo G. de los Santos, Jr.," ASU Retirees Association: https://asura.asu.edu/alfredo-de-los-santos

Almaguer, Tomás. Racial Faultlines: *The Historic Origins of White Supremacy in California.* Berkeley: University of California Press, 1994.

Almendros, Nestor. *Man with a Camera*. New York: Farrar, Straus and Giroux, 1986.

Alou, Felipe. *Alou: My Baseball Journey.* Lincoln: University of Nevada Press, 2018.

"Altuve Agrees to Deal Running until Age 29," *Houston Chronicle*, 7 February 2024.

"Ambasz Has Been the Subject of a Dozen Books and Numerous Articles. A Green-Architecture Pioneer. Emilio Ambasz Creates Buildings That Belong to the Landscape," *The New York Times*, 7 May 2023.

"The American Council of Spanish Speaking People," Texas State Historical Association: https://www.tshaonline.org/handbook/entries/american-council-of-spanish-speaking-people

"Américo Paredes," *Humanities Texas*: https://www.humanitiestexas.org/programs/tx-originals/list/americo-paredes

"Amleto Monacelli PBA Library," Bowlers Mart: https://www.bowlersmart.com/category/pba-tour/pba-bowling-player-video-library/amleto-monacelli-pba-library/

"Ana Roqué de Duprey," National Women's History Museum: https://www.womenshistory.org/education-resources/biographies/ana-roque-de-duprey

"Ana Mendieta: Cuban-American Performance Artist, Sculptor, Painter, Photographer and Video Artist," *The Art Story*: https://www.theartstory.org/artist/mendieta-ana/

"Andy Jauregui," National Rodeo Hall of Fame: https://nationalcowboymuseum.org/

collections/awards/rodeo-hall-of-fame/inductees/5102/

"Angela Ginorio," University of Washington: https://gwss.washington.edu/people/angela-ginorio

"Angelico Chávez," *Dictionary of Literary Biography*, Volume 82: *Chicano Writers.* Detroit: Gale Research, 1989, pp. 86–90.

"Anthony D. Romero Is New ACLU Executive Director; First Latino to Head Premier Civil Liberties Group," ACLU: https://www.aclu.org/press-releases/anthony-d-romero-new-aclu-executive-director-first-latino-head-premier-civil

"Antonia Novello," National Women's Hall of Fame: https://www.womenofthehall.org/inductee/antonia-novello/

"Apuntes," SMU Scholar: https://scholar.smu.edu/apuntes/about.html

"Aric Almirola Wins Inaugural Xfinity Series Race at Sonoma," NASCAR News: https://www.nascar.com/news-media/2023/06/10/aric-almirola-wins-inaugural-xfinity-series-race-at-sonoma/

"Artist Jesús Moroles," *SAAM*: https://americanart.si.edu/artist/jesus-moroles-5827

"Artist Manuel Neri," *SAAM*: https://americanart.si.edu/artist/manuel-neri-6624

"Aspira's Legal Landmark Cases," Aspira: https://aspira.org/about-us/aspiras-legal-landmark-cases/

Avila, Alex. "Freedom Fighter: Dr. Hector P. García, Founder of the American G.I. Forum," *Hispanic*, January/February 1996, pp. 18-22.

Avila, Pamela, "Eva Longoria, Director, Producer, Champion for Latino Community, Is Woman of the Year Honoree," *USA Today* 29 February 2024: https://www.usatoday.com/story/entertainment/celebrities/2024/02/29/eva-longoria-woman-of-the-year/72308679007/

B

Baez, Joan. *A Voice to Sing With*. New York: Summit Books, 1987.

Balderrama, Francisco, and Raymond Rodriguez. *Decade of Betrayal: Mexican Repatriation in the 1930s*. Albuquerque: University of New Mexico Press, 1995.

Berger, Max. "Education in Texas during the Spanish and Mexican Periods," *Southwestern Historical Quarterly*, Vol. 51, No. 1 (Jul., 1947), pp. 41–53.

Bernstein, David (2005-08-01). "A New Multiplex Is Aiming to Capture a Bilingual Audience," *New York Times,* 1 August, 2005.

Bernstein, Fred A. and Paul Goldberger, "Cesar Pelli, Designer of Iconic Buildings Around the World, Dies at 92," *New York Times* 20 July 2019: https://www.nytimes.com/2019/07/20/arts/cesar-pelli-dead.html

"The Best South American NBA Players of All Time," Ranker: https://www.ranker.com/list/south-american-nba-players/ranker-nba

"Beyoncé, Adele and Bad Bonny in Position to Make History," *Houston Chronicle*, 5 February 2023.

"Biden Taps 2, Including 1st Hispanic, for Roles in Fed Board," *Houston Chronicle*, 13 May 2023.

"Billionaires: Jorge Perez," *Forbes* 8, October 2023: https://www.forbes.com/profile/jorge-perez/?list=forbes-400&sh=a8a9542100b2

"Bishop Roberto O. Gonzalez, OFM," Diocese of Corpus Christi: https://diocesecc.org/

bishop-roberto-o-gonzalez-ofm
Blake, Robert Bruce, "Terán de los Ríos, Domingo," *Handbook of Texas*: https://www.tshaonline.org/handbook/entries/teran-de-los-rios-domingo
"Bonnie Canino 2019 IWBHF Inductee," International Women's Boxing Hall of Fame: https://www.iwbhf.com/photosinductees/canino.htm
Boyer, Peter J., "The Double Life of Frank Lorenzo," *Vanity Fair* (December 1989): https://archive.vanityfair.com/article/1989/12/the-double-life-of-frank-lorenzo
Brady, James, "Jimmy Smits (Tv and Film Actor)," *Parade Magazine* 2 January 2005: http://www.parade.com/articles/editions/2005/edition_01-02-2005/in_step_with_1
"Brief – McDonald's Board of Directors Names Enrique Hernandez Jr. Non-Executive Chairman." *Reuters*. 26 May 2016.
"Broadway's Hardest Working Man," *New York Times*, 4 June 2023.
Broyles-González, Yolanda. *El Teatro Campesino: Theatre in the Chicano Movement*. Austin: University of Texas Press, 1994.
Burke, Siobhan, "An Artist of Ordered Excess," *New York Times,* 16 April 2023.
"Bustos Makes a Comeback," *Media Moves*, 27 January 2011: https://www.mediamoves.com/2011/01/bustos-makes-a-comeback.html

C

"Cachao," *Hispanic Arts News*, October 1995, p. 12.
Calderón, Roberto. "Tejano Politics," *Texas State Historical Association*: https://www.tshaonline.org/handbook/entries/tejano-politics
Cameron, Bailey, "Blucifer: The Story of Denver Airport's 'Blue Mustang' Sculpture from Luis Jimenez": https://www.uncovercolorado.com/blucifer-blue-mustang-statue-denver-airport/
"Camilo José Vergara Photographs: Tracking Time to Document America's Post-Industrial Cities," *Library of Congress*: https://guides.loc.gov/vergara-collection-guide
Campa, Arthur L. *Hispanic Culture in the Southwest*. Norman: University of Oklahoma Press, 1979.
"Carlos Alvarez," Texas Business Hall of Fame: https://texasbusiness.org/wp-content/uploads/2019/07/TBHF_2010_Legend_Bios.pdf
"Carlos Lozada of The Washington Post," The Pulitzer Prize: https://www.pulitzer.org/winners/carlos-lozada-washington-post
"Carmen Herrera: Structuring Surfaces": https://www.mfah.org/exhibitions/carmen-herrera-structuring-surfaces
Canby, Vincent, "The Screen: 'El Super,' A Cuban American Tale: The Cast," *New York Times,* 29 April 1979.
"Captain Robert Campos Treviño, Ret.," *Houston Chronicle,* 15 October 2023.
"Cardcorner: 1972 Topps Preston Gómez," National Baseball Hall of Fame: https://baseballhall.org/discover/card-corner/1972-topps-preston-gomez
Carter, Thomas P., and Roberto Segura. *Mexican Americans in the Public Schools: A History of Neglect*. Princeton, NJ: College Entrance Examination Board, 1979.
Castañeda, Carlos. *Our Catholic Heritage in Texas, 1519–1936*. Newark, NJ: Arno Press, 1976.
Centro de Estudios Puertorriqueños: https://centropr.hunter.cuny.edu/

Chabrán, Rafael, and Richard Chabrán, "The Spanish-Language and Larino Press in the United States," in Kanellos and Fabregat, *Handbook fo Hispanic Culture in the United States: Literature.* Houston, TX: Arte Publico Press, 1993, p. 378.
"Chang-Díaz, Franklin," Internet Archive Current Biography Yearbook 2011: https://archive.org/details/currentbiography0000unse_z0h6/page/120/mode/2up
Chipman, Donald E., "Damián Massanet," *Handbook of Texas*: https://www.tshaonline.org/handbook/entries/massanet-damian
Chipman, Donald E. *Spanish Texas, 1519–1821*. Austin: University of Texas Press, 1992.
Cine Festival: https://guadalupeculturalarts.org/cine-festival/
Clark, Lesley. "Citing Health Care, Debbie Mucarsel-Powell Wants to Be Part of Florida's Blue Wave," *McClatchyDC*: https://www.mcclatchydc.com/latest-news/article219016890.html
"Conoce a uno de los hispanos que están detrás del famoso McRib de McDonald's," *People en Español*, December 12, 2022: https://peopleenespanol.com/noticias/familia-hispana-produce-carne-para-mcrib-mcdonalds-dueno-eduardo-sanchez/
"Congresswoman Nydia Velázquez: Biography": https://velazquez.house.gov/about/full-biography
"Congresswoman Sylvia García": https://sylviaGarcía.house.gov/about
Cordova, Alfredo C., and Charles B. Judah. *Octaviano Larrazolo: A Political Potrait*. Albuquerque, NM: Department of Government, Division of Research, 1952.
"The Corporation for Public Broadcasting Honors NPR's Lourdes Garcia-Navarro with the Edward R. Murrow Award": https://cpb.org/awards/corporation-public-broadcasting-honors-nprs-lourdes-garcia-navarro-edward-r-murrow-award
Cotera, Martha. *Profile of the Mexican American Woman*. Austin, TX: National Education Laboratory Publishers, 1976.
Coy, Cassie. *Dennis Chávez, The First Hispanic Senator*. Houston, TX: Arte Público Press, 2017.
Crawford, James. *Bilingual Education: History, Policy, Theory and Practice*. Trenton, NJ: Crane Publishing, 1989.
"Cristina Rivera Garza," Hispanic Studies, University of Houston: https://uh.edu/class/spanish/faculty/rivera-garza-c/
Crocchiola, Stanley F. L. *The Civil War in New Mexico*. Denver, CO: World Press, 1960.
Cruz, Gilbert C. *Let There Be Towns: Spanish Municipal Origins in the American Southwest, 1610–1810.* College Station: Texas A&M University Press, 1988.

D

"Daniel Suárez," NASCAR: https://www.nascar.com/drivers/daniel-suarez
Davis, William C. *Inventing Loreta Velasquez: Confederate Soldier Impersonator, Media Celebrity, and Con Artist*. Carbondale: Southern Illinois University Press, 2016.
"Del Rio ISD v. Salvatierra," *Texas State Historical Association:* https://www.tshaonline.org/handbook/entries/del-rio-isd-v-salvatierra
Deming, Mark, "José Feliciano Biography," All Music: https://www.allmusic.com/art-

ist/jos%C3%A9-feliciano-mn0000271113#biography

Diner, Hasia. *The Jews of The United States, 1654 To 2000*, Internet Archive: https://archive.org/details/diner-hasia-j-auth-the-jews-of-the-united-states-1654-to-2000

Dobkins, Betty Eakle. *The Spanish Element in Texas Water Law*. Austin: University of Texas Press, 1959.

Dolan, Jay R, and Allan Figueroa Deck. *Hispanic Catholic Culture in the United States: Issues and Concerns*. Notre Dame, IN: University of Notre Dame, 1994.

Dolan, Jay R., and Gilberto M. Hinojosa. *Mexican Americans and the Catholic Church, 1900-1965*. Notre Dame, IN: University of Notre Dame Press, 1994.

"Donna de Varona," National Women's Hall of Fame: https://www.womenofthehall.org/inductee/donna-de-varona/

"Dr. María Rosario Jackson," National Endowment for the Arts: https://www.arts.gov/about/leadership-staff/dr-maria-rosario-jackson

"Dr. Mario E. Ramirez - Biography of a Doctor," UT Health/The Libraries: https://libguides.uthscsa.edu/c.php?g=924869&p=6704801

"Dr. Miguel Cardona, Secretary of Education—Biography," U.S. Department of Education: https://www2.ed.gov/news/staff/bios/cardona.html

"Dr. Pedro Sánchez," World Food Prize Foundation: https://www.worldfoodprize.org/en/laureates/20002009_laureates/2002_sanchez/

"Drama," Arte Público Press Catalog, pp. 64-65: chrome-extension://efaidnbmnnnibpcajpcglclefindmkaj/https://artepublicopress.com/wp-content/uploads/2023/10/2023-Complete-Catalog_final-with-cover_9-7-2023.pdf

Duffy, Michael. "Campaign '96: Alex Castellanos Has a Crisp, Clear Way of Going for the Juglar," *Time*, 16 September 1996, p. 44.

E

"Ed Pastor, Arizona's First Hispanic Congressman, Dies at 75," *Washington Post,* 28 November 2018.

"Edge of a Dream," *Time*, 18 March 1996.

"Eduardo Mata Is Dead at 52," *New York Times*, 5 January 1995.

Eligon, John."Running for the House on Pride in His Roots, and Pure Energy," *New York Times,* 18 June 2012.

"Emilio Sánchez Biography": https://emiliosanchezfoundation.org/sanchez.html

"The Empanadas Are Just to Die for," *New York Times*, 9 July 2023.

Enciso, Carmen E., and the Hispanic Division, Library of Congress. *The History of the Congressional Hispanic Caucus*. Washington, D.C.: U.S. Government Printing Office, 1981.

"Escobedo v. Illinois, 378 U.S. 478 (1964)" Justia U.S. Supreme Court: https://supreme.justia.com/cases/federal/us/378/478/

"Eva Longoria Awards," *IMDb*: https://www.imdb.com/name/nm0519456/awards/

"Evangelina Vigil," *Dictionary of Literary Biography*, Volume 122: *Chicano Writers*. Detroit: Gale Research, 1992, pp. 306-12.

"Ezequiel Cabeza de Baca," *New Mexico History*: https://newmexicohistory.org/2012/06/30/ezequiel-cabeza-de-baca/

F

Faber, Nancy. "Candy Costie and Tracie Ruiz Are at Their Most Buoyant When They Get that Synching Feeling." *People*, 16 April 1984.

Fabre, Genvieve, ed. *European Perspectives on Hispanic Literature of the United States*. Houston: Arte Público Press, 1989.

"'Fame' and 'Flashdance' Singer-Actor Was Genius," *New York Times*, 27 November 2022.

"Feeling Grand: Some Milestone Highlights," *Houston Chronicle*, 3 November 2022.

Fernández, Roberta. *Twenty Years of Hispanic Literature in the United States*. Houston, TX: University of Houston, M. D. Anderson Library, 1993.

Fields, Darrel, and Brooke Hodge, eds. *Carlos Jiménez: House and Studio*, Cambridge, MA: Harvard Graduate School of Design, 2006.

"First Step, for Three Years, Michael Gonzales …," *Los Angeles Times*, 16 June 1992.

Florida Department of State. *Florida Cuban Heritage Trail*. Tallahassee: Florida Department of State, Division of Historical Resources, 1995.

Fontana, Bernard L. *Entrada: The Legacy of Spain and Mexico in the United States*. Albuquerque: University of New Mexico Press, 1994.

"Former APA President Pedro Ruiz, M.D., Dies," *Psychiatric News*: https://psychnews.psychiatryonline.org/doi/10.1176/appi.pn.2023.05.5.14

"Founder Dr. Roberto Cruz Bio," The Foundation for Hispanic Education: https://www.tfhe.org/apps/pages/index.jsp?uREC_ID=378967&type=d&pREC_ID=2030062

Fox, Tom. "Maria Contreras-Sweet on Running the Small Business Administration," *Washington Post,* 30 January 2015.

"Francisco Cigarroa, Chair, Board of Trustees," Ford Foundation: https://www.fordfoundation.org/about/people/francisco-g-cigarroa/

Friedman, Vanessa. "Independence Fortifies a Survivor," *New York Times*, 26 November 2023.

"From Mexican Army Colonel to Union Brigadier General," American Civil War Forum: https://www.americancivilwarforum.com/from-mexican-army-colonel-to-union-brigadier-general-556.html

"Full Circle: 'Fast' Freddie Ends Career Where It Began," Velo: https://velo.outsideonline.com/road/full-circle-fast-freddie-ends-career-where-it-began/

Furtaw, Julia C., ed. *Hispanic Americans Information Directory: 1992–93*. Detroit: Gale, 1992.

Futuro Media: https://www.futuromediagroup.org/

G

"Gabriela Alaniz Defeats Marlen Esparza by Split Decision, Wins Ring Lightweight Championship," *The Ring*: https://www.ringtv.com/current-issue/

Galarza, Ernesto. *Farm Workers and Agribusiness in California: 1947–1960*. Notre Dame, IN: University of Notre Dame Press, 1977.

Gallegos, Bernardo P. *Literacy, Education and Society in New Mexico, 1693–1821*.

Albuquerque: University of New Mexico Press, 1992.
García, David, *Arsenio Rodríguez and the Trasnational Flows of Latin Music*, Philadelphia, PA: Temple University Press, 2006.
"García, Hector Pérez (1914–1996)," Texas State Historical Association: https://www.tshaonline.org/handbook/entries/García-hector-perez
García, Ignacio M. *Héctor P. García: In Relentless Pursuit of Justice*. Houston, TX: Arte Público Press, 2002.
García, Lisette, "County Judge Attains New Benchmark," *Miami Herald*, August 29, 1999.
García, María Cristina. *Havana USA: Exiles and Cuban Americans in South Florida, 1959–1994*. Berkeley: University of California Press, 1996.
García, Mario T., *The Making of a Mexican American Mayor: Raymond L. Telles of El Paso*, El Paso, TX: Texas Western Press, 1998.
García, Mario T. *Memories of Chicano History. The Life and Narrative of Bert Corona*. Berkeley: University of California Press, 1994.
García, Robert. *Man of the People: the Autobiography of Robert García*. Houston, TX: Arte Público Press, 2023.
Garza, Beatriz de la. *From the Republic of the Rio Grande: A Personal History of the Place and the People*, Austin: University of Texas Press, 2013.
Gates, Anita. "Anthony Quinn Dies at 86; Played Earthy Tough Guys," *New York Times* 4 June 2001.
Givhan, Robin. "Alexandria Ocasio-Cortez Shared Her Personal Story and Revealed Our Collective Trauma," *Washington Post*, 2 February 2021.
Gladys Roldán-de-Moras, Artist: https://www.roldandemoras.com/about
Gleiter, Jan, and Kathleen Thompson. *David Farragut*. Milwuakee, WI: Rountree Publications, 1989.
Gómez-Quiñones, Juan. *Roots of Chicano Politics, 1600–1930*. Albuquerque: University of New Mexico Press, 1994.
Gonzales, Juan L., Jr. *Mexican and Mexican American Farm Workers: The California Agricultural Industry*. New York: Praeger, 1985.
González, David. "A Family Divided by 2 Words, Legal and Illegal," *New York Times*, 26 April 2009.
Gordon, Gregory, and, Ronald E. Cohen. *Down to the Wire: UPI's Fight for Survival*. McGraw-Hill, 1989.
Grant, Linda,"Coke Chairman's Pay Is Called Hard to Swallow," *Los Angeles Times*, 20 March 1992.
Greising, David. *I'd Like the World to Buy a Coke: The Life and Leadership of Roberto Goizueta*. Wiley, John & Sons, 1989.
Griswold del Castillo, Richard, and Richard A. García. *César Chávez: A Triumph of Spirit*. Norman: University of Oklahoma Press, 1995.
Griswold del Castillo, Richard, Teresa McKenna, and Yvonne Yarbro-Bejarano, eds. *Chicano Art: Resistance and Affirmation, 1965–1985*. Los Angeles: Wight Art Gallery, University of California, Los Angeles, 1991.
Guerra, Joey. "The Return of Just 'Dora,'" *Houston Chronicle*, 16 April 2024.
Gulvas Swarden, Carlotta. "College Head Leaving After a Turbulent Year," *New York Times*, 4 September 1994.

Gutiérrez, Carlos. "Carlos Gutiérrez: Business Man and US Secretary of Commerce," *Latino Leaders Speak: Personal Stories of Struggle and Triumph*, eds. Ibarra, Mickey, and Maria Pérez-Brown, Houston, TX: Arte Público Press, 2017.

Gutierrez, Félix F., and Jorge R. Schement. *Spanish Language Radio in the Southwestern United States*. Austin: Center for Mexican American Studies, University of Texas, 1979.

H

Hackel, Steven W. *Junipero Serra: California's Founding Father*. New York: Hill and Wang, 2013.

Hammond, Pete, "The Critics Choice Is 'Barbie' with 18 CCA Nominations; 'Oppenheimer', 'Poor Things' Follow with 13 Each," *Deadline*: https://deadline.com/2023/12/critics-choice-film-nominations-2023-1235665954/

"Harold Medina, U.S. Judge, Dies at 102," *The New York Times*, 16 March 1990.

"Héctor López, 93, Dies; Manager Who Broke Baseball Color Barrier," *New York Times* 2 October 2022.

"Helena María Viramontes," *Dictionary of Literary Biography*, Volume 122: *Chicano Writers*, Detroit: Gale Research, 1992, pp. 322–28.

"Helped Refine 'the Pill,'" *New York Times*, 16 February 2004.

Henderson, Ann L., and Gary R. Mormino, eds. *Spanish Pathways in Florida*. Sarasota, FL: Pineapple Press, 1991.

Henderson, Kathy. "Lindsay Mendez," Broadway Buzz: https://www.broadway.com/buzz/6633/lindsay-mendez/

"Henry Cisneros," Bipartisan Policy Center: https://bipartisanpolicy.org/person/henry-cisneros/

Herbert, John R., ed. *1492: An Ongoing Voyage*. Washington, DC: Library of Congress, 1992.

Hernández, Irene Beltrán. *Heartbeat Drumbeat*. Houston, TX: Arte Público Press, 1993.

Hispanics in U.S. History: 1865 to the Present, two volumes. Englewood Cliffs, NJ: Globe Book Company, 1989.

Hispanic, September 1993, pp. 50–54; March 1994, pp. 14–18; July 1994, pp. 9, 54; November 1994, p. 43; October 1995, pp. 28–32; July 1995, pp. 15, 22–26; August 1995, p. 28; September 1995, pp., 30–31; October 1995, pp. 28–32, 68–72; December 1995, p. 12; March 1996, p. 9; December 1996, pp. 8–9.

Hispanic Business, October 1993; October 1994, p. 70; March 1996, pp. 18; April 1996, p. 66 and 68; May 1996, pp. 8, 27, 28; June 1996, p. 150; October 1996, p. 58; December 1996, p. 58.

Hispanic Link Weekly Report, 19 June 1995, pp. 2, 8; 26 June 1995, pp. 3, 4; 14 August 1995, p. 3; 15 and 28 August 1995, p. 4; 29 August 1995, p. 1; 16 October 1995, p. 1; 22 January 1996, p. 1; 13 May 1996, p. 8; 9 September 1996, p. 4; 7 and 14 October 1996, p. 1; 13 January 1997, p. 8.

"Hispanic Playwrights Project," Southcoast Repertory Theater: https://www.scr.org/about/about-scr-landing/the-scr-story/scr-production-history/history-landing-page/

play-reading-history/reading-landing-page/hispanic-playwrights-project-history/
"Historia," Instituto de Cultura Puertorriqueña: https://www.icp.pr.gov/historia/
"History," El Museo del Barrio: https://www.elmuseo.org/about/history-mission/
"History," National Museum of Mexican Art: https://nationalmuseumofmexicanart.org/history
"History of Bilingual Education," *Rethinking Schools*: https://rethinkingschools.org/articles/history-of-bilingual-education/.
"History of the CHC," Congressional Hispanic Caucus: https://chc.house.gov/history-of-the-chc
Hoffman, Benjamin. "Albert Pujols Passes Willie Mays in Home Runs, if Not Dominance," *New York Times*, 18 September 2020.
Holden, Stephen (May 24, 1991). "Review/Film; Homeboys Hangin' Downtown," *New York Times* 24 May 1991.
Holt, Chandler. "Amy Rodriguez to Coach Utah Royals FC in 2024 NWSL Season," KSL Sports: https://kslsports.com/500588/amy-rodriguez-to-coach-utah-royals-fc-in-2024-nwsl-season/
Huetteman, Emmarie, "Dangers Propelled Norma Torres to Move to U.S., Then to Politics," *New York Times*, 15 February 2015.
"Hugo Castello, Coach at N.Y.U., Dies at 79," *New York Times,* 29 March 1994.

I

"In U.S. Politics, Even the Storied Phrase 'the American Dream' Divides," *New York Times*, 21 August 2022.
"Island Diplomacy, from Mayagüez to Micronesia: The Journey of Esperanza of Ambassador Carmen Gloria Cantor," National Museum of American Diplomacy: https://diplomacy.state.gov/stories/ambassador-carmen-gloria-cantor/

J

"J.C. Trujillo," National Rodeo Hall of Fame: https://nationalcowboymuseum.org/collections/awards/rodeo-hall-of-fame/inductees/j-c-trujillo/
"Jackie Nespral," *Miami Herald,* 5 February 2014: https://www.miamiherald.com/latest-news/article1959536.html
Jamieson, Stuart. *Labor Unionism in American Agriculture*. New York: Arno Press, 1976.
Jasinski, Laurie E., "San Antonio, Tx.," *Handbook of Texas*: https://www.tshaonline.org/handbook/entries/san-antonio-tx
Jenkins, John H. *Basic Texas Books: An Annotated Bibliography of Selected Works for a Research Libarary*. Austin: Texas State Historical Association, 1983.
"Jesús T. Piñero, 1897–1952," *Biographical Dictionary of the United States Congress*: https://bioguide.congress.gov/search/bio/P000361
Jiménez-Castellanos, Oscar, and Lawrence O. Picus. "Serrano v. Priest 50th Anniversa-

ry: Origins, Impact and Future," *BYU Education & Law Journal*: https://scholarsarchive.byu.edu/cgi/viewcontent.cgi?article=1057&context=byu_elj

"John Quintana," National Rodeo Hall of Fame: https://nationalcowboymuseum.org/collections/awards/rodeo-hall-of-fame/inductees/5383/

"John Velásquez," ESPN: https://www.espn.com/blog/onenacion/post/_/id/541/latino-jockeys-in-the-hall-of-fame

Jomantas, Nicole. "Maria Laborde Makes History with Silver at World Judo Masters," USA Judo: https://www.usajudo.com/news/2023/august/04/World-Masters-Day-1-Results

"José Antonio Villarreal," *Dictionary of Literary Biography*, Volume 82: *Chicano Writers*, Detroit: Gale Research, 1982, pp. 282–88.

"Jose Coronado Obituary," San Antonio Express-News: https://www.legacy.com/us/obituaries/sanantonio/name/jose-coronado-obituary?id=10038664

"Joseph Domínguez": https://www.constellationenergy.com/our-company/leadership/executive-profiles/joseph-dominguez.html

"Juan Salinas," National Rodeo Hall of Fame: https://nationalcowboymuseum.org/collections/awards/rodeo-hall-of-fame/inductees/5199/

Juárez, Tina. *Call No Man Master*. Houston, TX: Arte Público Press, 1995.

"Julian Samora." Institute for Latino Studies, University of Notre Dame: https://latinostudies.nd.edu/about/history/julian-samora/

"Julie Stav," *Latino Leaders Speak*, pp. 255–260.

"Ambassador Julissa Reynoso," U.S. Embassy & Consulate in Spain and Andorra: https://es.usembassy.gov/ambassador-julissa-reynoso/

K

Kanellos, Nicolás, and Pérez, Cristelia. *Chronology of Hispanic American History: From Pre-Colombian Times to the Present*. Detroit: Gale Research, 1995.

Kanellos, Nicolás, and Claudio Esteva-Fabregat. *Handbook of Hispanic Culture in the United States.* Four volumes. Houston, TX: Arte Público Press, 1994-95.

Kanellos, Nicolás. *Hispanic American Literature*. New York: Harper Collins, 1995.

Kanellos, Nicolás. *A History of Hispanic Theater in the United States: Origins to 1940*. Austin: University of Texas Press, 1989.

Kanellos, Nicolás. "Introduction," *Nuevos Pasos*. Houston, TX: Arte Público Press, 1989; pp. v–ix.

Kanellos, Nicolás. *Latinos and Nationhood: Two Centuries of Intellectual Thought.* Tucson: University of Arizona Press, 2023.

Kanellos, Nicolás. *The Latino Almanac*. Detroit: Visible Ink Press, 2022.

Kawahara, Matt, "Road to History," *Houston Chronicle*, 21 August 2023.

Keller, Gary D. *Hispanics and United States Film: An Overview and Handbook*. Tempe, AZ: Bilingual Press, 1994.

"Kid Chocolate," The Cyber Boxing Zone Encyclopedia: http://www.cyberboxingzone.com/boxing/kidchoc.htm

Kimitch, Rebecca. "Solis, a Woman of Many Firsts, Had a Steady Rise through California's Political Ranks," *San Gabriel Tribune*, 7 January 2009.

Kloss, Heinz. *The American Bilingual Tradition*. Rowley, MA: Newbury House, 1977.
Knippling, Alpana Sharma, ed. *New Immigrant Literatures in the United States: A Sourcebook to Our Multicultural Heritage*. Westport, CT: Greenwood Press, 1996.
Kozinn, Allan. "Celedonio Romero, 83, Guitarist Who Formed a Family Quartet," *New York Times,* 11 May 1996.
Kuehner-Hebert, Katie. "Under CEO Oscar Munoz, United Airlines Holdings Inc. Ups Its 2019 Guidance." *Chief Executive*, 18 November 2019.
Kushner, Sam. *Long Road to Delano: A Century of Farmworkers' Struggle*. New York: International Publishers, 1975.

L

La abeja, 5 April 1831.
"Ladislas [sic] Lázaro." *Biographical Dictionary of the United States Congress*: https://bioguide.congress.gov/search/bio/L000153
Lanman, Charles. *Dictionary of the United States*. Philadelphia: J. B. Lippincott, 1859, p. 882.
Latina/o Studies Association: https://latinxstudiesassociation.org/about/
"Latino History is US History": https://latino.si.edu/gallery
"Latino Power List: 45 Trailblazers Making Waves in Hollywood," *The Wrap*: https://www.thewrap.com/latino-power-list-eva-longoria-jenna-ortega/#helmers
"The Latinos Who Made History in the Midterm Elections," Axios: www.axios/2022/11/09/midterms-latinos-firsts
"A Latinx Resource Guide: Civil Rights Cases and Events in the United States," *Library of Congress Research Guides*: https://guides.loc.gov/latinx-civil-rights/mendez-v-westminster
"Lau v. Nichols–The Law in Education," Intercultural Development Research Association: https://www.idra.org/education_policy/lau-v-nichols-the-law-in-education/
Lavner, Ryan. "Abraham Ancer officially announces move to LIV Golf," NBC Sports: Golf: https://www.nbcsports.com/golf/news/abraham-ancer-announces-move-liv-golf
LeCompte, Mary Lou. "The Hispanic Influence on the History of Rodeo," *Journal of Sports History*, 12 (spring 1985); pp. 21–38.
"Leo Tanguma: An Interview": https://zingmagazine.com/blog_posts/leo-tanguma-interview/
"Leon B. Poullada, Ex-Envoy and Afghan Expert, Is Dead," *New York Times,* 23 July 1987.
"Leon Ichaso, 74, Latino Filmmaker Who Explored Assimilation and Exile," *New York Times,* 28 May 2023.
Lescaze, Zoe. "Striking a Balance," *New York Times*, 28 April 2024.
Lewis, Edward, "Tony Gonzalez to Be Inducted into Chiefs Hall of Fame," Around the NFL: https://web.archive.org/web/20180127015145/http://www.nfl.com/news/story/0ap3000000911162/article/tony-gonzalez-to-be-inducted-into-chiefs-hall-of-fame
"Lin-Manuel Miranda," Biography.com: https://www.biography.com/actors/biography-lin-manuel-miranda-community-heroes
"Linda Alvarado." National Museum of Americana History: https://americanhistory.

si.edu/profile/3104

"Linda G. Alvardo," National Women's Hall of Fame: https://www.womenofthehall.org/inductee/linda-g-alvarado/

"Linda Ronstadt," *Parade*, 11 September 2022, pp. 8–9.

Links, Zachary. "Marlins Manager Edwin Rodriguez Steps Down," MLB Trade Rumors: https://www.mlbtraderumors.com/2011/06/marlins-manager-edwin-rodriguez-steps-down.html

"Lionel G. García," *Dictionary of Literary Biography*, Volume 82: *Chicano Authors*, Detroit: Gale Research, 1992, pp. 123–24.

Llinás, Rodolfo, ed. *Neurobiology of Cerebellar Evolution and Development*. Chicago: American Medical Association, 1969.

Llinás, Rodolfo R., and Churchland, Patricia S., *Mind-Brain Continuum: Sensory Processes*, Baltimore, MD: The MIT Press, 1996.

Lombardi, Frank. "Freshman State Sen. Espaillat Going to Bat for More Than 1M Tenants from Rent Regulation Changes," *Daily News,* 14 April 2011.

Lomelí, Francisco, and Carl R. Shirley, eds. *Dictionary of Literary Biography,* Detroit: Gale Research, Vol. 82: *Chicano Writers,* 1989; Vol. 122: *Chicano Writers*, 1992.

"Lopez-Dorada Foods Names Gonzalez CEO," *The Journal Record*, June 1, 2022: https://journalrecord.com/2022/06/01/lopez-dorada-foods-names-gonzalez-ceo/

"Los Tigres del Norte," California Museum: https://californiamuseum.org/inductee/los-tigres-del-norte/

"Loyalty and Labor: Nydia Margarita Veláquez," *New York Times*, 16 September 1992, p. B6.

"Love Is in the Aria," *Vanity Fair*, June 2012: https://www.vanityfair.com/culture/2012/06/stephen-costello-ailyn-perez-opera-duets

M

MacDonald, Victoria-María. "Demanding their Rights: The Latino Struggle for Educational Access and Equity," *American Latino Theme Study: Education*, National Park Service: https://www.nps.gov/articles/latinothemeeducation.htm

Machado, Yolanda. "'La Bamba' and the Lives It Changed," *New York Times* 3 May 2021.

"The Man Who Didn't Invent Flamin' Hot Cheetos," *Los Angeles Times,* 16 March 2021: https://www.latimes.com/business/story/2021-05-16/flamin-hot-cheetos-richard-montanez

"Manuel Ortiz," The Cyber Boxing Zone Encyclopedia: http://www.cyberboxingzone.com/boxing/ortiz-m.htm

"Manuel Trinidad Pacheco," The University of Arizona: https://president.arizona.edu/person/manuel-trinidad-pacheco

"Marcelo Balboa 2005 Inductee," National Soccer Hall of Fame: https://www.nationalsoccerhof.com/players/marcelo-balboa.html

"Mariachi at HGO," *Houston Grand Opera*, Vol. 63, No. 2 (2022): pp. 20–23.

"Marina Rivero, Pitcher," National Baseball Hall of Fame: https://baseballhall.org/hall-of-famers/rivera-mariano

"Mario A. Martinez," *Californian*: https://www.legacy.com/us/obituaries/thecalifornian/name/mario-martinez-obituary?id=10039824&fhid=2348

"Mario Davidovsky, Composer Who Made Electronics Sing," *New York Times*, 30 August 2019.

"Mario J. Molina—Biographical," The Nobel Prize: https://www.nobelprize.org/prizes/chemistry/1995/molina/biographical/

"Marta de la Torre, CEO & Founder," *Hispanic Media:* https://www.echispanicmedia.com/martha-de-la-torre-biography/

Martín-Rodríguez, Manuel M. *Life in Search of Readers: Reading (In) Chicano/a Literature*. Albuquerque: University of New Mexico Press, 2003, p. 18.

Martínez, José, and Christin Devine, "Hispanic Blood: An Interview with Robert Rodriguez," *Creative Screenwriting,* 21 December 2015: https://www.creativescreenwriting.com/hispanic-blood-an-interview-with-robert-rodriguez/

Martínez, Rob. "Education in New Mexico Has Long, Tenuous History," *The New Mexican* 4, June 2021: https://www.santafenewmexican.com/news/local_news/education-in-new-mexico-has-long-tenuous-history/article_f9621b04-c3ec-11eb-b8cd-9f0bfdb1bc48.html

"Martin Sheen Biography," *Monsters & Critics*: https://web.archive.org/web/20131105095713/http://www.monstersandcritics.com/people/Martin-Sheen/biography/

"Master Builders," *Humanities,* May/June 1995, pp. 29–30.

Mathews, Jay. *Escalante: The Best Teacher in America*. New York: Henry Holt, 1988.

Matsumoto, Valerie J. "Vicki L. Ruiz Biography," American Historical Association: https://www.historians.org/about-aha-and-membership/aha-history-and-archives/presidential-addresses/vicki-l-ruiz/vicki-l-ruiz-biography

"Mauricio Gutierrez, One of 16 Hispanic CEOs in the Fortune 500," Business Insider: https://www.businessinsider.com/mauricio-gutierrez-nrg-ceo-interview-diversity-sustainability-2021-12

Maxwell, Erin, "Satellite Award Winners Announced," *Variety,* 17 December 2007.

Mayorquín, Orlando. "Lourdes Portillo, 80, Documentary Filmmaker Who Was Nominated for an Oscar," *New York Times*, 28 April 2024.

"Mayra Flores." *The Texas Tribune*: https://www.texastribune.org/people/mayra-flores/

"McDonald's Board of Directors names Enrique Hernandez, Jr. Non-Executive Chairman," *Reuters,* 26 May 2016: https://www.reuters.com/article/idUSASC08RIS/

McDowell, Edwin, "Reinaldo Arenas, 47, Writer Who Fled Cuba, Dies," *New York Times*, 9 December 1990.

McElroy, Lisa Tucker. *Alberto Gonzales, Attorney General*. Minneapolis: Millbrook Press, 2006.

McFadden, Robert D. "Herman Badillo, Congressman and Fixture of New York Politics, Dies at 85," *New York Times*, 4 December 2014.

McGlone, Peggy. "Smithsonian Selects Miami Museum Leader as Founding Director of Latino Museum." *Washington Post,* 4 February 2022.

McKnight, Joseph. "Law without Lawyers on the Hispano Mexican Frontier," *The West Texas Historical Association Yearbook,* 64 (1990); pp. 51–65.

McKnight, Joseph. *The Spanish Elements in Modern Texas Law*. Dallas: J.W. McKnight, 1979.

McNeill, Leila. "The Woman Who Revealed the Missing Link between Viruses and Cancer," *Smithsonian Magazine*, 17 June 2019: https://www.smithsonianmag.com/science-nature/woman-who-revealed-missing-link-between-viruses-and-cancer-180972427/

McWilliams, Carey. *North from Mexico: The Spanish-Speaking Peoples of the United States*. Philadelphia: Lippincott, 1949.

Mead, Kevi. "Obama Names Aponte to Top US Post at Organization of American States." *Caribbean Business,* 3 August 2012: http://www.caribbeanbusinesspr.com/news/obama-names-aponte-to-top-us-post-at-organization-of-4merican-states-99225.html

Meares, Hadley Hall. "The Love Goddess: Rita Hayworth's Tragic Quest," *Vanity Fair*, 23 September 2020.

"Meet the Chief Scientific Officer of BiotiQuest," BiotiQuest: https://biotiquest.com/pages/dr-raul-cano

Meier, Matt S., and Feliciano Rivera. *Dictionary of Mexican American History*. Westport, CT: Greenwood Press, 1981.

Meier, Matt S., and Gutiérrez, Margo, *Encyclopedia of the Mexican American Civil Rights Movement*. Westport, CT: Greenwood Press, 2000, pp. 64–65.

Mengiste, Maaza, "The Dream of Oscar Isaac," *Esquire,* 30 March 2022.

Meyer, Michael C. *Water in the Hispanic Southwest: A Social and Legal History: 1550–1850*. Tucson: University of Arizona Press, 1984.

"Miki García," ASU Search: https://search.asu.edu/profile/3211210

"Milwaukee Police Chief Philip Arreola," Milwaukee Public Library: https://www.mpl.org/blog/now/milwaukee-police-chief-philip-arreola

"Modesto A. Maidique," FIU/Business: https://business.fiu.edu/about/directory/profile/maidiquem

Mónica Muñoz Martínez: https://monicamunozmartinez.com/about/

"Montana Levi Blanco Costume Design": https://www.montanaleviblanco.com/about

Montes Huidobro, Matías, ed. *El laúd del desterrado*. Houston, TX: Arte Público Press, 1995.

Mora, Pat. *The Desert is My Mother/ El desierto es mi madre*. Houston: Arte Público Press, 1995.

Moreno, Carolina. "The Real Meaning behind the 'Macarena' Will Crush Your '90s Soul," *HuffPost*: https://www.huffpost.com/entry/the-macarena-meaning-crush-90-soul_n_55e738c9e4b0b7a9633b491d

Moreno, Rita. *Rita Moreno: A Memoir*. New York: Penguin, 2013.

Moritz, Charles, ed. *Current Biography Yearbook, 1963*. New York: H. W. Wilson, 1963.

Muñoz Marín, Luis. *Memorias: Autobiografía pública, 1940–1952*. San Germán, Puerto Rico: Universidad Interamericana, 1992.

"Museum Architect Wins Award," *Houston Chronicle*, 29 April 1996.

Museum of Fine Arts, Houston. *Hispanic Art in the United States: Thirty Contemporary Painters and Sculptors*. New York: Abbeville Press, 1987.

"Myth, Magic, and Spirit, *Houston Chronicle Zest Magazine*, 20 October 1996, pp. 8–9, 15.

N

"NASA's New Astronaut Leader to Help Pick Next Moon Visitors," *Houston Chronicle,* 2 February 2023.
"Natalia Clovis," Olympedia: https://www.olympedia.org/athletes/20993
"National Gallery of Art Announces Appointment of New Chief Curatorial and Conservation Officer E. Carmen Ramos," National Gallery of Art, 13 May 2021: https://www.nga.gov/press/2021/carmen-ramos.html
"National Heritage Fellowships: Eduardo "Lalo" Guerrero," National Endowment for the Arts: https://web.archive.org/web/20200521082518/https://www.arts.gov/honors/heritage/fellows/eduardo-lalo-guerrero
"National Hispanic Heritage Month: Olga E. Custodio," Transportation History: https://transportationhistory.org/2017/09/22/national-hispanic-heritage-month-olga-e-custodio/
National Image, Inc: https://national-image.org/
"National Park Service Announces 19 Additions to the Underground Railroad Network to Freedom in 10 States," National Park Service: https://www.nps.gov/subjects/undergroundrailroad/national-park-service-announces-19-additions-to-the-underground-railroad-network-to-freedom-in-10-states.htm
Nava, Julian. *Julian Nava: My Mexican-American Journey*. Houston: Arte Público Press, 2002.
Nelly Galán: https://nelygalan.com/about-nely/bio/
"New Faces of 1998," *Newsweek*, January 1996.
"New Members, New Districts," *Congressional Quarterly*, 7 November 7 1992, p. 52.
"New Mission, New Leaders for Hispanics," *Houston Chronicle*, 7 January 1996, pp. A23–24.
"New Technologies Could Ensure Safer Flights," *Houston Chronicle*, 3 September 1996.
"News and Notes," *Texas Library Journal*, summer 1996, p. 100.
Newton, David E. *Latinos in Science, Math, and Professions.* New York: Facts on File. 2007.
"The 1999 Pulitzer Prize Winner in Investigative Reporting," The Pulitzer Prize: https://www.pulitzer.org/winners/staff-44

O

"Obituary: Evelyn Margaret Rivera": https://www.dignitymemorial.com/obituaries/east-lansing-mi/evelyn-rivera-6300469
"Ochoa Reflects on Historic Career, Lauds Current Diversity," *Houston Chronicle*, 8 April 2023:, pp. 1, 5.
Olivares, Julián, ed. *International Studies in Honor of Tomás Rivera*, Houston, TX: Arte Público Press, 1985.
Olivas, Daniel. "Spotlight on Michael Nava," La Bloga: https://labloga.blogspot.com/2006/04/spotlight-on-michael-nava.html

Olivas, Michael A., ed. *"Colored men" and "hombres aquí": Hernández v. Texas and the Emergence of Mexican-American Lawyering*. Houston: Arte Público Press, 2006.

"100 Influentials," *Hispanic Business*, October 1996, p. 62.

"El origen de la instrucción elemental en la frontera norte de Coahuila," *El periódico de Saltillo,* April 2014: http://www.elperiodicodesaltillo.com/2014/abril%2014/origen.html

"Orozco Retiring as Chicago Fire Chief at Month's End," *Chicago Tribune*: https://www.chicagotribune.com/1996/11/03/orozco-retiring-as-chicago-fire-chief-at-months-end/

"Our America: The Latino Presence in American Art": https://americanart.si.edu/exhibitions/our-america

"Our History and Mission," National Conference on Puerto Rican Women: https://www.nacoprw.org/about/our-history-and-mission

P

Palomo Acosta, Teresa, "Conferencia de Mujeres por la Raza," *Handbook of Texas*: https://www.tshaonline.org/handbook/entries/conferencia-de-mujeres-por-la-raza

Pantoja, Antonia. *Memoir of a Visionary*. Houston, TX: Arte Público Press, 2002.

Paredes, Américo. *With a Pistol in His Hand: A Border Ballad and Its Hero.* Austin: University of Texas Press, 1958.

Pareles, Jon. "Another Year of Innovation for Latin Pop," *New York Times*, 25 December 2022.

Parker, Garrett, "Ten Things You Didn't Know about Rochard Gonzalez," *Money Inc.*: https://moneyinc.com/abbvie-ceo-richard-gonzalez/

"Patricia Rodriguez Art": https://patriciarodriguezart.weebly.com/biography-bibliography.html

"Pau Gasol Biography: Life, Career, Stats & Facts," Lakers Nation: https://lakersnation.com/pau-gasol-biography/#google_vignette

"Pedro A. Sanchez: Director, Tropical Agriculture and the Rural Environment Program," Columbia Climate School: https://www.earth.columbia.edu/articles/view/2784

Peña, Manuel. *The Texas-Mexican Conjunto: History of a Working-class Music*. Austin: University of Texas Press, 1985.

Pendas, Miguel, and Harry Ring. *Toward Chicano Power: Building La Raza Unida Party*. New York; Pathfinder Press, 1974.

Pérez-Firmat, Gustavo. *Life on the Hyphen: The Cuban American Way*. Austin: University of Texas Press, 1993.

Philipps, Dave. "Catherine Cortez Masto Wins Nevada to Become First Latina Senator," *New York Times*, 9 November 2016.

Piana, Ronald. "Alfredo Quiñones-Hinojosa, MD: From Migrant Farm Worker to Neurosurgeon in Search of a Cure for Brain Cancer," The Ascot Post: https://ascopost.com/issues/july-25-2023/alfredo-qui%C3%B1ones-hinojosa-md-from-migrant-farm-worker-to-neurosurgeon-in-search-of-a-cure-for-brain-cancer/

Pimentel, David, ed. *Global Economic and Environmental Aspects of Biofuels.* Abingdon-on-Thames, Oxfordshire, England: Routledge, 2012.

Polzer, Charles W. *Kino Guide II: A Life of Eusebio Francisco Kino, S.J., Arizona's First Pioneer, and a Guide to His Missions and Monuments*. Tucson, AZ: Southwest Mission Research Center, 1982.

"President Biden Announces His Intent to Nominate Robert Santos for Director of the U.S. Census Bureau, The White House: https://www.whitehouse.gov/briefing-room/statements-releases/2021/04/13/president-biden-announces-his-intent-to-nominate-robert-santos-for-director-of-the-u-s-census-bureau/

"Pulitzer Prize Winner Oscar Hijuelos Dies at 62," *The Guardian*: https://www.theguardian.com/world/2013/oct/14/pulitzer-prize-winner-oscar-hijuelos-dies

Punds, Marcia Heroux. "How Deal-Maker Cheryl Miller Rose to Become AutoNation's New CEO," *Seattle Times,* 11 August 2019: https://www.seattletimes.com/business/how-deal-maker-cheryl-miller-rose-to-become-autonations-new-ceo/

Putnam, Frank B. "Teresa Urrea, The Saint of Cabora," *Southern California Quarterly*, September 1963, pp. 245–64.

Q–R

Quevedo, Jane Allen. "Hi Bithorn," Society for American Baseball Research: https://sabr.org/bioproj/person/hi-bithorn/

Quirarte, Jacinto. *Mexican American Artists*. Austin: University of Texas Press, 1973.

Racine, Karen, *Francisco de Miranda: A Transatlantic Life in the Age of Revolution.* Wilmington, DE: Scholarly Resources, 2003.

"Rafael Campo," poets.org: https://poets.org/poet/rafael-campo

"Ralph Alvarez," Lilly: https://www.lilly.com/leadership/board-of-directors/ralph-alvarez

"Raymund Paredes, Texas' Higher Education Commissioner, Will Step Down Aug. 31," *Texas Tribune*: https://www.texastribune.org/2019/01/24/raymund-paredes-states-higher-education-commissioner-will-step-down-au/

Rayner, Alex. "Love and Rockets Rides Again: 'We Influenced a Whole Lot of Cartoonists,'" *The Guardian,* 10 August 2016: https://www.theguardian.com/books/2016/aug/10/love-and-rockets-california-punks-jaime-gilbert-hernandez

"Record-breaking Army Astronaut Receives Rare Qualification Device," U.S. Army: https://www.army.mil/article/273930?a

Reddy, Marlita A., ed. *Statistical Record of Hispanic Americans*. Detroit: Gale Research, 1995.

Reichler, Joseph L. *The Great All-Time Baseball Record Book.* New York: Macmillan, 1993.

Reinhold, Robert. "John Serrano Jr., et al, and School Tax Equality," *New York Times,* 10 January 1972.

"Rematch Is Set for Valley Seat," *Houston Chronicle,* 16 July 2023.

"Remembering Sister Ida Torres," CUNY School for Labor and Urban Studies: https://slublog.org/2016/06/08/remembering-sister-ida-torres/

"Review by: Janet Pérez," *Hispania*, Vol. 79, No. 4 (December 1996), pp. 810–12.

"Rey Saldaña," Communities in Schools: https://www.communitiesinschools.org/about-us/our-leadership/profile/rey-saldana?_z=1718051324882

Reyes, Luis. "Hollywood's Hispanic Heritage," *DGA News*, August/September 1994, pp. 16–20.

Reyes-Velarde, Alejandra. "Romana Acosta Bañuelos, First Latina U.S. Treasurer and Mexican American Pioneer, Dies at 92." *Los Angeles Times*, 22 January 2018.

"Reynaldo Guerra Garza," Federal Judicial Center: https://www.fjc.gov/history/judges/garza-reynaldo-guerra

"Ricardo Alberto Maldonado," Poets.org: https://poets.org/poet/ricardo-alberto-maldonado

Riccardo Hernández – Scenic Design: https://www.riccardohernandez.com/bio

Richard Blanco: https://richard-blanco.com/

"Richard E. Cavazos," National Museum of the United States Army: https://www.thenmusa.org/biographies/richard-e-cavazos/

"Richard Montañez," *Latino Leaders Speak: Personal Stories of Struggle and Triumph*, edited by Mickey Ibarra and María Pérez-Brown, Houston, TX: Arte Público Press, 2017, pp. 149–60.

Richardson, Bill, with Michael Ruby. *Between Worlds: The Making of an American Life—An Autobiography*, G. P. Putnam's Sons, 2005.

Rivera-Ashford, Roni Capi. *Raulito, the First Hispanic Governor of Arizona*. Houston, TX: Arte Público Press, 2021.

Rodríguez, Eugene. *Henry B. Gonzalez: A Political Profile*. New York: Arno Press, 1976.

Rodriguez, Lori. "New Mission, New Leaders for Hispanics," *Houston Chronicle*, 7 January 1996; pp. A23–24.

"Romualdo Pacheco." *Biographical Dictionary of the United States Congress*: https://bioguide.congress.gov/search/bio/L000153

Rosaldo, Renato, Robert A. Calvert, and Gustav L. Seligmann. *Chicano: The Evolution of a People*. Minneapolis, MN: Winston Press, 1973.

Rosales, Arturo. *Chicano! History of the Mexican American Civil Rights Movement*. Houston, TX: Arte Público Press, 1996.

"Rosario Dawson," *Biography.com*: https://www.biography.com/actors/rosario-dawson

Rosazza, Marisa. "Distinctive Contributions of Hispanic Catholics," *Texas Catholic Herald*, 23 August 1996, pp. 20-21.

Rossi, Madison, "From Street Performer to Disney Star," *Time*: https://time.com/collection/american-voices-2017/5042022/american-voices-anthony-gonzalez/

"Ruben Padilla," Trampoline & Tumbling National Team: https://members.usagym.org/pages/athletes/nationalTeamTT.html?id=266189

Ruiz, Vicki, and Virginia Sánchez Korrol, "Latina U.S. Treasurers," *Latinas in the United States: A Historical Encyclopedia,* two volumes, Bloomington: Indiana University Press, 2006, pp. 374–75.

Ruiz de Burton, María Amparo. *The Squatter and the Don,* edited by Rosaura Sanchez and Beatriz Pita. Houston, TX: Arte Público Press, 1993.

Ruiz de Burton, María Amparo. *Who Would Have Thought It*? edited by Rosaura Sanchez and Beatriz Pita. Houston, TX: Arte Público Press, 1995.

Ryan, Bryan, ed. *Hispanic Writers: A Selection of Sketches from Contemporary Authors*. Detroit: Gale Research, 1991.

S

Salazar, Francisco. "José Carreras & Placido Domingo to Reunite for Concert," OperaWire: https://operawire.com/jose-carreras-placido-domingo-to-reunite-for-concert/#google_vignette

Salomon, Carlos Manuel, *Pio Pico: The Last Governor of Mexican California,* University of Oklahoma Press, 2010.

San Miguel, Guadalupe, Jr. *Desegragation of Black and Hispanic Students from 1968 to 1980*. Washington, DC: Joint Center for Political Studies, 1981.

Sánchez, Linda, and Loretta Sánchez. *Dream in Color: How the Sánchez Sisters Are Making History in Congress*. New York: Grand Central Publishing, 2008.

Sánchez, Pedro. *Memories of Antonio José Martínez*. Santa Fe, NM: Rydal Press, 1978.

Sánchez-Grey, Alba. "El Tema del Desarraigo en el Teatro de Iván Acosta." *Círculo: Revista d e Cultura,* 24 (1995): p. 119.

"Sandra de la Riva," Olympedia: https://www.olympedia.org/athletes/32929

"Sarah Robles Becomes First U.S. Woman to Win Tao Olympic Weightlifting Medals," USA Weightlifting: https://www.teamusa.org/USA-Weightlifting/Features/2021/August/02/Sarah-Robles-Becomes-First-US-Woman-to-Win-Two-Olympic-Weightlifting-Medals

"Saul Alvarez," BoxRec: https://boxrec.com/en/proboxer/348759

Schement, Jorge R., and Ricardo Flores. "The Origins of Spanish-Language Radio: The Case of San Antonio, Texas," *Journalism History*, February 1977, pp. 56–58.

Secretary of Defense, *Hispanic America's Defense*. Washington, DC: U.S. Government Printing Office, 1990.

Sheridan, Thomas E. *Los Tucsonenses: The Mexican Community in Tucson*. Tucson: University of Arizona Press, 1986.

Schmal, John P., "The Four Latino Mayors of Los Angeles," *Hispanic Vista*, 23 May 2005.

Schwartz, Dana, "Mary Elizabeth Winstead Is a Comedian Who Blurs the Line between Life and Art in *All about Nina*: EW Review," *Entertainment Weekly*: https://ew.com/movies/2018/09/28/mary-elizabeth-winstead-all-about-nina-review/

Shapiro, Leonard. "Say Hello to the Ochoa Era," *Washington Post*, 27 April 2007.

Shinn, Peggy, "The History of Breaking." Team USA: https://www.teamusa.com/news/2023/november/04/the-history-of-breaking

Simmons, Helen, and Cathryn A. Hoyt, eds. *Hispanic Texas: A Historical Guide*. Austin: University of Texas Press, 1992.

Simmons, Marc. "Spanish Irrigation Practices in New Mexico," *New Mexico Historical Review*, 47 (April 1972), pp. 138–39.

Simonhoff, Harry. *Jewish Notables in America, 1776–1865*. New York: Greenberg, 1956.

Slatta, Richard W. *Cowboys of the Americas*. New Haven, CT: Yale University Press, 1990.

Smith, Steve. "Pauline Oliveros, Composer Who Championed 'Deep Listening,' Dies at 84," *New York Times*, 28 November 2016.

"Sobre Nosotros; Festival Casals," Internet Archive Wayback Machine: http://www.festcasalspr.gobierno.pr/abouteng.html

Sonmez, Felicia, Amy B Wang, and Marianna Sotomayor, "House Ethics Committee investigating Reps. Cawthorn, Jackson, Mooney," *Washington Post*, 23 May 2022.

Sorell, Victor. "Barrio Murals in Chicago: Painting the Hispanic-American Experience on 'Our Community' Walls," *Revista Chicano-Riqueña*, 4/1 (1976), pp. 51–72.

Sosa, Lionel. *Think & Grow Rich: A Latino Choice*. Napoleon Hill Foundation, 2006.

Sotomayor, Sonia. *Turning Pages: My Life Story*. New York: Philomel Books, 2018.

Soule, Alexander. "CT Native Tasked with Leading the Finances of Nation's Largest Defense Conglomerate," *CT Insider,* 24 September 2022: https://www.ctinsider.com/business/article/CT-native-leads-finances-for-Lockheed-Martin-17457260.php

Southwest Voter Research Notes, fall 1995/winter 1996, p. 1.

"Steve Van Buren, Philadelphia Eagles Player, Pro Football Hall of Fame Inductee," *Washington Post*, 24 August 2012.

Strachwitz, Chris, and James Nicopolus. *Lydia Mendoza: A Family Auobiography*. Houston, TX: Arte Público Press, 1994.

T

Tabor, Mary B. W. "Loyalty and Labor: Nydia Margarita Velazquez," *New York Times*, September 16, 1992, p. B6.

Tallet, Olivia P., "A Giant and Legend: UH Community Mourns the Loss of Professor Emeritus Michael Olivas," *Houston Chronicle*, 27 April 2022: https://www.houston-chronicle.com/news/houston-texas/houston/article/Scores-of-people-mourn-the-loss-of-a-University-of-17126210.php

Tapia, Richard A. *Losing the Precious Few: How America Fails to Educate Its Minorities in Science and Engineering.* Houston, TX: Arte Público Press, 2022.

Tardiff, Joseph C., and L. Mpho Mabunda, eds. *Dictionary of Hispanic Biography*. Detroit: Gale Research, 1996.

Tatum, Charles, M. *Chicano and Chicana Literature*. Tucson: University of Arizona Press, 2006.

"Tejano Conunto Festival 2024," Guadalupe Cultural Arts Center: https://guadalupe-culturalarts.org/tejano-conjunto-festival/

Telgen, Diane, and Jim Kamp, eds. *Latinas! Women of Achievement.* Detroit: Visible Ink Press, 1996.

Termini, Christina. "100 Inspiring Hispanic/Latinx Scientists in America": https://crosstalk.cell.com/blog/100-inspiring-hispanic-latinx-scientists-in-america

"Texan Becomes First Latina on Appeals Court," *Houston Chronicle*, 5 December 2023.

Texas Hispanic, November 1994, p. 43; 26 May 1995, p. 53.

"Texas Originals/Jovita Idar," HumanitiesTexas: https://www.humanitiestexas.org/programs/tx-originals/list/jovita-idar

Thorpe, Helen. "Lydia Aguilar-Bryan and Joseph Bryan," *Texas Monthly*, September 1995, pp. 116–17,148–49.

"Tom Fears," Pro Football Hall of Fame: https://web.archive.org/web/20111029014225/http://www.profootballhof.com/hof/member.aspx?PlayerId=66

"Tomás Rivera Center Collection," Trinity University: https://archives.trinity.edu/tomas-river-center

"Tony Jimenez Finds Success through Calculated Risks," *Hispanic Executive,* 8 August 2022: https://hispanicexecutive.com/tony-jimenez-microtech-2/

"Top Women: María Ríos": https://top30women.com/maria-rios/

U

Ugwu, Reggie. "Benicio Del Toro, Hollywood's Instant Antihero, Goes the Distance," *New York Times,* 27 June 2018.

"Universo Radio Program to Cease Regular Production," *UT News,* 6 July 2011: https://news.utexas.edu/2011/07/06/universo-radio-program-to-cease-regular-production/

Unterburger, Amy L., ed. *Who's Who among Hispanic Americans, 1992–1993,* 2nd edition. Detroit: Gale, 1992.

"U.S. Poet Laureate Ada Limón Appointed for a Historic Two-Year Second Term," Library of Congress: https://www.loc.gov/item/prn-23-040/u-s-poet-laureate-ada-limon-appointed-for-a-historic-two-year-second-term/2023-04-24/

V

Valdez, Luis, and El Teatro Campesino, *The Early Works*, Houston, TX: Arte Público Press, 1990.

Vando, Gloria. Pomesas: *A Geography of the Impossible*. Houston, TX: Arte Público Press, 994.

Van Hyning, Thomas E. *Puerto Rico's Winter League: A History of Major League Baseball's Launching Pad.* Jefferson, NC: McFarland & Company, 1995.

"Vaquero": https://www.si.edu/object/vaquero%3Asaam_1990.44

Varela, Félix. *Jicotencal*, edited by Luis Leal and Rodolfo Cortina. Houston, TX: Arte Público Press, 1995.

"Victor Ochoa's Biographical Sketch," Smithsonian Education: https://smithsonianeducation.org/scitech/impacto/graphic/victor/man.html

Vigil, Maurilio E. *Chicano Politics*. Washington, DC: University Press of America, 1978.

Vigil, Maurilio E. *Los Patrones: Profiles of Hispanic Political Leaders in New Mexico History*. Washington, DC: University Press of America, 1980.

Viola, Herman J., and Carolyn Margolis, eds. *Seeds of Change: A Quincentennial Commemoration*. Washington, DC: Smithsonian Institution Press, 1991.

"Voting Rights Act (1965)," National Archives: https://www.archives.gov/milestone-documents/voting-rights-act#:~:text=This%20act%20was%20signed%20into,as%20a%20prerequisite%20to%20voting.

Weber, Bruce, "Roberto Suarez, Founder of El Nuevo Herald, Dies at 82," *New York Times,* 10 June 1910: https://www.nytimes.com/2010/07/11/business/media/11suarez.html

"Who We Are: Michael Nava," *Publishers Weekly*, 30 September 1996, p. 49.
"Whose Media Is This Anyway?" *Hispanic*, December 1996, pp. 53–58.
Wilcox, Joyce. "The Face of Women's Health: Helen Rodriguez-Trias." *American Journal of Public Health*. April 2002, pp. 566–69.
Wile, Rob. "From 'Unknown' to Wealthiest Hispanic-American—And Now, He's Moving Back to Miami," *Miami Herald*, 15 October 2018.
Winter, Metta. "Animals Point to Nature's Medicines," *Cornell Focus*, 5/1 (1996); pp. 5-7.
"A Writer's Hidden Gem in Houston: Arte Público Press," *Houston History Magazine,* Fall, 2022.
Wroth, William. *Furniture from the Hispanic Southwest*. Santa Fe, NM: Ancient City Press, 1984.

X–Z

"Ximenes Traviño, Vicente (1919–2014)," Texas State Historical Association: https://www.tshaonline.org/handbook/entries/ximenes-vicente-trevino
Young, Jan. *The Migrant Workers and César Chávez*. New York: Julian Messner/Simon and Schuster, 1972.
"The Young Lord's Organization/Party," Library of Congress Research Guides: https://guides.loc.gov/latinx-civil-rights/young-lords-organization
Zarya, Valentia. "PG &E's Bolt of Energy," *Fortune,* 15 June 2017: https://fortune.com/2017/06/15/fortune-500-pge-geisha-williams/
Zavala, Iris M., and Rafael Rodriguez. *The Intellectual Roots of Independence: An Anthology of Puerto Rican Political Essays*. New York: Monthly Review Press, 1980.

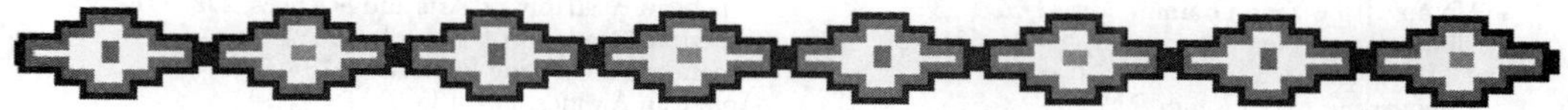

INDEX

Note: (ill.) indicates photos and illustrations.

C

D

E

G

I

M

N

O

P

S

T

X–Y

Z